Adventures and Discoveries

The Books and Monographs of Carleton S. Coon

1931 Tribes of the Rif

1932 Flesh of the Wild Ox

1933 The Riffian

1935 Measuring Ethiopia and Flight into Arabia

1939 The Races of Europe

1942 Principles of Anthropology (with Eliot D. Chapple)

1948 A Reader in General Anthropology

1950 The Mountains of Giants

1950 Races

1951 Cave Explorations in Iran 1949

1951 Caravan

1954 The Story of Man

1957 The Seven Caves

1958 Faces of Asia

1962 The Origin of Races

1965 The Living Races of Man

1968 Yengema Cave Report

1971 The Hunting Peoples

1980 A North Africa Story

1981 Adventures and Discoveries: The Autobiography of Carleton S. Coon

Adventures and Discoveries,

The Autobiography of Carleton S. Coon

Prentice-Hall, Inc., Englewood Cliffs, New Jersey

Adventures and Discoveries:
The Autobiography of Carleton S. Coon
by Carleton S. Coon
Copyright © 1981 by Carleton S. Coon

Printed in the United States of America
Prentice-Hall International, Inc., London
Prentice-Hall of Australia, Pty. Ltd., Sydney
Prentice-Hall of Canada, Ltd., Toronto
Prentice-Hall of India Private Ltd., New Delhi
Prentice-Hall of Japan, Inc., Tokyo
Prentice-Hall of Southeast Asia Pte. Ltd., Singapore
Whitehall Books Limited, Wellington, New Zealand
10   9   8   7   6   5   4   3   2   1

Library of Congress Cataloging in Publication Data

Coon, Carleton Stevens, date
  Adventures and discoveries.

  Bibliography: p.
  Includes index.
  1. Coon, Carleton Stevens, 1904–   .   2. Anthro-
pologists—United States—Biography.   I. Title.
GN21.C66A33   306'.092'4 [B]   81-2746
ISBN 0-13-014027-9   AACR2

Contents

Carleton Coon's Anthropology

As I am one of the oldest living anthropologists, my editor has asked me what has happened to the discipline during my lifetime. When I was a lad in my late teens and early twenties, anthropologists were so few that almost all of us knew each other; few outsiders knew what anthropology was or what anthropologists did.

The British summarized it neatly by dividing the subject into three parts: bones (physical anthropology), stones (prehistoric archaeology), and dirty stories (ethnology and ethnography). I worked equally in all three, convinced from the beginning that all were interdependent parts of a whole.

In my youth we still read and respected giants of the past like Charles Darwin, Sir James Frazer, Edward Westermarck, and Sir Arthur Keith, soon followed by D'Arcy Thompson (*Of Growth and Form*), and such archaeologists that I could know personally as Andrew Reisner, Joe Spinden, A. V. Kidder, and Sylvanus Morley. Edward Sapir and Benjamin Whorf dominated linguistics, Alfred Kroeber and Robert Lowie and the Seligmans ethnography, then Radcliffe Brown and Bronislaw Malinowski ruled social anthropology.

We were taught to view the study of man as a whole. Meanwhile the snake of racial consciousness had raised its head out of the central European bulrushes, largely through the cult leadership of Franz Boas. His devotees leaked introspection into our curricula, turning both physical and social anthropology into political forums, while archaeology began to fade as a rich men's hobby and its practitioners lingered as members of a club.

As time went on and the Boasite doctrine spread, expeditions, research, and publication gradually ceased to be funded by the elite and well-to-do. Public money had to be sought, and the subjects had to meet the public's taste. Why give X tens of thousands of dollars for research on the blue pigment of the horseshoe crab? Or to measure the heads of the Beni Flan u Flan tribe of southern Arabia? What had these things to do with cancer? Would they offend some minority?

To use a trite phrase, anthropology is needed now more than ever. But what kind of anthropology? In my opinion the old-fashioned

anthropology that saw the world as a whole, just as my generation—
now mostly dead—was taught to see it. My vision still encompasses
latitude, longitude, altitude, the weather, the evolution of races and
cultures on the sliding grid of time, and the reasons why. I have stood
still, and fads have risen and fallen around me. If I am a monument to
continuity, perhaps it is because my feet are of New England granite, as
solid as it was when anthropology was just a couple of Greek words.

Anthropology is fragmented and in the public domain. But
this statement is not all my editor wanted. Because I am the subject of
this book, modesty prevents me from introducing myself. By lucky
chance I found a suitable advance obituary of my life so far,* in both
the third person and the past tense, and have edited it to add a few
items my Boswell may not have known, and shortened it to a length to
fit the fact that most of what is mentioned will be covered at greater
length in the following text.

*Coon worked in three fields: cultural anthropology, prehistoric archae-
ology, and physical anthropology. He not only published in all three but also tried to
bring them together into a coherent whole. In this sense he was primarily a
historian.*

*Coon's career in cultural anthropology began with fieldwork in Morocco
between 1924 and 1928, culminating in the publication of an ethnography of the
Riffian tribes. He continued on this line with a similar study of the North Albanian
mountaineers and other hard-to-reach highlanders in Ethiopia, Yemen, and
Hadhramaut. His* Caravan *(1951) is a synthesis of information about Middle
Eastern cultures used as a text by diplomats and others concerned with the countries
from Morocco to Pakistan.*

Before World War II Coon collaborated with Eliot D. Chapple in writing
Principles of Anthropology *(1942) in which they attempted to analyze human
behavior in terms of patterns of interaction and the requirements of institutions to
preserve equilibrium, through the operation of the law of least effort. After the war
he simplified and elaborated his ideas about these principles in an appendix to his* A
Reader in General Anthropology *(1948).*

*While thinking about these matters overseas during the war, Coon
conceived the idea that human beings convert energy derived from outside their
organisms into social structure at a predictable rate of acceleration, culminating in
quanta of energy and global institutions since achieved. He expressed this idea in
lecture courses, then in an exhibit at the University Museum of the University of
Pennsylvania, and finally in his book* The Story of Man *(1954).*

---

*McGraw-Hill Modern Scientists and Engineers, *Volume I, pp. 224–225, 1980.

As companion piece to this discovery, Coon further demonstrated that, without man's knowledge or control, the use of energy versus time followed a constant slope on a double log chart, from the first use of fire to the first nuclear explosion. After that its slope rose more steeply. He published this study in 1970 in an article "Human Evolution and the Avalanche of Culture" in C. McC. Brooks, ed., The Changing World and Man, *Gramond/Pridemark Press, Baltimore, Md.*

Coon's contribution to archaeology consisted mainly of excavation of caves in parts of the world previously unexplored in this sense, and discovery of new cultures. In Morocco he found a succession of Aterian phases (bifacially flaked points like Indian arrowheads) under the Neolithic in the High Cave of Tangier. In Iran he found in Bisitun the first Levalloisio-Mousterian reported from that country, and in two neighboring caves on the Caspian shore, Belt and Hotu, a sequence of cultures running from the Epipaleolithic through the Mesolithic and Neolithic to the Iron Age. In these caves he also found the bones of what may have been the earliest domestic animals and worked out techniques for distinguishing them from wild ones of the same species. In the cave of Kara Kamar in Afghanistan he found an Aurignacian culture older than any in Western Europe, and a Mesolithic over it. In the cave of Jerf Ajla in the Syrian desert he found a transition from Levalloisio-Mousterian to Aurignacian.

In 1967 Coon excavated a cave at Yengema in Sierra Leone that contained a sequence of miniature replicas of a Middle Paleolithic hand axe industry that overlapped a Neolithic industry. The latter began about 2200 B.C. when the cave was flooded and abandoned near the end of the Pleistocene. Also, on his archaeological expeditions, he measured and photographed his workmen whenever he could.

In 1950 in his book Races, in which S. M. Garn and J. B. Birdsell participated, Coon propounded the theory that many of the physical differences between races are results of adaptation to environment. This hypothesis, then received with ridicule, has been demonstrated many times by physiological research. Coon himself went to southern Chile in 1959 with a team of physiologists who confirmed the superior adaptation of the Alakaluf Indians.

In 1962 Coon's The Origin of Races *appeared, provoking controversy between racists and segregationists although it had nothing to do with race relations in the United States. The publication of that book was the culmination of decades of work in the study of fossil human remains, a task greatly helped by the availability, in the University Museum in Philadelphia, of rubber and plaster molds of many fossil specimens. As a result of these researches Coon came to the conclusion that* Homo sapiens *is divided into five subspecies, and that these same subspecies also existed in his immediate ancestor,* Homo erectus. *The transition from one species to the other involved initial changes in one organ only, the brain. Because each subspecies was physiologically adapted to its environment in other respects, the* acquisition of a new gene or genes favoring higher intelligence permitted the then existing subspecies to cross the erectus-sapiens threshold independently. Subsequent work by paleontologists on other mammalian species has confirmed this discovery. For it Coon was given in 1962 the Gold Medal of the Philadelphia Athenaeum.

The sequel to The Origin of Races, entitled The Living Races of Man, appeared in 1965. In it Coon reviewed the racial and cultural history of the world with new data and many photographs obtained and taken on his and Mrs. Coon's trip to east and south Asia in 1956 and 1957.

Coon's next book, The Hunting Peoples (1971), showed modern peoples' debts to their preagricultural ancestors. His latest to date, A North Africa Story (1980), is a diary-like account of the author's undercover activities as an OSS agent, saboteur, and guerrilla fighter during World War II. By trying to free and help the native peoples, his activities were a form of "Applied Anthropology." The Army rewarded him with a Legion of Merit. To add to his supply of precious metal, The Harvard Travelers Club awarded him their gold medal for a lifetime of exploration. He did not climb mountains "because they were there," but to study the people on the other side, and to look for caves.

Adventures and Discoveries

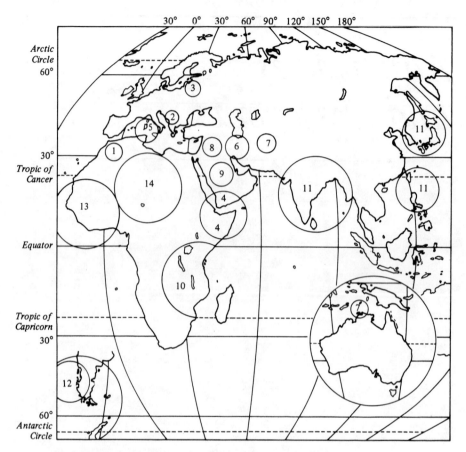

REGIONS VISITED PROFESSIONALLY IN PEACE AND WAR*

1. Morocco, 1924–28, 1942–44, 1962
2. Albania, 1929–30
3. Russia, 1933, 1964
4. Ethiopia, S. Arabia, 1933–34
5. Tunisia, Corsica, Bari, 1943–44
6. Iraq-Iran, 1948–51
7. Afghanistan, Australia, 1954
8. Syrian Desert, 1955
9. Saudi Arabia, 1955
10. East Africa, 1955
11. E. & S. Asia, 1956–57
12. S. E. Chile, 1958
13. Sierra Leone, Ghana, Nigeria, 1965
14. Chad, Cameroon, Tibesti, Acacus,
    Libya, 1965–66

---

*This map was created by Dr. Coon based upon a projection of John Morris's.

1. *My Childhood and Early Education*

From 1904 when I was born, to 1919 when I was sent away to school, most of my time was spent in Wakefield, Massachusetts, a town then of about fourteen thousand population, lying athwart the main Portland line of the Boston and Maine Railroad. By its track Wakefield was ten miles north of Boston, and many of its inhabitants—including my father—commuted to the city, but most of them worked in the factories which produced cast-iron stoves, knitted underwear, rattan furniture, pianos, and paper boxes. These factories did not greatly mar the landscape.

Wakefield had two lakes, Quannapowitt and Crystal, the former then being the scene of sailboat races in summer and iceboat races in winter, with much canoeing and skating during the appropriate seasons. Because Crystal Lake was the town's water supply, these activities were barred from it. On the outskirts of the town still stood a few farms and dairies, some extensive pine forests, and swamps full of muskrats—even an occasional mink was trapped there. In various candy and cigar stores we could buy red pennants stamped with white letters, reading "Wakefield, the Best Town," and many Wakefieldites who had not seen more than twenty or thirty towns believed this to be true.

A large white gingerbread house on South Main Street had belonged to my great-grandfather, John Coon, born in Cornwall, England; a Victorian one on Chestnut Street to my other great-grandfather, Amasa Hall, a native of Maine; and an early colonial farmhouse on Elm Street which had burned down before I was born, to my maternal grandfather, William A. Carleton, a relative newcomer from Fitchburg. Although it was the oldest branch of my family in terms of local residence, the Coons had lived in Wakefield little more than seventy years when I was born, yet I was as much a local boy as the youthful Eatons, Hartshornes, and Whites, whose ancestors had moved there from Lynn about 1636.

Coon is only one of many monosyllabic Cornish names, like Chin and Lugg and Glubb; all Cornish surnames do not follow the rhyme that Tre-, Pol-, and Pen- are the Cornishmen.

On the Common my grandfather's name could be read on the

Civil War monument, and the granite soldier towering above the carved inscription resembled him so closely that I firmly believed he had been the sculptor's model. I am not yet sure that he was not, because my grandfather was a striking figure prominent in the Grand Army of the Republic and other patriotic organizations like the Ancient and Honorable Artillery Company of Boston, of which he was once captain.

The Common provided a number of green park benches, on one of which, on sunny afternoons, my great-uncle, Henry Hall, was often to be seen chatting vigorously with his antique cronies. As I passed by, my ears picked up such archaic abbreviations as: "Tiza," "Tainta," and "Si." These meant, in the same order: "It is her," "It ain't her," and "Said I."

On the Fourth of July fireworks were set off on the Common. One year I was precociously and most appreciatively allowed to launch the rockets. This was much fun, because they detonated and hissed outward and upward the moment the cap touched the bottom of the hole, and I had to get my hands and head out of the way quickly. This lesson in precision and celerity in handling explosives did me no harm later on.

Like Gloucester, where I now live, Wakefield was a very patriotic community. Our chief enemies were not, as one might have supposed, the southerners whom men still living in our midst had conquered a thousand miles away, but the British who had invaded our sacred soil, and whom our more remote but still remembered ancestors had licked close by, on the holy battlefields of Lexington, Concord, and Bunker Hill. We were never told of the tens of thousands of other New Englanders who had remained loyal to the British crown and emigrated to Canada, making room for immigrants from other parts of Europe.

Enthusiastic and fresher support for our anglophobia was tendered by the Irish, and from our point of view it was their only good quality. Our parents shunned them and looked down upon them for their popish ways. In the 1910s ecumenia was not yet a pink spot on the eastern horizon.* Once when my father was praising a man named

---

*Readers younger than myself (as I hope most of them will be, if only for sales purposes) may wonder that I have placed so much emphasis on the twin issues of religion and ethnic origin, of which religion was the greater. It is not through personal interest on my part as much as through a desire to paint a faithful portrait of the life of the 1900s in a New England town, a prototype of the Ulster of the 1970s, with some mayhem but little bloodshed. Few Americans in their twenties or thirties will believe it. Their brains have been washed, but in a different direction and with a different brand of soap.

My father, John Lewis Coon, 1878–1941, born and died in Wakefield, Massachusetts. He traveled widely, especially in Europe and Egypt. His hair turned white during his late twenties.

My mother, Bessie Carleton Coon, 1880–1964, born in Fitchburg, Massachusetts, died in Wakefield; daughter of William Abel Carleton and Anna Whiting Stevens Carleton.

Moloney, I had the cheek to say: "Dad, Mr. Moloney is Irish. I thought you hated the Irish."

My father looked down at me and spat out a pungent wad of masticated cigar. "Moloney is not Irish," he replied. "He is a Congregationalist."

Now this brief conversation made several things clear. My father had not been to church for many years. On Sundays he played golf, walked around the lake on rainy days, or went riding in an antique (as of today) vehicle. Religion was a prime symbol of social status.

In addition to ourselves and our sparring partners, the Irish, who stood at the two poles of the social spectrum, Wakefield then contained a sizable minority of southern Italians, including John Volpe, in turn governor of Massachusetts, secretary of transportation, and American ambassador to Italy.

There were also French-Canadians, a number of Poles, and a few Scandinavians. While the last named were absorbed by the Yankees almost on arrival, the others tended to keep their own company in separate parts of the town, although we all went to school together.

As in Mr. Moloney's case, the Catholic-Protestant dichotomy was the critical social item rather than nationality or minor differences in physical appearance, although wealth and education were also important. One wealthy Italian family lived in the hallowed Park, an exclusive section, and was accepted by its other inhabitants, all Yankees. They were north Italians and Congregationalists. A Neapolitan-Sicilian splinter group of Baptists had its own church in Guineaville, but this religious switch did them little good in terms of the local rank situation. A Polish family on our street was socially acceptable as Protestant, while a rich family of huge, blond Congregationalist French Canadians stood near the social apex. Years before my birth, one of my grandmother Coon's sisters married a Protestant Spaniard, and their son became a Congregational minister.

As I recall it, I was aware of only four Jewish families in Wakefield, one of which attended services now and then in the Universalist church. All these families were highly regarded and their virtues often extolled. When my grandmother Carleton invited the children of her Jewish neighbors to Saturday night supper, she baked her beans with olive oil and an onion instead of pork, and that was all.

There were two colored families in Wakefield. The widow and children of Colonel Braxton, a Civil War hero, lived in a choice part of town, near my grandchildren's great-great-grandfather, Brigadier General Greenleaf A. Goodale; these two retired officers had been good friends. I met a daughter of Colonel Braxton at my mother's funeral in

1964. The only other colored person I knew was a boy named Cummings, captain of the high school baseball team. No one to my knowledge ever tried to discriminate against him, and if they had, they would have received no support.

With this early training, I can truthfully say that both anti-Semitism and racial discrimination were unknown to me before I left home at the age of fifteen, and zero to fifteen are formative years. The only social barriers I had been exposed to were the Catholic-Protestant wall, and a few differences in wealth and manners.

During my infancy my mother hired a young woman named Bertha to take care of me, and Bertha taught me to read before kindergarten. I entered the first grade nearly a year earlier than most of the other pupils because my birthday fell on June 23. Had I been born a few days later, I would have had to wait another year.

Being youngest in the class had one disadvantage. Also being tall for my age and skinny, and probably fresh, I became a perfect target for the resentment of mentally retarded stay-behinds. One of them, named Raymond, was already sporting a few stiff whiskers on his upper lip, and his voice was changing. It was his pleasure to knock me down, to try to crush my chest, and to twist my limbs, but he did not do this often because Bertha soon formed the habit of appearing in the school yard at recess and when it was time to go home.

The school had two stories, two rooms, and two teachers, each handling two grades. Out back was a four-holed privy for boys and another for girls. Early in my first year it was impressed on me that my uncle Max Carleton had fallen through a hole in the boys' privy and remained below for some time before being rescued. This experience had obliged him to stay home several days with a fever.

I never met Uncle Max because before I was born he had been killed by a train during a snowstorm. He was commuting from the Massachusetts Institute of Technology in Cambridge, and walking home down the track from the station. Owing to the storm, the northbound track had not been plowed; the train had been switched to the southbound track and came up behind him. In later years every time I drove my mother over Deadman's Crossing, where Uncle Max had been hit, she became visibly nervous and said, "Be careful, dear."

At the beginning of the first school year I had another problem just as serious as Raymond's hostility. I am left-handed. The teacher tried to make me write with my right hand. Had I not already been writing for several years, I might have weakened and changed, but I refused, and she tied my left hand behind me. At that point I refused to write at all, and we were deadlocked—with a little switching thrown in—until Bertha came once more to the rescue.

My grandfather, William Lewis Coon, born of Cornish parents in Charleston, Massachusetts, in 1840, died in Wakefield in 1912, also traveled widely to Egypt, the Holy Land, and Europe. Here he is seen sitting on his back doorstep, blind from glaucoma, wearing his Civil War Grand Army of the Republic uniform, and holding the author on his knee. With a paper cap on my head, I am sticking my tongue out saucily at the photographer.

One of my happiest moments in that school was on a Memorial Day, when Civil War veterans used to address the children. On one such occasion the speaker was my grandfather, William Lewis Coon, who had to be led in because he was blind. As I remembered it in 1939, when I first wrote it down, his story ran something like this:

"It is appropriate on this day that I should say something about our martyred President, Abraham Lincoln. I recall the time I saw him with my own eyes in Washington. Troops were marching through, and old Company A from Wakefield among them. There was Abraham Lincoln standing in a carriage, with his tall hat in his hand, though it was blowing plenty from the east and getting set to rain. I mind how the light shone on his big, wide forehead, and how tired he looked. Sitting up all night with his cabinet, and yet he had time to come out and give us boys a word of cheer.

"I suppose that you want to hear about marching through

Georgia. Well, I was with Sherman, and I got wounded on that march. Yes sir, I got wounded by my own quartermaster; he gave me a pair of shoes too small for a baby. Lord knows what size men they thought they had in the Army. Made me walk like a Chinese woman, or a toe dancer. First night we stacked our rifles and set up our tents, I said: 'Sergeant, you've got to issue me some larger shoes or I'll join the cavalry.' S'e: 'That's all there is.' S'I: 'Then I'll go barefoot.' 'You do that and you'll sleep in the guardhouse, it's agin regulations.' Well, I walked in those shoes, and my feet have never been right since.

"On that march we had to rustle our own food. We used to start out in the morning with a canteen full of water, and when the sun came up, we drank it off fast. Then we found some hens' nests in a barn, or some turkeys', and got the eggs. We cracked these right over the canteens, and come dinner time we just poured the eggs out straight into the frying pans. They got shaken up on the walk and came out scrambled.

"And you should have seen the colored people that came out to greet us. There were old darkie men with curly white hair and whiskers like sheep, and fine big girls with red handkerchiefs on their heads. And all smiling and lifting up their hands and showing their big white teeth. Some of them fell down on their knees and grabbed us around the ankles. We boys were overcome. We didn't know what to do with them. They wanted to come right home to Wakefield with us.

"There were plenty of colored people around, but not many white ones. Johnny Reb kept well out of sight. One day the captain sends for me and he says: 'Corporal Coon, you see that big white house up there, with all the columns on it? You go on up and set fire to it.'

" 'Yes sir,' I says, for it don't pay to disobey a captain, and I assembled my platoon and led them up there. Well, it was a beautiful house, with big, high rooms and white panelings, and the walls covered with oil paintings. We didn't have time to look at all the pictures, but I thought, someday I'll come back here and take a good look at 'em. Then I remembered that they wouldn't be here, because I had to burn the place down.

"Up in the second story, in a front room with the sun shining in the windows, we found an old lady. She was setting up in bed, in a loose shawl and nightcap. She was a cross old lady, with a cane in her hand, and she shook it at us as if she'd knock our heads off. Would have had a nose or two if we'd got within range.

" 'Get out of here, you damned Yankees,' she said.

" 'Well,' I said, 'Madam, I know this is your home, and it's very likely you've lived in this fine place for a long time, but I have my orders to set fire to it. So I request you, madam, in the name of the United States Army, to remove yourself from these premises. If you ain't strong enough, madam, or have any ailment that prevents you from getting out of bed, I have some very strong and gentle soldiers here, and they can carry you.'

" 'Carry me, hell's fire and damnation!' (Excuse me, Miss Austin [the teacher], but that's what she said. These southern ladies ain't brought up like the rest of us.) 'You may carry my dead body, but you won't move me out of here alive. Go ahead. Stick a bayonet through me. If you're afraid to do that, set a fire and toast me.'

"I never seen a woman like that in all my days. She was thin as a straw and light as a feather. Her eyes were sparklike, sharp as lightning. I turned to my men and asked them: 'Has anyone here got a match?' They all said: 'No we ain't, Corporal.' I felt in my pocket and pulled my matches out, and cut my finger. A flask of water I was carrying had broken and soaked them. I struck them one by one against the side of a table, but the heads fell off all of them. Then I turned to the old lady and asked: 'Madam, maybe you've got a match? We're under orders to burn your house down.'

"She sat straight up in bed and said: 'Young man, I don't carry matches. Truth to tell, though, if I had one I'd give it to you, for you're a man that does his duty. It's your job to burn this house down, and if I was able, I'd see that you followed your orders, for my husband was an officer. But I'm very much afraid, suh, that I can't help you.'

"Then I said: 'Madam, I'm no Indian, I can't light a fire with two sticks, and I haven't got a burning glass. So I bid you good day.' So I took off my hat to her, and my men followed suit. 'One moment before you go,' says she, and she reached out her hand as if to shake with me. I reached out mine, suspecting nothing, and she dropped a gold ring into it.

"When we passed out of the room, we heard her yelling behind us. 'Just walk through the cellar on your way out,' she said, 'and help yourselves to some bourbon whiskey. There's two barrels down there.'

"Whatever you think about her, that woman was an American lady, even if she was a rebel. The house was an American house, and American people are living in it. I'll bet you her grandsons have gone to Annapolis or West Point, and are officers in the United States Army or Navy. You're all Americans the same as she was and I was. When the time comes and there's another General Sherman, you'll all go marching to whatever place he leads you to, but it won't be Georgia. That war is over. This country is united. No dynamite or anything else can ever blow us apart again."

My grandfather had not blinked once during this narrative, but now he took out his handkerchief and wiped his eyes. They were not the only wet ones in the schoolroom. I walked home in a dream, my feet feeling as if they never touched the ground.

Only once do I remember having seen my grandfather before he went blind, and then I was sitting in a baby carriage waiting for him to turn the corner and come home. Until I was eight I spent all the time I could in his house. There he told me marvelous tales, for he had traveled in the Middle East and Europe, and had forgotten nothing that he had ever seen or heard. He knew Stanley's book on Africa almost by heart, and before I was six I knew it too. After he had died, when they wheeled his body down the street on a caisson to the slow beat of muffled drums, I felt that I too was dead.

My poor brothers never shared the experience of knowing my grandfather, because they were born after his death, but my cousin Billy, who was six months my senior and lived in another town, remembers him most vividly.

But I have a private memory of my grandfather that Billy couldn't share, for obvious reasons.

One afternoon when I was very small I took a nap on my grandfather's bed. The shades had been drawn to let me sleep, but I awoke suddenly. The room was bright enough for me to see everything in it without raising my head off the pillow.

And then I saw a little man dancing just in front of the footboard. His skin was dusty black, his hair was very curly, and as the little man smiled, the rims of his eyes and his teeth glistened as white as my grandfather's shaving cup.

Although I watched him closely as he was dancing, he didn't notice me at all, nor did he make a sound. It was as if he and I were in two different worlds, just accidentally come together. When he disappeared through the door into the back hallway, I felt very sad, and didn't go to sleep again.

When I told my grandfather about the little man, he said, "Of course, he was a Pygmy. They live in Africa." And then he told me all about them, and many other wonderful things that I knew I had to see before I died.

In the fall of the year of my grandfather's death I was moved to the fifth grade in a large brick schoolhouse, farther than the last one from my home. Although it had inside plumbing, it offered worse perils than privies: If, as I often did from then on, I wanted to visit my grandmother Carleton after school, it was not as easy as going to Grandfather Coon's, because I now had to run the gauntlet between a dozen or more Irish boys walking home by the same route. Sometimes

I was able to follow a circuitous, secret path through a swamp and between houses, but this was not feasible when the ground was covered with snow or slush. Once I reached my grandmother's house only to find it surrounded by enemies.

My grandmother had a habit of tying half grapefruit rinds to a forsythia bush outside her dining room window, and filling them with suet for the birds. The day was spongy and wet, and the grapefruit rinds were full of water mixed with mushy suet. Safe inside, I reached out the window and removed the fragile yellow cup, to clamp it upside down on the rufous pate of a particular foeman. As the Irish boys could not get into the house, donnybrook was delayed.

The next time I visited my grandmother, I knocked one of the boys down with a stone inside a snowball, and removed an eyeball from another with an undisguised rock. This second bit of mayhem cost my father two thousand dollars. Although I then gave up calling on my grandmother immediately after school, the Fenian foe followed me home one day by my regular route, through pure Protestant territory, and chased me up a twenty-foot stone pylon, one of the so-called park gates. There I remained until after dark, when my father came searching for me and I climbed down unmolested.

By the time I reached high school, these doctrinaire and microethnic rivalries had abated, to be replaced by concerns which then seemed more important, one of which was sex. On the positive side, the small neighboring town of Lynnfield sent its students to Wakefield High, and most of the Lynnfield students were girls. Just as Wakefield was a dry town and Lynnfield a wet one, so the new, exotic Lynnfield girls exuded more glamour—or so we thought—than the familiar local crop.

On the negative side, one afternoon all of the boys were herded into the YMCA to hear the famous Homer Rodeheaver, Billy Sunday's trombonist. Mr. Rodeheaver pursed his plump lips and blew out a rolling hymn. Then, sweating in embarrassment, he lectured us on sex in general and masturbation in particular, stating as his principal theme that semen and cerebrospinal fluid were a single liquid connected by the spinal cord, a common duct. Every emission from below drained the supply at the top, and lowered forever the mental ability of the ejaculator. Thus we must take care never to play with ourselves, in order to ensure the continuity of the human race. Following this somber mendacity, Mr. Rodeheaver again picked up his trombone and blew out another hearty hymn, and we walked shamefacedly home— except for some of the boys who had never heard of masturbation and decided to try it.

In the last two years of grammar school, we boys were allowed to choose between carpentry and printing, and I chose printing. Before long I was able to set type, compose pages in a chase, and run a hand press. When I started high school, I found an old printing press in my grandmother Coon's attic, and my father bought me several cases and enough fonts of type of various sizes to fill them. I established myself as the proprietor of the Star Press, and as editor and publisher of *The Freshman Gazette,* established on March 25, 1918, published weekly, with advertising costing three cents a line, and selling for one cent a copy. This enterprise terminated when my assistant editor and publisher broke the handle off the press.

After that I spent most of my time out of school in the woods and other odd places, making trips by bicycle to visit my great-uncle, Aretas Hall, in the Soldiers' Home in Chelsea, and exploring a so-called cave in the Lynn Woods. For two years I never took a schoolbook home, doing all of my homework in reading periods; what reading I did elsewhere was of my own choice. Wakefield High School gave excellent instruction. There I had one year of French, two of Latin, one of Greek, and one of English composition. There was nothing wrong with the teachers or the teaching, only that the assignments were too easy, and I was bored when the work was done.

I became fractious and misbehaved, throwing stinkballs in class and pouring ink in a boy's seat while he was standing up, thus ruining his trousers when he sat down. Finally I hit a male teacher in the middle of his forehead with a pencil propelled by elastic bands, and was sent to see Mr. Howe, the principal—who, incidentally, lived across the street from us.

Charlie Howe, then an old man with a long white mustache, pointed to a chair-and-desk set screwed to a movable board platform in a corner of his office. "Carleton," he said, "this is your homeroom and that is your desk. It is where your uncles, the Carleton boys, sat."

Life was closing in on me. Finally one day I went down to the boys' toilet in the basement and hung by my arms from the pipes overhead, like an ape. The pipes fell down, the basement was flooded, and I was expelled.

I strode quietly, deep in thought, down to the shore of Lake Quannapowitt, and out onto the porous, melting ice. It began to crack. I came ashore, walked home, and faced my parents. There was no scene.

My father consulted an old friend, Theodore Eaton, a lawyer with whom he played bridge every workday morning on the train to Boston, and often golf on weekends. Mr. Eaton told my father that I needed discipline and that the best place to get it was at Andover. My

The author in his early teens, holding a lost dog on the beach in front of the family's summer house at Rexhame Terrace, Marshfield, Massachusetts.

father sent in the applications, I took the entrance examination and was admitted, with a condition in plane geometry. Two years later I was admitted to Harvard with the same condition, and before I had worked it off, I was on probation and the dean's list at the same time.

It took me only a few minutes of life at Andover to realize that I had entered a world almost as new to me as the surface of the moon before the first landing of the astronauts. No sooner had I unpacked my belongings in my small single room in Taylor Hall than an older boy burst in demanding money. He had, he claimed, lived in that room the previous year, and had supplied the radiator out of his own pocket. If I wanted the radiator, I would have to pay him for it or he would take it out. I cannot remember exactly what I said, but I did not pay him, and he left. As soon as I stepped out-of-doors, I was accosted by a group of older boys, saying: "Come here, prep, carry my suitcase." And carry it I did.

We preps were not allowed to walk down Main Street between the school buildings and the shopping area, but had to approach the latter by back streets. In the dormitory discipline was at a minimum. Our house master, whom we called Mudpuppy behind his back, usually came around once every night to make sure all hands were on deck, and seemed to have been almost totally deaf. When we dropped cakes of ice down the stairwell to smash on the floor near his back door, he paid no attention, but he came leaping up one night after we had hung a string of alarm clocks, set to go off at fifteen-minute intervals, down his fireplace chimney. Not many clocks had rung before he flew into action.

Mudpuppy taught a course on ancient history, which I enjoyed very much indeed. When the time came to take the final examination, I found that I had left my glasses in my room and received his permission to go get them, but it was a long way and would have taken a long time. As I left the room, I was faced by a portly but kindly looking old gentleman, Warren K. Morehead, who was wearing a pair of old-fashioned pince-nez. He asked me my trouble and I told him. "Try these," he said, handing me his pince-nez. They worked perfectly.

Insofar as I was capable of thinking about it at all, it seemed to me then that the wonderful discipline mentioned by Mr. Eaton must have slacked off since his school days, which had been in the 1890s. Our masters appeared to pay little if any attention to the boys outside of class, and to be utterly oblivious to our pranks, antics, and fears. But I was wrong. Since then I have learned that they have always had a good idea of what is going on and interfere only when someone is likely to be seriously hurt. But now and then they underestimated our violence, as we shall see shortly. As I soon found out in a very hard way, the overt or direct discipline exerted on us came from our peers.

A boy on my floor named Zimmer, who was two years older than I and much heavier, propped my ski pole against the inside of my door, so that when I forced it open the pole broke. This act of insolence was destructive as well as humiliating, unlike the simple stacking of my furniture which happened almost every time I left the door unlocked. So I gave Zimmer a great deal of lip, and hounded him until he reluctantly agreed to fight me. It was not fear that made him reluctant, but his obvious physical superiority.

The only room large enough to fight in was a scholarship room between two small corner singles. Its inhabitants pulled their cots against the walls, and one of them, who was from South Africa, produced a pair of thin, hard boxing gloves he had brought from that country. I had been taking boxing as a sport, and had learned how to use my left hand to advantage with right-handers, but until we had started fighting I did not know that Zimmer was also a southpaw. Soon after I made this important discovery, he landed a left punch square on the bridge of my nose, and I did not wake up until the following morning.

Alec Sutherland, the boxing coach, was vexed with me because people might think my nose had been broken in his boxing class; indeed, Zeus Benner, the Greek professor, made that assumption. I had only one consolation: My parents were in Egypt. As soon as I could get an out-of-town pass, I took the trolley car to Wakefield to see the aunt who had been left in charge of me during my parents' absence. She sent me to a doctor, whose activities in straightening my nasal bones were much more painful than Zimmer's punch—and the pain lasted longer.

Although a severe concussion, the first of many I have had, was a high price to pay for a lesson, I had learned never to challenge a reluctant adversary, however wrong he may be, if he has superior armament. If you must punish him, there are subtler and less costly methods, also more likely of success.

Another lesson I learned was not to show off my intellectual prowess, such as it was. At that period Andover had many fraternities, whose members surveyed the new boys carefully for recruitment. A prestigious boy on my floor belonged to such a fraternity. One day I wrote down the three Greek letters of the fraternity's name and tried to imagine what words they stood for, on the ground that whoever had chosen them knew little Greek. I was right, and guessed the words in a few minutes. So far so good, but I should have kept this information to myself, or at least not revealed it to an important member of the fraternity. Like an ass I told him. His face took on a very serious mien, and he called a council of members. As he told me later, they were torn between letting me in, now that I knew their secret, or beating me up; they compromised on a horrendous threat of instant destruction if I should murmur my discovery to another human being.

That was not the only trouble Greek got me into. In Zeus Benner's class we were reading the *Iliad,* which I loved almost as much as I had my grandfather's stories. On some days Zeus would give us sight reading. Flipping the pages at random, with eyes averted, he would pick out a page and a line, and ask for volunteers to translate the following passage. While I tried not to volunteer too quickly, the reader was always myself because no one else could do it. One day after class, a posse of the larger and huskier members of the class waylaid me and beat me, on the grounds that Benner and I had laid this show on be-forehand. Here I was in a real dilemma—to tell on the boys, which would lead to a worse beating, or to disappoint Zeus, who was inordinately proud of me. Word of my punishment must have leaked to the faculty, because the problem solved itself. We had little more sight reading, and no more assault and battery over it.

It was clear that I was not much of an athlete. In trying to play football, my head was stepped on and I lost consciousness. I won my numerals in the half mile in track. I came in first, but when I staggered up to the bleachers after crossing the finish line, I threw up on the shoes of the director of athletics.

But I came out well on a clandestine sport. Every spring the seniors walked to the shore of Pomp's Pond, over toward Ballardvale, to hold a farting contest. In my class the winner was a boy who later became president of a bank in Boston. A quarter of a century later one of my sons came in first, but my grandson William has reported that in his effete day the contest had been given up.

Because both my father and grandfather had been connected with Egypt in one way or another, almost as soon as I had arrived at Andover I decided to learn the ancient Egyptian language. By coincidence the man who had or knew where to get the necessary books was Ned Bartlett, an Andover resident who had a bookstore on Cornhill in Boston, now foolishly torn down. He was a bridge-playing commuter friend of my father's, and before long I had more books on the subject than I could assimilate.

When I was not doing my own work or cramming football players for examinations—this service was gratis, and my only pathway to prestige—I was bent over Egyptian texts, dictionaries, and grammars. To my immense satisfaction, before I graduated I could read many passages in hieroglyphs (never hieratic). While to the vast majority of mankind who cannot read hieroglyphs this achievement may seem miraculous, I will let the reader in on a secret. It is easy—much easier than Russian, for example, and infinitely easier than Chinese. It is almost as easy as Spanish.

The nouns have gender and number, following regular rules with almost no exceptions. The verbs are equally simple and regular, the sentence structure a sequence of subject, verb, and object. As for the writing, there are alphabetic signs, syllabic signs, and determinatives which may be pictures of the action itself; e.g., the verb *MS*, to give birth, has a determinative showing a woman doing that very thing.

One summer when he took me to Europe, my father bought me more Egyptian books in Berlin, and then paraded me in front of Cleopatra's needle in Paris. There he demanded that I translate the inscription, much to my embarrassment because the performance soon drew a crowd. Although this attention greatly pleased my father, it made me feel like jumping into the Seine.

It might have been better if I had broken the pipes in the Wakefield High School basement a year earlier than I did, because then I might have had three years at Andover instead of two. These were the most critical years of my life. Besides receiving excellent—and in one subject inspirational—teaching in categories of learning essential for a broad general education, I was transformed, I hope, from a confused, spoiled, overconfident adolescent into a youth capable of taking care of himself under most circumstances, although with little social grace. These years were my puberty ceremony, an age-old rite of passage incorporating the three standard and successive factors of isolation, ordeals, and eventual incorporation into a new biological and social condition.

In the wide world of man that anthropologists study, puberty rites are automatic and standard procedure, because they are necessary for the development of an adult personality at an impressionable age. In our frontier days, depicted over and over again in western movies and television shows, life on the frontier was a puberty rite in itself, and the interest of urban and suburban youth in these dramatic presentations is a vicarious substitute for the same.

A society that omits these rites is diseased, but I shall pursue this subject no further here because this is a book of memoirs, not a jeremiad. In any case, the school that whipped me more or less into shape was of that kind that Xenophon wrote about in his *Cyropedia*, in which he himself taught the sons of the Persian elite. Andover was an overseas counterpart—but not an imitation of—the English public schools, which, in a lemming-like mood, the British Labour Government of the late 1960s tried to downgrade.

It may be added that the rite of passage through which we went produced some results unexpected to us, but not unpredictable to others. We did not know, but the faculty probably did, that the names of the boys voted most likely to succeed would be as scarce in *Who's Who* as names beginning with X. Benjamin McLane Spock, whose books about rearing babies are found on at least as many shelves as *Fanny Farmer's Cookbook*, received less notice than even myself, who was listed as the Class Grind.

2. Harvard

In those days most Andover graduates went on to Yale. Harvard was unpopular, and only a half dozen of us chose it. I entered Harvard with a condition in plane geometry which I did not lose for over two years, when I was on the dean's list and probation at the same time. I finally passed the course by going to the Widow Nolan's cramming school on Massachusetts Avenue, right across from the Yard. The Widow said, "Just imagine you are a sailor sitting on a bench on Boston Common. A pretty girl comes along and sits on your lap. That is how you superimpose two triangles." From then on plane geometry was duck soup. I took the exam in College Boards, passed it, lost my condition, and went up to Andover to collect my diploma.

Well before going to Harvard, my father used to take me with him on business trips, for company. One day during my freshman year he insisted on my cutting classes and accompanying him to Fall River for another purpose—as interpreter. He was taking along an Alsatian representative of a textile machinery house. The Alsatian spoke no English, and my father no French or German. I was to explain things to the Alsatian in schoolboy versions of both languages.

The Alsatian was a short, plump man with a considerable paunch. His jacket was a little too tight for him, and he could fasten only one button. The proprietor of the factory showed my father and the Alsatian a new spindle he had just invented, of which he was modestly proud. He was not quite sure of his patent rights, and pledged the Alsatian to secrecy. A pile of these spindles stood on a table, and when both the proprietor's and my father's backs were turned, the Alsatian quickly grabbed one of the spindles and put it under his jacket, just over his ample buttocks and under his lumbar curve, which was considerable, and he had his one button back in place before the proprietor and my father turned around. I was the only one who saw this theft, but I did not want to expose the Alsatian at that point, and could not think of what to do.

While we were on the return trip, we passed through a wooded section in a township where a few Indians still lived, and I said to the Alsatian, "We are now passing through redskin country."

"Are they dangerous?" he asked tremulously.

"Very," I replied. "They hide behind trees and shoot arrows at people."

The Alsatian dropped immediately to the floor of the backseat where he and I were riding, the button popped, and the spindle rolled out on the floor. I quickly picked it up and handed it to my father.

In order to distract the Man Who Was Afraid of Indians even more, I said, "As a matter of fact my father's chauffeur is an Indian, too, but he is relatively harmless."

Like my first statement, this one had an element of truth in it. My father's chauffeur was the son of an Iroquois father and a Gaelic-speaking Scottish mother. As we neared Boston, the Alsatian got up, holding his jacket together because of the lack of a button, and never mentioned the spindle, which my father had secreted in the glove compartment.

During my freshman year, I took Egyptology 1 with Professor Andrew Reisner, which meant a long subway and trolley ride to the Boston Museum of Fine Arts. The other members of the class were graduate students. There the other students laboriously learned to read hieroglyphs, but as I could already read them Reisner gave me more advanced work to do. He was a thickset, vigorous man with rather prominent brown eyes, which never blinked, and he frightened nearly everybody. He spent much time denouncing all his rivals, particularly Sir Flinders Petrie, who, he said, had gotten his job because he was a king's bastard, and did not know how to excavate. One of the other students, who spent a season at the Pyramids with Reisner, said that at that time Reisner was excavating a section of earth, known as the Harvard Concession, at the foot of the Great Pyramid. One morning he was in the expedition house working over his notes when one of his assistants rushed breathlessly in, crying, "Professor Reisner, Professor Reisner, a man has fallen off the Pyramid and broken his neck."

"Did he land in the Harvard Concession?" asked Reisner.

"No, he fell in the French Concession."

"Then don't bother me," said Reisner. "I have work to do."

Two years later Reisner gave a general course in Egyptology, this time in the Peabody Museum. I took it, and he invited me to join his team in the field, but I declined because I wanted to study living peoples, and not work in a single area.

In my freshman year I had another stroke of fortune. Having failed to pass an exam in English composition (now called creative writing in most colleges), I had to take English A—freshman English—and was put in a class under Grant Code, a poet and inspiring teacher. From him I learned about writing, including Chester Greenough's rule about unity, coherence, and emphasis, and particularly not to start writing a composition until I had outlined it in full. In my sophomore year Grant wangled me into Charles T. Copeland's English 12, a class limited to fewer than twenty students, all of the others graduate students.

In my freshman year I also took History 1 (compulsory) with the late Friskie Merriman, a tall, blond man of impressive mien who had a habit of pronouncing *R* like *W*. My chief memory of this course was Friskie's statement: "Gentlemen, we will now consider the pwivate life of Cathewine of Wussia. Gentlemen, Cathewine of Wussia had no pwivate life."

This course required much outside reading, and all the books were in the basement of Widener Library, reached by a separate outside door. It was presided over by a small, wiry, and elderly man named Mr. Mahady. Once when I was in there, Mr. Mahady asked me to give him a sample of my signature. As the piece of paper was large, I wrote large. He then produced a number of slips for books that had been taken out. All were signed "Carleton S. Coon" in a cramped space, for there was little room for a signature on the slip.

"You have deliberately faked this signature," said he, holding up the piece I had just signed. "You have stolen these books!" He grabbed me by the throat and hit me in the face, saying, "You bastard, I will have you kicked out of college for this."

In a state of near shock, I walked across the yard and up the stairs of University Hall to the office of Chester Greenough, dean of the college. Dean Greenough was Wakefield born, and a close friend of my Aunt Grace Carleton's husband. I told him my story, which he believed. Later on the missing books were found in a student's room, along with many others also taken out under other students' signatures. What happened to the thief after that I never learned, but in any case this episode made me allergic to Widener Library, which I never entered again, except once or twice when I was on the faculty. Later on, if I wanted any books from Widener, I ordered them through the Peabody Museum Library. But I did no more reading for History 1, and flunked it with a D.

That same year I took Paleontology 1, with a handful of others. All we had to do was draw pictures of dinosaurs and mammoths. I got an A, and believe that most if not all the others did, too. The next year about one hundred students signed up for Paleontology 1, but steps were taken, and that was the end of that gut course.

During my sophomore year I repeated my Andover practice of tutoring gratis members of the varsity teams who were in danger of being barred from the playing fields for poor marks. Their trouble was not that they were stupid, but that they worked so hard at athletics every afternoon that in the evenings they were too tired to study. In this way I compensated to a certain extent for my lack of athletic prowess.

In my freshman year I had gone out for freshman crew and absentmindedly stepped through the floor of a shell, which began to sink immediately. Bert Haines, an Englishman and the freshman coach, fixed me with his steely blue eyes. "What intelligence," he said. My father had to pay for the damage to the shell.

During my sophomore year I went out for fencing, but was barred after the second lesson on the grounds that I was left-handed. This ended my athletic career at Harvard.

That same year I took Philosophy A, also required. The lecturer had a speech impediment, and seemed to be talking mostly about the question of whether or not we actually existed. Again the assignments were in Widener, so I did no reading. I attended classes, but did not listen. My Arabic class followed the next hour, and I spent my time in philosophy class preparing for it. I bluffed the final exam in Philosophy A and got a C double minus.

Arabic interested me in three ways: I wanted to learn a language spoken all the way from the Atlantic to the Persian Gulf. I wanted to know how the Muslim peoples' minds worked. Most of all I wanted to learn to pray flawlessly so that when I became an explorer I might pass as a proper Muslim, like my fabled heroes, Sir Richard Burton and Charles Doughty.

When I started I was a little over eighteen, probably a year or two too old to be able to learn to pronounce all the critical consonants gargled in the back of the vocal cavity, or roughened by humping the tongue in the roof of the palate. But I practiced them as assiduously as I was able, to my roommates' annoyance, more or less as a concert pianist exercises his fingers. The result was equivocal. I may have fooled Muslims whose native tongues were no more Arabic than mine was, but never tried it in Arabia, where I was most obviously a Christian.

The sophomore year held many compensations, not only in Arabic but in English 12 and Anthropology 1. Copeland's English class met at 2:00 P.M. twice a week. Copey, as he was called, was a short man with a huge head covered with a derby hat, and he wore starched white shirts with stiff collars attached, not held on by collar buttons. He had a mustache and carried a bamboo cane. During classes he talked about almost anything except English composition—including his problems with having his shirts laundered—but he was always interesting. Sometimes he read to us from his favorite books, and he was a magnificent reader; in fact, he sometimes gave readings in one of his rooms in

Hollis Hall to all who could crowd in. Now and then he had guest speakers, including Robert Benchley and Robert Sherwood.

These meetings were far from being the heart of the course. Once a week he had each one of us come to his rooms and read to him a new composition. He would listen carefully, and then dictate a critique. Some of these were devastating, but all were to the point. Among the tricks of the trade he taught us were: Rely heavily on the senses, particularly sight, sound, and smell; every fourth sentence or so must be a periodic sentence, to sustain suspense; if you can find an Anglo-Saxon word to replace one derived from Latin, use the Anglo-Saxon one. My chief trouble was not putting in enough periodic sentences, at least in the first draft, and there was hardly time each week to rewrite a composition.

Copey once said to me: "Coon, all Cornishmen are natural writers, and you are a Cornishman. Make the best of your natural gifts." He then told me to read the books of George Borrow, one of which was *Lavengro* ("There's wind on the heath, brother"). He was also partial to Irish students, to whom he ascribed comparable gifts. One of them, named Gilligan, wrote a bloodcurdling account of a day in an undertaker's embalming room, which Copey read to the class with gusto.

One of Copey's friends on the faculty was George Pierce Baker, who ran the famous 47 Workshop in Massachusetts Hall, which had been gutted by fire and was a magnificent empty shell, perfect for making stage sets and trying out plays written by the students, who came from far and near. Don Oenslager, the famous set maker, was there, and Eugene O'Neill came from time to time. Although English 47 was also a graduate course, Copey connived to get me in during my junior year.

Alas, all this effort was for nothing. The powers that were decided to rebuild the inside of Massachusetts Hall and make it into offices for the administration. There was no other place for George Baker to set up his workshop, and he resigned and went to Yale. Aside from George Baker, no one could have felt more let down than I did, because his graduate students could go with him. In late April 1972, Massachusetts Hall was occupied by about fifteen black students protesting Harvard's ownership of some Gulf Oil stock, because Gulf does business with Angola. Had George Baker been still alive, it might have amused him to see Massachusetts Hall once more the scene of a drama.

In my sophomore year I also took Anthropology 1 under Earnest Hooton, a great and inspiring teacher, as all who have studied under him know. Changing my concentration from English to anthropology, I took every course in the department, helped Hooton in his laboratory (especially with Guanche skulls from the Canary Islands which he had personally collected), and was a frequent visitor to his house, where Mrs. Hooton and he served tea to visitors every afternoon.

In those days everyone taking anthropology knew everyone else, and the faculty—consisting of Alfred Marston Tozzer and Roland Burrage Dixon as well as Hooton—knew us all, too. It was a far cry from the frenzied anonymity of many anthropology departments these days, where most professors do not know their students' names, and classes, instead of fewer than thirty, consist of hundreds of students, sometimes reaching the thousand mark. Hooton and Tozzer held "seminars" in their own houses about once a week, where we were privileged to listen to such men as Sylvanus Griswold Morley, who had excavated Copán in Honduras; Alfred Vincent Kidder, the father of southwestern archaeology and the restorer of Chichén Itzá; Bronislaw Malinowski; and Marcel Mauss, the French sociologist. I remember Franz Boas coming once, but he failed to inspire me as the others did. In return he ignored my existence.

In those same days the annual meetings of the American Anthropological Association were held at Andover during the Christmas vacation, when most of the students had left and dormitory rooms were available. We met in Peabody Hall, and ate in its basement in the Grill, where the food was first class, and where I had often eaten as a student when the beanery fare was insufferable.

Boas, Hrdlička, Weidenreich, Sapir, and other celebrities were usually there, and Hrdlička and Weidenreich usually got into an argument. Once Weidenreich was talking about the fetalization of tiny dogs, such as the King Charles spaniel. Hrdlička interrupted him in his usual fiery manner, shouting: "Vat do ducks haf to do vit antropology?"

Weidenreich replied: "I am not talking about ducks, I am talking about ducks [meaning dogs]."

It was a lot of fun, and well worth the drive from Cambridge to Andover.

From my sophomore year on, I kept on taking every course offered in anthropology and graduated *magna cum laude* at midyear early in 1925. History 1, Philosophy A, and the basement of Widener Library had ruled out a *summa*. Still occupying my old dormitory quarters, I continued on as a graduate student.

The transition from undergraduate to graduate status was uneventful. I had already begun seeing more of the graduate students than of my classmates, and had been to Morocco in 1924 and 1925. In April 1926 I took my general examination for a Ph.D. in the smoking room of the Peabody Museum basement. Present were the three professors of anthropology plus Kirk Bryan, professor of geology.

I went there with the mistaken idea that if I failed to answer one question, I would automatically have failed the whole examination, and would have to walk out. I was very nervous and sweating profusely. When Kirk Bryan asked me one that I could not answer at all (having never taken geology), I stood up to leave, and Tozzer asked me where I was going. I said, "Home. I have failed."

"Sit down," he said, "and finish the examination."

It took three hours. When it was through, I was told to wait outside. Nervously I paced up and down the basement corridor, but not for long. Tozzer emerged from the smoking room and asked me to come in.

"You have passed," he announced, and they all shook my hand.

Also in April Mary Goodale and I were married. She was a granddaughter of my grandfather's friend General Greenleaf Goodale. We moved into an apartment on Prescott Street, where we soon discovered that we were not alone. When Mary first opened the bedroom closet door, she saw on the floor a human embryo in a jar of alcohol. Mary was then a junior at Wellesley, and commuted there five days a week. But she dropped out before the end of her junior year because we were making plans for a trip to Morocco.

On the way home from that trip, in 1927, we stopped over in Paris. In the American Hospital in Neuilly, Mary gave birth to our first son, Carleton S. Coon, Jr., who has resented being called Junior ever since. He has had the good sense not to name any of his three sons C.S.C. III.

Our son's birth at Neuilly was eclipsed by another and vastly better known event. Charles A. Lindbergh, also a junior, landed in his *Spirit of St. Louis* at Le Bourget Airport, three weeks after our son's birth but while Mary was still in the hospital. As many of the nurses were Swedish and identified themselves with Lindbergh, this created a subject of continuous conversation.

From May 1927 to April 1928 I worked doggedly on my doctoral dissertation, entitled, at Tozzer's suggestion, "A Study of the Fundamental Racial and Cultural Characteristics of the Berbers of North Africa as Exemplified by the Riffians." I had wanted to call it simply "Tribes of the Rif" until Tozzer pointed out that the latter sounded purely descriptive whereas a Ph.D. thesis was supposed to be analytical, as mine really was. As usual, he was right.

At commencement in 1928 my Ph.D. was granted, with an M.A. thrown in as a dividend. Actually I got my diploma out of a drawer in the dean's office, as I had my Andover and Harvard undergraduate sheepskins, for I am allergic to ceremonies. Today I find only

one living anthropologist whose American Ph.D. antedates mine—
Harry L. Shapiro's, granted in 1926. Li Chi (1923) and Leslie A. White
(1927) died in 1975 and 1979, regretfully. If there are more ancient
survivors, please let me know.

One reason why Harry Shapiro and I both got our Ph.D.'s at
age twenty-four was the Harvard system of letting undergraduates take
advanced courses if qualified, and not requiring candidates to get an
M.A. first. Nowadays, the male Ph.D. candidate is likely to be married,
has one or more children, his wife has to work, and his career may have
been interrupted by military service.

As for working, I had one job that was particularly satisfying. I
shared it with my classmates Douglas S. Byers and P. T. L. Putnam, and
it was well paid in terms of the pre-Depression wage scale. It was editing
educational films for the Pathé Exchange, Inc., of New York. We were
sent can after can of 35-mm, black and white, silent prints of film shot
in Africa, Melanesia, Polynesia, and elsewhere. Among them was
Robert Flaherty's *Nanook of the North.*

Being too long for our purposes, we had to cut it, and we also
changed some of the captions for our own special purposes. In 1972 I
was horrified to learn that not only had the negatives of *Nanook* been
lost, but also that the copy we had tampered with had been the only
existing print. Mrs. Flaherty was justly upset by this negligence on the
part of the film companies. Had either of my companions or I been
able to see forty-three years into the future, the film we worked on
would never have been touched.*

Many other things happened during my graduate school days,
but only one of them seems worth describing in the space allotted me.
It is a true story which might, if written as fiction, have been entitled
"The Case of the Pickled Brains." I never wrote it down, but I remember it as if it happened yesterday.

While I was studying physical anthropology (Anthropology 2)
with Earnest Hooton, he had a glass jar in the lab at the head of the
fifth-floor stairs in the Peabody Museum. In the jar were three decapitated human heads one atop the other. One was that of an American
Indian, another of a Hindu, and the third, as I remember, that of a
Chinese. So tightly did they fit in the space that their noses were pressed
against the glass like those of children peering through windows to
await the arrival of the mailman. The important thing about these
heads was that they were one hundred years old, and had been pickled
all that time in alcohol.

Relax, Nanook lovers. A whole print has been found and the film reissued.

When I was in my senior year, or first term of graduate school (it was the same year), Hooton moved the jar out of the lab and set it up as an exhibit at the head of the staircase, which ended there. One day a pregnant woman who had climbed the five flights of stairs paused to catch her breath, saw those heads staring at her, and swooned. She claimed that she had suffered a miscarriage as a result, and threatened to sue Harvard. Hooton then took the jar back into the lab, but lost interest in the heads.

A little later a Polish medical researcher named Rodokievic, who was working at the Harvard Medical School on the effects of alcohol on the brain, asked permission to remove the brains and to take them to the medical school. Hooton granted him permission. Dr. Rodokievic removed them from the jar and placed them side by side in a glass tray.

The next problem was to get them to the medical school. I volunteered to help him. So we carried them downstairs to the front entrance, where my 1922 Cadillac was parked, and started our journey. We crossed the Lars Andersen Bridge over the Charles River without incident, but as we were driving along Brighton Avenue I was exceeding the speed limit. Soon we heard a siren, and a motorcycle policeman stopped me, dismounted, and came alongside.

"And where do you think you are going, young man, to be in such a hurry?" he asked in a friendly brogue.

"Officer," I said, "we're rushing them to the medical school," pointing to the glass tray Rodokievic was balancing on his lap.

"Sure," he replied, "then I'll give you an escort." And so he did, riding ahead of us, siren open, all the way to our destination.

This episode took place in either 1926 or 1927, between two of my fact-seeking trips to Morocco, where I did the work that won me my doctorate. Although there were temporal gaps between these excursions, I shall relate them seriatim, as I have just done with my formal education, for the sake of continuity.

3. With Gordon to Morocco

During my junior year at Harvard, Hooton, who had never been there, gave a half course on the races and cultures of Africa. In it he described in vivid terms the allegedly blood-thirsty habits of the Riffians. They were northern Moroccan Berber mountaineers, some of whom were blond, and how they had gotten there was a mystery I hoped to solve.

At that time they were in revolt against their Spanish conquerors, under their remarkable leader, Sidi Mohammed ben Abd el-Krim el-Khattabi, better known to the infidels as simply Abd el-Krim. Gordon Canning, the grandson of the liberator of Greece, had already gone to Morocco at risk of his life to negotiate a peace settlement, but without success. The American newsman Vincent Sheean had also made two trips in disguise to interview Abd el-Krim. I had read his accounts in the press, but his book *An American Among the Riffi* did not appear until 1926, when I was there on my third—and first successful—attempt to follow in the footprints of these two audacious men.

One evening in the spring of 1924 I heard a knock on my door in Matthews Hall, Room 1. When I opened it, along with the damp vernal air entered a young man whom I had not seen before. Athletic in build, with an aquiline nose and a shock of stiff blond hair that stood erect on his scalp, he looked at me and said: "I am Gordon Browne. I understand that you plan to go to Morocco."

"Yes, I do," I answered.

Although I had to face an examination the next morning, we stayed up late planning a trip for the coming summer. We have since seen each other many times in different parts of the world, and he is now living in vigorous retirement in Tangier. Two years before I first met him he had graduated from Harvard, where he had also taken Hooton's course. At that moment he was employed in the curious, for him, job of tasting tea. He was fed up. He wanted to go to the Rif as much as I did. We arranged to meet in Paris a few months later.

In the glare and baking heat of midsummer 1924 we stepped ashore from a Bordeaux packet at Casablanca, which was then a miniature city centered about a large square, Le Place de l'Horloge, named after a tall clock tower, behind which we soon located the American consulate. On the north side of the square stood the gates of the kasbah, and there was only one street of European shops, entering the square by the Hotel Excelsior. That is how I remember Casablanca. The last time I went there, in the fall of 1962, it was a maze of white canyons holding a million people.

We tarried there long enough to catch a bus to Fez, the first genuine Islamic city I had visited. General Lyautey had wisely forbidden both the construction of modern buildings and the use of wheeled vehicles within its walls. Instead, he had laid out the modern Fez Nouvelle some distance away; at that time it was still small.

The narrow streets of the old city twisted and turned, sheltered from the sun by lattices and grapevines, and they were lined with small shops full of tasty and beautiful merchandise. In the spicers' *suk* open baskets of cardamom, cinnamon, saffron, chilies, turmeric, and shiny Spanish flies cast their combined odors into the air, and anyone with half a nose who has ever slept in Fez will die remembering that allspice scent.

Through these tortuous corridors laden donkeys filed, their drivers shouting hoarsely, *"Balek! Balek! Balek!"* (Make way! Look out!; literally, Your attention!) When some of them cried: *"Balek ez-zīt"* we really looked out, for that meant "Look out for the oil!" Donkeys were carrying baskets of dripping ripe olives to the oil presses.

From Fez we rode a bus eastward to Taza, a small but strategic city on the watershed between the Atlantic coastal plain and the Algerian border, where the Riffian mountain chain to the north and the Middle Atlas to the south almost meet. Because both ranges were inhabited by warlike and hostile Berber tribesmen, it was—and remains—a most vulnerable spot. Its capture could block the fertile and populous western part of Morocco from its more arid eastern part, and from access to Algeria.

When we boarded the bus, Gordon and I could feel an atmosphere of uneasiness among the other passengers. Once we had left the cultivated land, the Trik al-Sultan, or Sultan's Road, turned into a fan of tracks crossing open country, and the driver steered his vehicle wherever the ground seemed most suitable. Some riders were muttering that Riffian patrols had been crossing it lately, and that if the Riffians were to catch a Christian they would bury him up to his neck in an anthill, after having castrated him totally, placing his genitalia between his teeth.

As I found out later, the first statement is untrue, and the second inapplicable to Christians, being reserved for fellow Muslims caught in adultery by cuckolded husbands.

While the bus rolled and bumped along, Gordon and I heard someone singing behind us in a voice loud enough to attract our attention. His song was: "Oh, the cowboy has his troubles, and the city fella too; but to sort of grin and bear it is the best that both can do."

The singer was a Frenchman, also newly arrived. He had been a cowboy in Canada, and he was looking for work.

In 1924 Taza consisted of a fortified hill inhabited by a small Moroccan community and a French garrison. On the flat land leading to the Royal Road stood a French Bureau of Native Affairs and the usual Hotel Transatlantique, in which we lodged. To the right of the road winding to the top of the hill was the mouth of a cave, gaping in the morning sunlight. Its name was Kef el-Ghar, a redundancy, because both words mean cave. It had been hurriedly excavated. In it I found one massive human jaw, which I brought back to the Peabody Museum.

But Gordon and I were bent on discovering other, virginal caves. To the south of the city, in a steep and narrow pass, Gordon spied one high on a ledge over a concave wall. He got up there, how I do not know, and of course it had no earthen floor. He had much more trouble climbing down. His safe descent amazed me as well as a posse of Berber horsemen from the Middle Atlas who were riding by. They seemed to be wondering whether or not they might be blamed, and I was writing a report in French in my mind.

A few days later I crawled through the mouth of another cave, just wide enough to let my head pass without scraping off my ears. Being then quite thin, I eased the rest of my body through the six-inch gap by twisting my shoulders and hips vertically. Inside, the cave began to widen, but before I could explore its inner recesses I heard a rattling. On the floor I found the long quill of an African porcupine; I took the time to pick it up and then hastily, if awkwardly, departed.

A third cave had a ground-level entrance both wide and high enough so that two men could walk into it without stooping. It might easily have had bones and implements in its fine-grained, soft brown floor, but we were not destined to find out. We heard the muffled footsteps of armed men wearing grass sandals. They were coming in our direction.

Peering out, we saw a Riffian patrol in yellow turbans and short brown jellabas. They were well armed, and could have whipped their rifles to their shoulders in a second. Gordon and I, aged twenty-two and twenty, had been toying with the idea of enlisting in Abd el-Krim's army, and we hesitated on the brink of stepping out. Which one of us held the other back, neither of us remembers. When the patrol had passed, we both let out a "Whew!"

As a Riffian officer told me two years later, we had made the right decision.

4. A Sheldon Fellow

In the next summer, that of 1925, I returned to Morocco on a Sheldon Fellowship from Harvard. It provided a stipend intended to enable a frugal honors graduate to spend a year studying quietly abroad. Although it was not nearly enough money for what I had in mind, it was a help.

When I arrived once more in Casablanca, I was not as starry-eyed as I had been in 1924. It had been a long ocean trip, and it would take me just as long to get home. I noticed this because I was in love with Mary Goodale, the granddaughter of Brigadier General Greenleaf A. Goodale, a veteran of many wars from the Civil to the Spanish, including Indian fighting in the West. General Goodale and my grandfather Coon were friends. They had had a rifle range on a hill in Wakefield, where they shot together.

Another reason for my diffidence was that the French had begun fighting the Riffians on the French side of the border that divided their zone from Spain's. Without hope of going there, I would have to mark time and find other places to go, other things to do.

That year's companion was a Harvard classmate from Chicago, Thomas Arnold Barrett Scudder, a huge amateur boxer who had won a prize in London and who had the makings of a heavyweight champion.

One of my earliest memories of Tom was when another classmate, Patrick Tracy Lowell Putnam, a nephew of sorts of President Lowell, popped out of a sixth-floor attic window of the Peabody Museum and ran out onto the two-foot-wide, downward-sloping zinc ledge outside, with Tom close behind him.

Pat ran around the sill of the whole building—geology, botany, glass flowers, zoology, and all. Near the starting point, where an audience of lip-biting spectators had assembled as if from nowhere, Tom caught Pat and they wrestled, but neither fell.

When Pat, Tom, and I met in Paris later that year, Tom volunteered to come with me to Morocco, but Pat had other fish to fry, like going to Dutch New Guinea to live among headhunters.

In Casablanca I bought a Model T Ford, a tent, and digging equipment. We drove to Rabat, where I presented my credentials to M. de Liouville, Director of Antiquities of the Protectorate. A most amiable gentleman, he readily agreed to let me excavate a Paleolithic site, and helpfully suggested one near Tit Mellil (Berber for White Spring), outside Casablanca. It was that city's source of water. Then capped, it had been a famous spring, known to Strabo the Geographer, and long before that the watering place of rhinoceroses and other Pleistocene fauna.

With the help of a few local men I dug out of it many Acheulean hand axes struck from lumps of quartzite, many rhinoceros horn cores, and other bones and artifacts. All are still in the Peabody Museum at Harvard. Although I tried to excavate layer by layer, as Reisner had taught me, there was no stratification. M. de Liouville had given me a disturbed site to practice on.

Meanwhile Tom wandered about with his Doberman, Piet-sche, collecting tortoises, snakes, and other "slow game"; but most of his time was spent sketching horses, mules, and donkeys, all in motion. He brought them all to life in split-second timing, and he was a most accurate, fast-sketching draftsman. Despite my protests, he thought he wasn't good enough—he would neither keep his sketches nor let me hold them for him. Before we left he tore them into pieces and burned them up.

We left because I was sick. One day we had gone boar hunting with a group of French colons, and became very thirsty. A French priest drank some water out of a pool covered with green slime. "It's good," he said. "I always drink this."

I followed his example and came down with amoebic dysentery. Furthermore, I had been excavating, bare to the waist, under the merciless rays of the early July sun. I started to get sunstroke. We broke camp and moved to Fedhala, then a small and fashionable seaside resort where the de Liouvilles stayed—monsieur, madame, and daughter Daisy, along with the British consul who walked naked, monocle in eye, on the beach where many Americans would die seventeen years later. The first time we went there, Mme. de Liouville had plucked a small octopus off my arm. This time, they had gone.

I went out of my head, raving, and must have remained in that condition for about a week before I came to my senses.

Later, when strong enough, I drove Tom to Casablanca on a shopping trip. He went to a gunsmith to buy ammunition, and we were to meet at the sidewalk café of the Excelsior. When we started, I felt uneasy about Tom's appearance. He had grown a beard, which emphasized the flatness of his broken nose, and he wore a wide-brimmed hat with a live snake tied around it as a hatband. I had tried to discourage him, but without success. Tom was late, and as I sipped a drink in the café I began to feel jumpy.

Finally a precocious Arab street boy, one of the sort we always used to see hanging around cafés to run errands and to dispense unsolicited information, approached me in agitation.

"El-maidāni, el-maidāni, fil hibs!" he cried, meaning: "The giant, the giant, he's in jail!"

I found Tom locked in a cell with a number of unlicensed Arab prostitutes who did not seem to mind his company. I then ran to the office of Mr. Russell, the American consul, who was not surprised, and who soon had Tom released. This is what had happened: Tom was walking across the Place de l'Horloge when three plainclothesmen grabbed him. They had mistaken him for a Russian deserter from the Foreign Legion whose description, they said, matched his. When they refused to believe that he was an American, he knocked their heads together and walked off, leaving them on the ground. Before he had neared the café where I was sitting, a whole squadron of uniformed police had captured him, and on to jail.

Soon after this we moved to Marrakesh, where we shared an Arab house with the two staff members of the local branch of the Bank of British West Africa. The house had a wide courtyard, in which I started to make anthropometric measurements of country people—just as I had done at Tit Mellil, where I had managed to get fifteen—but I gave up. I was still not strong enough. Tom and I used to sit in a café on the edge of the Jema'a el-Fnar (Meeting Place of Lanterns). There we ate liver kebabs broiled on bicycle-spoke spits and watched Shluh dancing boys, water vendors, jugglers, native healers bleeding and cupping their patients, and other diverting spectacles.

Among the many festivals enacted in Marrakesh was the dance of the Hamadsha, a splinter group of the Aissawa, or worshippers of a saint named Aissa (Jesus) buried at Meknes. In 1925 they were forbidden to perform in the Jema'a el-Fnar, but met behind an adobe wall on the edge of the city. There they danced themselves into a frenzy, frothed at the mouth, and sliced their own heads with axes.

Tom and I, still in my weakened state, went to this ceremony; I brought my Graflex, the big, old square box camera so rugged that once when mine bounced out of the Model T onto the road, it was not damaged. To use this camera, I had to hold it at waist level and look through a felt-lined opening in the top, a routine that left me quite vulnerable. Standing on the ground, I could see only the other spectators' backs.

So I climbed onto Tom's shoulders. He held my legs while I focused. It was not long before some of the head choppers spied me committing this sacrilege and tore through the crowd to chase us with their axes. Not waiting to set me down, Tom turned and coursed like a wolfhound until we reached the safety of a tinned-gasoline depot run by an old missionary British friend, Mr. Lennox. I jumped down, and we laid some loading planks from the curb to the middle of the street to trip the head choppers, should they follow us that far. Then we dashed out the back door, and the chase was over.

Shortly after that I was told of some lovely caves on a road running east from Marrakesh toward the mountains. As Tom did not opt to come, I drove alone in my Model T. Feeling weak from malaria, which I had also contracted, I ran my vehicle into a culvert and wrecked it. As I was surveying the damage I heard the steps of many men, coming from the mountains. So I crawled under the culvert and hid until the sound of their steps had died out. They may have numbered from fifty to one hundred. Later I heard that they were rebellious tribesmen on a raid.

After they had passed I crawled out and walked over to some Arab tents pitched a few hundred yards away. Their owners led me into one of them, where I collapsed, and they gave me sweet, thick camel's milk to drink. At that time my spoken Arabic was still rudimentary. I always carried with me my Moroccan-Arabic dictionary, written by the Reverend Budgett Meakin, and published in 1894. Its covers were bright red, its letters gold. When stuck for a word, I would look it up in Meakin and write it out in Arabic script.

Although few, if any, of them could read, this performance stirred them. They asked me to let them hold the book in their hands, and they passed it around, kissing it. When I was strong enough to leave, they escorted me out to my Model T. For an hour or more I stood beside it, until a truck rolled along. The driver towed the Ford to Marrakesh, with me beside him in the cab.

Within a few days the combined forces of amoebic dysentery, typhoid, and malaria immobilized me. I was admitted to the only hospital in Marrakesh, in a high-vaulted palace taken over by the French Foreign Legion. In order to get in I had to sign a paper, but am not sure what it said. If it made me a legionnaire I certainly would have heard of it later, because the hospital was so awful that I escaped, simply by walking out when the entrance was unguarded. I retrieved my Ford, which had been repaired, and drove back to Fedhala, then collapsed in my room in the hotel. One night I heard some men in the corridor discussing where they should bury me, a foreigner, Protestant, and all.

Somehow this conversation gave me the strength to escape once more, and I was taken to another hospital run by pretty French nuns. They cared for me with utmost kindness, and when I was beginning to recover they cabled my father. He telephoned my Uncle Will, then practicing medicine in Bridgeport, Connecticut, and when I stepped off the packet in Bordeaux, my father and Uncle Will met me. By then I was blind in one eye and walking with a cane. I was taken home and put to bed in my parents' home, where I studied for my Ph.D. orals. Soon I received a notice from the Harvard bursar's office, demanding part of my Sheldon Fellowship back. I had not stayed out a whole academic year.

Following my recovery, which included regaining the sight in my left eye, I passed my oral examinations and married my fiancée, Mary Goodale, a young woman of great beauty and a fiery disposition, who bore me two sons. Our marriage lasted eighteen years.

After leaving Marrakesh I never saw Tom Scudder again. He was off somewhere in pursuit of further adventures, doubtless with his dog, Pietsche, which probably survived him, because Tom was later shot in Chicago by an intruder who was attacking a kennel keeper's wife. The bullet lodged in his brain, and he died slowly, expiring on January 11, 1931, only five and a half years after he had saved me from the head choppers' axes. He might have become a great painter, had he tamed down a bit, and lived. I miss him.

5. A Hazardous Honeymoon

I returned to Morocco in June 1926, this time with Mary and her dog, a buff-colored Great Dane named Marduk. We got off the Algeciras ferry at Tangier, a gem of a city, then full of Riffian refugees. Some had been made homeless by the Abd el-Krim war; others had fled there earlier when their houses had been burned down by their victors in feuds. Still others had been born there, into the second or third generation. For the first time in Morocco I saw blond men who might have been Harvard football backs walking about in yellow turbans and brown jellabas.

The war in the Rif was barely over. Instead of waiting to barge in there and start measuring these racially exotic people, we could begin right away in Tangier. So I rented a small-time photographer's studio, and let the word drop that I would pay real Riffians a small fee for the privilege of recording their bodily dimensions.

One of our first subjects was an elderly *fqih* (cleric, clerk, schoolmaster) who had left his tribe on the run after having made a serious mistake while circumcising a baby boy. The Riffian technique is to stretch the prepuce over a still-moist sheep dropping perched on the tip of the infant's glans, and then to cut through foreskin and pellet with one practiced snip of a pair of sharp scissors. This poor *fqih* had placed his cut one lump too low.

One of our last subjects was a beardless youth with pink cheeks. I thought he might be a year or two too young, but I started to measure him anyway, fully clothed and barefoot, as usual. When it came to recording skin color with the help of a standard enamel matching plate, my routine was to observe both the exposed (and possibly tanned) parts of the body and the unexposed. For the latter I asked him to unbutton his shirt. When he did, I saw a pair of fully developed female breasts, and so did the other subjects awaiting their turns. Rumors spread quickly in Tangier, the city of potential pillars of salt.

I bought a secondhand automobile in which Mary, Marduk, and I moved south, to Marrakesh, where I already knew my way around. With the help of my banker friends I soon rented, for a ridiculously low price, a palatial house with a large courtyard. Our landlord, who lived next door, was an illegal slave dealer who wore, nevertheless, his traditional badge, a blood-red jellaba. His merchandise was not Negroes, but Shluh maidens from the mountains whose parents had sold them. They were learning to be musicians.

Their melodies accompanied my voice as I called off the numbers to Mary while I was measuring mountain men in the courtyard. But this way of life lasted only a few weeks. Abd el-Krim had surrendered. We took off for Fez, where I already had a rich and useful friend, Sidi el-Hajj Abd es-Slam (usually pronounced Abselam) Tuizi, an American protégé. As representative of the Singer Sewing Machine Company, he could not be harassed nor exorbitantly taxed.

El-Hajj fed and entertained us lavishly. He also helped us outfit ourselves for an expedition into the Rif. Besides equipment, he got us two riding and two pack mules, and two Riffian retainers, a muleteer and cook. They came from a village outside the city walls, where the Hajj owned gardens and orchards. This property was painstakingly worked by a clan of Riffian refugees named, in Arabic, Ulad (like Mac in Gaelic) Abd el-Mumen, after an ancestor who had first settled a steep, forested, previously uninhabited valley, the Vale of Iherrushen. For the sacrilege of shooting enemy clansmen on the Sabbath they had been exiled by their whole tribe, to the Hajj Abd es-Slam's profit, and our long-enduring good luck.

It was July—sweltering, shimmering hot. We sent the men and mules ahead and drove to Taza, to the Hotel Transatlantique, this time with a dog. I had already been issued a permit to travel north by the Bureau des Affaires Indigènes in Rabat. Colonel Huot, in Taza, commanded all of the territories to the north as far as the border of the Spanish Zone. The Vale of Iherrushen lay just inside the colonel's domain. He confirmed our permit, on two conditions. I should leave my measuring instruments in his office, to avoid creating a stir. If our foray was successful I could pick them up later for a second trip. Also, Marduk should be left behind. Although both these limitations irked us, I soon learned that in the second, at least, he was right.

We started out one morning on our mules, with the cook and muleteer jogging or walking alongside. But before we had gone more than ten kilometers, we heard a horse galloping toward us from the rear. It was a *mokhazni* (a mounted military policeman) sent by Colonel Huot to inform me that Marduk had developed rabies and had been killed.

We backtracked to Taza, left our staff and outfit behind, and drove to the antirabies clinic in Rabat, for Marduk had bitten us both and drawn blood. There followed two weeks of boredom and pain, with two shots in the abdomen each day—a poor routine for a honeymoon. A fellow patient didn't help much. He was a sergeant and had been bitten by his captain, who had soon died, in graphically narrated agony.

Meanwhile, my twenty-year-old bride had acquired a replacement canine companion, a German police dog named Duke. With him coursing in front of the mules, we made a second start for the Iherrushen on September 1, with the same permissions and restrictions as before, except that Duke could come along, for he had had rabies shots.

Our human companions were named Mohammed Amar and Hamid. The first one was the cook, who was taller than myself, thus over six feet, lean, brown, with long arms and legs and a sly sense of humor. Nothing daunted him. Hamid was a half foot shorter, barrel-chested, and walked quickly on the short, well-muscled legs of a mountaineer. His head was round, his complexion florid, his nose snubbed, his eyes a watery blue and somewhat protruding. His mouth was usually open, showing a few missing front teeth.

Everything bothered him. He was often sweating and arguing over what seemed to be trivia, but he was also often right. Having spent most of his life among a rather low grade of city Arabs, he fawned on and flattered those richer and more important than himself. "You are good!" he would say frequently. "You are *very* good!"

I tried to silence him by barking "*Stusum*" and "*Iskut*," meaning "Shut up!" in Riffian and in Arabic; *stusum* was the first Riffian word I learned.

Hamid, a pious man, would neither eat nor be in the presence of anyone eating pork, nor would he eat anything that came out of a tin, such as bully beef, on the reasonable assumption that the animal had not been ritually killed. Mohammed Amar was content to consume canned pork and beans while Hamid, from a distance, shouted to him that with every mouthful he was heading straight for the Fire, meaning hell.

We soon felt that we were there already, because we were moving over barren and desiccated country in almost incinerating heat, which could be seen rising in shimmering waves off the glaring white ground. Habitations were few, ramshackle, and widely spaced. The villagers had little food and not even enough fodder left to keep their livestock through to the winter rains.

Once at dusk I heard women shouting shrilly and saw Hamid running toward our camp, cupping some straw stolen from a haycock in the tail of his cotton tunic. I took the dry stems away from him and returned them to the women, over his hoarse protestations that without this fodder our mules would never reach the Iherrushen. I replied that if we were to be shot as thieves, we would be even less likely to attain our goal.

Past the plain we reached the foothills and an empty stream-bed, on the edge of which perched the French Bureau of Aknoul. It was staffed by a Captain Schmidt, who happened to be in Tangier; a lieutenant; a sergeant; and about a dozen or so Arab *mokhaznis,* who were taking turns watching a larger body of Riffian prisoners, whom both Hamid and Mohammed Amar recognized. Some were rich land-owners, most of them veterans of Abd el-Krim's army, and one was Hamid's cousin, the son of Bu Zkri, the sheikh of Iherrushen.

Within eyesight of the building, these prisoners were working on a new road, carrying bags of sand from one pile to another, and made to run on the way back. Anyone who tarried was beaten, and Hamid's cousin, who glanced back, was shot through both thighs. Two days later he died.

Neither officer saw this, for both Captain Schmidt and the lieutenant were absent from the post, and the sergeant had little control over the mokhaznis. We had to await the lieutenant's return, during which time Hamid and Mohammed Amar managed to sneak some of our food to the hungry prisoners.

When the lieutenant arrived he told me that it was absolutely impossible for us to go where Colonel Huot had said we could, because four Spaniards had just been killed over the international border in the tribal territory of the Beni Tuzin, and everyone on both sides was uneasy. After a bit he changed his mind, perhaps to get rid of us lest we report what was going on at Aknoul. He said: If you will sign a paper absolving the French Protectorate of any responsibility for your safety, you may proceed. The paper will be ready in the morning."

The next morning I signed it and we left. Before we had ridden very far, once more we heard the hoofbeats of a mokhazni's horse galloping after us. The rider handed me a message from the lieutenant, which read: "I have spoken on the phone with Taza, and they say that you may not cross a line between Suk el-Khemis [Thursday market] and Azru [the Rock]. Proceed to the Suk el-Khemis and await me there, and then I will inform you when you may move on."

As we approached the marketplace, we came to one of the two residences of the Kaid Midboh, the French-appointed chief of all the Gzennaya, the whole tribe, whose territory stretched from the crest of the Riffian Mountains to the barren southern plain. While most of the Riffians considered Midboh a quisling, he performed his duties well, for it was not easy to run the gauntlet between the French occupation forces and the trigger-happy tribesmen he was supposed to rule.

A retainer escorted us into the Kaid's audience chamber, where he sat on pillows, waited on by a Fezzi secretary who took dictation in Arabic. Midboh had a round face, widely spaced china-blue eyes, and a small nose, and his manner was easy and friendly. He fed us well, asked us many polite questions, and made us feel relaxed.

At the end of the meal a servant brought in a huge watermelon, the sight of which enhanced our thirst. When I asked him if he would eat some of it with us, he declined through his secretary, who said elegantly, *"Monsieur le Kaid est gonflé,"* meaning literally that the Kaid was blown up, like a tire. Neither the secretary nor we visitors knew that *gonflé* also means pregnant, which indeed he looked.

We each ate several slices of the watermelon without hesitation—we did not know what I discovered later: Offering watermelon to a guest and slicing it with a knife poisoned on one side is an old Riffian trick.

After the meal I repeated the lieutenant's message to Midboh, who replied that the lieutenant had sent him a message later than the one sent to us. It read that he, the lieutenant, was too busy to come to the market. He therefore delegated to the Kaid the duty of informing us that the way had been cleared for us to proceed as planned.

With his eyes twinkling, he added that he had personally ordered the Sheikh Si Moh wild el-Hajj Bukkeish at Tiddest, almost on the Spanish border, and several other notables along the way, to take good care of us.

Having thanked the Kaid for his hospitality and help in laying on the next leg of our trip, we left and walked about the market. It was very busy, because men from many clans were buying meat to eat on the Sabbath, the next day.

Unveiled women walked about as nonchalantly as women do in America and Europe. Some were selling eggs and handmade pottery, others buying needles and thread and scissors. When they saw Mary, some of them stared at her, for she was the first Christian woman they had seen. She did not have horns growing out of her forehead at all.

We had to choose among three trails that led from the Thursday market to the Vale of Iherrushen. One led to the left, another to the right. Both were long, circuitous, tedious, and physically safe. The first would get us into the Abd el-Mumen settlement by riding downstream; the second would require a stop at Tiddest, where its new sheikh, Si Moh, was supposed to be expecting us. The third was short and said to be perilous. It ran sheer across the Noisy Mountain of Akhfiligum, which towered directly overhead. This was the one that Midboh urged us to take, looking me straight in the eye.

Both Mohammed Amar and Hamid had crossed it before. The first was game; but Hamid protested hoarsely, and yielded begrudgingly, and only under duress. Had Hamid not been the one to object, I might not have ventured it. His disapprobation, plus the twinkle in

Midboh's eye, spurred me on. In hindsight, if I hadn't caught Midboh's message my life from then on might have followed a duller course.

Up the steep side of Akhfiligum we zigzagged, leading the mules, with our loads equally distributed on all four. As we climbed higher, we seemed to progress no farther forward because the houses of the last settlement we had left behind lay strung out below us like matchboxes set in line on a green carpet, with the now-silent river glistening down its scalloped bed. Up on the Noisy Mountain it was both hot and cold. The sun beat boisterously on our sweat-soaked heads, while a cool mountain breeze graciously fluttered our open-necked shirts.

Up through a chaos of granite blocks we struggled, pulling our bridles and beating the mules' rumps with switches, running to one side and then to the other to ease them around rocks, so that what little equipment we carried would not be crushed.

After hours of work, our heads swimming and our clothing soaked, we pushed the beasts over a shoulder of the mountain and paused to gaze at the panorama spread before us. Directly in front lay a patch of greenest grass, with a spring in its middle. This was the source of the Tighza, which raced madly down a dark cleft in the rock below. This precipitous canyon was to be our road.

Ahead, and over the course of the Tighza, we could see the cedared mountain of Iherrushen, brightly lit in the afternoon sun. A little to its right lay a bluish rise which, as Hamid pointed out, was the domain of the Beni Urriaghel, Abd el-Krim's kinsmen, and the terror of Spain.

We proceeded warily to the spring and cast ourselves down on the soft grass. Duke limped to the small trickle just below the pool and lapped noisily. After we had drunk our fill and cupped a fresh supply of clean water in the *gulah* (a porous water jug that keeps its contents cool by evaporation), we unbridled the mules to let them drink.

But there was little time for resting. Although it was but mid-afternoon, the trail was long and steep. The western wall of the canyon was already dim in black shadows, and the sunlight stretched but halfway down its eastern side. If we were to make Tiddest before sunset—and to travel this trail in the dark would be suicide—we must lose no time.

The trail down to Tiddest winds around rocks along ledges no more than a foot wide in places. In one place where a rounded boulder thrust its paunch over the trail, as far out as the sheer lip of the track, it took the combined strength and dexterity of us all to get the animals around it. Packs came off and went on again; each mule was held by its head and tail. Down below, chalky white in the near-darkness, we saw the bones of one that had not made it.

Past that rock the trail went into short, double zigzags to lose altitude. There it was steepest. At two bends the mules had to look directly over the edge. And in several spots the path was wet from hidden springs. As we descended water became more abundant. The trail was now lined with an irrigation ditch, and in several places the water was carried along hewn wooden troughs like our roof sills. One of them crossed the canyon overhead.

We saw terraces that looked no larger than billiard table tops, bright green with corn, and from the terrace edges squash vines hung over the cliff. The houses of the tillers of those terraces were perched on rock, long and narrow to waste no arable soil, and fitting the contour of the terrain.

The gorge widened. We splashed across the Tighza on our mules and entered a flat stretch bordered with walnut and olive trees. The first building we passed was a gaunt structure silhouetted against the blood red of the sunset. Out of its open door drifted the mysterious yet peaceful, harmonious yet discordant sounds of chanted prayer. The day was Friday. The building was a mosque.

Farther down we found a good camping place, slung the panniers off the mules' packsaddles, and pounded two iron stakes into the soft ground. We stretched a rope between the stakes and tethered the mules to it.

As we unfolded our sleeping tent and began to raise it with its poles, the door of a building across the stream opened and a black-hooded figure stepped out, walked across to us on stepping-stones, and greeted us rather shyly. It was the young sheikh Si Moh. We had not met, but I had caught a glimpse of him in the Thursday market the day before.

Being a young man of excellent manners, he almost concealed his surprise at our arrival from the rear, by that crazy route. As the evening wound on, we became increasingly aware that the Kaid Mid-boh had not told him we were coming, but his hospitality was as lavish as if he had been expecting us for a month.

Younger than my own twenty-two, he had succeeded his famous father, el-Hajj Bukkeish, only about two years before. Bukkeish had rivaled Abd el-Krim for leadership of the nascent Riffian nation and had been poisoned, allegedly at Abd el-Krim's orders. Bukkeish was a member of a widespread family, the Oshannen (*jackals* in Riffian), whose members were leaders in several tribes.

Si Moh was followed by about twenty others, all young and

sturdy. More of them issued from houses on either side of the stream, and soon we were surrounded by a group of nearly sixty men. They stood looking at us uneasily, and without speech, as if we were creatures fallen from the sky.

Si Moh spoke to us softly, using the old schoolmaster as interpreter into Arabic, for the young sheikh spoke only his native tongue. Once the formal greetings were over Si Moh began issuing orders. Four men set up our tent; a half dozen boys vanished and reappeared bearing flat baskets full of almonds, shelled them on rocks, and offered them to us in kerchief-fuls. A man scrambled up the bank dragging a goat by the horns and slaughtered it on the spot. A smirking young fellow with a short upper lip and a large white turban that completely covered his head brought a clay brazier full of red coals, and a teapot. Another man fetched a tray of glasses, a tin sugar box, and a brass hammer.

Someone lit a crackling fire just as the chill of evening was setting in. Others spread mats on the ground, and soon we were sitting on them—Si Moh, myself, the short-lipped one, and what appeared to be a select inner group—while Mary, missing the fun, rested in the tent with Duke. His tongue hung dry from his mouth, and his eyes glistened pathetically.

We mat sitters noisily sucked in the steaming tea, while Mary sipped hers in the tent out of sight. Soon we became a jovial company, with much broad humor, which I understood mostly through gestures and facial expressions. It seemed easy for me to understand men of another culture without language if our minds worked the same way. I soon found myself feeling more at home here than I had felt even in Europe, and my new friends expressed surprise and pleasure that I laughed at the right times and entered into their jests. They were as different from Arabs as night is from day, although I have learned to get along with Arabs too.

He of the short upper lip was the comic of Tiddest. Everything he said, with a sly twinkle in his eyes, evoked laughter. At length someone snatched his copious turban from his pate, and then I saw that he was a scabhead, a childhood victim of favus. Si Moh tapped the scarred one's glistening scalp with his fingers and said, with a serious look, "*Akshar.*" The whole company repeated this word with much laughter, and when I said it after them there was no end to their delight. Thus did I learn my second word of Riffian, following *stusum,* my silencer of Hamid.

From scabhead on, the next lesson was to learn the names of the parts of the body, beginning with the head and its various parts, such as eyes, ears, hair, mouth, teeth, lips, and so on. I repeated the words after them. My pronunciation brought a little laughter, but when we came to the intimate portions of the male anatomy, the mirth increased.

But the joking could not last forever. Finally I was asked, "Are you French or Spanish?"

"Neither, we are from America."

Great surprise and obvious disbelief followed this statement. Hamid hastened to confirm it with a lengthy speech which I could, of course, not follow, but which I could see was disbelieved.

"Where is America?"

"Far away, across the great sea to the west," I answered in Arabic. "It is noon there now."

There seemed to be a little confusion between *melikan,* their pronunciation of American, and *malakin,* meaning angels, which we obviously were not, but the context was religious, thus leading to the next question:

"You are Muslims, then. Let us hear you pray!"

This was just what I had been waiting for ever since Abdullah Thomson had coached me, so I rolled out the Fatiha, from the *Bismillah al-Rahman al-Rahim* through the tricky last line with its triplet *dāds* to a sonorous *amīn* (amen).

My tour de force seemed to surprise the locals, many of whom had never left the Rif, but I was still not sure they considered me a friend, partly because Hamid had warned me that despite my performance my jovial new companions planned to roll hand grenades under our tent flaps in the middle of the night. While I was evaluating his warning in light of his usual gloomy view of things, he pointed at a new face which had appeared at the fireside, just as I had spotted it myself.

It was a swarthy, intelligent face, with shining brown eyes, a firm chin, and a luxuriant black mustache with up-curling tips. He was not one of Hooton's exotic Nordics, but he was certainly a Riffian, because Hamid whispered to me hoarsely: "You see that man? He is a bad one, the worst in the Rif. He is my brother, may God damn him. Avoid him utterly. Have nothing to do with him."

The newcomer unobtrusively approached us. Si Moh made a place for him by the fire, and he sat down. Then he addressed me in fractured French as spoken among Moroccan troops like the Tirailleurs Marocains. The use of this patois annoyed me, just when I was doing so well with my Arabic and beginning to learn anatomical nouns in Riffian. He had chosen that language deliberately because it was the only one that he and I alone understood.

Our conversation may be translated as follows:

"Good evening. What are you doing here?"

"Just looking at the country."

"What country are you from?"

"We are Americans."

"That's really true?"

"Yes, I repeat, we are Americans."

"When I heard you talking with your wife I thought you were either Germans or English. These men think you are French or Spanish."

I assured him once more that we were Americans.

"What you say is true, then. Now I will have to persuade the others. If they don't believe me they will kill you both in the night."

"Oh, but why should they kill us?"

Our visitor looked surprised. "You are crazy, you! Don't you know? This country here has not yet submitted."

Ouch.

Our savior's name was Mohammed Limnibhy. He had fought in the French army in Europe during World War I, had done time in a French jail, and had been a centurion (captain of one hundred) in Abd el-Krim's army. Thus he himself was in almost as tenuous a position as the one he was bailing us out from.

What was his motive? Sheer compassion, some form of self-interest, or a mixture of both? I didn't worry about that item then, but in the years that have passed, Limnibhy's help sealed a pact between two clans, the Ulad Abd el-Mumen and the Ulad Coon.

As soon as my brain had cleared, which owing to my youth took only a few seconds, I heard Limnibhy persuading the Ikhuanen (*thieves* in Riffian), as the Tiddest men were called, that we were not foes, but friends.

The next morning we awoke rested and refreshed. By daylight we could see, down the valley, two small mountains. One was straight and pyramidal, the other shaped like an old woman bent over with a load of firewood on her back. Between the two runs the gorge that lets the blended waters of Ikhuanen and Iherrushen pour out to the sea.

Up on the water side of the Old Woman is a grotto called the Cave of the Ogress. If I couldn't measure people, I could still explore caves. Limnibhy, Si Moh, Hamid, Akshar the Scabhead, Sheikh Bu Zkri of the Iherrushen, whose son had been shot at Bu Zineb, and I climbed up to it, even though Bu Zkri had a wooden foot.

Most of the Ogress's passages were vertical, so that we had to do much jumping and lowering. Hamid went down one hole with the lantern and I followed him, with Si Moh, Akshar, and Limnibhy close behind. Hamid kept shouting at the top of his lungs, grunting, and making all sorts of other noises to scare off the afreet, or demon, that was believed to lurk there. As I had not yet heard of the *afreet,* I wondered if Hamid had finally gone off his chump.

But I was soon told. A successful afreet scarer is supposed to scatter salt and to click knives together, or if he has but one knife, to click it against rock.

Every time Hamid heard a noise he would blow out the lantern, turn, and knock me down. Once when dashing around a corner he let out a terrible scream, dropped the lantern, walked over me, and ran into Limnibhy and Si Moh, who held him firmly in the darkness, for what seemed to be half an hour. During that long interval Hamid forgot Arabic but babbled in his native tongue.

In his inimitable French, Limnibhy told me that Hamid had seen an afreet in the form of a huge dog with green, fiery eyes.

Then we decided to try another, possibly less haunted, hole. Hamid, whose courage had been restored, climbed down, but I could not follow him in my heavy boots. So Si Moh and Limnibhy made a rope of their two turbans tied end to end and lowered me into a chamber two turban-lengths and one body deep. Out of this opened another about twice as deep, but neither Si Moh nor Limnibhy would come down, even if Akshar's and Bu Zkri's turbans were to be added. It was too risky. Hamid eventually returned, reporting that he had reached water but had not seen the afreet again.

"You are good!" I said to Hamid. In speleology I gave him an unspoken A.

The afreet story was as follows. Once, about 1870, a Soussi (a Berber from southwestern Morocco) entered the valley of Tiddest with a box full of gold coins, and he took with him a since-deceased Iherrushen man, whose brother still remembered this adventure in 1926. They went down to the second passage as far as the water, where they buried the treasure, but as soon as they had finished, the same dog-faced, green-eyed afreet leapt on them and bit the Iherrushen man on the shoulder.

The Soussi disappeared. The Iherrushen man went to Fez in exile, and died there shortly afterward. The box of gold, therefore, is presumably still there. I learned later that this story is a common one; I heard it elsewhere in various forms. But it served its purpose. It made us, the strangers, friends with the men of two valleys. Until World War II, I thought no more of hand grenades in the night.

Mary and I spent the next few days wandering around the valley with our new friends—mostly Si Moh, Akshar, and Limnibhy— visiting, drinking tea, eating meals here and there, and laying plans for the future, for this glimpse of paradise could not go on forever.

On these walks we found that Si Moh was treated with much greater veneration than that accorded an ordinary sheikh, khalifa, or even kaid. He had what the Moroccans call *baraka*, a spiritual internal emanation, like one of saintly or royal blood, or both. Every day small noisy crowds came to kiss the hem of his jellaba; they knelt down to address their grievances to him, all talking at once.

One day, up on the pyramidal mountain, one hundred feet from the Beni Urriaghel land and the border of the Spanish Zone, two men who had been picking grapes came to him and began jabbering over an affair which concerned a woman. Si Moh paid no attention to them, but kept on fiddling with my Graflex, trying to focus on the mountains of Beni Urriaghel on the ground glass.

As soon as the grape pickers had gone and while Si Moh was still busy focusing, an old man appeared, looked at me sternly, held up his right forefinger, and said firmly: "*Wahad!*" (Number one).

"*La ilahu illa Illahi*" (There is no god but Allah), I replied.

Then the old man raised his middle finger, to which I instantly shot back: "*Inna Muhammadu rasul Illahi*" (Lo! Mohammed is the messenger of Allah).

That was all the old man wanted. Again, Si Moh paid no attention. It was quite clear that the "in" group, being Si Moh, Akshar, Bu Zkri, and of course Limnibhy, knew that we were Christians, but considered it of less importance than the fact that we were informally on their side. Although too late for action, this was what Gordon and I, and perhaps Midboh, had had in mind.

Members of this elite did not have to pick grapes or to plow fields. They were landowners who hired others to do such work for them, for a one-fifth share of the crop. Si Moh had four houses, but so far only two wives. Akshar had five wives, but apparently only one house. Bu Zkri, the sheikh of Iherrushen, had eight houses, and I did not know how many wives. One of his sons we had seen shot at Bu Zineb; another, age fourteen, already had one wife in Fez.

Limnibhy's father, the Hajj Mohammed, who was Bu Zkri's older brother, had three wives and seven sons. The Hajj Mohammed resembled the late J. Edgar Hoover, and Limnibhy's mother was tall, fair, and dignified. Her other son, Zarkan (Blue-eyed) was Nordic, already at the age of sixteen a noted dancer, and he is still alive. Limnibhy also had two blond sons by a blonde wife whom he had acquired from the Galiya tribe just outside the Spanish citadel of Melilla during the siege of that city by Abd el-Krim's troops. He had another son, of his own complexion, by another wife.

Collecting demographic data like those given above was one part of my Ph.D. requirements that I could do while my instruments lay idle in Colonel Huot's office. Each man whose pedigree I took down had a story of his own to tell, from which, with Limnibhy's help, I was able to reconstruct the history of the Ulah Abd el-Mumen, from its first settlement by their pious ancestor through many a hair-raising feud, followed by a dolorous exile to the outskirts of Fez, their eventual pardon by the combined tribal council, and the return of some, but—luckily for my dissertation—not all of them. And Mary sororized with the women, who had their own things to show, if not to tell.

Part of this information we obtained in Tiddest, and part in the houses of the Ulad Abd el-Mumen upstream in the Iherrushen, whither Limnibhy led us over Si Moh's protest, for he had offered us for two months the house we had seen him come out of during our first arrival.

We had come to the Vale of Iherrushen during the season of opulence, when grapes, figs, walnuts, almonds, and olives were plentiful. Men were grinding and squeezing tart-smelling oil from their olive wheels and presses; children were spreading fruits and nuts on rooftops for drying. Women (yes, women) were leading stocky bulls by their horns to freshen each other's cows, and the sheep were fat.

It was also the season of weddings: long, drawn-out, well-attended rites full of excitement, when the groom fights a more-or-less mock battle with rejected suitors, as well as with the bride's brothers. The women cry shrilly, "You! You! You!" Young men dance feverishly, and Zarkan gave the fieriest performance of them all. Professional musicians from another tribe, called The Shameless Ones because they performed for hire, drowned out all other sounds at times by the bagpipelike skirling of their shawms—wild-looking chanters tipped with wild sheep's horns.

One of the songs was sung antiphonally by two lines of men, one representing the Riffians and the other the Spaniards. One pair of verses went:

Riffians: *O soldiers, why did you come here? Why did you pitch your white tents between the crags covered with sweet-smelling trees?*

Spaniards: *To look at the girls of Temsaman walking by, girded with belts of many colors, and their skirts swishing.*

After all these years, I can remember only one short couplet, which I try to voice now and then during moments of mild chagrin. It refers to raids on Riffian settlements in 1925 by Spanish, French, and one insensitive American whom I had met in Fedhala. They bombed and strafed their targets from low-flying, cotton-winged biplanes, some of which were felled by Riffian marksmen shooting ball shot out of long-barreled flintlocks, which they steadied in crotch-handled walking sticks.

The couplet goes:

Ayará tiará, Mimi zibzibothshím,
Ateryénthi imúth, Asarhéntu izím.

Which means:

O airplane, why did you buzz like a bee?
Your lieutenant is dead. Your sergeant is wounded.

The climax of the ceremony came when the groom stepped out of the door, displaying the tokens of virginity on a shiny new piece of cotton sheeting stamped, in bright blue letters, CABOT. My contemporaries will know that this label refers to a textile milling company located along the Merrimack River, in Massachusetts.

At the sight of this symbol, most of the men standing in the courtyard fired their flintlocks in the air. (Their modern rifles had already been packed in oil and buried in secret places against a future chance to fight the Christian invaders.) At the same moment the female spectators began to ululate loudly ("You! You! You!") like a swampful of lady tree toads calling their mates.

As the night moved on I was forced, out of politeness, to drink too many cups of sugar-saturated mint tea. I felt an urge to step out into the darkness for a moment, but Hamid, who would not leave my side for a second, pulled me down as I started to rise. In a stage whisper he told me that it would be grossly rude of me to leave.

After several such thwarted attempts on my part, he mentioned to me that he had a severe headache, so I gave him a powerful laxative which I kept in my pocket for use in such an emergency. About ten minutes later we both left.

While we were at that wedding Mary was worrying about Duke. On Friday, when we had arrived at Tiddest, he had begun having fits; they recurred every hour or two during the day, and frequently during the night. He had been swallowing a lot of bones since leaving Taza because we could not find him enough to eat.

On the chance that he had a piece of bone stuck in his stomach or intestines, we gave him salt and water. This medication won the approval of Mohammed Amar and Hamid, who said that a jinn must have entered the dog's body and only salt could get it out. Still, it did not work.

So on Sunday I rode my mule up the Vale of Iherrushen alone for three hours until I came to a French outpost called Bou Zineb. It was perched on the top of a steep mesalike mountain, and commanded a view across the Spanish Zone to the Mediterranean. I went to the dispensary, and asked the doctor's orderly for some medicine for my dog. He gave me sulfate of soda.

As I was about to mount my mule and return, a captain spied me and stopped me. He then led me to his colonel to explain my presence. I did, and the colonel then invited Mary and me to come to lunch with him on Wednesday, and let me go.

When I got back to Limnibhy's house, he said that someone had poisoned Duke before we got to Tiddest, to find out how long his dose would take before using it on his human victim. He had chosen Duke because it would be easy to trace the movements of a Christian dog. Before we left, Duke died.

On Wednesday morning we rode to Bou Zineb, but were told on arrival that we were an hour late, the colonel had left for another post, Bou Red, and that we had to ride there to see the general. This made a total of about forty kilometers of mountain riding. At Bou Red the French officers put us in a tent and fed us in the lieutenants' mess.

Just before dinner the commandant called me into his office and began raking me over the coals as if he had just caught a spy.

He asked if I had been hired by the United States Army or by some other government agency, to which I said no. When I told him that we were on a scientific expedition for Harvard University, he snorted, exclaiming: "*Alors!* I never *heard* of Harvard!"

It was very dangerous in the Iherrushen, he said. He could not understand how we had managed to get there unobserved or why we had not been killed. Neither Colonel Huot nor Kaid Midboh had any right to let us go north of Taza. We must leave at once.

Mary and I were taken by truck to Midboh's house, where we had eaten watermelon, and then to Taza in a tiny Citroën wedged against the bulk of the Kaid himself. Limnibhy, Hamid, and Mohammed Amar rode and drove the mules overland to Marrakesh with our gear.

Our honeymoon was over. We had lived briefly among a friendly people who were still free, and who, with Midboh's help, had been allowed to meet a new and more compatible kind of Christians.

We were unable to return to the Rif until December, when the last clans had submitted—but not Limnibhy, who had chosen to move with us. In the meantime, we found other mountains and other peoples to visit and other things to do.

6. The Jinns Depart

Well before his pilgrimage, one moonlit evening Limnibhy's father was wading up the streambed of the Iherrushen to his home. Glancing ahead to avoid a dangerous waterfall, he spied a dazzling and irresistible water maiden standing in a pool. She invited him to join her in her secret chamber behind the fall, and when he left her she said, "I am an ogress, and I eat people. If you ever tell a living soul about me, you will drop dead."

Despite his promise the Hajj Mohammed, by then a wrinkled yet vigorous man, broke his silence after the five of us had returned from Marrakesh. He told his tale to his son Limnibhy, who passed it on at once to me.

And the Hajj Mohammed did not then drop dead, although many of his kinsmen had died when the Christians marched down the valley in their heavy boots, trampling the ripening grain. When the jinns smelled the intruders from afar, they left the land.

With them fled the green-eyed dog, and the Soussi's box of gold was gone, for the Rock of the Ogress had been shattered into slivers by a bomb.

A pall of silence had fallen on this jinnless land. Only the rushing of the stream did we hear, and a few cocks crowing. On the trip before I had faintly heard the last Riffian lion roar. Both Limnibhy and Hamid had agreed on this, so it must be true. Old Bu Haru himself, The Father of the Heart, stood hidden in a dense thicket, a holy game sanctuary surrounding an ancient tomb. Since then, hungry men had killed and eaten the boars on which Bu Haru had fed, and he had starved.

So now the no-nonsense time for work had come. I mounted and oiled my precious instruments, and unpacked three sets of five-by-eight blanks—for individual measurement, village data, and censuslike facts and figures of the personnel and possessions of individual heads of households, starting with Tiddest.

Its housing pattern was scattered and open, and it contained one official residence, that of our friend Si Moh. Its one mosque doubled as schoolroom and hostel for itinerant *tolba,* celibate students who lived on local charity and on the proceeds of peddling amulets and charms. They could not be listed as local residents because, in addition to being itinerants, most of them were not Riffians. They were Jeballis from the western mountains; kif-smokers and pederasts, tolerated for their magic.

Although Tiddest had a local, weekly market, it was held on Sunday, a poor day, and attended mostly by women who traded local produce with each other and bought imported sugar cones and candles.

The total population of Tiddest was somewhere between 400 and 500, and when we were there before, there may have been sixty or so men of military age and inclination left, but not all were visible in December. Among the latter was one example, Si Moh ben Amr, a rather colorless individual (after the fashion of survivors) who had been born there forty-odd years ago (few men knew their exact age), and who had one son and one daughter living, and one son deceased, the issue of his single wife.

He made his living both as a farmer and as a kind of notary public, employing one share-cropper from another valley and writing official documents in Arabic, covering the sales of land and the wedding certificates that stated the sizes of bride payments in Hassani or Spanish silver dollars. He lived in a large four-roomed house, with European glassware and teapots on display. He wore good clothing, and grew maize, barley, and many kinds of vegetables, as well as figs and olives, but had only a single cow. His father had been killed by the Ulad Abd el-Mumen in a feud, and he had personally been in all wars during his life span, but was never wounded. He owned an American rifle which, it was said, had bugs in its barrel, and when he heard a shot, he trembled.

When we had finished with Tiddest and the Ulad Abd el-Mumen we climbed westward up the Vale of Iherrushen to its head-waters at Telmest, filling out dossiers and measuring men all the way, covering a total of sixteen villages.

Finally, on December 11, we crossed the Franco-Spanish border just north of Bou Red, into the tribal territory of the Beni Amart, the blondest people of the Rif, and reputedly the most ferocious, although the Iherrushen men would deny this. They were said to be the country's most ancient inhabitants, and to have been heathen at the time the Iherrushen was first settled, and to have worn hide garments in place of cloth ones.

Having sent our mules back with Hamid and Mohammed Amar, we rode horseback over open, rolling country. This trail held no hazards remotely comparable to those met on our first ride over the Noisy Mountain from the Thursday market to Tiddest.

The author, Captain Sanchez Perez, and seated, Mary Coon, in the newly conquered Spanish outpost of Beni Amart. (Photo finishing by Harold Adams, Rockport, Massachusetts.)

On our arrival at Suk et-Tnine we were greeted by a young Spanish officer, Captain Sanchez Perez, one of the politest, bravest, and most dedicated men I have ever met.

He was holding an isolated post alone, with the aid of two Spanish corporals and a dozen or so mokhaznis. The Beni Amart had submitted only a few weeks earlier. The mokhaznis were all Riffians fresh out of Abd el-Krim's army. By his personal charm and his solicitude for his new charges, he had been able to keep the peace more firmly than with a hundred seasoned troops. He had one special advantage over his French counterparts south of the border: His mokhaznis, like his charges, were all Riffians, speaking the same language and understanding each other. They did not disparage, sneer at, or rob the local people as did the Arab mokhaznis by whom we had been "protected."

When we had dismounted, our conversation with Captain Sanchez Perez was somewhat limited. He had no French or English, nor did we two at that time have enough Spanish to be of much use. So we were forced to speak Arabic together, much to the amusement of all who witnessed this performance. The Riffian mokhaznis in particular were holding their sides in laughter and rolling on the ground. But Limnibhy and a Spanish-speaking mokhazni soon rescued us, so that our conversation passed from English (when Mary and I spoke together) to French to Riffian to Spanish, and back, without the need of any Arabic at all.

On December 15–17 we were measuring in Targuist, an Arabic-speaking enclave just north and east of Beni Amart. Many of its inhabitants were blacksmiths and gunsmiths. It was they who had repaired old rifles for Abd el-Krim, and he had had a motor road constructed between Targuist and his capital, Ajdir. As we rode into Targuist our nostrils were assaulted by the nauseous stench of a solid ring of human excrement surrounding the Spanish army camp, which apparently had no latrines. As we rode across it we passed several soldiers with their trousers down adding to the mess.

Targuist was also the home base of a wealthy family of *shorfa,* or descendants of the Prophet, the Ikhemrijen. They lived in a large compound of lofty buildings all gleaming white in the sun. These men, especially their leader, Sidi Mohammed n Suddik, possessed *baraka,* or great holiness and the power to heal the sick simply by touching them; an application of Mohammed n Suddik's saliva on an afflicted part was considered a sure cure. The Riffians living to the east of Targuist paid little attention to these living saints, who got most of their business from the local people and those living to the west. The latter were not Riffians, but Senhaja and Ghomara, some speaking their own Berber dialects and others Arabic. While we were there we were told that Mohammed n Suddik had lost his *baraka* because he had dined with Spanish officers—but that was what the Riffians said, and they were anti-Ikhemrijen anyhow.

From Targuist we rode down Abd el-Krim's motor road to his capital at Ajdir. The road had been built by Spanish prisoners guarded by Riffian soldiers, who apparently treated their charges no better than the Arab mokhaznis had treated their Riffian prisoners at Aknoul. One red-headed, hawk-nosed Riffian, who had been one of the guards and was now a Spanish mokhazni, told me that they had mixed dirt with the flour to make the prisoners' bread.

Near Ajdir, which was just a village, the Spaniards had begun to build a new town, Villa Sanjurjo, and had already constructed a dock. We camped on the beach opposite the Spanish island of Alhucemas, so covered with rectangular buildings of different heights that it looked like a ship. On Christmas day I stopped measuring people and hired a

Riffian boatman to row me over to the island to buy some supplies. I left Mary behind because she was pregnant, and I did not want to expose her to any more rough traveling than what she had already been through. As a Christmas present I bought her a bottle of brandy. Just as I was climbing out of the boat onto the beach, the bottle slipped out of my grasp and smashed on a rock. So we opened a can of pineapple instead, and offered a slice of it to a homeless old man who served us more or less as factotum and guard. He refused it in horror, on the grounds that it was pork.

Our next stop was Melilla, to which we shipped on a small coastal steamer as deck passengers, for no berths were available. Sharing the deck with a dozen or so mules and horses, as well as an uncounted number of Riffian women and children, we had hardly enough room to stretch out or turn around until the ship stopped near the shore at some place in Temsaman or Beni Said. There the horses and mules were pushed overboard. All of the mules swam straight for the beach and waded ashore, but two of the horses swam out to sea and drowned.

When we pulled into a dock at Mellilla someone shoved a gangplank out and we proceeded to disembark. This was not easy because the plank was narrow and had no rails. I followed Mary, but before I could get ashore a Spanish policeman ran up the plank facing me, without room for either one of us to pass. I was holding my passport aloft in my left hand, and the policeman, six inches shorter than I, made a grab for it.

Because it said inside the cover never to let it out of the owner's possession, I did not yield, but the policeman jumped for it and fell overboard with a loud splash. A squadron of his colleagues escorted me, still gripping the passport, to the police station, but on the way I managed to ask Mary to telegraph our consul general, the Honorable Maxwell Blake in Tangier. She did, and within an hour or two I was out.

Having retrieved our car from the French Zone, Mary, Limnibhy, and I lived in a hotel in Melilla and went out every day to cover the round of markets in every tribe of the Rif in the Spanish Zone east of Beni Urriaghel. We did this until we had made a complete coverage from Temsaman to Kebdana, near the Algerian border; knew every passable road like the palms of our hands; and had met the chief men of nearly every tribe. It was a kind of game, and these men remembered me.

This knowledge, which placed me in a unique position later on, was won only at the price of exhausting work: measuring, measuring, and measuring. At peak load it required about one hundred decisions per man one hundred times a day. I found myself able to gauge such dimensions as head length and head breadth by sight, either on the nose—so to speak—or at worst within two millimeters, but I measured them just the same to make sure.

We finished our measuring in the Spanish Zone just in time. Mary's burden was growing heavy. We hastened to Tangier, across the strait to Algeciras, and thence to Paris by train, arriving shortly before our first son was born, four days after Charles A. Lindbergh, Jr., had landed *The Spirit of St. Louis* at Le Bourget, as previously stated.

7. *Winter in the High Atlas*

During the six months in 1928 between our ignominious departure from the Rif and our return after total pacification, Mary and I found other things to do. When we returned to Marrakesh we soon learned that Limnibhy, Hamid, and Mohammed Amar had arrived ahead of us with the mules. We also were informed that my parents and my thirteen-year-old brother, Jack, were about to visit us via Tangier, and I had to drive up there at once in the Ford to fetch them. While my parents disapproved of our life-style, Jack had much fun, and Limnibhy spent much time keeping him out of trouble.

The months spent in Marrakesh were not spectacular, but very informative. No one stopped me from measuring men, and subjects were plentiful, for a special reason. Over half the female population of Marrakesh were prostitutes, catering to the mountaineers and other rustics who had come to the market to sell their produce, and were soon picked up by pimps who guided them to whorehouses. During the off-hours of daytime the pimps could work for me, and the visitors who had squandered their money on women could earn a little more to take home.

It was my job to take 28 measurements plus dynamometer pressure plus 66 observations, all for each man. Mary took 12 sociological observations, one or another of us took two photographs and drew some blood in a tube for ABO blood group testing—a rare thing in 1926. We got through 238 Shluh (Middle Atlas mountaineers and Soussis) and 93 Arabs. No city people or slaves were included. It was tiring work, but not so tiring that it failed to rouse our interest in the mountaineers of the High Atlas directly south of us.

By means of the twelve sociological items on the measurement blank, Limnibhy and I were able to tell where each man came from, what tribes and kinship groups they belonged to, and any division of labor that revealed itself under occupation. A second set of blanks used only in places we knew well gave us population statistics from house to house and village to village, with number of wives per man, number and sexes of children per wife, land and fruit trees owned, down to the last goat. While useful for genetics, this work was primarily concerned with cultural anthropology. I have taught more of the latter than I have of physical anthropology or archaeology, or of both wrapped together, and the combination of the three is my greatest interest.

Some of the men we measured were members of the Glawa tribe, directly south of us, whose country included thirteen-thousand-foot peaks gleaming in snow. As soon as our work had slacked off, we decided to go there despite the season. This meant travel by mule through the snow over bandit-infested country. A motor road was being built, but had not been finished. Nowadays, I suppose, tourists drive up the mountain to go skiing. In 1926 that was just a dream. We did it the hard way, and it was particularly rough on Mary.

On October 26, armed with a letter from the Glawi to his brother, who lived in the family castle at Telwet, just over the crest of the Atlas, we drove to the bend of the road where our men and mules awaited us. An English friend drove the Ford back to Marrakesh. Early the next morning we set out for Zerekten, camping in open country one night on the way. At Zerekten we pitched our tent, and that of the men, in a cornfield near the khalifa's castle. Also nearby stood two small, well-built stone flour mills. Under each of them a horizontal wheel was being rapidly turned by irrigation water on the turbine principle. A wooden shaft ran straight up through the floor to the millstones, which thus turned without gears. The shafts were attached to the upper stones not in the middle, but a little to one side, which gave them an eccentric grinding motion that allowed grain to be poured in through a hole nearer the center. These mills were being operated by Jewish women and Negresses.

On October 29 Limnibhy and I explored a cave, which was sterile; we also had to do something about food. What the khalifa had sent us was scanty and almost inedible, so we crossed the stream to the Mellah (Jewish quarter), a collection of houses built wall to wall, as in a pueblo. There we met Shlimu, sheikh of the Jews, who sold us mutton, chickens, bread, and vegetables, as well as fodder for our mules. Wishing to be closer to our food supply than we were, we moved our camp there.

It had rained on and off all that day, and also hailed. The next morning both our tents were afloat. Shlimu invited us to move into his house, which we gratefully did.

The Mellah is built on a terrace about one hundred feet above the streambed. It was inhabited by about thirty adult males, forty adult females, and an uncounted number of children. Shlimu the sheikh had entire control over the actions of his people. He was the thrall of the khalifa directly, and of the Glawi indirectly. When the khalifa got orders from the Glawi to furnish a sum of money—or mules, or produce—he forced Shlimu to hand it over by a certain date. If he did not, Shlimu went to the dungeon under the khalifa's castle to think about it. When he decided to fork it over, he was released.

Shlimu's brother was the rabbi, who conducted services in a special room. These Jews wore the traditional black caps and let their forelocks grow long, but otherwise they dressed like Glawa tribesmen in tightly woven black or dark brown sleeveless jellabas (silhams) with a large red embroidered eye or fish design on the seat of it. Their women wore the same type of costumes as those in the cities. I did not find out how much Arabic or Hebrew they knew, only that they spoke to each other in the local Shillhah.

Among the men were various kinds of craftsmen, such as blacksmiths and locksmiths, but most of them were engaged in agriculture and herding. In these latter occupations they were helped by four households of Muslim Berbers, who were thus helots of the Jews, just as the latter were thralls of the khalifa. I suspect that one of the reasons for this relationship was that the Muslims could do work on Saturday that the Jews could not, a situation we found later in the Yemen. The Jewish women did their housework, wore woolen garments and ground grain. Shlimu lodged us in a second-story room in his father-in-law's house. It had a flimsy floor of withes covered with beaten clay. I managed to step through it several times, just as I had stepped through a Harvard shell when a freshman.

It was on a Saturday that we moved in. The men would take turns coming to visit us, and the women concentrated on Mary, showing her their babies and their jewelry, which they put on her; they also blackened her eyelids with kohl. They told us that instead of having been bought, as Muslim women are, their fathers had given their husbands dowries to marry them, and one fat young bride said that her father had given her husband two thousand francs, a relatively large sum.

All day the men were nipping at two kinds of liquor distilled locally—one of figs and dates, the other of grapes. Limnibhy attended their religious services, in which more liquor was served. Afterward he was very downcast, because he said he remembered some ancient law laid down by the Prophet's nephew and successor, Ali. From now on for forty days he would be a Jew. Only on the forty-fifth day would he again become a Muslim. Were he to die within this critical period, he would be refused Muslim burial, and unless the Jews interred him, his body would be cast to the dogs.

On Sunday it was still raining, but in the morning the boredom was suddenly broken when the khalifa sent for Shlimu and all the other adult male Jews and locked them up in his dungeon. The women, however, didn't seem overly disturbed by this, which seemed to be a fairly common event. At first I thought it was all my fault, because Shlimu had been helping me fill out some sociological blanks about the Mellah and its occupants, but apparently it was not. It seems that the khalifa had ordered Shlimu to give him a certain number of mules and he had failed to do so. Now he had to rest in the dungeon until he had decided where he could find them. As soon as I learned this, I sent Limnibhy down to plead with the khalifa, saying that we needed Shlimu to provide us with food and fodder, but the khalifa answered that Shlimu was a very bad man and had to stay there. Nevertheless, he let them all out an hour or two later.

It took us two days to get to Telwet, with Shlimu as guide. He said that he had business to do there anyway, and no doubt was glad to have our company and protection, for there were many bandits about.

About 9:00 P.M. we arrived at the first village under the mountain wall. Limnibhy knocked at a door to ask for shelter, as it was too cold and windy to stay outside. A man opened the door and said he would fix us a room, then bolted the door and never opened it again. As this door was too hard to force, we pushed in another one, entering a room inhabited solely by women and children huddling in corners and behind a loom. Their menfolk had been taken away to work on the motor road being constructed to cross the pass, and they were terrified of bandits. The presence of Mary, and Shlimu's explanations, helped calm them down, particularly as three husky Riffians and myself could now be viewed as allies and protectors.

On Tuesday morning, November 2, we started out after the sun had had a chance to thaw the road a little. As we crossed the divide we rode through a region rich in minerals. Huge sheets of mica, blocks of gypsum, and little red stones that looked like coral lay along the whole road, but I saw no implements. This road ran along a ridge, with valleys on either side. At one point we passed between two almost identical settlements on the bottoms of parallel valleys. Each had a huge turreted castle in which dwelt the sheikh, with a cluster of smaller houses around it.

This was the time for plowing. Men were out furrowing the dark brown soil with teams of oxen, mules, horses, camels, and combinations of these. One man's plow was drawn by two cows. Up on the hillsides where we passed were boys with flocks of beautiful sheep and goats, which they herded with the help of large hairy dogs that looked like collies. Some of the boys were fondling the dogs affectionately, a rare sight in Morocco and in most other Muslim countries, where dogs are despised.

About three in the afternoon we came up to Telwet, which lay at the head of a flat, agriculturally rich valley. The men plowing there

Mary on a mule with Mohammed Limnibhy afoot in front of her, on the Tizi-n-Tishka Pass over the High Atlas in the winter of 1926–27. Limniby holds my 12-gauge shotgun loaded with solid shot. My riding mule stands behind his left shoulder, a pack mule with its load to the far right.

seemed to be mostly Negroid, probably Harratin serfs from valleys to the south. (Incidentally, the word *Harratin* means plowmen.) Telwet has two castles. The larger one, belonging to the kaid, is painted or washed in four primary earth colors—brown, red, yellow, and white. It is surrounded by a high wall, and reaches a height of at least five stories, judging from the outside. Some parts of it appear to be quite ancient, others new. It would be impossible to estimate exactly how many rooms there are in it; it is a small town in itself. The other castle is new and white, and belongs to the kaid's brother.

Across the streambed from the kasbah is an unwalled town occupied mostly by Jews, and behind the kasbah is another, in which the Harratin live. We passed through the first town and entered the kasbah, where I sent Limnibhy up to the khalifa with a letter I had obtained from the Pasha of Marrakesh, the Glawi himself. The main courtyard contained two shops and an open square on which many people were selling dates, dried figs, and manufactured knickknacks such as colored thread, small mirrors, matches, and much kif, the Moroccan equivalent of marijuana. What astonished me was to see at least fifty sloughis lying around in the sun, and no other kinds of dogs. One sloughi, unlike the rest, was slate gray and shaggy like an Airedale. He had a higher cranial vault than the other sloughis, and seemed to be an entirely different breed. In one day we had seen two kinds of dogs, a shepherd and a wire-haired sloughi.

Limnibhy soon returned with the khalifa's answer, the usual evasion. He could not read the Glawi's letter because it was addressed to the kaid, who was then in Marrakesh. Instead, he would loan us a horse and feed us as long as we cared to stay. A mokhazni named Abdullah led us to an Arab-style house in poor repair, with a garden.

No sooner had we sat down than another mokhazni popped in to tell us that the French lieutenant up at the post had just phoned down to order us to come up there at once. (There was a telephone between the Kasbah and the post, but none to the world outside, and apparently no radio. The lieutenant communicated via couriers mounted on mules who rode back and forth to Zerekten.)

The lieutenant's name was Paulin. He spoke English, having been connected with the American College in the army of France. He was assisted by a second lieutenant of North African-Jewish extraction, probably selected because of the Jewish majority in Telwet.

Lieutenant Paulin explained to us, in much more detail than we were usually given, that he had received instructions not to let us go south of Telwet because it was too dangerous, but we could stay in the town if we wished. Said he: "This post is entirely isolated and has no authority as the Glawa tribe has not yet submitted. Our government keeps it quiet by paying the pasha large sums of money."

I then asked the lieutenant if it would be possible for us to look at two sites within safe distance of Telwet, one being some "Portuguese" ruins and the other a promising cave. The lieutenant then asked me quickly, "Where did you get this information?"

I replied, "From Mr. Lennox in Marrakesh, who had been up here years ago working for the Sultan Mulay Abd el-Aziz." Then, most naively and gratuitously, I added: "And I have just confirmed it from the old watchman in our courtyard."

Lieutenant Paulin sent for the old watchman, but the khalifa would not let him come up. Then we returned to the kasbah. The old watchman was still there, and did his duty, but would give me no more information. I felt like sixteen Judases rolled into one. This game was not for me. I often wondered what this tight security was all about, for it went far beyond the bounds of personal safety. It might have been connected with the minerals we had seen along the trail that morning. The last tribe in the whole of southern Morocco submitted seven years later, in 1934, yet foreigners were not allowed to wander around there until independence came in 1956. During the intervening years a number of French mining companies had begun a profitable exploitation.

While we were his guests, the khalifa fed us abundantly and well. In the mornings it was coffee, big fat dates, fresh bread and butter; at noon and at night huge plates laden with mutton stew or roast chicken, and always tea and a giant mound of kuskus. After Limnibhy and Abdullah, the khalifa's mokhazni who had been assigned to us, were through with them, we fed the leavings to the two black slaves who had brought us the food, and they too fared well. Shlimu ate at the house of a fellow Israelite, except for bread and butter, which his religion permitted him to eat with us.

I took a lot of photographs, made a few ethnographic collections, and spent much of my time looking at the people around me. Abdullah supplied the clue. Although not at all Negroid, he was definitely partly Mongoloid. So were a number of other local Berbers, and some of the Harratin, but not the Negro slaves. There had to be an old Mongoloid-looking element in the indigenous population, for I had already seen some of it among the Riffians. This puzzled me for years, but now I know the answer: *The Mongoloid-looking element among the Shluh and the Harratin is descended from a pre-Berber population, related to the Bushmen of South Africa, who were pushed southward in fairly recent times.* Every scrap of existing evidence points in this direction, and none elsewhere.

On the morning of Thursday, November 4, we purchased seven loaves of sugar for the khalifa, as we had no other present to give him. Sugar is always acceptable, being a symbol of highest esteem. The khalifa asked Limnibhy for his Riffian jellaba, but Limnibhy said he had promised it to me. So he had, but I had mentally promised it to the Peabody Museum, where it was still hanging the last time I went up to the exhibits on the fourth floor.

After leaving the khalifa, we said good-bye to Lieutenant Paulin who, spying the old watchman, took him around a corner and told him that if he ever gave any more information to Americans he would throw him in jail. We went down to the Suk el-Khemis (Thursday market), the largest of the Glawa tribe. There Mary bought a Glawi jellaba—a good thing, for without it she might have perished from the cold before the day was over. We headed back over the Tizi Telwet, which was supposedly easier to descend than to climb, but we had to pass through drifts of snow five feet deep, and arrived at Zerekten at 7:30 P.M. too sore to sit down and too weak to stand up. My total profit from this arduous sortie was a certain amount of ethnographic information, a lot of photographs, and the germ of an idea.

8. A Riffian in America

By the time we had left Morocco to let our son be born in an American hospital near Paris, Mary and I had collected enough data to let me write my dissertation and to be granted a Ph.D. degree. However, the data was not complete enough to satisfy my curiosity about the tribes to the west of the Rif, so we left our firstborn in the care of a grandmother and returned in the spring of 1928.

We were joined almost immediately by Limnibhy, who knew when and where to find us by some underground so-called *Poste Hassani,* by courier and word of mouth.

The three of us rode horseback from Targuist to Tangier, passing through the tall forests of the Senhaja Srir and the scrub-covered hills of the Ghomara, whose tribes reach the sea. Incidentally, *srir* means gun stock, which these sylvan craftsmen fashioned for the Riffian's rifles.

The inhabitants of both regions spoke Berber languages of their own, and the Ghomara in particular were rapidly becoming Arabized. The most interesting tribe we visited was the Beni Bu Nsar, who, as their name implies, believed they were descended from Christians. Encouraged by this rationalization, they ate pork and alcoholic grape jelly.

Instead of felling the beautiful hemlocks and cedars to clear the land and grow crops, they obtained most of their staple foods by trade. They lived well, for they were skilled craftsmen, and their products were much in demand. They forged long-barreled muskets out of old pipes and pieces of metal, fitted them with beautiful polished stocks, made bullets and gunpowder, tanned cowhides and goatskins, and fabricated the fringed Taghzuthi shoulder bags that every Riffian warrior had to carry. It was they who carved the forked walking sticks that doubled as gun rests, and carved the sides of bellows with floral designs in bold relief.

So friendly were they and so intriguing was their artistry that I would have loved to have been able to stay with these people as long as I had with the Riffians, but the clock was running out. Mary came down with malaria, and we went home, taking Limnibhy with us. I needed what lay still untapped in his head. Without him I could not have written my first three books, and I believed he might be a little safer in Massachusetts than in Morocco because of his record in the French colonial books. For that reason I had a little trouble exfiltrating him, so to speak, but we made it.

When we reached Boston on an American export ship out of Casablanca, we had no home to go to. Receiving no pay from Harvard during our absence, Mary and I had given up our lease in Cambridge. So, with Limnibhy, we joined our son in my parents' house in Wakefield.

My father was at first reluctant to let Limnibhy in, and he would not let him sleep upstairs. Instead he made him bed down in a game room in the cellar. Before he had been there many nights, Limnibhy saw a ghost, internally illuminated in some mysterious way. It emerged from a coal bin beside the furnace, walked straight through the door into the game room without opening it, and on through the outside door in the same way, never letting out a sound. Although this was a bad omen, Limnibhy did not complain, and continued to sleep in the game room until we found a place of our own in Cambridge.

It was on Upland Road, facing the northern end of Washington Avenue. The other half of the duplex was occupied by an elderly German with a strong accent, who disapproved of us heartily; he, posthumously, has my sympathy. Besides Mary, Carl Jr., myself, and Limnibhy, our dwelling was also occupied by a German nursemaid-governess, Pat Putnam and his chimpanzee, and often Gordon Bowles and his horned owl, which sat on Gordon's shoulder as he ate, pecking his ear until it bled. To this, Gordon—being a proper Quaker missionary child from Japan—could only say "Good grief." Frequent visitors were Gordon Browne, Fred Johnson, Jo Brew, Owen Lattimore, and Oliver La Farge. In my darkroom in the cellar, Owen enlarged his negatives taken in Central Asia, some of which he used in his book *The Desert Road to Turkestan*. Oliver was already famous for his best-seller, *Laughing Boy*. Fred Johnson became director of the Peabody Foundation at Andover, Jo Brew of the Peabody Museum at Harvard.

The goings-on in that house hardly provided the proper atmosphere in which to indoctrinate a centurion of Abd el-Krim's army for life in America, and Cambridge itself was not a community like those in which he had been bred. He had already identified himself with Wakefield; he had acquired a deep attachment for my father and liked to visit his larger and more elegant house.

Walking twenty-eight miles from house to house and back again was child's play to him, and he never lost his way, although the route was extremely complicated. Stimulated by Limnibhy's example, my father sometimes walked back with him, for now they were good friends—there was no more sleeping in the game room. On one such walk they took a short cut through a Jewish cemetery, I believe in

Woburn, where Limnibhy spied some gravestones with conical holes cut into their upper parts. Inside each hole, well protected by glass, was a photograph of the deceased in formal clothes. This impressed Limnibhy deeply.

America was a wonderful country. What he wanted most was for me to take him out West, to see the *gharbiyyin* (westerners), both cowboys and Indians, but I failed him. The nearest we came to it was when Fred Johnson, Gordon Bowles, and I drove him to Oldtown, Maine, in the middle of winter to visit Fred's old friends, the Penobscot Indians. It was cold on the way up from Cambridge, and Limnibhy said, "This is poison." When we got into the deep snow, he said, "This is death."

We stayed with the chief, Gabriel Paul, who spoke French. They had a wonderful time comparing cultural notes until long into the night, coming to the conclusion that the Indians and the Berbers were really the same people. When they were discussing ways to skin animals, Limnibhy said: "When we kill a sheep, goat, or even a cow, we cut a hole in the skin of a hind leg and blow into it with our mouths, while hitting the side of the body with the flat of a knife. That loosens the skin so that you can pull it off over the neck without having to slit the skin." To this Gabe replied: "You may do this with tame animals, but you can't with wild ones, because blowing them up makes them look foolish. One of our men once blew up a rabbit that way, and he has never killed another rabbit since." Then he added for Fred's benefit, "I don't think I ever told that to Frank Speck."

Frank, who was chairman of the anthropology department of the University of Pennsylvania, was at the head of the list as number-one authority on the Penobscots, and Fred, his former student, was runner-up. So a Berber from North Africa had extracted a piece of information out of a Maine Indian that no American had done. Limnibhy was a natural ethnographer; this episode convinced me, if I had any doubts, of the accuracy of his data on the Rif.

In Cambridge, Limnibhy went to night school to learn English, which he did rather rapidly, and incidentally met some female French-Canadian friends with whom he could converse more freely from the beginning. When we went to my parents' summer house in Rexhame Terrace, Marshfield, he used to sit on the beach in a bathing suit and fez. Girls strolling by from Brant Rock or Ocean Bluff would gaze at him, whereupon he would say, "Me Araby sheikh." As this happened during the Valentino period, they understood what he meant.

Shortly before I was due to depart on my next expedition, this time to northern Albania, it was also time for Limnibhy to go home. He missed his wives and children, and had his own property to take care of. One night in a dream he saw his favorite uncle, who told him to come home.

Before he left, he appeared one morning wearing my raccoon-skin coat, and carrying my anthropometric kit and some measuring blanks.

"I am going to Boston Common," he said, "to measure some Americans. Then I can take the blanks home to let my friends there know what kind of people the Americans are."

Everyone present thought this was a good joke, and a wonderful substitute for tears.

I booked him an American Export ship and saw him off. I never saw him again, although I have seen Zarkan and other members of his family.

Not long after his return Limnibhy was invited to a dinner party in Fez. He shouldn't have gone there, but he did. Someone poisoned him. He barely made it back to his beloved Iherrushen, where he died. Although Gordon Browne and I had held many suspicions and heard many rumors, we never found out exactly who did it, although I did learn who had ordered it done.

One day during World War II I went to the cartographic office of the protectorate in Rabat to buy some maps. After I had signed my name, the French officer on duty told me quite candidly without my asking that it had been necessary to liquidate Limnibhy because he had been drinking heavily, playing around with other men's wives, and generally creating unrest.

Through clenched teeth I thanked the officer for his information and walked out with my temples throbbing. It was not wine nor women that did Limnibhy in, but a heady aftertaste of freedom—with whom but me to blame?

Shortly after Christmas in 1974 my firstborn son, his wife, Janet, and the three youngest of my grandchildren—Lizzie, Ellen, and Richard—went on a pilgrimage to the Vale of Iherrushen, that my son had first visited in his mother's womb. At the Thursday market the current kaid fed them as lavishly as Midboh had my son's parents, and there he saw a ghastly sight.

Although the jinns had long since departed, the Volkswagen had replaced them. Having little work to do at home, the sons and grandsons of the warriors we had measured had driven from the Netherlands, where they toiled in factories, across France, Spain, and the Strait of Gibraltar to spend their holidays at home.

An American reforestation expert driving a four-wheeler met

the Coons at Boured, and carried them down the Iherrushen to almost a mile above Limnibhy's house. When they walked in they saw Zarkan, the great dancer of the 1920s. His sons were in Holland, where they had married Dutch girls, and had not returned.

Deforestation and floods had left Limnibhy's house half hanging over a bank. Most of the olive trees had been washed away and the oil press lay dismantled and abandoned. No one danced. The Laiya Labouya was not sung. A youthful bride was suggested for Richard, and when they left at least two of the visitors had wet cheeks. I am glad I wasn't there. It would have been too much.

9. To the Mountains of Giants

Hardly had Limnibhy left us than I was off again, postponing my writing of the books about the Riffians that I could never have written without his information. This next trip was to Ghegnia, or northern Albania, another of Earnest Hooton's favorite places, although he visited it only vicariously through my eyes, ears, and camera.

Although Albania is separated from the heel of Italy by less than forty miles of water (the Strait of Otranto), and it borders on Greece and Yugoslavia, in 1929 it was by far the least-known country of Europe, and its northern Gheg mountains (the Mountains of Giants) were virtually unexplored. Simply exploring these mountains was one reason for the expedition, if the least important one anthropologically.

The Ghegs who lived in them were reputed to be men of great stature with long, lean faces and heads flattened to the rear. This was the archetype of the Dinaric race, so named by the Franco-Russian anthropologist Joseph Deniker. From Albania northwestward Dinarics were to be found all the way up the Illyrian Alps to Switzerland. One of my jobs was to confirm and to explain this odd combination of cranial traits.

This search would be aided by the fact that, perhaps uniquely in Europe, the mountaineers still followed a rigid patrilineal kinship system with local exogamy (marriage outside the paternal line, sometimes to the hundredth generation) and often cross-cousin marriage (getting one's bride from the groom's mother's line). By questioning each subject measured, it would be possible to explain local similarities and differences.

We took no blood samples there. This was during the early days of blood sampling when blood groups were supposed to replace anthropometry in racial studies. I had taken blood in Morocco, and found the ABO groups totally unrelated to any physical measurement, index, or observation. So I abandoned the system, which was just as well because drawing the blood of Ghegs is either a ritual making the participants blood brothers for life, or a hostile act to be avenged by the blood letter's death.

My other problem involved the local geology, that contained

contrasting regions of limestone and granite, among other rocks, in very steep mountains that looked higher than their maximum of 9,068 feet. In 1929 the Ghegs grew all their food locally, except for sugar. This situation was also true a century ago in marginal regions of France. In 1866 Pierre Paul Broca, the great French anatomist and anthropologist, found that people living on the produce of granitic soil were shorter than those reared in limestone country. I wanted to look for the same correlation between soil and stature in Ghegnia, and I confirmed it.

Historical and archaeological records show that the Ghegs were probably the least mixed Hallstatt Iron Age people left in Europe. The Hallstatt people were the Illyrians who had and worked iron several centuries before the rise of the La Tène people, who were the Kelts. The Hallstatt center was in Bosnia, where a pre-Slavic language close to Gheg survived into historic times. A linguist from the University of Paris, Dr. Zacharie Mayani, has related Etruscan to Illyrian through a comparison between Etruscan and Gheg,* and he paid tribute to my work on that expedition by writing: "To the Professor Carleton S. Coon, in recognition of his help of vital importance to this research."

Before 500 B.C. the Gheg mountains were heavily forested and probably thinly inhabited or seasonally visited by hunters. The first Hallstatt settlers moved down the chain from Bosnia, bringing their ironwork and the designs of their wooden chairs hewn out of beechwood with adzes and files.

The Romans built a road across Ghegnia south of the river Drin, the northern fork of which drains the plain of Kossovo in Yugoslavia; the southern fork drains the north-south valley out of Lake Okhrida. The combined waters of the White (northern) and Black (southern) Drin rush through a deep gorge. Still used, this road runs along the southern rim of the gorge. It is too narrow and too steep for the passage of wheeled vehicles, but it is crossed with packhorses.

The Romans also introduced Catholic Christianity, just as Orthodox Christianity was brought to the Toscs by the Byzantines. Catholicism had little effect on the Gheg way of life—if anything, it reinforced their exogamic mating system. At several periods outsiders seized control of the Drin highway, principally Slavs and Turks. The Turks massacred many Ghegs in the northwesternmost region, the Malsia ë Madhe (Great Mountains) country. In the sixteenth century the

---

*Z. Mayani, Les Etrusques Commencent à Parler, Paris, B. Arthaud, 1961.

wholly and partly empty villages were repopulated by immigrants from Bosnia. These were Catholic tribesmen who spoke the parent language, Illyrian, in a semi-Romanized form. It differed little from the local Gheg. These newcomers were a reinforcement from the Gheg home-land, thrust out by pressure from Slavs and Turks, becoming a second wave of migration.

The Turks introduced firearms and fortified castles (*kullas*), thus increasing the tempo of feuding. They also converted many of the tribesmen to Islam. This meant that Muslim Ghegs could circulate freely in other parts of the Ottoman Empire, where some of them achieved high rank in the Turkish forces. The last dynasty in Egypt, which ended with Farouk, was Albanian. The Ghegs who clung to Catholicism, mostly in the relatively impregnable heights of Mirdita and Dukagin, took a risk when they went to the towns bordering the mountains, such as Scutari and Dibra, and used double names: Kol Prenga at home was Ali in the town. Like a Christian in the Rif, he had to be ready to rattle off the Profession of Faith at the rise of two successive fingers.

In 1929, when I decided to go, things had not changed much. The Turks had been out of power since the Balkan War of 1912, and the powder-puff king, the erstwhile Prince of Wied, ruled only a few months in 1914 before the outbreak of World War I. Italians and Yugo-slavs invaded Albania and were forced out. A shaky parliament was convened, and one of its premiers was Bishop Fan Noli, who founded the Autocephalous Autonomous Orthodox Church in Boston, and had returned to Albania for that purpose. He headed the state from June through December in 1924. Back in Boston I consulted with him fre-quently, and he was a great help to me in preparing for my expedition.

The bishop was ousted by his rival, Ahmad Zogu, a Mati tribal chief who fled to Yugoslavia and returned with henchmen from that country. Although his dependence on his country's previous enemies made Zogu unpopular with his people, he made himself premier in 1925, and King Zog I in 1928, just a year before our arrival. By the time we got to the capital city of Tirana he was sending doubles out to ride in his automobile to be shot at, and through fear of poison, accepted food only from his mother.

When we departed Mary had to be left at home until she should feel strong enough. She was still suffering from bouts of malaria contracted in Morocco. My first companion was Frederick E. Farns-worth, a Coloradan who had graduated from Harvard in anthropology that June.

We traveled by ship to Germany, by rail to Trieste, and by ship again down the shallow, stormy Adriatic, as far as Durrës, a pathetic little landing place, from which a dilapidated taxi took us to Tirana. It had a population of probably less than fifteen thousand. The capital sported one hotel, which fell far short of rating a *cordon bleu*. Without wasting much time, we presented ourselves at the American ministry. There we met the Honorable Julius C. Holmes, chargé d'affaires. The minister, who was absent, was my old friend, the Honorable Maxwell Blake of Tangier. The legation was spacious, and Jim Holmes lonely. It did not take him long to invite us to be his guests; it took us even less time to accept.

One wise step that King Zog had taken was to employ four British officers to set up a gendarmerie. They were General Percy and Colonels Stirling, Martin, and Glegg. Colonel Stirling's name will be familiar to readers of Colonel T. E. Lawrence's books *Revolt in the Desert* and *The Seven Pillars of Wisdom*. A small garrison of gendarmes stationed at Tirana were the first to feel the touch of my calipers, but they did not form a good sample because they had been selected for their jobs because of their physical fitness, and because most of them were from Mati, the king's own tribe, and thus theoretically were men he could trust.

In order to measure a valid sample of at least one hundred men from each of the ten Gheg tribes, we had to get government permission to travel in the north. It was the usual tedious runaround, and I mention it here only because it was humorous and pathetic.

In our fifteen days of battling a new and creaky bureaucracy, the course was marked by one unique event. Toward the end of the fracas Jim Holmes, white tie, tall hat, and all, went straight to the king to explain to His Majesty what we were doing, and Zog exclaimed: "That is unnecessary. I have just issued a decree abolishing all tribal boundaries. Now all Albanians are identical."

When Jim finally won and we departed, we took along as guide and interpreter one Anthony Stevens, a clerk in the legation. He had been born in the village of Gonaj* in the tribe of Has—in 1929, as now, a part of Yugoslavia. Most boys in Gonaj learned the baker's trade, including Anthony. In his youth he migrated to Cleveland, Ohio, to work in a bakery, but he lost his right arm there when it got caught in the machinery. His baking career thus ended, he studied to become a government clerk, and was eventually sent with his family to Tirana. At the time of our imminent departure, he was due a vacation. It made good sense for him to spend it taking care of Farnsworth and me. Our

---

Pronounced Johnny.

route, of course, was plotted to include a visit to his tribal kinfolk at Gonaj.

Steve spoke both Albanian languages/dialects (depending on which linguists you believe) as well as flawless Serbian and Ohio English. With one arm he could ride a horse better than I could with two, but I will not extend this comparison to Farnsworth, born and bred in Colorado. Above all, Steve was a born diplomat and had a delicious sense of humor.

Before taking us away from the legation gates, it may be apropos to mention that the kullas* that the Turks had introduced included a special safety device, a chivalrous element. To reduce the danger brought with firearms, they had built privies into the upper story walls in the form of flying wings with their drainage holes made crooked to prevent any sniper below from shooting a foeman unsportingly. The Turks also introduced *hans,* or rural inns, studded along major trails in Muslim country to lodge travelers and their beasts in safety overnight; and *kirajis,* or horse renters, who were in charge of the transport trade. The latter were a group of hard-bitten, disillusioned men who owned horses and rented them for perilous journeys anywhere, to be ridden and/or packed. They always insisted on reserving one or more steeds to carry fodder for the others; they personally walked, urging on and guiding their beasts.

Naturally, the kirajis had to be paid, partly in advance and partly at more or less stated intervals en route. Therefore we had to carry bags of silver currency; this exposed us to the machinations of fancied bandits conjured up by the kirajis, as well as to their simpler demands, in tight spots, for a raise.

This money included an interesting collection of coins from Turkey, many European countries, and even Canada and the United States. Unacceptable was the Albanian paper money issued in 1925. The acceptable unit of whatever coinage was a Napoleon, valued at twelve gold French francs or four gold U.S. dollars, as of before World War I.

The night before we left, while standing in front of the legation, we saw four men walk by carrying on their shoulders a large plank. On the plank lay a corpse with a great erection showing under his shroud, like the veiled periscope of a one-man submarine. The sad story ran as follows: The body was that of a man from Valona who had caught a rival toying with his wife. The cuckold tried to kill his rival, but was prevented. Then he chased the adulterer to Tirana and there, in the

---

*Spelled kullë *in Albanian.*

open marketplace, shot him six times. The victim died, and the dishonored husband was promptly hanged, as the erection indicated. When we saw the latter being carried horizontally, he was on his way to the cemetery.

Farnsworth, Steve, several kirajis, four horses, and I set out around noon the next day. We soon noted that one of the horses was a pregnant mare. First we had to traverse a barren region of sandstone eroded by water and by winds from several directions into fantastic shapes, like a petrified topiary garden. In a way it resembled Farnsworth's native Colorado's Garden of the Gods. After about an hour the road rose and before long we were climbing on foot. Steve fell off his horse when the packsaddle turned, and landed on his back between the hind hooves of his horse. Chick (Farnsworth), Mustafa (the head kiraji), and I hauled him out without further injury.

About dusk we went over a high, narrow, twisty trail in a pass, with a deep, steep canyon to the left, almost as sweat-raising as the trail over the Noisy Mountain to Tiddest. We eased our way downward in the dark, into a high-lying river valley, and passed three hans before finding the right one at Zalli. The han was a two-storied building: The lower floor was a stable and cheap lodging; upstairs was the expensive room, with an open fireplace and the dwarfish *hanji,* or host, squatting beside it. We rolled out our blankets by the fire and waited for the hanji to make us an olive oil pilaf. The hanji, Mustafa, Murap (a kiraji), and others sat up all night talking. The hanji explained this the next morning by saying that he suspected the others of being thieves. Steve said that news traveled fast there, and they were already discussing the murder in Tirana the day before.

The men at the han agreed that the murderer should have been hanged—not for having killed his wife's lover, but because he had shot two more bullets into him after he was dead.

As we were going over the pass the preceding afternoon, the fact that we had a pregnant mare with us reminded Steve of the story of Kol Prenga and the Speech of Animals, as follows.

One day Kol Prenga and his wife went to market, and started home over a mountain trail. Kol was riding his stallion. His wife, also pregnant, was lagging along on the mare, and the woman was complaining of her discomfort most of the time. This annoyed Kol Prenga considerably. Finally they came to a bend in the trail and saw, right in front of them, a huge, beautiful owl. Kol exclaimed to his wife, "What a beautiful bird. It is the loveliest creature I have ever seen." His wife snorted and replied, "It's just an ugly old owl."

When the owl heard itself complimented, it said to Kol, in a language that his wife could not understand, "You are the first human being that has ever called me beautiful. For this favor I shall reward you. From now on you shall have the power of understanding the speech of animals. But there is one condition: If you ever tell anyone else, and particularly your wife, what the animals have said, you will instantly die."

At that point, Kol heard the stallion complaining to the mare: "Why don't you get along a little faster, you slowpoke?" To this the mare replied, "I am carrying four and you are only carrying two. There is no justice. I will be glad when this trip is over."

When he heard this, Kol could not help laughing, and his wife demanded: "What is so funny? Are you laughing at me? If not, what is it? I must know."

After being pestered for several hours, Kol admitted that the owl had given him the power to understand the speech of animals and that he had been laughing at the conversation between the mare and the stallion.

"What did they say?" his wife further demanded.

"If I tell you, I will die at once. Do you want me to die?"

"No, but I have to know just the same."

This went on until they arrived home. Then Kol got a shroud and some candles. He lit the candles and placed them in the proper positions, lay down, and pulled the shroud over him.

"Now I will tell you, and then I will die," he said.

At this point his dog burst in, howling: "Don't tell her, master, don't tell her, we need you alive."

Then his cow ambled in, licked his face, and said the same thing. And his pig, and his sheep, and all the other animals, including the stallion and mare, who declared they would never have said anything to each other had they foreseen this result. But none of this moved Kol Prenga from his purpose, with his wife still standing over him and repeating her demand, when in flew the cock, followed by his hens.

"Ki! Ki! Ki!" (Albanian for *cock-a-doodle-do*) crowed the cock. "What a fool are you!" And he mounted his hens, one after the other.

Kol Prenga leaped to his feet, knocking the candles over, threw his wife on the floor, lifted up her skirt, and mounted her, pregnant or no. And everyone lived happily forever after.*

---

*Only in 1975 did I discover that I was scooped in this story by Paul Fenimore Cooper, in his Tricks of Women and Other Albanian Tales, *New York: Morrow, 1928,* pp. 75–85. The details are different; the plot's the same.

Steve had other stories too, which he either remembered from his youth, picked up as we went along, or both, and he always told them in moments of anxiety, when the trail was dangerous or bandits "imminent," to distract us. They were by no means hilariously funny, but grim and a bit homiletic, each with a sharp punch line suited to the mood and tempo of the scene and time.

The next morning we set out early to cross another divide, a very high one. Squat by the crest stood a wattle-and-daub coffeehouse next to a new barracks, still being built. The trail led through a forest of beech trees, two to four feet in diameter, their leaves now yellow. Inside the coffeehouse a mandolinlike instrument called *qyteli* (pronounced *chyoutelli*) hung on the wall. A man in a soldier's uniform took it down and played it for us. It had two strings, one of which produced a tune with brief intervals between stops, while the other went on and on, on the same note, like a bagpipe drone. It was quite a different instrument from the *gusle,* which we heard farther north. This is a smaller instrument with a single string, held against the singer's cheek for resonance, to accompany epic poetry, spontaneous or old.

The first place at which we measured was Gur i Bardh (the White Stone), where we met some opposition, owing to general suspicion on the local people's part and inexperience on ours. The second was Klos. There we gave a party in the han, handing out *mastika* (anisette) to all comers, and measuring about half of them the next morning. But that was too expensive to keep up indefinitely.

At Bulçiz we hit the jackpot. First we made contact with the chief elder of the village, who simply produced the men. If my memory does not fail me, it was here that the praying game first arose, wholly unwittingly on my part. As I was reading off the measurements to Chick—one-ninety-two, one-fifty-four, one-zero-two, one-thirty-two, etc.—my voice took on a special tone and pace, for there was a long line ahead of me. I must have sounded somewhat like a tobacco auctioneer, and this seemed to have a partly hypnotic effect. The men formed in line voluntarily, and beamed with pleasure when I had finished with them.

"Keep it up," said Steve out of a corner of his mouth. "They think you are praying for them."

One man had less pious thoughts in mind. While I was taking his hip breadth he asked me if I would like to measure his *membrum virile* as well, but I pretended not to understand.

Among our prayed-over subjects was an albino. In the Gheg

country albinos are said to be produced by a union between women and ghosts, and are called ghost children. They are said to be the only ones that can see ghosts and are hired to shoot them when domestic animals die mysteriously, or the crops fail.

Our next stop was the town of Peshkopi, otherwise known as Little Dibra. Big Dibra, the original market center of the tribe of that name, lay across the river a few miles to the south. It had been given to Yugoslavia in the notorious treaty that followed the Balkan War, and the Dibrans inside the present boundary had built Peshkopi as a substitute. The last few miles of the trail had been widened into a six-foot road. The town boasted a real hotel with separate rooms and iron cots, and one general dormitory in which a dozen men could sleep, as in a hospital ward. There were butcher shops, shoemakers' booths, a barbershop, and hardware stores, all that a market town really needed, on a minor scale.

In the hotel we had plenty to eat, including meat. In the hans we had subsisted mostly on beans, hard maize bread, and sour, soft cheese. Now we could sleep on beds, in a smokeless room. As soon as we got in we visited the prefect, who promised to send us men to measure the next day, and so he did. So far it had rained every day and every night, but now the weather improved, and we were measuring on reasonably flat, hard earth.

Our next stop was the castle of one of the two most important men in the tribe, Major Çen Eleze. As we approached, we heard gunfire. Chick and I, walking at the beginning and end of our procession, held our rifles cocked and ready, but it was a false alarm. Outside the castle stood three men, the major himself and his two sons, all about six feet four, who were shooting at targets. They invited us to join them. Although all three were crack shots, Chick equaled them, but I did not.

Çen Eleze and his sons had been feuding with the other big man of Dibra, and that was what the rumors of rebellion had been mostly about, although neither of them had much use for King Zog. We were royally entertained, did our measuring, and continued on our way, proceeding through the rest of Dibra and various settlements in Luma to the north. This depleted our ammunition, because at both Çen Eleze's and one stronghold in Luma, there were many toasts. After each one the host, Chick, and I were supposed to shoot a clip of cartridges out a window. But we halted this exchange as soon as possible, lest we run out of ammunition and become defenseless against bandits—or, more likely, irate tribesmen on the lookout for Zog's tax collectors.

We walked and rode northward to where the Black Drin and White Drin met at Kukës. From there their combined waters rushed westward toward a gorge to Scutari and the Adriatic, which it entered by several mouths. At Kukës Chick had a critical ailment requiring expert medical service, so we crossed the border into Yugoslavia after a considerable argument with the Serbian guards, who thought that Chick was a Croat or a Slovene and thus their enemy. Finally we were allowed to be jolted to Prizren in an oxcart and rode by train from there to Belgrade.

Meanwhile, Steve visited his kinfolk at Gonaj. Once back at Prizren we measured the men of Has—Steve's tribe—in and out of jail, but not the townsmen of Prizren, who are Turks. As Steve's vacation was over, we returned to Tirana, where I had my own medical problem, Vincent's angina of the gums. Because the local dentist could not cure it I went to Vienna, where a specialist did so, and thence to Cuxhaven, Germany, to meet Mary. The two of us arrived in Tirana the day before Christmas.

My next job was to find a new interpreter. After some search I discovered that there was no Gheg available with whom I had a common language. Finally I was forced to break a firm principle and take along a Tosc, one Stavrë Frasheri, a professor at Dr. Irwin's American University at Durrës. This university was founded by a Methodist preacher, but had folded for lack of funds, and Stavrë was out of a job. He had studied at Roberts College in Istanbul, spoke English perfectly, and soon adapted himself to Gheg. He had studied anthropology and knew a great deal about magic and folklore, and wanted to collect data for a future book on the subject. As Chick was just getting over a bout of jaundice, he stayed at the legation.

Just after Christmas Mary, Frasheri, and I started out with the usual horses and kirajis through Mati, partly over old trails and partly over new ones, the latter being new country for the kirajis. In order to get to the last han in Mati, we had to ford the southern branch of the Fan River, which rose in Mati territory, the northern one rising in Mirdita. A local guide led us along the river bank, which twisted and turned. To save time and distance, the guide made us ford the river five times. We all got soaking wet, particularly the kirajis and myself, who were on foot. On the last fording I fell into a hole in the riverbed and was totally immersed.

When we finally arrived at the han after dark, the hanji insisted that I should have a tot of *raki* to warm me up. He drew this from a keg in a low-ceilinged room, which he naturally kept under lock and key. I leaned over to pick up the glass, and as I straightened up to drink the firewater, I hit my head smack on a protruding nail and fell flat. A local who had witnessed this mishap thought it was the funniest thing he had ever seen, and laughed uproariously. Still dazed, I stood up and punched him in the solar plexus, flattening him in turn.

My act disturbed the hanji, who said: "That man has kindred hereabouts. I am not going to let you sleep in the han, but you will have to hide under a pile of straw in the stable, and you must be off well before dawn lest they shoot you."

When the sun rose we were well out of range, and out of Mati as well, inside the bounds of Mirdita. Once we reached this region of granite, the vegetation changed from scrub to dense forests with giant beech trees in the lower land, then to pines on the slopes of the mountains. Some of the beeches were so thick-trunked that the Mirditans could carve a one-piece circular tabletop over six feet in diameter out of a single plank, to be laboriously carried to Scutari for sale.

The high point of this journey came when we reached the impressive residence of Preng Jon Markojon, the hereditary Prince of Mirdita, a town inhabited solely by Catholics. When we arrived, Jon Markojon sat outside his doorway on a beechwood throne of pure Hallstatt Iron Age design, surrounded by his family, including his wife and mother. Among other things, he said to me, "There is only one woman a man can trust—his mother." Thus he echoed the sentiment of his rival King Zog, who paid him off handsomely not to raid the lowlanders of their cattle in winter. Like the king, the prince would accept food only from his mother, for a reason previously stated.

Measuring one hundred Mirdita men was easy, with the Prince's cooperation. When we had finished, we moved northward to Puka where we were again put up in the local han. Measuring in Puka was also easy, because the regional judge was holding court there, and many people had gathered to present grievances and to have settlements made.

One day the judge asked me quite casually the age of a boy I was measuring, who turned out to be a prisoner. I replied, equally casually, "About twenty-two or so."

"Thank you," said the judge. "Then he will hang."

It seems the young man had murdered two people in payment for a beating-up his brother had received six months previously. He had said he was thirteen, and hoped to get only a jail sentence on account of his immaturity. When he and his brother heard that he was to be hanged, the "boy" shook all over and had a mild fit from fear. The brother was all for killing me, obviously without success.

On Saturday, January 21, Mary and I left Puka very early, took an automobile from Scutari to Tirana, and that night attended an international ball. Sunday night Mary came down with chills and fever. On the twenty-seventh I put her on a boat to Bari, to rejoin her after the expedition was over.

The only tribe we had not measured was Dukagin, the northernmost, least accessible, and least known. Like Mirdita it is wholly Catholic. It consists of two major *bairaks,* Shoshi and Shala, and several smaller ones with which these two could intermarry.

On February 2 Chick, Frasheri, and I tried the lowest pass into Shala, from the Malsia ë Madhe side, with four horses lightly loaded, and when we got to the top the snow was waist deep. Beyond that stretched a plateau with about four feet of snow, and it was still snowing hard. We had passed people hiding in caves and rock shelters all the way up. We could have gone on alone, breaking a trail, but the horses were wallowing in drifts up to their panniers, and threw their loads. So we turned back in order not to lose the horses, since we couldn't have made it lugging a minimum of instruments, grub, and bedding on our backs.

We came back, and the next night arrived in Tirana. The whole north was snowed in. We spent the following day inquiring about all the routes into Mati and Dibra, the southernmost tribes, and found one road to be open, the one we had taken the previous fall. We planned to leave the next morning if we could get horses. Had we brought snowshoes and a toboggan, we might have gotten through on foot. But wishes won't build toboggans, even in Albania, and we had to give this route up.

Then we planned to do the projected trip backward, so to speak—Mati, Dibra, Luma, Malsia Jakoves, and Dukagin (Shala), taking a chance of getting stuck. We couldn't wait for spring because we would run out of cash.

We left the next day, setting off through Mati with our usual horses and kirajis, but soon discovered that we had companions. An enterprising publican was accompanying a string of horses laden with spindly tables, Sunday school chairs, and what was most important, several cases of Löwenbräu beer. When thirsty, all Chick and I had to do was to reach over and remove a bottle of beer each, taking care to leave the loads trim and to pay the publican. By the time he reached Burelli, the new government administration center where he had planned to set up his café, the publican had to send his rented horses back to Tirana for a new shipment of beer.

We measured more men at Guri Bardh and Bulçiz and finally

reached the bank of the Black Drin River. There we were received in the usual friendly fashion by Major Çen Eleze and his giant sons. I had brought the major a few boxes of ammunition from Vienna, partly as a present and partly to keep him from shooting off all of my own. During the feast that ensued, which included a whole roasted sheep, my host tried to pop one of the sheep's eyeballs into my mouth. The mind was willing but the stomach refused. As graciously as possible, I rejected this kind offer.

All the way up the Black Drin to Kukës we measured, completing our series for Dibra and Luma. As we approached Kukës from the south, the trail was steep and the kirajis were particularly fretful because it was getting dark; furthermore it was Ramadan, the Muslim month of fasting. They had not eaten a bite nor drunk a drop of water since 6:00 A.M. In Albania, at least, where the length of daylight varies considerably during the year, instead of fasting from dawn to dusk as the Holy Koran (properly Quran) requires, the faithful fasted from 6:00 A.M. to 6:00 P.M., thus equating the seasonal variations, for the month of Ramadan crawls around the calendar as measured by the moon.

As I had been unofficially chosen as timekeeper, with a real old-fashioned pocket watch instead of just a wristwatch, the kirajis kept asking me: "What time is it? Isn't it six o'clock yet?" Finally I got bored with constantly having to pull out my watch. At exactly 5:00 P.M. I said: "Now the fast is over."

The procession halted abruptly. The kirajis had their water jugs out of their packsaddles in a flash. After an initial gurgling, they began nibbling on bread and cheese. We moved along in the dusk at a quickened pace, until at exactly six o'clock we heard a loud rolling of drums ahead of us. We were entering Kukës, where a band of gypsies was beating large drums as hard as they could to announce the end of the fast. To say that I was unpopular would be an understatement, but gendarmes were about; luckily, we stayed in Kukës a week measuring men of many tribes who had come there on shopping trips, and this gave the kirajis a cooling-off period.

From Kukës we departed on February 22, wending our way, such as it was, through the tribes of Has and Malsia Jakoves. First we crossed the White Drin over an elegant Turkish footbridge of three arches, just upstream from the confluence of that river with the Black Drin, then we followed the usual tortuous trails, measuring people as we went. Food was scarce. Our usual fare was unleavened corn bread almost too hard to chew, so we dipped it in melted pork fat (when we were among Christians), and it was hard for each of us to keep from taking more than our share.

At length we arrived at a tributary of the combined Drin, a roaring, whitecapped freshet swollen by melted snow and too swift and deep to be forded by men or horses. The only way to cross it was by walking a slippery pole, which luckily had another pole set up as a handrail about four feet higher and a foot upstream. At this point we paid off the kirajis, lumped the packsaddles and their contents across the pole, and set our loads down on the other side.

But we had not long to wait. A half dozen huge men soon appeared, picked up the packsaddles, threw them over their heads like ponchos, and we were off, pushing our way through the snow in the wake of the porters. The accumulation was waist deep when we came to the crest of the pass dividing Malsia Jakoves from Dukagin. Being Christians, the porters paused for a smoke, and a snack to boot. Before us to the west stretched a relatively flat valley, Shala to the north and Shoshi dead ahead. Another silver-crested range rimmed the valley to the west. The sun was low and bright, and the details of the scene stood out in high relief.

We worked our way down to the flat land, where the snow was spotty. Walking between plowed fields already beginning to turn light green, we heard an unusual sound—the tolling of church bells. They issued from a small stone chapel, from which emerged a somewhat bedraggled looking priest, his vestments clean but worn, for he had no way of getting new ones. He greeted us warmly, and in German. An Austrian by birth, he had studied at Rome, and had devoted his life to caring for the lives and souls of these isolated mountaineers.

Beside him also appeared a genial elder named Tom Tushi, who led us to his house and made us comfortable. He seated Chick and me in two of the same kinds of handsome, Iron Age, hand-hewn, thronelike chairs that we had seen in front of Prince Jon Markojon's house in Mirdita. Later I informed the priest that I would consider it a great honor to take a pair of these thrones home.

He replied, "Those here are all in use, but I will have a pair made and ship them to you by way of Scutari after the snow has melted."

"How much will they cost?" I asked.

"Whatever you wish to give," he answered. "The money will go to the poor of this parish." I paid him what I could.

Toward the end of the summer that followed, I received a notice from the Boston customs house bidding me to come to their warehouse to pick up a pair of chairs. When I got there I found my chairs, uncrated and unblemished. On the bottom of each seat were painted my name and address. On each of them sat an elderly customs officer, both Irish.

"I see your name on the bottom of the seat," one of them said. "Are you by any chance related to Billy Coon?"

"He was my grandfather," I said.

"He was one of us, and we remember him well. He was a fine man. Incidentally, how much did you pay for these chairs?"

"I don't rightly remember, but I really paid nothing, for I gave the money to a Catholic priest to distribute among the needy of his parish."

"God bless you, boy, and take them away."

I did. They have been a wonderful ornament and conversation piece in whatever house I have lived in, ever since.

We remained at Tom Tushi's place for about five days, measuring men from the two major bairaks of Shoshi and Shala, as well as from the smaller ones of Plani, Kiri, Dushman, and Toplana. While Shoshi, Shala, and Mirdita are all theoretically descended from three brothers, Shoshi and Shala nevertheless regularly intermarry because, they say, these two *fis* (patrilineages) are separated by more than one hundred generations. Both also intermarry with the four smaller and unrelated fis.

Yet the Mirditans say that they cannot intermarry with Shoshi or Shala because they reject the one-hundred-generation cutoff, intermarrying instead with their own smaller fis. But the chances of a Shoshi- or Shala-Mirdita union are close to zero, because they live on either side of the uncrossable Drin, and are further separated by the Muslim tribe of Puka.

Early in March we left this hospitable aerie, climbed down to the Drin, and arrived in Scutari by dugout canoes, sculled gondolier-style—a fitting finale to a brave and tragic journey. Although I had been there less than half a year, I felt like an emigrant with a pack on my back, setting forth to a new world.

Mary and I met in France and went home. There my father told me about the stock market crash, and the Great Depression had begun. We did not go out again for three years. Chick Farnsworth joined the State Department.

Having studied no Shqip before leaving home, I was mostly dependent on Steve and Frasheri for communication. Steve called a spade a plow; Frasheri, missionary-style, made it a trowel. But gestures, expressions, and general wavelengths communicate many things that words hide. I can always tell a liar when I don't know his language. Liars were as scarce as palm trees in Ghegnia. The eagle men are too proud. Still, before we left, I could understand more than I let on.

Once when we were sleeping upstairs on a wooden floor—which had an open fire pit in the middle—Chick and I crawled into rather expensive felted blankets doubled and sewn up both sides, an awkward kind of sleeping bag. Three other men lay on the hard floor in front of us, crowded under a single blanket, with their bare feet sticking out.

No sooner had our trail-weary bodies become comfortably settled in their twin cocoons than our roommates burst into almost hysterical laughter.

"What's wrong?" I asked, as I sat up with difficulty.

"What'll you do," one of them gurgled between gasps, "when the house catches on fire?"

On our last day before our gondola ride to Scutari I was standing on the riverbank, gazing (rather rudely, I must admit) at the most beautiful young woman I had seen in Albania, when a man approached me. He stared at my underpinnings, clad in knickers and long stockings, and asked: "How do you keep from falling down, with such skinny legs?"

Frasheri assured me that the young woman was a (ahem) prostitute, blushing as he said it. I thanked Zoti (Albanian for My Lord) that it hadn't been the leg inspector's wife.

The same wry spirit that permeated such encounters may also explain why we heard so much about bandits who never materialized; I am convinced that for anyone who didn't look like King Zog, the whole of Ghegnia was safer for travelers like us than forty feet of Massachusetts Avenue in Harvard Square.

The October 2, 1930, number of *The Harvard Alumni Bulletin* carried an article by Earnest A. Hooton entitled "An Untamed Anthropologist Among the Wilder Whites." It was twelve pages long, and each page was half text and half one of my photographs. The first seven pages were about the Rif, the last five about Albania. After a lot of flattery, he says on page 41:

I watched Coon getting more and more restless, yearning more and more obviously for the society of the uncivilized and unwashed. I could see it was a case of savages or bust. So we picked out the wildest spot we could find in Europe, with the toughest and least known population of two-gun men. We planned an anthropometric survey of Albania. . . .

He ends up with:

Coon is quite as energetic in the analysis of his material as in the collecting of it. He goes at it with a kind of divine frenzy, inventing new methods of analysis, improving on old ones, cursing, tearing his hair when he gets into difficulties, yet always emerging, disheveled but triumphant. He is a bit like Colonel Lawrence [sic] and a great deal like Sir Richard Burton, possibly a little erratic, and with more than a spark of genius. . . .

After that I might just as well have dropped dead, particularly when I saw the sneers on the faces of my contemporaries and rivals for promotion. The rest of the article contained excerpts from a few of my more extravagantly worded letters, posted in the field. Some of them I have used here to stir my jaded memory, because I kept no diary other than the dates on the measurement blanks, which served as a calendar.

My book *The Mountains of Giants* was published in 1950, as Volume 23, No. 1, of the Peabody Museum (Harvard) Papers. It did not take me long to write it. The delay was caused by paucity of funds, although funds were not lacking for statistical and editorial work. Forty-four members of the Excavators' Club of Harvard and Radcliffe raised the money, and it appeared at a time when anthropometry was being labeled racism, and blood-group studies were in the ascendancy.

The first half of the book covered the Ghegs' social and political structure, and the second half their physical attributes. As stated earlier, I confirmed Broca's fundamental discovery that, all else equal, stature is a function of the amount of calcium present in the local soil and available in the local diet for bone growth and has little to do with race. As for the Dinaric problem, I solved that too as far as Albania was concerned. Gheg mothers carry their babies in horizontal cradles with the backs of their heads pressing on the cradle boards. This practice flattens the head behind and thrusts the nasal skeleton forward. If one side of the occipital region was flattened more than the other I could check this assymetry against handedness by asking the subject to throw a stone. Back in Cambridge, I found some Albanian families living in Somerville. They were Toscs, who are Dinarics too. Those born in the old country had occipital flattening. Those born in America and un-cradled were also unflattened; if seen in a crowd no one would suspect from their appearance that they were Albanian by ancestry.

As for Joseph Deniker's Dinarics farther north into Switzerland, I do not know how many have been cradled and how many derive their craniofacial form from a purely genetic source. There may be as many ways to get a Dinaric head and face as there are to skin a cat. I only know that from Lebanon to the Oxus river country, people cradle their babies, who grow up with flattened heads; Armenians born in

America, who remain uncradled, do not usually have Armenoid (the equivalent of Dinaric) heads; and that some prominent Americans who were born of missionary parents in the Near East and raised by doting local nursemaids can always be identified by the shapes of their heads.

All in all my trip to Albania was profitable from a scientific point of view. I learned a lot and came to admire the courage and spirit of the Ghegs, their truthfulness, honor, and virility, but can never feel quite as much of a meeting of minds with them as I did with the Riffians. Both are brave and honorable. Perhaps it can be best expressed by comparing their senses of humor. Things that amuse the Riffians amuse me too. Things that set the Ghegs into roars of laughter, I find cruel. Farnsworth enjoyed their company more than I did, however, and he was not cruel.

Nor was Stavrë Th. Frasherie, our second and last interpreter. He scooped my book by twenty years by publishing *Permes Mirdites Ne Djëmer* with the Peppo-Marko Press in Korçe, 1930. It has taken nineteen years to get it translated finally, by the scholar Peter Prifti, and it will be published in English as a Peabody Museum (Harvard) Paper, comparable to *The Mountains of Giants,* as soon as funds can be found.

In it he begins by saying that all that southern Albanians know about their northern neighbors is that their country is wild, impassable in winter, and haunted by ferocious beasts. He recounts our travels (in which he plays the leading part) and then settles for a history of the tribe of Mirdita. This is followed by details of the kinship system and other ethnographic details similar to what I gave but perhaps somewhat more accurate because I got them from him. He mentions an American lady and gentleman as his companions on the first page, but names neither of us until about halfway through the book.

In the few pages where he mentions me by name, I seem to take shape as a stumbling, awkward, clumsy character, like a conventional dude among cowboys, or a Laurel and Hardy comedian.

The casual southern Albanian reader must have been left in some doubt as to who was the leader and who was the employee in this narrative. When I read it for the editor of the Peabody Museum Press in 1979, I was reminded of Robert Burns's lines in "To a Toad":

> *the power the giftie gie us*
> *to see ourselves as others see us!*

10. Farwell Place

When we returned from Albania in 1930, Mary and I rented a house from Radcliffe College on Farwell Place, a short, dead-end street running from Brattle Street to the Christ's Church graveyard, parallel to and between Church Street and Appian Way. Gordon and Eleanor Browne lived across the street, and a business associate of Gordon's two houses away. His name was Randolph Mohammed Guesus, the son of a wealthy Arab textile importer from Fez and a British mother who was the prototype of women's lib in Fez at the turn of the century. As our house was very handy to Harvard Square and the Yard, we had frequent visitors who used to come and sit on the floor practically every day. It was while we were living in that house that our son Charles Adams Coon was born, on June 2, 1931. Adams was his maternal grand-mother's maiden name. She lived until a few days short of one hundred years, and at ninety-nine received a letter of congratulation from Jimmy Carter.

My memories of expeditions and battles are as keen as mustard, but the opposite is true of time spent at home. Although I had an office in the Peabody Museum and worked there, I do not remember what my title was. My entry in *Who's Who* reminds me that between 1934 and 1948 I rose from instructor to assistant professor to associate pro-fessor to full professor, all of which are paying jobs. If I had any title it could have been a museum one, because I arranged an exhibit of my Moroccan specimens on the fourth floor, and went with a museum curator to a lady's house to appraise some precious specimens.

As to who paid me during those two and a half years, it must have been mostly my father, who kept on giving me $250 a month despite his catastrophe in the 1929–1930 stock market. In terms of its 1930 value, three thousand dollars might modestly support a small young family like mine.

My first job was to get my book *Tribes of the Rif* ready for the Harvard University Press. Funds for the analysis were provided by the Bureau of International Research, headed by George Grafton Wilson; the publication was paid for by Mrs. Oric (Natica) Bates, whose de-ceased husband's book on blond Berbers (*The Eastern Libyans*) started me on this quest. Lavishly illustrated, *Tribes of the Rif* was published in 1931.

Part I, Culture, covers 187 eleven-by-eight-inch pages. It deals with everything from geography to religion. Part II, Race, covers 234 pages, and includes the measurements of 539 Riffians, 197 Senhaja (living south and west of the Rif), 73 Ghomara (a coastal group of other Berbers to the west), 27 citizens of Sheshawen, who claim that their ancestors were expelled by the Spaniards from Grenada, 93 "Arabs," and 277 Shluh measured in Marrakesh. At the end are plates 33 through 67, each with front view and profile Graflex photographs of six men, or two hundred and ten men. There are other photographs scattered through the text. I only wish that Limnibhy could have seen it.

Three young Riffians, grandchildren of Limnibhy's generation, having reached America as students, have come to see me lately, and *Tribes of the Rif* is the first thing they want to see. Although the first edition is out of print, a reprint house makes excellent reproductions. All three of them now have one.

My conclusions to the historical, cultural, and physical analysis of the Riffians is that they resemble northern Europeans more than they do southern Europeans or Arabs. Their measurements put them closest to the Norwegians and the British. They are not the descendants of Vandals, who didn't land on their shores, but mostly settled in Tunisia. They came from the south and east into thinly inhabited, forested mountains. The designs on their clothing are the same as those on the Old Kingdom tattoos on the blond Libyans depicted in Egyptian bas-reliefs. Their hairdos are also the same. Thirty-three years after the publication of *Tribes of the Rif* I saw and photographed cave paintings of blond Europeans riding in chariots, in the barren Acacus Mountains of southern Libya.

The most reasonable answer is that the Libyans, Acacus charioteers, Riffians, and other blond Berbers are the remnants of one wing of a westward invasion out of the steppes of eastern Europe and adjacent parts of western Asia, while the northern wing constituted an invasion of central and northern Europe by the same kind of people. The local climate favored the retention of blondness more in Europe than in Africa, where it was finally limited mostly to dwellers in misty mountains too steep for chariot driving, although still possible for riding horses, especially their hardy barbs. How to fit this answer into European Bronze and Iron Age prehistory is the prehistorians' problem.

Once *Tribes of the Rif* was in galley proofs I began writing *Flesh of the Wild Ox*. How I did it is briefly stated in the following answer to a letter from my granddaughter Ellen January Coon, a student at Bryn Mawr. The date is February 10, 1980. My answer reads:

Dear Ellen:

How did it feel to be writing about Africa in the 1930s?

I can only answer this by telling you what happened. Limnibhy went home to his death in 1929, the year Nana Mary and I went to Albania. In 1928–9 I had debriefed Limnibhy of all the information he could tell me, as well as what he had told me in Morocco, and (having written my Ph.D. thesis in 1928) I rewrote it as Tribes of the Rif *and I cut the saga of the Ulad Abd el-Mumen into two books, both about Limnibhy. In* Flesh of the Wild Ox *he was Moh Umzien. It took me 14 Sunday mornings from about 5 to 11 A.M. to write it, before going to my parents' house for Sunday dinner with Jack and Maurice and your papa and Uncle Chick as soon as he was portable. I just wrote it. It came right out of my head and heart. I was like a medium. I never changed a word of it except when Mr. Morrow, the publisher, made me cut out* A Pasture of Thorns. *I published this excerpt in* Story *along with a story by Hemingway and one by Michael Arlen. Then I wrote* Ali the Jackal, *which turned out to be called* The Riffian, *published by Atlantic-Little Brown.*

While Moh Umzien, a cripple, stayed at home, Ali the Jackal went to France, the Middle Atlas, and all over. He was the adventurous half of Limnibhy. I wrote this second book with the same combinations of organs as in Flesh.

Nothing I have written ever since compares with these books because I was a Riffian.

Love, G.P.

Incidentally, the title of the first book was taken from an old Riffian proverb: "They that partake of the flesh of the wild ox will grow in courage, and he who eats of its brain becomes crafty."

For many years I thought that the wild ox was some kind or species of cattle. It was not. It was *Alcephalus buselaphus,* the northern hartebeeste, a relative of the gnu.

While Morrow published *Ox* and Atlantic-Little Brown *The Riffian,* Jonathan Cape of London published both. Reviews of both on either side of the Atlantic were copious, for example that of Compton Mackenzie in the *Daily Mail.*

The Riffian carried me along with such breathless interest into a world as remote from ordinary experience as the planet Mars that my gratitude to the author makes me most anxious to persuade other readers to give themselves the pleasure I had. . . . There is something of the Odyssey in The Riffian, *something of* The Arabian Nights *and something that is common to all tales of mountainy men, as they call them in the kingdom of Kerry. . . . When you have read this novel you will feel a little pale and flabby, but you will do well to read it. It is a good book.*

My highest praise came from Vincent Sheean, one of the most sensitive writers of his day, who had been in the Rif before me. He reviewed both books. In a file kept by my mother I have found a letter and a pair of copies of his review of *The Riffian.* I had left for Ethiopia when it came, and my father answered Sheean, thanking him for his kindness and promising to deliver the letter to me on my return.

In an explanatory note, Sheean said (no date given):

Dear Mr. Coon.

Just in case my review of your book gets cut in the Herald-Tribune *office—cut so as to tone down my enthusiasm—I am sending you a carbon-copy of what I really did write. It was mailed today, and ought to appear in the Sunday Tribune of September 10th, probably—on account of its length—in a pretty prominent place. I wrote to Irita Van Doren and told her also that this was the best book she had ever sent me to review, and that it deserved plenty of space and prominence. She knows that I am not given to easy or undiscriminating enthusiasms. Often my reviews have been so nasty—so oversevere—as to be unprintable. So I think this one will somewhat surprise her.*

Anyway, good luck to you.
V.S.*

Somewhere in Africa, many years later, an archaeologist named William Lawrence asked me an unusual question—how old I was. He said that he and his brother had thought me much older because of the way I wrote. His brother was Colonel T. E. Lawrence, the Lawrence of Arabia. Before the colonel died, he had sold most of his books, but *Flesh of the Wild Ox* and *The Riffian* were found by his bedside after his death.

On the eve of our departure for Ethiopia, just before Vincent Sheean's review had appeared, a New York literary agent phoned me to tip me off that Warner Brothers was about to offer me five thousand dollars for the movie rights to *The Riffian,* but if I would let her handle it, she would jack it up to ten grand. I had no choice.

She jacked it up, and Warner Brothers turned her down.

In the fall of 1932, after I had received bound copies of *Flesh of the Wild Ox,* it became clear to me who was responsible for my finances,

---

*James Vincent Sheean died on March 15, 1975, aged 75.

Harvard or my father, and the latter won. To put it in another way, which came first, my family or my work? I was to be my brother's keeper, but that job was to be combined with an academic duty.

My brother Jack's ebullient spirits had rendered his education difficult in American preparatory schools, and my father felt that he needed a touch of Old World discipline. He was in the same boat that I had been when I was sent to Phillips Academy, Andover. So I was commissioned to take Jack to Germany to find him a school.

When news of this free trip reached my superiors at Harvard it seemed to them an excellent way to send me still farther, to settle a library exchange with Russian institutions that had fallen into a stalemate. A few years earlier an envoy from Penn had made a library exchange between the Peabody Museum library and the University Museum library of the University of Pennsylvania, on the one hand, and libraries in Leningrad and Moscow on the other. The earlier envoy seemed to have made some promises that he had not kept, and I was given a sizable package of publications to distribute in order to break the logjam. This double mission was, to put it mildly, double trouble.

The leisurely boat ride to Bremerhaven was made much more attractive than any jet trip that could be taken today, because of a curious sex ratio among the young and nubile passengers. Young females outnumbered young males almost three to one, and the females were all beautiful. They had to be, for most of them were members of an Albertina Rasch dancing team. The poor German captain, aristocratic and very correct, did not have an easy crossing.

Jack and I went to Freiburg im Breisgau where I left him, but he did not stay there very long. Finding nothing that suited him there, or vice versa, he bought a secondhand motorcycle with no brakes, and rode it to Munich via Ulm. Going downhill, when he could not brake it enough with the motor, he dragged the soles of his shoes on the surface of the road. When he reached Munich his shoes and socks were ruined, and his feet bloody.

Meanwhile I went on to Berlin and got on a small plane with six passenger seats, bound for Leningrad. It was unpressurized and had no seat belts. Only the pilot and I were aboard. It was the season of dense Baltic fog. First we flew to Königsberg, thence to Kaunas in Lithuania, to Riga in Latvia, and to Tallinn in Estonia. The land was completely socked in all the way. On one of these hops the plane hit an air pocket, and I levitated. My back was pressed against the roof of the cabin. When we hit the bottom of the pocket, I was catapulted down so that my solar plexus struck the upper rim of a seat, and I threw up.

The pilot recognized Riga by the steeple of a cathedral piercing the fog. As for Tallinn, he had to fly over to Finland, where there was no fog, and back to hug the low-lying ground in order to reach the landing field. We rode into Tallinn in the only motor vehicle that we saw. The road was covered with oxcarts and pedestrians, and there seemed to be no question of driving to the right or to the left; everyone went where he pleased. Never have I seen elsewhere so many buxom, rosy-cheeked, flaxen-haired women as I did that day. They all looked alike, and it would be hard to pick a winner in a beauty contest. This mass of pulchritude seemed to make no impression on the pilot, who was exhausted. We spent the night at the Kulde Löwe (Golden Lion) Inn, where I had a marvelous dinner. The captain went straight to bed, saying: *"Schlafen ist die beste Nerventonik"* (Sleep is the best nerve tonic).

The next morning we were three. According to Soviet regulations a Russian pilot had to fly the plane into Leningrad, and so he did. I stayed in the Astoria Hotel, visited the Hermitage Museum for the first time, made my book exchanges, and also went to the Institute for Northern Peoples. There I met a collection of nearly but not quite all of the peoples of Siberia: Eskimo, Chuckchi, Tungus, Koryaks, Yukhagir, Goldis, Yakuts, Samoyeds, Ostyaks, and Voguls. I had ready about all of these peoples, but here they were in full life, studying in order to help their own people make an orderly transition into modern life with the least possible disturbance. New alphabets had been devised for their languages, and books printed in them. I asked for a photograph of each person, got them, and have been using them ever since.

The next stop was Moscow, by train, in one of the well-known broad-gauged sleeping cars, the most comfortable I have ever been in. I was sent to the Novo Moskova Hotel, and assigned the usual female guide-interpreter-amanuensis. Inevitably, I was also sent to the opera, in this case *Boris Godunov*. There I met a number of fellow countrymen who insisted on taking me to the International Hotel bar afterward, where trouble began. My guide begged off. An Armenian-American who spoke Russian had a guide of his own, who said that he would take care of all of us and see that we got to our various beds. After a while it became clear to me that the party would last long into the small hours, and I wanted to sleep because I had a fairly early morning assignment.

I wanted to leave, but didn't know how to reach my hotel alone. A man who said he was Robin Glendenning Kincaide, a journalist, offered to take me in a droshky. When we emerged into the cold, open air, it was snowing, with soft, large flakes and no wind. Then I discovered that a pickpocket had relieved me of all my money. Kincaide told me that didn't matter. The droshky seat was narrow, really wide enough for only one large passenger, and neither of us was small.

After a while Kincaide said, "Here is your hotel," and pushed me out. The droshky horse trotted off, and I found myself in Red Square, in front of Lenin's tomb.

What to do without a ruble, or even a kopeck, and no Russian? I simply stood and waited, until a vehicle miraculously loomed through the snow. It was a garbage wagon, with two men aboard. They picked me up. I said over and over again: "Novo Moskova, Novo Moskova." "Da, Da," they replied, nodding their heads sidewise, as Albanians do, meaning "Yes."

The rest of that night I helped them collect garbage, which gave me some helpful exercise, dispelled the fumes of the International Bar from my head, and taught me that the Muscovites throw away less good food than Americans do. Shortly before 7:00 A.M. their rounds took them to the door of the Novo Moskova, where I dismounted and tried to thank them.

But the door of the hotel was still locked. I sat on the doorstep shivering until it opened a half hour later. Barely had I reached my room and tried to dry my clothing, shave, and generally prepare for another day when my female guide strode in, catching me undressed.

"What have you been doing?" she asked. I told her, and she laughed uproariously.

We were a little late at the museum, where she insisted on telling everyone present about my nocturnal adventures. Professor Gyorgi F. Debetz in particular, a Siberian bear of a man, was greatly amused. Far from upsetting them or making me lose face, this episode broke the ice at once, and Gyorgi Debetz and I remained friends until his death on January 19, 1969.

Gyorgi and I met again twice, once in Philadelphia and my home in Devon, Pennsylvania, the other time in a UNESCO meeting and in his apartment in Moscow. His wife Natasha was a charming lady, and he a splendid man. Whatever our politics, which we never discussed unless necessary, we were good friends, and I am grateful for Jack's adolescent behavior that brought Gyorgi and me together.

And as for Jack, I dropped in to see him in Munich. He was living quietly and doing well. Later he went to Mulhouse in Alsace to learn the textile-machinery-making trade, and to Bradford in Yorkshire. Eventually he took over my father's business. He died on January 1, 1981.

11. The Commander of the Faithful

Three long, desk-bound years passed before I went into the field again, and I had plenty of time for planning. One concept guided me more than any other. I longed to study people who were still free, or who had been during the lifetimes of living men. More specifically, I had two primary interests: to push my study of what Hooton had called "The Wilder Whites" past the Rif and Ghegnia eastward into Asia; or to unveil the intricacies of a fully functioning, classic Islamic state.

Plan One seemed the more fragile and immediate. I knew of only one such manner of people who had survived, culturally intact, almost until the time I was born. They were the one hundred thousand, more or less, inhabitants of Kafiristan—the Land of Heathen—whom the fiery Afghan king Abdur Rahman Khan had conquered in 1896, converting them by the sword. He renamed their country Nuristan, Land of Light.

My source of information was a beautiful book, *The Kafirs of the Hindu-Kush,* by Sir George S. Robertson, British Agent, Gilgit.* (Its vivid lithographs are still sharper and better-composed than most stop-press photographs, and are placed opposite the pages where they belong).

The Kafirs were muscular, wiry people, looking more or less like Riffians and Ghegs. About one fourth of them had blue eyes and blond mustaches, and their skin remained fair because they were shielded from the sun by the steep forests and cloudy atmosphere protecting their five high valleys, accessible from the lowlands only by precipitous, easily defended footpaths. Kabul, the capital of Afghanistan, was only a hundred miles southwest of their fortress-home.

There these stalwart heathen burned hecatombs of goats to their gods, built three-story wooden houses from their abundant timber, and lived, on the whole, more nutritive and varied lives than the Muslim tribesmen herding sheep below. Governed like the Riffians by councils of tribal elders, each valley was independent; in each local leaders arrogantly or slyly vied for power, and with their kinsmen fought feuds on foot, armed with bows and arrows.

London: Lawrence & Bullen, 1890.

Sir George visited this anachronistic pocket twice, and had his book published before Abdur Rahman Khan made it officially the Land of Light, which physically it became, in a literal sense, as its forests were gradually shorn—but some shade might be left, in 1933, where old men who had been young before Abdur Rahman's visitation might tell another young man what had been etched in his mind before the scimitar cleft the bow.

Hooton thought this a great idea. So did Waldo Forbes, an undergraduate who was finishing his junior year and wanted to take another one off, in travel and exploration, before becoming a senior. His uncle and guardian, the Honorable W. Cameron Forbes, first American Governor General of the Philippine Islands, agreed, but as he was to finance the expedition, he also wanted to look over the leader, who must have seemed pretty young.

With this in mind, Waldo took us down to Woods Hole, and then by family launch across the swift current to the Forbes emirate of Naushon.

After a little conversation, the governor led me to the stable, where he kept some horses from his ranch in Wyoming, and led out as mean-looking a mustang as ever I had seen. Luckily I had spent a summer myself in Wyoming between Andover and Harvard, and ridden in Morocco and Albania, so I rode my mount until I tired it, without falling off or pulling leather; and without any expression of emotion, the governor let us go.

But Naushon was not Cambridge. Within the Kremlin of the Peabody Museum's inner walls, Donald Scott, its director, and Alfred Tozzer, chairman of the anthropology department, dumped cold water on poor Earnest Hooton's head. The reason given me was that Afghanistan was too dangerous, a factual error on their part.

Hooton must come up quickly with the name of another place safer for us Coons to take an undergraduate Forbes to. In a desperate hurry, he proposed Ethiopia—a nice, tidy Christian empire in Africa ruled by that enlightened monarch Haile Selassie, of whom, to quote the late Ogden Nash: "Many fine things we've heard."

It seemed, at this point, to the senior members of the committee that Earnest was beginning to talk a little sense. They perhaps failed to realize that his most up-to-date information came from the mouth of a youthful Ethiopian undergraduate at Harvard, who would like a free round tour to his native land before resuming his studies. It seems quite doubtful that Desta told the professor about the slave trade in that country; that the Lion of Judah's rival, Ras Hailu, was still wallowing in chains in a straw hut; that almost no roads were available for wheeled traffic; or that the rich tribal chiefs were the only possible protection against bandits.

I knew some of these things, but they did not bother me as much as the idea that my guide and interpreter was to be an African from Harvard, rather than one I should choose myself when I arrived on the spot. And he was too young. Also, I knew that most Ethiopians physically resemble Arabs and Berbers, with skins of various shades plus what is now called Afro hair. But Makonnen Desta was fully black, with a large head, bulbous forehead, and hands and feet nearly as small as the emperor's, which were almost those of a ten-year-old child.

Before I had had a chance to talk with him for more than a few minutes, he was off to Paris to visit his friend the Ethiopian ambassador to France, and I did not see him again until we met in Marseilles, where Waldo also joined us after a season of digging in Ireland.

Once we had exchanged greetings, trouble began. A man of Desta's noble blood and social position had to travel first class. Second was good enough for Mary, Waldo, me, and for Pat Putnam and his bride, Mary Linder, who had unexpectedly appeared on their way to Mombasa and thence to Pat's camp among the Pygmies in the Ituri forest, his home.

Desta's filibuster was shadowed by Pat's uproar when the purser tried to put him in a cabin with other men and his Mary in a female cabin. Shaking his beard angrily as he towered over the uniformed official, he won. Desta's motive, perhaps subliminal, for wanting to go first class might have been that there he could get a single cabin. In second a double was the most private. Waldo solved the problem by volunteering to bunk down with Desta, who had refused to share his cabin with any white man. Desta reluctantly agreed, and Waldo tactfully slept most nights in a lifeboat.

One evening Desta appeared on deck in an impeccable dinner jacket, starched shirt, and patent leather shoes. He was going to crash first class. He tried, but soon returned.

In the Suez Canal, while the ship was tied up to let the northbound traffic through, Pat created a diversion by leaping naked into the canal. He swam to the east bank and back, while the whistle blew. Emerging dripping at the head of the pilot's ladder, he shook himself and said, "The water is too warm."

This set Desta somewhat at ease, as did Pat's general manner, for he had been living in the Congo for about five years.

On the Swiss cogwheel train from Djibouti to Addis Ababa, our guide-interpreter balked again; he would not ride second class. But he had to. The first-class compartment was completely occupied by a group of American engineers, hopefully contemplating a trip of exploration as ill-omened as our own.

This time Desta explained his need to ride first class by declaring, "There will probably be a crowd of my friends and supporters at the station in Addis Ababa to greet me. This is a bit dangerous, because I may be suspected of challenging the emperor for his throne. They cannot see me come out of the second-class carriage."

But his fears failed to bear fruit, for two reasons: Our train was delayed on a siding at Diredawa, to let the downbound train through. According to Desta the queen mother was aboard it, on her way to Jerusalem for a pilgrimage, and the train stopped several hours longer than usual to let her greet her subjects. Among them, he reported, was Desta, who said that she had brought him up as a child.

When we arrived late at our destination, Makonnen walked out through the first class, to find no cheering throng. Bill Farrel, the second in command at the American Embassy, was awaiting us, and had been for some time. He conducted us to the Imperial Hotel, in which Desta refused to lodge because its proprietor was a Greek.

But he was on hand early next morning to accompany us to our interview with Mr. Addison Southard, the American minister, and managed to dart into the boss's inner office with us, where he declared that he was in charge of our arrangements with his own government.

This perhaps unprecedented event caused Mr. Southard to write a report to the Department of State declaring me a person unfit to be allowed abroad. For nine years I was unaware of his action, and it almost kept me out of World War II. Outwardly, however, Mr. Southard did his best to get me interviews with various ministers, most of whom were absent when I called; one on the excuse, relayed by his secretary, that he was being dewormed after a feast on raw beef.

After several weeks of futile attempts to penetrate the wall of evasion and delay (for time was on their side), I obtained two permits. One was to measure Ethiopians in some inconspicuous place, the other to mount an expedition into the interior, on which we must keep moving. For the second we bought eleven mules and hired muleteers, cooks, and armed guards. While awaiting the final papers for this trip, we started measuring—first in a rented room, where a crowd gathered, and then in an annex of the Hotel Imperial. While I was measuring the head length of one rustic Galla a great commotion arose in the courtyard.

Still holding my spreading caliper, I stepped out. Four soldiers were beating the candidates for anthropometry unmercifully with sticks, while the latter were trying desperately to escape. Seeing me towering over him with a shiny instrument in one hand, the commanding sergeant pulled a pistol and pointed it straight at my face. I stupidly advanced toward him, telling him to leave my subjects alone, and he backed up, keeping the same distance between us as we moved. When his back was about three feet from a whitewashed wall—and it was clear to everyone except myself that a bump on the back would make him pull the trigger automatically—my loyal caravan leader and chief muleteer seized me from behind and threw me into the measuring room, locking the door on the outside.

Needless to say, that was the end. Desta had long since left us, having finally given up his pretenses and his excuses, but I am convinced that he really tried. The last time I saw him was at breakfast in the Imperial Hotel one morning, when he told me, with great dignity: "You will never understand the complexities of the relationships within the royal family."

Whether he belonged to it or not, he was right.

In later years, Desta's political career was a continuous ride on a roller coaster. It reached its peak with his elevation to the rank of Dejesmatch, or minister, and its nadir when he died in America, unbeknownst to me, of leukemia, after a long illness, according to the *Ethiopian Herald* of October 22, 1966. He was fifty-eight. As stated in his obituary, "He was honored for his patriotic deeds against the Fascist invaders. He spent the war years in exile."

So did his emperor, who held his shaky throne, guarded by an imperial lion, for eight more years. On August 25, 1975, he and his dynasty died.

We sold our mules at a profit to the leader of a hopeful German expedition, and paid off, with a bonus, our loyal men, who were in tears. They were as honest, straightforward, and brave as the bureaucrats were not, and we hated to leave them, but we had no choice.

While we glided down to Djibouti twice as fast as we had chugged up, the lowering of altitude relaxed our nerves a little. Mary, Waldo, and I plotted furiously, in our second-class compartment, about where we should go next. Looking out the windows, we saw the Bāb el Mandeb glittering pale blue in the background. Right in the harbor ahead of us we spied smoke puffing up out of the stacks of the S. S. *Explorateur Grandidier,* building up a head of steam. Quick as a flash, Waldo snaked our rifles out of the customs, where we had been forced to leave them, and we clambered aboard just before the gangplank was pulled.

While plotting on the cog train, we decided on Phase Two. It had to be the quickest and cheapest plan, which was also the one with the least predictable chance of success. It was nothing less than to crack the xenophobic wall of a nearby mountain kingdom almost as forbidden as Tibet, lying in sight of thousands of seamen and passengers each year, passing through one of the world's most crowded sea-lanes.

It was the holy Imamate of Yemen, ruled by the Imam Yahya, the leader of the Shi'a branch of Islam, whose three million subjects were outnumbered only by the Persians, and were reviled by the Sunni Arabs throughout most of the Islamic world. A Yemeni pilgrim to Mekka, we were told, had once vomited on the sacred Black Stone in the Ka'aba, and had been instantly killed.

The strongest wall was religious, but it was reinforced by natural barriers. A forty-mile strip of steamy seacoast was enervating and malarial, and a ten-thousand-foot escarpment rising almost sheer behind the coast was easy to defend. From its crest the land sloped gently eastward across cool, well-watered, fertile fields to the edge of the Empty Quarter. Another forty miles east-northeast separated San'a, the Imam's capital, from the deserted city of Ma'rib. It was the fabled seat of Bilkis, Queen of Sheba, mother of Menelik I of Ethiopia, whose country we were then leaving, with relief and regret.

The S. S. *Grandidier* slid out of Djibouti Harbor over water as smooth as glass. It was exactly 4:00 P.M. At 4:00 A.M. the next day, a sleepy Portuguese proprietor let us into an Aden hotel. At 9:00 I walked to the American consulate, where I found Mr. Callahan, the American consul, a fellow Bostonian of about my own age, packing papers busily, for he was due to leave his post the next day.

I told him our plan. He then informed me that in order to visit the Yemen, I must send off a wire to the Imam in San'a, asking his permission. Then we would have to wait two or more weeks in the steaming heat of Aden for a reply. Our chances were, he added, rather poor.

So I suddenly requested Mr. Callahan to dispatch a wire, stating simply that we were coming, and that His Majesty might expect us in two weeks' time. This bit of effrontery amused Mr. Callahan, who did as I had asked, and bade me good-bye.

I had made this decision on blind instinct abetted by desperation. In a few minutes I learned that the next coastal steamer bound for Hodeida would not even dock in Aden for two weeks. So we walked the waterfront, looked over the native craft tossing a little at their moorings in the tidal swell.

Not one of their skippers had planned to go to Hodeida,

although the monsoon was blowing steadily out of the Indian Ocean, and at the Bāb el Mandeb it veered north-northwest and scooted up the Red Sea as far as Jidda, twice as far as we needed to go. Why, then, I asked them, wouldn't they go? "No cargo," they said sadly, shaking their heads.

Then either Waldo or I (I forget which) had another cosmic thought. As we were so desperate, why not shoot the wad and charter an unloaded ship? That brought action right away. Captain Ahmad al-Yamani, a small gray man with hennaed fingernails and his eyes cast on the ground, offered to do it for two hundred and fifty rupees, or fifty dollars. And he wanted to sail the next morning at dawn.

Action, action, and more action followed, through an almost sleepless night. Mary sorted and packed. We got clearance papers—not only for the ship, but for ourselves. Although no British subject could leave Aden bound for Yemen without a good reason, we—being Americans—could go freely. I taxied to the Crater, an extinct caldera, and Aden's hottest section, to ask a Greek banker to convert American dollars into Austrian ones—the silver Maria Theresa dollars used on both sides of the Red Sea.

When he heard where we were going, and taking a woman along to boot, he almost blew a gasket, and refused point-blank. But after fanning himself a little, he mellowed enough to call in a Jewish moneychanger, a tired elderly man with a sad expression and nimble fingers. He had brought more cartwheels than we needed, in a heavy canvas sack. So we counted them out together, rejecting the worn ones, which the sharp-eyed Yemenis might refuse.

We did not slip out unnoticed at dawn as Captain Taffrail, as we now called him, had planned, but it was not his fault. The harbor master's deputy refused to let us leave without permission, and our plea that as Americans we were free to go fell on deaf ears. Meanwhile a crowd had gathered, gawking and cheering, adding to the general confusion. Waldo tried to persuade the deputy, who insisted on talking by telephone with his boss, who was still abed. Finally our cook, whom I had hired the previous day, stepped ashore, and spoke with the deputy in their native tongue. Both were Somalis, the Sikhs, so to speak, of the British protectorates flanking the strategic sea-lanes.

Our ship, the *Shaikh Mansur,* was a *sumbuq,* sixty feet overall, with a twelve-foot beam, and three feet of freeboard at the waist when fully loaded, as the *Shaikh Mansur* had unexpectedly become overnight. With this weight it shipped not one drop, no matter how hard the monsoon blew, nor in luffing, when we had to come about. It bore a tall, forward-slanting mainmast and a mizzen stepped just abaft the poop deck; in about the same position as in a modern ketch. Both masts were rigged with lateen sails, triangular in shape, lashed to diagonal yards, and without booms—their lower corners were made fast to stanchions on the gunwales.

Both bow and stern were decked, but amidships the open hold was crammed with merchandise stuffed in striped sacks. Perfectly camouflaged in a cloak striped in the same colors squatted a fat, anxious-looking merchant—not exactly a stowaway, but a cheap loader, whom we had scarcely noticed in the stew of boarding ship. All the way to Hodeida he kept his own company; once there, he disembarked quickly and disappeared.

The most conspicuous man aboard was our cook, Jama'a, who had approached me with a sheaf of enthusiastic recommendations. He stood about six feet four, was bald, with graying, straight hair along the fringe; his nose was knifelike, and a pair of thin lips covered, when silent, a magnificent array of gold teeth. He had worked in Buffalo, New York, and in Australia; he spoke English, Arabic, and Somali—although, like some other Somalis, he had a curious habit of scrambling his consonants. He admired the British administration of his own country, expressing his approval by frequently saying, "Good show, Brishit."

He had traveled as field cook for other Americans, and had been to San'a.

"Imam, he's a good bloke, sir," Jama'a informed me. "He treat you werry nice, sir, decent condition. But you don't want to trust these Arab fellers, sir. They cut your t'roat in no time. Believe me, sir, I take good care of you. I been used to American gentlemen."

His actions were as good as his word. While he was with us nothing was stolen, and if anyone had had any intention of harming us, his physical appearance and his hoarse, bellowing voice would have kept almost any miscreant away. His arms and legs were of egregious length, and his hands and feet fell into the category of prodigies. Walking with a rolling motion from the hips, he covered immense distances with a rocking stride, and alone of all men I had seen, could keep pace with a camel without breaking into a trot. In his right hand he wielded a stout, knobby stick. A jinn leaping from behind a rock would have seemed almost harmless compared to our cook.

The applause from the dock faded slowly as we sailed out of Aden Harbor, in high spirits after the strain of the last few weeks. As the six seamen, not counting the ship's cook and helmsman, swung their small bodies from the main halyard (the mizzen was already up) Jama'a and Waldo added a third of a ton's weight and the mainsail was soon set, a triangular sail with a long spar that crossed the mast

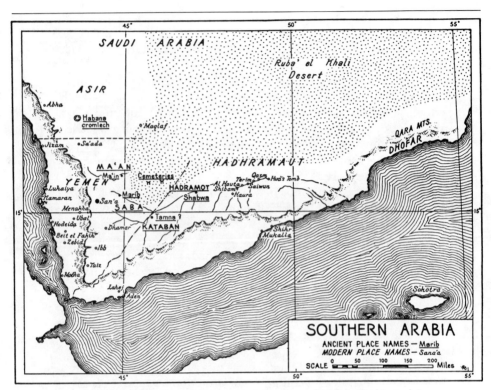

This map shows the locations of the pre-Islamic kingdoms of southern Arabia, and, in italics, the modern political units (as of 1939), including places that we visited: Hodeida, San'a, Aden, and Mukalla.

diagonally, about halfway up. Captain Taffrail brought the main sheet around to port and made it fast to a stanchion just forward of the poop deck, on which we passengers sat, ate, and slept. The mainsail bellied and filled. We glided past the breakwater at a steady six knots.

Along the grim, black-duned shore we coasted, with the monsoon fair behind. Captain Taffrail and his mate squatted politely on the edge of our ground cloth and engaged us in conversation, telling us the names of the parts of the ship, and their own names. The crewmen were all natives of a small fishing village named Beni Abbas, just north of Hodeida, near the British-owned island of Kamarān.

The ship's cook, a six-fingered boy, brewed us some coffee, which he served us in tiny, handleless Chinese cups. It was brewed not from coffee beans—which were packed for export—but from their husks, mixed with ginger. It was delicious, tasting like hot, strong, ginger beer. Then he handed us a cake of his durra bread, hot from his herring-barrel stove, and autographed by the mark of his six fingers on the crisp upper crust.

In return, we opened a tin of fruit to eat with the captain and mate. They nibbled at it cautiously, but their looks of puzzlement changed to smiles when we offered them a tinful of Huntley and Palmer's biscuits. Captain Taffrail deftly extracted one piece for each member of his crew and tossed it to them, more or less in order of rank, saving the last for himself. The box was soon empty, but what was a tin of biscuits compared to good fellowship aboard?

Captain Taffrail was especially interested in our scientific equipment. Cameras intrigued him. Watches and binoculars had to be examined and explained. When Waldo explained to him the workings of the aneroid barometer, he caught on immediately. He handled our whole kit meticulously, almost reverently. Then he began thumbing over the pages of the magazines we had brought aboard, pointing to the pictures and asking the meaning of each. As he finished each one, he passed it to his crew.

Meanwhile the *Shaikh Mansur* sailed on marvelously, and almost timelessly, until the biological clocks ticking in our inner organs rang a strident gong. We looked at each other, and no one of us dared ask the pressing question, "Where is the head?"

Jama'a took the initiative, and I was chosen to go first.

From the port rail of the poop deck a peculiar contraption projected overboard. It was a small wooden box open at the top and braced by two narrow slats at the bottom, the whole held clear of the hull by two slender poles. Having the heaviest body aboard, if I could make it, anyone could.

As I arose and stepped into this contrivance, the modest sailors turned their heads away. My knees and thighs stuck so that I could not extract them, heave and strain as I might. A low gurgle interspersed with muffled laughter gave evidence of Mary's and Waldo's interest, and as I turned to rebuke them a loud cracking proceeded from the supporting poles. As the whole device broke loose, I reached and clutched an awning pole in both hands. There I dangled, the box still clamped around my legs, a few inches above the water.

At this point the modest Arabs could no longer contain their nonchalance, and folded with laughter. As soon as Captain Taffrail and the mate could regain the use of their hands, they rushed to the rail and released me. Jama'a, who had been slumbering with his bald head on our moneybag, raised it and exclaimed: "I say, sir, you were properly stuck, sir."

That night we sailed through the lesser strait of Bab el Mandeb, between Perim Island and the Arabian mainland. The moon was in its first quarter, and the stars shone brightly. The captain sat on the poop deck with us, giving us a lesson in Arab astronomy. Waldo—who had been studying Arabic, and knew the most astronomy—carried the ball for our team, and the captain wanted to learn the English names for the stars and constellations. Thus we all began to understand how the Arabs, and the Phoenicians before them, were able to make such long voyages as they did, and so successfully. It was all very quiet and peaceful.

The next morning we passed Mocha, the famed coffee port, which was falling into decay because of its sandbars. Hodeida had taken most of its trade. Behind the clusters of palm trees and a few white buildings loomed the mountains, blue and capped with clouds.

Toward sunset the monsoon blew up into a gale. A sudden gust tore a wide rent in the mainsail. Now the whole crew pitched in, and all of us with them, to lower it. They stowed the torn sail under the poop deck, and bent a new one onto the yard. When we had all raised this, we looked aloft and read the blue legend: PEPPERELL MILLS, BIDDEFORD, MAINE.

As the wind did not abate, the captain put into the lee of a spit of land, where we went ashore in a dugout canoe. The beach was littered with many species of mollusk shells, and there was one species of live invertebrate, tubular and green, about eight inches long. I picked one up to look at it, and it squirted water in my face. The sailors laughed, and one of them said, "*Zibb al-baḥr*" (Penis of the sea).

The third morning we awoke under sail, and sighted Hodeida

before sunset—its white houses with grass penthouses seemed to be perched, as in a mirage, directly on the water and deceptively close by. It was too late for us to land because the port authority would have been closed.

Instead we tacked to starboard and anchored in the lee of another spit, on which several fishermen were supping. We went ashore and walked over to them. They had been catching sharks. We had seen many swimming about as we paddled in. The fishermen were drying shark fins, as well as trepang (the saucy creature that had squirted me), on poles behind a fire where a boy was roasting shark meat. The fins and trepang were to be shipped to China for soup.

Early the fourth morning we cast anchor off Hodeida, and the sails were stowed. The mate and two sailors went ashore, and about noon a small dhow sailed out to hail us. From it a man in European clothes and a Turkoman kalpak with a gold-braid cross on its crown boarded the *Shaikh Mansur.*

He was a Turk left over from the old regime, and the chief of police. He had blue eyes and a long, gray mustache. He greeted us politely, asked for our passports, and bade us come ashore with him. We transferred our baggage, shook hands with the crew, and paid the captain, with largesse for all hands.

Hodeida had no harbor. All ships, steam and sail, anchored out in the roadstead. As we approached the pier the sky suddenly darkened and black clouds swooped in from the west. Without further warning, a terrific gale began to blow and large raindrops fell. All the small craft near the breakwater lowered their sails, and we did the same, with difficulty. Boats banged together. Waldo stood in the bow, paddle in hand, pushing us away from the hulls that rushed by.

We made a sharp turn and drew up flush to the pier, where a dozen gigantically muscled Negroes plunged in and held our hull out so that it would not crash or shatter. Thus we entered Yemen in the teeth of a storm, and hoped that it would be a propitious beginning. Jama'a jumped and rushed about the narrow pier, checking our luggage, over which the squat black stevedores with bulging biceps fought to carry.

Led by the police chief, we marched down the waterfront street through a large, curious crowd to the customs house, where we found two dignitaries seated on a high platform. One was a plump man with blue eyes, a blond mustache, and a very red face, who greeted us in perfect English. He turned out to be another Turk. He introduced his neighbor, the kadhi (*Qādi*), meaning literally "judge," as follows: "This is the mayor of Hodeida. He has come to welcome you. First you will have to go through the customs. Please open everything and show it to that man."

Small, sharp-faced, and quick as a ferret, the customs officer neglected nothing, disturbed nothing, and paused only once—he had never before seen Kotex. He pressed it a little to see if it contained anything metallic, and then he and his assistants helped us repack. Finally he spoke.

"Give me eighty silver thalers," he said. That was the eight percent tax on silver.

"Give them to him," said the red-faced man on the dais, whose cheeks were now even redder. "This is just a formality. You will get them back." And we did.

When it came to our firearms, the officer lost his air of instant decision, not knowing which weapons to keep and which to let pass. Here the kadhi helped him. It was finally decided that we might take along my shotgun, my Winchester .405, Waldo's 30-40, and the ammunition for the shotgun and .405. We must leave behind our three pistols and their ammunition, as well as that for the 30-40.

This seemed like a random decision, as if made by someone who knew nothing about firearms, which made no sense. (Later we found that it made much sense indeed—they knew what would happen, while we were in the dark.)

Finally the red-faced Turk told us that we could pick up what we had left in bond on our return.

"What if we come back down some other way?" I asked.

"There is no other way," he replied.

After we had passed the customs and repacked, the Turk introduced himself. He was Ahmad Tahar, associated with a Parsi shipping firm that owned the steam packets servicing the ports of the Aden Protectorate and of the Red Sea. He led us to a waterfront building where he installed us in a commodious apartment on the third, and coolest, floor. As soon as we were comfortable, two servants sent by the mayor arrived, to wait on us and to feed us at government expense.

Because this hospitality seemed excessive after my undiplomatic message, we wondered why we were receiving it, and hoped to find the answer before our scheduled call on the governor the following day.

Meanwhile, we took advantage of a free afternoon by strolling around the city, accompanied by a sizable but friendly throng, whose physical appearance interested us as much as ours did them.

The well-dressed townsmen, members of old, seafaring families, who lived along the waterfront and within the city wall, were more or less alike; they had thickset bodies; short, bandy legs; yellowish skins; shaven heads as round as ostrich eggs; snub noses; and strong chins.

Also short and round-headed, the sailors were variable, but one kind of face predominated. Some of them had rakish profiles; small chins; prominent, hooked noses; and sloping foreheads rising to a peak behind. This was how, one might imagine, the fabled Sinbad had appeared.

Both the shipowners and seamen were half a world apart from the Highland people represented by a few of the Imam's soldiers—tall, erect, thin-faced, and bearded, and curiously ill at ease in this unfamiliar environment.

Before very long we walked down the only through street facing inland, between a pair of towers flanking the city wall. Atop one tower stood a bugler who blew out patchy calls at odd moments,with no visible response from the populace milling about down below on an open square facing a line of outdoor cafés. Behind the latter rose a tangle of straw huts with shed roofs. This was the African quarter, inhabited by the muscle-bound stevedores who carried two or three heavy coffee bags at a time out through the breakers to load them in dhows, day after day. As a result, the peaks of their foreheads had become permanently grooved and their toes splayed out like frogs'.

Two other kinds of black people also stood out in this almost cosmopolitan scene: the Somalis, of whom Jama'a was hardly typical; and the Zeraniks, small, delicate-looking tribesmen from the coast north of Hodeida. The Somalis strode by on long legs, trim, erect, and elegant. The Zeraniks were short and perfectly formed; with small hands, feet, and teeth; curly or frizzy hair held in place by silver rings and topped by brown, pleated conical caps.

What surprised me was their facial features. Some Somalis were quite European looking and others, as I found out later, were like some of the aboriginal tribes of southern India and the Veddas of Sri Lanka, while the Zeraniks resembled in some ways the Andaman Islanders. Coastal Yemen was a racial refuge area, with layers of racial history piled up in living strata. When I began to mutter about unpacking my calipers, Waldo reminded me that I had yet to see the Imam.

That evening after dinner we heard a knock on our apartment door. It was an Englishman, the only one in Yemen, who invited us across the street to his place for a drink. He lived above the office and warehouse of a coffee-importing company. His only companion was an Italian, with whom he worked side by side all day, although they ate their meals and spent their evenings separately. He had only two months more in Hodeida before his leave came up.

First he showed us around his living quarters, which were full of beautifully carved wooden beams, wall posts, and panels, all from Java, where the Arab merchantmen had sailed to trade, bringing home more than merchandise; they also returned with wives and children. This accounted for the exotic physical appearance of some of the burghers we had seen outside. He also explained the presence of the small, delicate-looking men in the straw dunce caps, and all decked out with silver, including silver-sheathed and -handled daggers set with gleaming agates. All in all they carried themselves with an air of confidence, one of aristocratic tourists in a foreign city.

"They are tribesmen from the plain north of Hodeida," he said. "They have powerful chiefs, and are good fighters. The Imam keeps them from raiding by holding some of the chiefs' sons as hostages in San'a."

Before we left, our host remarked, "By the way, you are not the first Americans to go up to San'a to call on the Imam. A few years ago a rich plumbing manufacturer named Charles R. Crane made the trip. Afterward he built a motor road at his own expense, up over the escarpment and onto the plateau, as far as San'a. His men also set up windmills for the farmers to irrigate their fields."

Walking back to our own apartment, the air suddenly felt cold. What had we to offer the Imam? Roads? Windmills? What? And I, at least, tossed and thought and thought, during an almost sleepless night, before we tidied up our few respectable garments to wear during our audience with His Highness the Governor and Prince, Saif al-Islam Abdallah, the Imam's son. *Saif* means "sword," used in beheading criminals and enemies of the Divine Kingdom.

Led by Jama'a, we trudged a dusty mile beyond the city gates to the yellow palace. Outside the door, on a platform, reposed an antique stagecoach like one shown in western movies, and beside it a new Ford roadster.

The gate was well guarded by mountain men in turbans and black frock coats, armed with antiquated Martini rifles. A secretary led us up to the third floor, into a room lighted by high glass windows; plush-bottomed chairs had been backed against its walls on all sides. In the center of the room stood an ornate table.

No sooner had we been seated than His Highness the Sword of Islam entered. Waldo, close behind me, whispered, without moving his lips, "Sword, hell. Penknife."

The prince was a small, thin, and pallid youth, about twenty years old, with a thin face, a thin, incipient beard, and thick glasses. A large white turban, like the cap on a mushroom, matched the ample white robes below.

His Highness started out in French, but with little success, and then Jama'a took over.

"This bloke the prince, *he* says," boomed Jama'a in decibels that bounced back from the ceiling.

"The prince is not a bloke," I cut in.

"Werry well, sir. This guy says that he's trying to learn French, sir, but it's no good to him."

After a brief statement by me to Jama'a, we held pleasant chitchat with Abdallah, both with and without Jama'a's modulated assistance. The prince told us that he was profoundly bored with Hodeida and hoped to return soon to the delights of his native San'a. His father the Imam had sent him instructions to shunt us up there immediately. He insisted on sending us in one of his own vehicles. If we needed another for baggage, we would have to pay for it ourselves. The food and lodging would be on the royal house.

After numerous polite exchanges he said: "You will depart at dawn. May peace be upon you."

To which I replied, "And upon you the peace."

Just when the eastern sky over the crest of the mountains had begun to lighten, two four-doored Fords drew up—one for us to ride in, the other to carry our baggage. The price for the second one was seventy-five rupees, or twenty-five dollars—very cheap.

Two soldiers climbed atop our belongings to protect them and us, but they would have to do so with knives alone. As Waldo and I inspected their antique Martini rifles, we found that neither would work. And our own two guns were at the bottom of the heap.

This reminded us that twelve hours earlier, just after our return from our afternoon stroll, we had seen a flagless, nameless, smokeless motor vessel glide silently into the Hodeida roadstead and unload a cargo of heavy boxes in lighters that had been waiting for it, and which crowded around it like puppies nuzzling a bitch. Stevedores immediately carried the boxes ashore, not through the customs, but directly onto the backs of a long line of kneeling camels. The boxes bore the stenciled label, MADE IN CZECHOSLOVAKIA. When we returned from the Englishman's quarters, both the ship and the camels had left.

No wonder the Sword of Islam wanted to go back to San'a. A new element had been added to a situation already complicated enough.

Quite literally, we took off in a cloud of dust. Our driver jammed his foot on the accelerator and kept it there until the speedometer hit sixty miles per hour. The car might have broken down because it had been driven only 500 miles. Through the narrow, crowded streets flew the Ford, first on its right wheels, then on its left, scattering people, camels, and chickens, with Jama'a on the front seat and we three infidels helpless in the rear. Because of baggage on the floor, our feet were stretched out straight to the back of the front seat. We tried to brace ourselves, but this annoyed the driver.

When I shouted to him to slow down, he speeded more. When I thumped the back of his neck he looped completely around several buildings, whereupon Jama'a turned his head around and said: "You see, sir, he's a Turkey fellow. They got very bad temper, these chaps. That's why we call them in wartime 'Terrible Turks.' You can't do nothing about it, sir. Please don't say any more, sir, and before long he quiet down again."

We rode along the sandy shore for about a mile, then turned sharply right to follow a camel trail inland. The country was barren and desolate, and we had to cross a few sand dunes, where our driver's speed kept us from being stuck. Soon we reached a plain on which durra was growing on ten-foot stalks. We passed a few straw villages, and several deep wells out of which women were drawing water with buckets on the end of long leather ropes. Then we paused at a small town named Obal, where four dancing women approached, pock marked and dirty, and one with but a single eye. They beat on tambourines and sang as they danced. We gave them some *buksha* (the plural is *bakshish*), each worth one fortieth of a Maria Theresa dollar, and they clamored for more. When we tried to photograph them, they scurried away.

Like the other women of the low plains, they were unveiled. Those seen in the fields wore blue trousers and blue smocks hanging to their knees. On their heads, Mexican-sized sombreros shaded their faces. The men, in contrast, wore only breechclouts and small round straw caps, grimy from sweat and much handling.

Fifty miles out from Hodeida the trail turned into the beginning of Mr. Crane's road. Here, too, we passed between fields of low-growing millet and alfalfa, turnips and onions. As the slope increased the open fields yielded to terraces. Some of the farmers were plowing with teams of two oxen, while others smoothed furrows with ox-drawn stone boats. The freshly turned earth smelled damp and rich.

Gradually we worked our way up into a region of higher and more majestic mountains, with more natural vegetation alongside the road. Beside mimosas and thorn bushes we saw bottle-shaped trees, six feet high, leafless, but with five brilliant red flowers sprouting from the top of each. In their swollen bases, healed cuts showed that travelers had tapped them for water. Tall gray-barked trees with shiny thick green leaves grew in gullies along with scrub palmettos and reddish aloes. In the dampest places banana plants were crowded, with bunches of small green fruit.

Farther up on the now-twisting road we found ourselves in a region of high castellated peaks, like giant fingers carved of sandstone and raised aloft to bid the faithful say: "There is no god but Allah."

The very place was like a domeless mosque, with an almost visible ladder tapering to a point as it pierced the ice-blue sky.

Under tilted strata of shaly rock lay inhabited caves. Their occupants were given a little privacy by durra-stalk screens set in the caves' black mouths. Smoke curled out in thin wisps, and children sat on the edges in front of the screens, their small feet dangling, close to the road. Had these caves been occupied as far back as the Paleolithic? How I longed to stop the Ford right there, find an unoccupied cave with a fat floor, and sink a test trench!

But we did not even slow down. As we climbed higher the terracing that faced the steep concavities of the mountains became more intricate, and in some places one hundred or more tiny terraces, each contained by its own stone wall, rose without interruption, one above another, from the river's edge to the feet of steep cliffs.

Now the one- or two-storied houses became tall, square structures, four to six stories high, with battlemented roofs, slit holes for musketry in the lower walls, and whitewash-bordered windows higher up. These houses were perched on the tops of spindly spires of rock and the lips of cliffs.

As we approached the topmost terrace we found an old man transplanting onion seedlings from a bed six feet wide to another just below it, ten feet in width. Then we crested the range at our aneroid reading of 8,700 feet. In the dying light we braced our bodies for the descent, but it went down only a few hundred feet. The mountains were not a range but the lip of an immense plateau gently tipped toward the desert in the east. As we continued over bumpy grainfields a jackal's eyes gleamed in the headlights, and we made out his gray body scampering behind a wall.

At about nine we reached Ma'bar, where we were led into a third-story room in a large stone house and introduced to a dozen tall, silent men standing against the walls with their arms folded over long silver-sheathed knives. We took off our shoes, ate supper, and drank some milky brew of coffee husks and stalks which made us sleep. We awakened in a windowless high-ceilinged room diffused with soft, white light. Its rays were filtered through three long sheets of thin alabaster set in the walls.

Hitherto we had ridden almost due east, and now it was only forty miles to San'a, over the improved old road from Ta'izz, Ibb, and Dhamār, running north-northwest.

It was easy to see why Yemen was the envied breadbasket of the Arabian peninsula, as we viewed the panorama lying ahead. It was cool at 8,400 feet, ribbed by several 8,700-foot ridges, and corduroyed by innumerable irrigation ditches trenched across the road. Pueblolike villages, more multistoried keeps, minarets and domed roofs of mosques and tombs, and circular towers, were all built on rock to spare the arable soil. Some of the villages were inhabited by Jewish farmers, identifiable by their small black caps set on the backs of their heads, and their side curls. We saw a new (to us) breed of camel, with long, silky dark brown hair; our drivers drove at them as fast as possible to make them shed their loads. Beyond the last ridge we saw our first real Arabian horses, being exercised by their city-dwelling owners' grooms. Our drivers did not try to stampede these noble steeds.

Straight ahead in the distance we saw what seemed to be a lake, pierced by iridescent masts and spars. It was San'a, set in a depression. Not until we were quite close did the mirage dissolve and its aerial projections connect themselves to structures on the earth below.

Our Fords briskly skirted the city walls until they passed through a gate into a large square, which separated the main city from the Ka'a el-Yahud, or Jewish Quarter. A second gate led to the center of the city, where we stopped in front of the Imam's six-story palace. To one side stood the tomb of an earlier Imam, with three decorated domes, and just beyond it a larger multiple-domed structure already completed—like a pharaoh's pyramid—in anticipation of its future occupant's decease.

Our drivers stepped down and entered the palace, while the expected crowd collected, milling and shouting. Fathers held their children over the heads of the throng to gaze at these curious Christians with their funny hats. An old farmer, clad in a one-piece garment woven of goat hair and as thick as a carpet, paused for a moment, shook his head, and plodded on, mumbling.

The drivers came back carrying papers, drove us to an alley in the Jewish Quarter, and led us down it to an inconspicuous house. At its door we met our host, Israel Suberi, the kingdom's richest and cleverest Jew. He had been told, in the middle of the preceding night, that he had to quarter us and feed us until we should depart—at his own expense.

Not knowing what manner of Americans to expect, he was on the alert for a split second, then—seeing how young and innocuous we looked—his red cheeks widened, and he smiled. The outwardly inconspicuous house was inwardly palatial. Mary and I had a private bedroom; so did Waldo; while Jama'a was assigned to another room below, next to the kitchen. A Jewish boy named Ma'er became our factotum, and from sundown Friday to sundown Saturday his place was taken by an Arab counterpart whose Sabbath was just over.

One of Israel's first kindnesses was to order kalpacks made for Waldo and me, who had both begun growing beards. The combination made us inconspicuous in the streets, for ours was the garb of Turks. From the very beginning we all got along splendidly with Israel, and soon found ways to communicate easily. Israel spoke Arabic, Hebrew, and Italian. Having been to Morocco, he could understand my Arabic perfectly. If worst came to worst and he had to use an Italian word, I could usually catch it from the Spanish, French, and Latin I knew. Thus we built up a private jargon, as I had done earlier with Limnibhy, and the percentage of Yemeni words we used increased as we moved along. Sometimes Israel translated for us via our jargon into local Arabic, when I was stuck for a phrase or word.

Before lunch on that first day I sent a message to Raghib Bey, minister of foreign affairs, requesting an interview, and another to His Majesty to thank him for his hospitality and to request an audience. While awaiting the first reply, Israel used our time to his—and our—advantage: I became his private tutor, filling in some gaps in his general education, with Mary and Waldo kibitzing when I was stuck. I spoke slowly, and he wrote down every word in a large ledger, in Hebrew characters. His questions pushed us to the frontiers of our own combined repertoires, and sometimes beyond. As long as we stayed in San'a we continued this tutoring, and I hoped that to Israel it was worth our board and keep.

After two days' waiting we were granted our interview with Raghib Bey. At his door we were met by His Excellency in person—a large, dignified man of fine bearing and handsome features with light blue eyes, pure white hair and beard, a pinkish skin, aquiline nose, thin lips, and craggy brow. On his head rested a large snow-white turban; a long blue kaftan stretched from his shoulders to the floor. Having greeted us in flawless French, with an old-fashioned, courtly manner, he led us upstairs to his audience room.

Raghib Bey had been Turkish governor of the Yemen, but he

did not get out in time. When the Imam came into power, he was taken prisoner, which he still was in 1934. He was also foreign minister and chief adviser of his master, who needed him too much to set him free.

His youth had been spent in Turkish chancelleries in many European capitals, and his first post as ambassador was Cetinje, Montenegro, where Turks were loathed; but he learned Serbian and became friendly with Montenegro's massive monarch, King Peter. Next he was sent to St. Petersburg, where his Serbian turned to Russian in a few months. At the czar's court he became extremely popular for his good looks, manners, and biting wit.

Twenty years in virtual isolation in San'a had made him hungry for conversation with some educated people, even with us, fresh from the stir of the outside world.

He asked us many questions about global politics, world economics, and other international subjects. Being an avid reader, he knew most of the answers already; it was only about countries and problems with which we had had personal contact that we could hope to be of much help. When he heard that Waldo had spent the last summer in Ireland, Kadhi Raghib leaned forward to ply him with queries about that country, which seemed to hold a special interest for him.

In the midst of this conversation he arose and asked Mary to spend a few minutes in another room with the elder of his two wives. Before he returned a slave girl brought in a tray of fragrant (real, not stem) coffee. On his return he broached at once the question, Why had we come there?

I told him that we wished to measure a statistically valid sample of the people of Yemen in order to determine their exact racial character, stating that so far only a few sailors from the coast—who were not typical of the Highland tribesmen—had been measured in Aden, thus giving the world a false impression.

He saw no objection to this work and, in fact, declared himself enthusiastically in favor of it. He said that he would arrange an audience with the Imam, and would discuss the matter with His Majesty in advance. Furthermore, he outlined to me the proper method of approach, telling me which arguments would appeal to His Majesty and which ones might antagonize him.

Before we left, I broached the subject of archaeology, for it was well known that several pre-Islamic cities within the nation's boundaries lay in partial ruins, with buildings, statues, and inscribed stones. These included Ma'rib, the Queen of Sheba's capital, which stood bleak in the desert, unpeopled and intact.

"Unfortunately," he replied, "His Majesty has not yet passed antiquities laws comparable to those in Egypt and Persia. After our diplomatic and economic situations shall have improved, then will come the time for archaeology. Our ruins are buried in the earth, where they are safe. Let us save some surprises for the future."

On parting he told us, with a smile, "This is a paradise. The Imam's principle is to oppose modernization, or any change from a blissful Islamic state. Here all is quiet. One lives and one dies. There is nothing to cause upset, stimulation, or excitement."

So sorry did I feel for this caged paragon that my eyes were moist. On several occasions when we met later, he told many stories of his earlier life. If only I had written them and published them. I had hoped that he would somehow spring his cage and publish them himself, but it was too late. But not for his biography: As I learned in 1979, it has been published in Turkish. I hope to read it someday in translation.

After our audience with Raghib Bey, things happened fast. This unoriental celerity might have meant either that the Imam wanted to be rid of us quickly or that we fitted into his order of events.

The next day was Friday, the Muslim Sabbath, during which we had hoped to relax. But hearing the distant rumble of drums and blare of trumpets, we walked to the center of the city, attracting no attention, although Mary was unveiled. Perhaps the onlookers thought she was my son.

The event was a mixed one, half May Day parade at the Kremlin, half the Pope's ride in a palanquin at Easter. First came drummers and buglers, led by a boy in a white uniform who was extremely dexterous with his drumsticks. Then along marched several hundred Highland men and boys wearing antique Italian frock coats and new leather bandoliers, all singing in a quavering falsetto as they tried to keep lines of ten abreast, with Turkish (or Circassian) officers alongside, themselves attired in khaki uniforms and black kalpaks. In the middle of this martial body a dozen or so men carried parts of four or five machine guns. Was this the Imam's total manpower and armament, or all he chose to show us Americans?

In any event, the second part of the procession was certainly uncensored and original. After, the soldiers rolled an ancient coach, drawn by four handsome horses. In its pillows sat a small man with a long beard and twinkling eyes. He waved at us as he passed. Not knowing how to return His Majesty's greeting, we stood at attention and saluted.

After lunch we were invited to the Italian consulate, where we were ushered into a windowless room with a life-sized portrait of Mussolini on one wall, and Victor Emmanuel's on the opposite, with numerous Italian flags in between.

About a long table sat eight men, some in black shirts. Three Russians and two Germans who had also been invited failed to show. The eight at the table arose at our arrival, with much bowing and heel clicking and hand kissing. Pleasant chitchat went on in French and German, but nothing important was said. They seemed to be simply looking us over, and as soon as we could do so politely, we left. One of the Italians was the consul. Some of the others were gunsmiths, whose job it was to repair the ancient Martinis that needed it, like those of our two guards on our ride up.

The Imam's Sabbath ended on Friday at sundown, the moment when Israel's began. At midnight Israel was rudely awakened by a thunderous pounding on his gate by a messenger of the Imam. Waldo and I were to appear in His Majesty's audience chamber at eleven o'clock.

In our sleep-befuddled state, we thought this fair warning and started to go back to bed, but Israel and Jama'a stopped us. In Arab time 11:00 is 5:00 A.M. The day begins and ends at sunset, which, so close to the equator, is 6:00 P.M.

With Mary's help (for ladies were not invited) Waldo and I tried to press, clean, and polish our meager garments, all except our socks— for one simple reason: We had worn them to bed to keep our feet warm. Meanwhile, Jama'a had whipped us up a pre-cock-crow breakfast, and we made it on time.

A uniformed guard at the gate carried our invitation in his hand as he led us through a massive portal into the palace courtyard, where forty or fifty petitioners and soldiers lounged and shivered; across the open space we climbed a massive set of stairs, walked down a long stone corridor, and then turned left into a side passage. In a room at the right some twenty clerks squatted below low desks, writing out official documents; then, at their left, was the door to the audience chamber.

Before entering, the guard motioned us to remove our shoes, thus showing our sox. We each saw that there were holes in both pairs, and my right big toe was completely exposed. Both pairs were also dirty, but Waldo's, being gray, looked the cleaner, as he took pains to point out.

The door opened, and we walked down a long, narrow, high-vaulted chamber, with a simple throne of cedar wood set at the far end. It was empty. The Imam sat cross-legged on a pillow on the middle of a long bench against the left wall. His Majesty's small body was draped in a long kaftan of finely woven brown cloth, austerely embroidered along its edges with gold braid, and girded by a golden belt. His head was capped with a large white turban, somewhat askew, under which reposed his small brownish face of dignified and intelligent appearance. His brown, piercing eyes were surrounded by a network of intricate wrinkles which, when he smiled, gave him a look of deep humor and benignity. He was, in sum, every bit a king.

Raghib Bey, who had been standing behind his master, walked slowly over to us—in his clean, new, white stockings—to lead us to the Imam. His Majesty held out his right hand, and when I extended my own, he clasped it between both of his and raised it symbolically in the direction of his lips. I muttered an Arabic salutation which I hoped was appropriate, having forgotten the one Israel had taught us. Waldo remembered it, to his great satisfaction.

Then a secretary firmly planted a Sunday school chair under each of us, mine in such a position that my right big toe stuck out about thirty inches from His Majesty's delicate nostrils. As nothing could be done, we both pretended to ignore it.

On the Imam's right sat Kahdhi Abdallah Amri, prime minister and minister of war, a handsome, stern-looking man who exuded an air of crisp authority. He and the Imam recommenced where they had left off at our arrival, discussing and signing papers stacked in a small pile on a low table between them. After each signing, the Imam dipped all fingers of one hand into a pot of red pigment, to smear it diagonally across each document. These wavy lines, looking as if done in blood, made the document official and binding.

After a few minutes of this, the Imam asked us the usual polite questions. How did we like the Yemen? Was it too cold? How were our quarters? Were we being well treated? How many days had it taken us to come from America? Which did we prefer, Ethiopia or the Yemen?

The Imam knew the answers, and he had little time to waste. He could be doing it to size us up. Except for the sock business, we thought we got A— each.

Then he asked me bluntly why we had come to the Yemen, but before I could get very far, Raghib Bey took the lead. It was my purpose, he said, to prove and to demonstrate before the world that the Yemenis were the purest branch of the Arab race.

The Imam seemed to like this, for he nodded pleasantly at us both. At his own prompting I said: "Arabia is a land from which migrations have gone out, and to which none has come. In North Africa and other countries live many Arabic-speaking tribes and peoples claiming Arabian descent. I have measured some of them already, but cannot test their claims until I have measured the Yemenis too."

At this point the Imam and Raghib Bey fell into a rather lengthy discussion of the works of al-Bekri, Ibn Khaldūn, and other authorities, in which both men showed that they knew their stuff. What I had said might well be true. (As a matter of fact, it was.)

Having reluctantly abandoned this literary tête-à-tête, the Imam asked me briefly: "What is the commercial or practical monetary goal of your mission?"

"None," I replied.

"Do you know how to tell gold if you find it?"

"No," I repeated.

"That's a pity. I would like someone to find gold for me."

"If you wish to employ a mineralogist, I can send for one," said I.

Said the Imam, "We will talk about that later."

He, Raghib Bey, and Kadhi Abdallah Amri went into a brief but serious huddle, after which the Imam announced: "You have my permission to measure my subjects. Fortunately I have a large standing army in San'a assembled for the purpose of defeating Ibn Saud, king of the Najd. You may measure all of these men and more, as they arrive from the outlying districts. It will not be necessary for you to travel about the country. Conditions are too disturbed, and I cannot at the moment permit it. I appoint the Kadhi Abdallah to take charge of your work and to see that the men come to you properly."

Saturday was a quiet day in the Jewish Quarter. Late that afternoon we went to Israel's house, where many of his relatives were sitting around eating walnuts and raisins and drinking red wine, white wine, and their version of brandy. Alcohol, one of them said, was their only weapon against the Arabs, because any one of importance who came to a Jew's house to drink dared not risk exposure. (I saw that in action; one of Imam's sons came to call on me, killed my last bottle of Scotch, and wove his way back to his palace slowly.)

They also told me that Ma'rib, the Queen of Sheba's city, was still standing, and one man present had actually been there. The desert around Ma'rib was protected by a fierce tribe of Jauf, pagans who spoke only in poetry. Ibn Saud's soldiers could never attack San'a from that direction, nor via 'Asīr to the north; its mountaineers were fiercely independent. The Saudis' only access to the Yemen would be by sea. This would cut the invaders off from their base in Jidda, and although they might take Hodeida—which was virtually defenseless—they could never climb the escarpment, but would sicken in the damp heat of the coast. As events were soon to demonstrate, these Jews were dead right.

On Sunday evening Israel, Waldo, and I, following a summons, walked to Kadhi Abdallah's office, where we found him seated in a swivel chair in front of a modern desk. At his request we measured each other to show him the routine. Then he said that he would send recruits every day but Friday to be measured between our eight o'clock and five, with two hours out from eleven to one. They would come in two squads, the first at eight, the second at one. Squad One would knock off at eleven to eat lunch, chew *qat* (the narcotic leaves of the shrub *Catha edulis**), and sleep it off, while Squad Two took over.

On the following morning, two uniformed officials arrived, one decked out in a gaudy opéra bouffe uniform with gold epaulets and a long sword, over which he frequently tripped, and a "straight man," wearing ordinary clothing and holding his whisht. All day Number One sat in our best chair, alternately smoking a hookah and chewing *qat*. His companion took no drugs.

And for two long days, no soldiers came.

Israel had the answer. First he persuaded me to send my Winchester .405, with its ninety rounds of ammunition, to the Imam. Then he bought a Zeiss twenty-power binocular from an Italian engineer, which we sent to the Kadhi Abdallah. He thanked us and also asked for a flashlight.

According to a court rumor, the Imam had immediately taken his new weapon to an enclosure within the palace walls and shot off all ninety rounds before stopping. When I heard this, it occurred to me that His Majesty's right shoulder must be very black and blue. Either he had not really fired them all, or his right hand had not been affected, for he requested me at once to send him one thousand more rounds.

I replied that I would have to order them from America, over his signature, on a finger-smeared document. The matter was dropped, and the recruits began to arrive.

While we were still eating breakfast, we heard many voices raised in high-pitched, quavering song. The sound grew in volume as the singers surged down the alley, and became almost deafening as they burst into our living room, which was simultaneously inundated with

---

**These leaves are supposed to put the addict into a state of religious ecstasy, but their physical by-products include drooling, semen leakage, and early impotence. From Israel's point of view, the green refuse messed up his real estate—our living room. Kadhi Abdallah did not chew them himself.*

the blended bouquet of Caucasian male sweat, soaked starch, and aniline dye—a startling olfactory experience.

The singing sweaters were raw recruits from the edge of the desert, half farmers, half shepherds, with kohl around their eyelids against the sun's glare, and sheets of what had once been stiff blue cloth slung around their torsos, and kilts below.

While we were processing them, they each broke three tabus: letting an infidel touch his body with metal; standing in the presence of an unveiled infidel woman; and having his picture snapped, doubly sacrilegious when the snapper was an infidel too.

As I was measuring him, each man held his right hand on his dagger hilt, and each time he felt the anthropometer bar or a caliper graze his skin, the shining blade of his knife moved out of its scabbard a little farther. It was not easy for me to keep my eyes on the instrument bar and on the dagger blade too.

A few days later we were visited by a company of regulars from the tribe of Hamadan, farmers from the High Plateau. All of them were mature—some even middle-aged—men, tall, erect, well-dressed, clean, and of dignified mien. They marched in solemnly, sat down quietly, were measured without trouble, and left as they had come.

Meanwhile, one of Israel's brothers had formed the habit of leading in some civilians at about 6:00 A.M. On empty stomachs and with minds still fogged by the tag ends of dreams, Waldo and I mechanically measured and photographed dozens of camel drivers and farmers, semistupefied by the cold. Many of them promised to bring their brothers, sons, and friends, and did so.

Whatever else it was worth, this extra work gave us a wider spread of the regional populations, a better sample than soldiers alone could do, and a supplement to our total figures. But it did not last forever. In the third week repeaters began to present themselves under false names, and the time to quit had come.

So far, our visit to the Yemen had followed a standard adventure-story script. We had chartered the *Shaikh Mansur* on a desperate, paper-thin chance. With the inadvertent help of Mr. Crane, and the friendly connivances of a Turk and a Jew, we had come out on top.

But the game was not over. Every thriller worth its jacket price must have its villain, and ours was made to order. Not the butler, for this was Arabia, but a wheedling, chiseling courtier who played his king against the foreigners, particularly the Italians and us Americans. His double-agent machinations were hard to foresee or to thwart. His name was Ahmad Jillali, the Imam's secretary, whom we had first met during our holes-in-stockings interview, and that gaffe on our part may have led him to figure us as a pair of simple louts.

He must have had something on his master or he might not have run as many risks as he did; but on the other hand, he probably did not know that Israel had dealt our team a pair of aces that gave us a fighting chance. Ace one was the Imam's itch; ace two, his insurance policy.

In the middle of the hollow between the shoulder blades of His Majesty's back lay a patch of scruffy raw skin that he could not scratch, nor could he rub it against anything during his lengthy sessions on his pillow while holding court. So he secretly asked Israel if we had any ointment that would give him relief. We had it, and it did.

Although officially at war with Britain, he held an insurance policy on a London bank. The money he had stashed away was unlikely to benefit his mediocre sons, but more sensibly to insure his survival in exile if, for example, he might lose the impending struggle with his neighbor to the north. His premium was due, and someone who could read and write English, and was at the same time reliable, had to fill it out. That someone had to be me.

Crudely speaking, through my agency Israel had His Majesty by his royal balls, and insofar as the latter could control Jillali, which was not very far, our success and our safety were assured.

During our earlier measuring sessions Jillali appeared in our living room nearly every day to fill us in with the latest court gossip, which we did not want to hear. At Israel's suggestion we gave him twenty rials a throw for this service. If it was meant to be nuisance money, it worked to the extent that only three attempts at extortion followed, with all of which our team coped. These three were over a nonexistent photograph, a skin, and a box.

One day, while we were hard at work, an emissary of the Imam appeared and ordered us to stop work. The reason was that the chief rabbi had complained that Waldo had snapped a picture of the Imam out of our window when His Majesty was riding in his coach to Friday prayer in his mosque. Israel immediately bearded the chief rabbi, who admitted that he had not seen the foul deed himself, but a Christian in one of the European consulates had. It turned out that Jillali had persuaded the Christian to make this accusation to the chief rabbi, when all he had seen was Waldo changing a roll of film. The Christian apologized to me in person, and the soldiers came back, at no expense to us.

The skin game was a more serious enterprise. In reward for my gift of the Winchester .405 and its ninety rounds, the Imam sent me a message that he was giving me a black leopard skin in return. Yemeni leopards are very large and very scarce; black ones are even scarcer. Except as a specimen for the Harvard Zoological Museum's collection, I did not particularly want it, but I had to accept it gracefully.

Before Jillali got around to delivering it, the news reached the Italian consul, who complained to the Imam that a black leopard skin was exactly what Il Duce needed; that its ferocity and blackness would make a perfect background for Mussolini's staged appearances. We never got it; nor am I yet sure whether or not the Italian consul did.

While this skin jockeying was going on, I had another bout over photography to cope with. Before leaving Aden I had left some 35-mm negative rolls with a local photographer, to develop and blow up to standard size. Just after our departure on the *Shaikh Mansur* he had written me a letter, to be carried to Hodeida on the next packet. In the letter he said that he could not enlarge the Leica frames without cutting them apart. If I agreed to this I should wire back "COON YES"; if not, "COON NO." I wired the latter.

Having intercepted this, the consul told the Imam—presumably through our villain, who brought me a request from His Majesty to explain this ominous message to his enemy. I sent the original letter, by other and safer hands, directly to the Imam. Within a few hours the consul paid us a visit, and after a few formalities, said, "Thank you, thank you, for clearing up this sensitive matter. You may have no idea how many signals have passed through the air between Asmara, Rome, and here!"

Operation Box had nothing to do with the Italians, and it was a long, drawn-out affair, complete with a regular Hollywood chase. As soon as we had heard about the Saudis' plan to land at Hodeida, our escape hatch might be blocked. So we had requested—and been granted—permission to have the box containing the weapons and ammunition, which we had left in the customs in Hodeida, sent up.

The box was made of polished mahogany, long enough for three rifles: about two feet wide and eighteen inches deep. Despite its size, it was light, because it contained only three pistols, their ammo, and the ammo for Waldo's 30-40—which we had to carry with us; it was as useful as a club. All we had to shoot with was my Belgian FN double-barreled shotgun, bought in Meknes, Morocco, in 1926, and about two hundred rounds of birdshot and buckshot, with no birds or bucks to shoot. It was dandy for Ethiopia, but only a mild deterrent where we were.

Instead of riding back the way we had come up, we were given permission to climb down the escarpment diagonally to the coastal plain. We would be able to see that most interesting terrace country where the coffee trees grew, the castles, and the people, at a slow enough pace to take it all in. We were to ride on mules supplied by Kadhi Abdallah, with soldiers for guards.

Two days before our departure date the box had not come, despite several messages from the Imam that it was on its way. Through sources of our own, however, we knew that it was in San'a, but we didn't know exactly where.

Waldo and I then went to bid good-bye to His Majesty, and he immediately asked us, "Were you pleased with your weapons? Were they all there?"

"We have not seen them," I replied.

The Imam's cheeks grew very red. "I gave them to Ahmad Jillali to take to you two days ago," he said, looking at his secretary.

Jillali turned gray, began sweating, and trembling all over, a lot of trembling for a loose-jointed man. Then he spoke very rapidly in a wheedling, nasal singsong, of which I caught nothing other than the confirmation that he was a cowardly louse.

When he had finished, the Imam turned to the Kadhi Abdallah and asked him, "Did that Christian understand?"

"He understands everything," said the Kadhi Abdallah, looking at me intently, with a smile on his face.

"I don't think so," said His Majesty, who then turned to me and said, slowly and distinctly, "There has been a mistake. The arms are still on the road, but you may leave tomorrow. I will give you a permit to search all upcoming caravans until you find them."

No sooner had we reached home than Jillali burst in with Israel in tow. If I would give the secretary my Colt .45 he would see that we would get the rest of the guns at once. But this would be like paying blackmail, with no end in sight, so I refused. Then he demanded twenty rials not to tell the Imam that I was a British spy. I tossed him these coins, one by one, with Israel's winked approval, letting some fall on the floor. His bony arse made a tempting target as he stooped to pick them up.

At my insistence Israel, Jillali, Waldo, and I walked to the palace, but only the first two went in. When they came out Jillali was beaming. He insisted on holding hands with me and walking with fingers entwined, swinging our arms like buddies for all in the courtyard to see. How I kept my temper, I have no idea.

After dinner Waldo, Israel, and I again went out, this time to call on the Kadhi Abdallah. He told us that our precious box was in the next room, but that he could not give it to us. "Ahmad Jillali will be here this evening and take it to you. That is the best way."

Once outside, Israel said, "Let's go call on Ahmad Jillali and act friendly toward him. He still has lots of influence with the Imam, and if he should say you were an English spy, what could we do?"

Jillali's house was large. He came downstairs with a candle in one hand, asking in a high-pitched voice, "Who is it? Who is it?"

Upstairs he greeted us like long-lost brothers, in a large room with four narghilehs in the center, and pinups from European magazines covering the walls. He and Israel went into a huddle in a corner, and after we had left Israel said that Jillali had promised to deliver the box to us that very night.

To no one's surprise, he didn't. In the morning Kadhi Abdallah's soldiers and mule men were there, all anxious to depart. Then Israel left us for a while, and soon returned. Jillali had taken the box from Kadhi Abdallah, and had ridden a fast horse down the road to Menākha with the box over his pommel. He would undoubtedly leave it at the first sleeping place and then ride back to San'a over another route.

There was nothing left to do but follow, and we packed the mules, leaving three saddled for Mary, Waldo, and me. Just as we were ready, Israel insisted that we should go to his own house for a farewell ceremony, for we might never meet again. Raisins, walnuts, and "cognac" were nibbled and sipped. His mother and his brothers all bade us godspeed in a most emotional manner, and when we finally reached the mules and soldiers—not to mention Jama'a—it was already high noon.

But after he had said good-bye, Israel seemingly changed his mind. Out from the alley he led the largest jackass that any of us had ever seen, navy gray, with a black stripe down its back. "I will ride a little way with you," he said as he climbed aboard. Ma'er, our servant boy, followed on foot, along with a dozen or so beggar boys, one with a wooden leg.

Waldo and Israel tried out their steeds, giving them a short run, to the dismay of farmers bringing in bags of grain on smaller donkeys and guiding others precariously loaded with newly fired pots. Waldo pretended to play polo with Israel, crowding against his jackass and crying, "Ride 'em off, Izzie!" Cathing on to this sport immediately, Israel attacked the farmers, shouting, "Ride 'em off!"

There had to be an end to this. Our beasts ambled on well past the place where Israel had said he would leave us, but he did not, until we had recovered our box. How that happened would make a long scenario, as it took two days. False leads succeeded one another, our party got split into three segments, until finally we met in a towering castle, where Waldo and I and Jama'a trudged in last.

The castle belonged to the kadhi of Mefhak, whose servants had already installed Mary in comfort. She had stuck by Israel, which showed good sense. As soon as we were assembled our host joined us from his top-floor observatory, and the bargaining began. The kadhi was a pleasant man of about thirty, wearing spotless white garments cut in city fashion, and with a well-trimmed beard.

The kadhi admitted that he had the box, but the Imam's paper was worthless. He wasn't afraid of that old man. But he could see that we were nice people, and he would let us have it for sixty rupees ransom. I offered twenty, and he came down to fifty. Then I bid thirty. He said forty—thirty-five was out of the question; I must give forty or our box would stay up on his rock.

I peeled off forty rupees and handed them to our host. Then we sat back in comfort, drinking more tea, eating well, and holding a pleasant conversation. Like most of his peers, he showed a keen desire for knowledge of the outside world, particularly about geography, also mechanical inventions and their potential applications.

The box came downstairs. Only five rounds of 30-40 ammunition were missing. As we started downhill for Hodeida, we said goodbye to Israel, who took the high road back to San'a. We never saw him again, although we received a photograph from the land of his name. He looked thin, wan, and anxious; his wife brave; his children uneasy and bored. In the accompanying letter he made one request. Would we sponsor a German-Jewish friend of his, his wife and daughter, so that they could leave Hamburg? We would and did. They lived in Sudbury with us until the man of the family found work. The last I knew, which was just after the war, he was running a rubber-footwear company in Texas. But what was Israel doing? I am not sure that I would like to know.

The rest of this story is anticlimax. We measured in Hodeida, got out just before the Saudis came, measured again in Aden, and again in Mukalla, a beautiful white city on the Hadhramaut shore. Waldo got malaria, Mary a spot on her cheek that looked like the beginning of a Baghdad button—a disfiguring kind of boil. Except for Jama'a, who was there already, we all went home. From Aden to Boston by freighter took twenty-eight days.

When we got back, the news was full of the Italians' preparations to invade Ethiopia, which they bordered both to the north and the south by their colonies in Eritrea and Somaliland. Ted Weeks, editor of the Atlantic Monthly Press in Boston, wanted a book to meet the public interest. Right away I rattled off *Measuring Ethiopia and Flight Into Arabia*, which he published early in 1935. I devoted almost as many pages to

Ethiopia as to southern Arabia, unlike my present coverage. Those who wish to read it should note that I have changed a few names—Makonnen Desta was called Zaudu; Mike and Matilda were Pat and Mary Putnam—and all three have died.

The book sold well, but not well enough. Owing to the political crisis it had to share the field with six other books written mostly by library-seat polishers who had never been to Ethiopia; but it got good reviews. Before the book's publication, *Story* magazine ran my fictionalized version of what happened to us in Addis Ababa just before the measuring incident that precipitated our departure. It was in the October 1935 number, twenty pages long, and occupied one third of the issue. Anyone who desires to read it, and can find a copy, should be told: Although a tale, it tells the plain unvarnished truth. Its title is "The Man in the Purple Suit."

As a counterpart to the historical and cultural sections of *Tribes of the Rif* and *The Mountains of Giants,* I wrote *Southern Arabia, a Problem for the Future.** It came to about twenty-two thousand words, and was cleverly condensed into a version of about seven thousand words in Publication 3793 of the Smithsonian Institution in 1945.† It gave a review of the four pre-Islamic kingdoms of Ma'an, Saba, Kataban, and Hadramot, whose capitals were, in the same order, Ma'in, Ma'rib, Tamna (?), and Shabwa. Shabwa presumably was the seat of Bilkis, the fabled Queen of Sheba, rather than Ma'rib, if only because the living Ethiopian languages are related to that of Hadramot rather than to Sabaean. Only Hadramot supplied frankincense and myrrh, a valuable cargo which they sent north and west by camel caravans around the southeastern corner of the Empty Quarter, along with other precious merchandise, picking up local camel-loads of cereals and precious stones destined for marts as far afield as Greece and Rome. The Greeks, in turn, sent back sculptors, some of whose statuary was still visible in the Imam's boarded-up museum, which I visited on days when measuring was slack. The Romans sent an army, which perished in the sands.

During the winter of A.D. 449–450, the famous dam at Ma'rib burst, never to be repaired. With irrigation gone, Saba was impoverished, and the capital moved westward to San'a eventually, if not at once. About the same time the camel trade was cut by the opening of

*C. S. Coon and James M. Andrews, IV, eds, Studies in the Anthropology of Oceania and Asia, (Dixon Memorial Volume), Peabody Museum Papers, Vol. XX, 1943, pp. 187–220.
†Smithsonian Report for 1944, pp. 385–402.

shipping up the Red Sea as far as Jidda—as on the *Sheikh Mansur.*

In addition to these archaeological and historical notes, *Southern Arabia, a Problem for the Future* has information on the social and political organization of the ancient South Arabians; as well as the Zeraniks whom I fleetingly saw in Hodeida; and the cattle peoples in Dhofar, halfway up the Indian Ocean coast beyond the Hadhramaut, who still speak South Arabian.

Finally, it reported the origin of the name of the Muslim God. *Il* or *Ilah* was the moon god. The sun was an insatiable goddess, whose periodic demands on her partner made him wane and wax. Under Muhammad's tutelage, *Ilah* became *Al-Ilah, The* God—or Allah, the Supreme Being—now revered by over half a billion Muslims from Morocco to Mindanao and Turkestan to Tanzania, with congregations as far afield as Chicago and Brazil.

12. Suburbia, 1934–1939

On our return from southern Arabia in 1934, Mary and I quit Cambridge to live in the suburbs. First we moved to Waban, then to Weston, and finally to Sudbury, where we remained until World War II. Waban was inhabited purely by commuters, and was easily accessible from Cambridge, even by students, who came on skis. Weston had a large commuter population also, although we had the advantage of living on the grounds of a golf club. One student landed an airplane on the golf links in front of our house. Old Sudbury, where we lived, was still rural, while South Sudbury was already becoming overpopulated, perhaps because the commuter train that stopped there also stopped at Porter Square, Cambridge, on its way to Boston's North Station.

Because the Porter Square station stood at the head of Oxford Street, which is flanked by many Harvard buildings, the commuters who got on and off that train included many distinguished scientists and scholars: the head of the Harvard Zoology Department, a Jesuit seismologist from the observatory in Weston, a young physicist who told me about the A-bomb before it was labeled top secret, a precocious baby dean, and my close friend Hallam L. Movius, Jr., already a well-known Paleolithic archaeologist.

On these trips, Hallam and I usually tried to sit together because we had much in common to discuss. The third occupant of our four-seat compartment made by facing one seat backward was Lawrence Winship, editor of the Boston *Globe*. He spent most of his ride tearing articles out of other papers, marking them with a heavy crayon, and stuffing the excerpts into his breast pocket. Number four was Arthur Howe, a jute-mill operator, who later became the captain of the Sudbury company of the Massachusetts State Guard, before Hallam and I were sent overseas after Pearl Harbor.

One thing I learned from Larry Winship was a modicum of discretion. Although he heard many scandalous things that would make glaring headlines, he passed his own judgment of what was fit to print and what wasn't. One evening the Moviuses and Coons were invited to the Winships' to dine with a member of the United States Supreme Court, Felix Frankfurter. Hallam said something that didn't seem quite logical to the justice, who ridiculed him mercilessly. Larry calmly stopped this cruelty.

I began to feel very much at home in Sudbury and was once elected to the school committee. My rival was the janitor of the high school, who knew all about roofs and nothing about books. It did not take me long to discover that the agenda of the meetings concerned his special knowledge and not mine. I resigned in his favor. The schools were good for the boys, who did not have to change every year. We were living as a family, a wonderful thing.

After Mary, our sons, and I had settled down in suburbia, I began seriating my new measurements in my office while writing *Measuring Ethiopia and Flight Into Arabia* at home. Before I had finished either job, in 1934 Earnest Hooton, as expected, conjured up another.

It was nothing less than to rewrite *The Races of Europe, a Sociological Study* (Lowell Institute Lectures), by William Z. Ripley, Ph.D., Assistant Professor of Biology, Massachusetts Institute of Technology; Lecturer in Anthropology at Columbia University in the City of New York. It was published by D. Appleton & Company, New York, with no date, although Ripley's introduction was dated Boston, April 25, 1899.

I went to see Dr. Ripley about this proposal, and he agreed with Hooton that I should take it on, despite my hesitation that it was too big a job. He could not tackle it himself because he was up to his ears in railroading, a big item in the social-relations field in 1934. Then I made an appointment with the editor of Appleton to discuss terms, and for this purpose I rode a train to New York. When I presented myself at Appleton's office, on the dot for my appointment, the secretarial lioness at the grille stepped out for a few minutes and said: "Mr. X is too busy to see you."

Because the copyright had expired anyway, I hied me to Macmillan's, where their text-department editor, Ted Morehouse, received me and gave me a contract.

Ripley's book was a marvelous 608-page (not counting the index) piece of prose, which must have kept the audience at his Lowell Institute Lectures clinging to the armrests of their seats. Also it must have amused the liberals to hear him debunk the search by German scholars for the homeland of the Aryans, somewhere between the Pamirs and the Baltic.

In essence and in sum, Ripley was a lumper, not a splitter. He recognized three European races only, the Nordic, Alpine, and Mediterranean. And he used as his sole criterion the cephalic index (head breadth times one hundred divided by head length), stature, and pigmentation. In his Appendix D, he cited some stop-press publications of Dr. J. Deniker, librarian of the Museum of Natural History at Paris, whose final work had not yet appeared. Deniker had split Ripley's three races into four, with three subraces tucked in to boot.

While he decried this fragmentation and called Deniker's categories only types, Ripley admitted the potential validity of two. One was the Adriatic or Dinaric, with the flat occiputs and pointed heads, of which he wrote (before he had heard of Deniker) "the side views . . . show the shortness of the head. . . . At the same time the cranium is high, the forehead straight, sometimes overhanging. *It seems as if pressure had been applied, front and back, the skull having yielded in an upward direction*" (pp. 123–4).

I should have read this when I was a student, or before I wrote *The Mountains of Giants,* but I didn't read it until the day before I typed this page. That's what comes from jumping ahead too fast. In a trite manner of speaking, I had reinvented the wheel, or at least moved it off the drawing board onto the road.

His second tentative agreement with Deniker was to split the Mediterranean race into an Atlanto-Mediterranean, as in the British Isles, where it presumably preceded the Nordic; and an Insular-Iberian, meaning Spaniards, Portuguese, Corsicans, and Sardinians. He admitted that his agreement was based on stature, a minimal distinction.

Ripley was a sociologist, I a physical anthropologist with considerable field experience who worked with many measurements, indices, and observations, with little thought of the current sociological consequences of racial studies. So I told both Hooton and Ripley that I had to tear the handsome Victorian mansion down and build in its place something less elegant without but more complicated within. Both agreed, and said they would let me work alone.

Many heads, faces, and bodies had been measured since the turn of the century. Many skeletons had been exhumed and studied. Just to bring my data up to date required a massive library search. Mary Ruby, my assistant, studied Slavic languages to cope with the almost unknown (to us westerners) Russian and Polish literature, some of which I had collected myself on the spot in an interlibrary exchange tour in 1932, when I visited Leningrad and Moscow.

In Leningrad I had communed with Professor Boris Vishnievski, an outstanding physical anthropologist who was later exiled to the Urals. He was particularly helpful. We had conversed in German, which my lady guide-interpreter didn't understand.

Boston and its environs, known proudly as the Hub of the Universe and the Athens of America, contained many ethnic spokes to its wheel, including Greeks. I also had a Rolleiflex, an automobile, and the gall of a Fuller Brush salesman. I put all three to work. In my spare time I roamed from ethnic club to ethnic club, pressed door bells, and snapped and clicked. The photographic supplement of my own *Races of Europe* contains forty-six plates of from four to eight portraits each.

Most of my subjects were proud to pose and happy to have their smiling faces printed in a book. Only a few subjects played hard to get. Three were Turks, in this country illegally, fleshing smelly hides in a tannery. The other was the consul of a European nation. He called me "My good man," and at first refused to cooperate. Then, when he turned to have his profile shot, I saw that he had hardly any chin. His pictures were not used.

Besides photographing each such man, I measured him and recorded his figures in a table following the plates. These figures included his age, stature, weight, and eleven head and face dimensions, four indices, and the color of his skin, hair, and eyes. Appendix I lists twenty-one measurements and indices for fifty-three cranial series from the Upper Paleolithic to Roman and medieval times for most of Europe, Western Asia, Egypt, and North Africa. I know of no other such coverage in a single-volume, "semipopular" book.

The bibliography lists 271 individual books and 585 authors. There being no room to print all the papers cited in the footnotes, I simply listed the abbreviations for the journals in which they appeared, from *AA* (*American Anthropologist*) to *ZWAK* (*Zbior wiadomości do antropologii krakowéj*, Komisya anthropologiczna, Akademija umiejetnosco, Krakow.) They numbered 234. Tucked in between *A* and *Z* were a few I referred to frequently, like *BUMP* for the Bulletin of the University Museum, Philadelphia, and *PMP,* Peabody Museum Papers, some of which contained my own work.

Early in this period at home I sometimes taught summer school, even if it meant commuting from my family's summer place in Marshfield, where Limnibhy used to loll on the sand dunes. One morning between 5:00 and 6:00 A.M., when I was heading for Cambridge on the Rexhame road, I stopped when I saw a mother skunk carrying her litter of newborn pups across the pavement. There were six. She would pick up the hindmost gently by the scruff of its neck and place it in front of the foremost, then scramble back for the next one. Fearing that a milkman or someone else who had an eight o'clock class at Harvard would drive up and crush this little family, I helped her, and between the two of us we got them across the road into safety. She seemed to understand what I was doing and showed her appreciation by not squirting me.

One summer, when Limnibhy's friend Fred Johnson was my

assistant in Anthropology 1, the final examination was held in Memorial Hall, along with those of several other courses too small to merit rooms of their own. Before the proctors handed out the examination papers, whereon the questions had been printed by the Harvard University Press in total secrecy, one of my former students (who was earning much more than I did) sat down inconspicuously near the rear door that led to the toilets. He was a professional tutor. He boasted that he could always tell in advance what questions I was about to ask, and crammed his customers the night before for a lucrative fee. His trick was to sit down, raise his hand to get an examination paper, read and memorize the questions, and then head for the john where students who were not sure of the answers could meet him and be quickly briefed. If he had failed to read my mind the toilet would be a particularly busy place.

Before the tutor had a chance to leap up, I asked Fred to go to the john to tell the students that it was no use, because their rump teacher couldn't come. He couldn't come because I pushed him back in his seat and held him there, forcing him to wait a full hour before I escorted him out of the building. He protested loudly and threatened me for unlawful detention. Shortly afterward he was put out of business for having illegally sold verbatim notes of law-school lectures.

There were and probably still are three kinds of tutors within gunshot distance of Harvard Yard: the great teachers like the Widow Nolan, who got me through plane geometry; the cheats like the one I held down in Memorial Hall; and the official ones, like myself, on the Harvard faculty.

I kept office hours in the Peabody Museum, seeing tutees and freshmen advisees from both Harvard and Radcliffe. Among my tutees were Eddie Goodale and Norman Vaughan, who drove dog teams to the South Pole on the Byrd expedition. E. Wyllys Andrews IV, recently deceased—a great Maya archaeologist as well as an OSS hero in northern Italy—was once threatened with expulsion because he invited a Dunster House waitress, who had been fired, to a Dunster House dance, clad in a Maya *huipil,* a rather flimsy garment by the standards of those days. It took me much effort to keep him in college and on with his brilliant career.

One sad case involved a member of another house, who was also going to be expelled because he had taken a Radcliffe girl to his room. He had been wheeling her along Memorial Drive in his car when, to avoid a head-on collision, he had hit one of the lovely plane trees that line that road right in front of his own dormitory, and the girl was knocked unconscious. So he picked her up, carried her to his room, and immediately called his uncle, who was a doctor, and who arrived before the girl had regained consciousness. His uncle took care of her, and for this act of quick thinking and intelligent action the young man was in danger of being kicked out of college. He might have been had I not myself vigorously and rapidly intervened.

Two other tutees I am proud of are both named Purcell, although they were not related. Richard Purcell, possibly partly because of my example in the Rif and Yemen, learned Arabic so well that he could pass for an Arab. One summer he joined a caravan in Libya and went to Kufra Oasis and back in disguise. Returning to Harvard, he was wrestling with another young man on the top landing of one of the Smith halls, lost his balance, and fell to the bottom to his death. His parents came to my house in Weston, and I spent an afternoon in my study trying in vain to console his mother.

The other Purcell is John, who was a Time-Life reporter in China in World War II, later editor of *Natural History,* and now an editor of *The Scientific American.* Kenneth MacLeish, Archibald's son, was not my tutee, but he was John Purcell's friend, and I saw much of them together.

My Radcliffe tutees were mostly beauties, especially three that we called the Three Graces. One of them married my older son and bore my six grandchildren. Many of my Radcliffe tutorial visitors had personal troubles, mostly concerned with amorous affairs, or just plain sex, which they discussed with me freely, as if I were in my sixties instead of my late thirties, possibly because of my premature white hair. Only one, of foreign nationality, was silent on this subject, but I discovered that she was paying her way through college by performing personal services. I first learned of this from her dentist, who was also mine. While I was reclining in his chair playing "Open wider, please," he told me that she had proposed to pay his bill that way—but he preferred cash.

Although I have no statistics to back my estimate, I reckon that the percentage of virgins in Radcliffe then and recently may not be significantly different, but my evaluation may be of little value. In any case, if girls had not always been girls the human species might long ago have become extinct.

During this period of life in suburbia five other jobs kept me on my toes. Three were of long duration; two took only a day or two apiece. I shall start with the case of the African stowaway, which was reported in the Boston *Sunday Globe* of March 20, 1938. During the previous week I was sent to the immigration station in East Boston to interview a stowaway of obvious African origin who had been found hiding on a Dutch cargo ship when it docked at Boston. With me went George Harley, M.D., a former medical missionary in West Africa who spoke several local languages. Because the man held papers issued him in Dakar, French West Africa, the French consul in Boston had interviewed him, without success. George Harley tried his Berlitzkrieg of languages, also to no avail. So I tried asking him in the lowest form of dockside pidgin French audible in Casablanca: *"Ti parle fransa, toi?"*

"Oui, monsieur," he replied, and then spilled his tale. It was customary for men like him to stow away on French cargo ships bound for Marseilles, where they would scramble ashore, make some money, and hitch-sail home again. He had made these round trips several times, but this time he made a mistake. He did not notice that the white stripe in the middle of the ship's flag ran horizontally instead of vertically. This was an easy mistake to make, with the ship in dock and the flag hanging limp without a breeze. The immigration man gave me a fifteen-dollar fee. I took it to an exchange booth where I traded it for francs, which I slipped into the stowaway's pocket when no one was looking. It was against the museum's rules for an employee to accept a gratuity.

Two years earlier the summer of 1936 ended in rhapsody with the Harvard Tercentenary celebration. To it came pundits from other lands, attired in caps and gowns that rivaled a tropical aviary. The Swedes and the Italians easily led the field, but the Italians won by a nose because their headpieces resembled the leaning tower of Pisa.

The guest who interested me most was also the star performer—Bronislaw Malinowski of London, born a Pole. During World War I he had been interned in the Trobriand Islands as an enemy alien. This gave him ample time to lay the ground for his studies in functional anthropology and to write his famous books, *Argonauts of the Western Pacific* and *The Sexual Life of Savages,* two knockout titles.

Of all the writers on social anthropology, at least in English, he produced the clearest and most palatable prose—an anthropological Joseph Conrad. Unlike the latter, whom I once met in an elevator, Malinowski not only spoke without an accent, but could imitate anyone else's.

At first he stayed with Leverett Saltonstall, governor of and later senator from Massachusetts, but he found it more useful to move into my humbler domain. Mr. Saltonstall was campaigning for reelection, and Malinowski volunteered to speak in his behalf to the Poles in Clinton, Massachusetts, but that idea was reluctantly turned down.

I was more useful to Malinowski, and for a special reason. He had to give a key speech at the tercentennial celebration, and being a

Catholic, his special role was to make the local Catholics from Cambridge and Boston—particularly the Irish ones—feel a little less resentful about Harvard. We decided that his Oxford-BBC accent would remind them of the Black and Tans and antagonize them—and then he hit upon the idea that my local, unaffected, and unconscious non-Harvard pronunciation would pull more heartstrings. My father, who also considered this a good idea, loaned us his car and chauffeur for this purpose. We were driven to Revere Beach and the North Shore, around and around, but Malinowski took little time off to view the scenery. He produced a copy of his speech in which he had written here and there "joke," but I told him that unless the wit was spontaneous there was no use in labeling it.

I read the speech aloud to him over and over, and each time he repeated it, until finally he had mastered my accent, such as it was. When he stood up on the platform, he was speaking his words in my voice out of his own mouth. It worked, and he won great applause.*

In December 1936 Professor Roland Burrage Dixon died suddenly and without warning, at his home in Harvard, Massachusetts. He was a bachelor, cared for by his chauffeur and the latter's wife. He always wore a coarse-textured, rust-colored Harris tweed suit, and how he could tolerate the scratching on his legs we could not understand. Some of the students thought he had only one such suit, but actually he owned several that were identical and alternated them. Between and after classes, he used to stand on the museum's granite steps answering questions, and while thinking he would hold his pipe in his left hand and place his right index finger alongside his nose. He was considered infallible, and within the limits of his subjects, he probably was.

He, his chauffeur, and the chauffeur's wife played different musical instruments in the evenings to amuse themselves and each other. Once a year he had all the graduate students come out to his house—a large, hunting-lodge type of building with a fireplace big enough to take cordwood—and extensive grounds, including a rustic pond. On his worktable in his living room—which was also his study—stood an antique Hammond typewriter with a golf-ball head that jumped around as he typed, with alternate balls containing several alphabets, including linguistic symbols. It was the prototype of the IBM Selectric, on one of which I am composing this page.

When Dixon died, someone had to take his place at once. He was giving a course on the races and cultures of North America, and

---

*Another but not identical version of this story appeared on p. 3 of "Overview" in the 1977 edition of The Annual Review of Anthropology.

was in the middle of his lectures on the Eskimo. He also gave courses on the races and cultures of South America and of Asia, but those could wait. Someone had to leap into the breach with one day's notice, for his classes were held on Mondays, Wednesdays, and Fridays, and he had lectured on the morning of the day he died.

That someone was I—not out of choice, but from necessity. I was the only person available with a Ph.D. and had shown that I could lecture in summer school. I had never seen an Eskimo, and most of what I knew about them came from Dixon's lectures, from Robert Flaherty's *Nanook of the North*, and from the *National Geographic*. I had to sit up all night before the lecture, working. Unfortunately Dixon's notes were unavailable because he had stipulated in his will that they be burned immediately after his death. They were not burned, and I was given them later, but they were of no use to me because they were fragmentary and out of date. Apparently he had been lecturing mostly off the top of his head, which contained an encyclopedia of ethnographic information.

After that I had to give the races and cultures of the whole world, by continents, as Hooton had turned Africa over to me, too. In this forced teaching I learned a lot, and from scratch, and that is why it took me so long to finish *The Races of Europe*. Eventually I had to give Anthropology 1, the sophomore introductory course, both at Harvard and Radcliffe—and separately, dashing across Cambridge Common in seven minutes between the two lecture halls in rain or shine, snow or slush. The lectures required shouting to large classes without a microphone. For this I received a little more than a common laborer, but less than a good carpenter. The prestige of teaching at Harvard was supposed to compensate for the poor pay, but prestige is inedible.

Before I started giving Anthropology 1, Hooton had doubts about the suitability of my voice for lecturing before large classes at Harvard. It was rough and gravelly (ideal for TV later on), and he wanted me to change my accent to a phony Harvardese, as spoken by some western-born professors except when suddenly awakened from a deep sleep. This I refused to do. But I was willing to take steps about breathing, volume, and the like; and to achieve this end, he did what may seem to the reader to be an incredible thing.

He sent me to a woman on Beacon Street in Boston who was a cripple, with spaghetti legs and hands as strong as a gorilla's. Sometimes she rode in a wheelchair, but at other times she grew impatient and walked on her hands like an acrobat. She worked on my breathing mostly, and one day she shoved both her thumbs into my diaphragm so hard that I felt something give, and it was very painful. Actually she ruptured my diaphragm; my liver descended halfway down into my abdominal cavity through the aperture, and my stomach was pushed downward, too. For years I thought that my liver was simply enlarged from malaria, alcohol, or both, but a recent liver scan has shown that it is actually small for my body size, only misplaced.

Anyhow, despite Hooton's warnings, there was one Radcliffe girl who did not mind my voice. She sat in the front row, knitting and smiling. One day I asked her why she took no notes, and the girl next to her said, "Because she is stone deaf and cannot read your lips. Later she will read my notes."

In 1939 I finished my *Races of Europe* and it was printed. It had required an immense amount of work, and has recently been reprinted. At that time the age of blood groups had begun to dawn, and conventional physical anthropology was on the wane, mostly because of counterprejudice owing to Hitler's treatment of minorities and his resurrection of the Aryan dream. Like most professional Nordic-lovers, he was not one himself.

While writing *The Races of Europe,* I found that I was thought to be on the wrong side of the fence, through several revealing episodes. Hooton offered to take the book away from me and author it himself, but I refused. Richard Walsh, Pearl Buck's husband and the editor of *Asia,* asked me to write an article on race prejudice as part of a trilogy with Franz Boas and Harry Shapiro, and he stated the fee to be paid to me. I regarded this as a valid contract, otherwise I would not have bothered to write it. Then Walsh refused to print my article or to pay me, because he didn't like what I had written. I stated that racial prejudice was a natural phenomenon common to mammals in general, a behavioral isolating mechanism important in the origin of species via subspecies, or races. This was perfectly true and still is, particularly now that zoologists recognize the importance of behavioral differences in animal taxonomy.

For example, it was once thought that the wildebeeste or gnu was a member of the cattle family, but Richard Estes found that it is not, but rather a gazelle, for its mating behavior is close to that of the hartebeeste. Those who say that man's possession of culture negates nature need only observe what is going on in Northern Ireland, where Catholics are killing Protestants and vice versa. Cultural differences, as in religion, can make members of the same race act as if they were members of different species; Boas, if not indeed Walsh, should have known that.

One morning, before I had finished my manuscript, I received a letter addressed to me by my editor. When I opened the envelope I saw that the letter inside was addressed not to me, but to a sociology professor at the University of Chicago. It outlined a plot to take the authorship of *The Races of Europe* out of my hands, by some devious means, and to give it to the Chicago professor. The latter was to defuse my work to prevent the accusation of racism. The letter also stated that another letter had been written to me, to soft-soap and confuse me, so that I would be lured, like a silly fish, into the conspirators' net. That letter was presumably sent to Chicago.

After reading the letter that came to me, on foot in the front hall of the museum near my mailbox, I headed for the nearest telephone and called the editor. He answered in a whisper, saying, "I can't talk with you because I have laryngitis."

"Good," I said. "You don't need to talk, just listen." What I told him then could be heard by visitors looking at the totem poles in the hall of the American Indians. He backed down at once, and I forwarded the letter to its destination in Chicago, but the sociologist did not return my courtesy. No sly trick that had ever been tried on me in the Middle East could match that dramatic ploy for perfidy.

When the book came out, Franz Boas was sent a review copy, as editor of the *American Anthropologist*. Ralph Linton, a truly great and no-humbug anthropologist, whose works could be understood because he wrote simple English, saw a copy of my book in Boas's office and asked if he might be allowed to review it. The maestro said no, that he was going to review it himself, but he never did. I have no evidence that he even read it. If he had, he would have found that I made no mention of racial differences in intelligence, which was his bugbear. If he had a conscience it was guilty, because in 1894 he had given a vice-presidential address before the section of anthropology of the American Association for the Advancement of Science, in Brooklyn, entitled *Human Faculty as Determined by Race,* published by George A. Aylward, The Salem Press, that same year on pp. 1–29 of Volume 43 of the *PAAAS*, where anyone who cares to look can find it. On page 28 he wrote: "We have shown that the anatomical evidence is such that we may expect to find the races not equally gifted."

Despite Boas's pocket veto, *The Races of Europe* sold for twenty years, and is on sale again from the Greenwood Press, Westport, Connecticut.

In 1939 the powers that were began to realize that they had overworked me and decided to give me a half sabbatical on full pay. This meant not only that we could take the boys with us wherever we might choose to go, but that we could also keep our house in Sudbury until our return. The boys would be able to have some continuity of schools and playmates, something they badly needed and should have had long before.

13. The Azores and the High Cave

Six years of hard work at Harvard had followed our return from Arabia, and I was given a half year's sabbatical in January 1939, starting at the end of the examination period. We asked various friends where the cheapest place to relax in might be, and the answer was, the Azores. An Italian ship took the four of us—Carl Jr. was twelve and Charles eight—as far as Ponta Delgada in São Miguel, the island from which most of the non-Brava Portuguese around New Bedford, Massachusetts, came. We went out to the hot springs at Furnas, where we experienced a minor earthquake during the night. The boys didn't even wake up, and berated us the next morning for having let them sleep through it.

São Miguel was not the island for us. We took a smaller Portuguese steamer to Horta in Faial, stopping at most of the intermediate islands on the way. Faial and its neighbor Pico, whose cone is so tall that it is capped with snow in winter, are where most of the Gloucester, Massachusetts, Portuguese come from—or came from, for many have been here a good three generations, have had their names anglicized by the city clerk, and have intermarried with Yankees, which, in fact, many of them have become.

When we arrived in Horta we rented a large furnished house, complete with a maid, for what the maid alone would have cost in Massachusetts in 1939.

We had little language trouble because many of the Faial people spoke English, or rather Cape Ann American, even saying "Ayah" for "Yes." Even the local Portuguese was not very difficult because it sounds like a Frenchman trying to speak Spanish. For example, *vino branco do Pico* (Pico white wine) comes out something like this: *"vinh branc de peek."* It is the strongest unfortified wine I have ever tasted. It is grown on the slopes of the volcano, with each vine growing in its own stone-walled enclosure, where it gets the heat of the sun reflected by the stones, if not some of the volcanic heat itself.

The Azores consist of nine islands: Santa Maria, São Miguel, Terceira, Graciosa, São Jorge, Pico, Faial, Flores, and Corvo. Santa Maria, the easternmost, is flat. It is like an aircraft carrier of red stone, a broken-off piece of Africa. The others are all volcanic, with one or more calderas; Pica alone is an active volcano. When discovered in or before 1452, the islands were uninhabited; had a unique, endemic flora; and their fauna consisted of one species of lizard, possibly either dropped by sea birds or drifting in on logs. Neither theory is too convincing; we just don't know how they got there.

As the Portuguese spread their empire to Brazil, various parts of Africa, to India, Ceylon, and Macao, among other places, they soon ran out of personnel. Therefore they picked up colonists from other parts of Europe. São Miguel received a large proportion of Spaniards, while Flemish people went to Faial (where the principal valley is called Flamengos), Pico, and Terceira. In 1939 there were still some Flemish names left in Horta—like Brum, Statmeyer, Goulart (probably a Portu-guese version of Gevaert). Most of the Flemish names, however, had been translated into Portuguese; in America they have been retrans-lated into English ones like Wood, Rogers, and Perry.

Horta is the mid-Atlantic relay station for the British cable company, and all messages were read there, and some re-sent if needed. The cable company had a compound with about a dozen families, and these families had an English school, which Carl Jr. and Charles attended.

I went alone on a ship that visits the outer islands of Flores and Corvo twice a year. We went ashore on Flores, an island without auto-mobiles, only oxcarts, and I saw and photographed a fair number of people. They looked entirely different from the Mediterraneans of São Miguel and the husky blonds of Faial and Pico. They were fairly short, with massive heads, craggy features, and much red hair, in some cases curly. At Corvo the seas were so high that we could not go ashore, but two longboats reached us. They were rowed with two men to an oar, and there being only about twenty houses on Corvo, the crews were probably almost the entire adult, able-bodied male population. They did not stay alongside much longer than it took to transfer the semi-annual mail pouches and a few packages, but they looked entirely different from the Flores people, smaller and darker. On Santa Maria, São Jorge, and to a certain extent western Pico, another breed of men was evident: tall, lean, bony, hawk-faced, blue-eyed, and with red or brown hair. They looked for all the world like men from Galway, and particularly the Aran Isles. Taking note of all these different kinds of people reminded me of Darwin's observations on the finches of the Galápagos, which led him to his main theory about the origin of species. Much could still be done by population-genetic studies of these islanders. Like a Darwin in miniature, I got a few ideas out of seeing them too.

Carl Jr., Mary, and Charles Coon sitting in the sun at El-Farhar English Pension on the mountain at Tangier.

When I returned from this last voyage I felt restless again and found my family restless too. Mary wanted the boys to see Morocco before the impending war should break out, and we wanted to visit parts of the southern regions that had been forbidden us in the 1920s.

One event served as a grand finale. It was the arrival of the first Pan American Clipper to cross the Atlantic, its route being via Bermuda and Horta to Lisbon. A ground crew of Americans had been there for some time making preparations. Everyone in Faial, and many in Pico, were excited, including especially Carl Jr. and Charles. We were all up early, particularly the boys, and Carl Jr. took an 8-mm movie of the plane's appearance, descent, and landing on the water. Charles still has the film.

Shortly afterward we left by ship for Gibraltar, via Madeira, and ferried over to Tangier, where we planned to stay only long enough to rent an automobile and drive southward. But fate was to have it otherwise.

Renting a car took some time. There was only one garage where this could be done, it had only one car for rent, and that one had to be put in shape. Instead of staying in the city we went up on the mountain to the west, to El Farhar* English Pension, a large villa with a magnificent view over the strait and the twin Pillars of Hercules, Gibraltar, and Jebel Musa gleaming white in the distance. The pension was run by Winthrop Buckingham, a World War I veteran from Chicago, and his charming wife, Ellen, who had been born in Smyrna, Turkey, of English missionary parents. Her maternal grandfather had been a Yankee skipper from Salem who had settled and married in Smyrna. Beside the house they had a row of separate cottages—a proto-type of a motel—and a private bathing beach.

One evening shortly after our arrival the Buckinghams and some other Farharites took us to an outdoor dancing pavilion, the Emsalah Gardens, and it too was an informal place. People were cir-culating from table to table introducing themselves and choosing partners. At one point when Mary was dancing with someone else I spied a good-looking young blonde at another table, sitting with some older people, and I invited her to dance. When the music stopped I led her back to her table and she introduced me to her father, a handsome man. He was the Honorable Hooker A. Doolittle, U. S. consul general, and her name was Katya. Her mother, Veka, was the daughter of the czarist General Bergman, who had led a White Army over the Caucasus into Georgia. Hooker was then U. S. consul at Tiflis, and he promptly married the general's daughter, thus making her an American citizen. At that time and for long after Mme. Bergman and another daughter lived in Casablanca. Several years after this meeting Katya married my youngest brother, Maurice Putnam Coon, who died in February 1980.

The next day I went to call on Mr. Doolittle at his office, which I should have done a day or two earlier. While we were discussing our projected trip to the south and other subjects, I noticed him fingering a black, shiny object on his desk. It was a Neolithic polished axe.

"Where did you get that?" I asked.

"Out at the caves of Hercules, at Ras Ashagar, just south of Cap Spartel. I excavated it with Dr. Ralph Nahon."

Ralph Nahon, M.D., had an office in the American Cinema building, where his father, who had been born in Tangier, had a movie

---

*The terminal R is an anglicization. The Arabic original is el-Farha or el-Farhah, meaning "happiness," which it really was.

theater, and the top floor of which was occupied by Freddy's New York Night Club. Freddy was a Czech, a former member of the French Foreign Legion, and he knew his way around. Ralph had been born in New York and educated at Columbia, and he was married to a British admiral's daughter.

When I went to call on him at his office he looked over his list of appointments and found nothing urgent enough to keep him from showing me the cave at once. Tangier is always exciting because it is never twice the same. I had not been there since 1928. Tall buildings had begun to appear on the slope west of the Socco Grande, and the narrow road over the Wed el-Yahud (Jews' river) and up the mountain was as much used by automobiles as it was by donkeys and mules. Spaniards, Sephardic Jews, Riffians, and Arabs, in their many-colored and distinctive garments, mingled as indifferently as gnus, giraffes, and Thomson's gazelles on an East African plain. Square minarets, as white as if carved of chalk, pointed to the westward-moving billows of clouds overhead. All the flowers of the Mediterranean were out at once, crawling and hanging on walls, blanketing the perennial smell of stale urine with their overpowering medley of bouquets.

On top of the mountain we came to a lookout rock in which steps had been carved. From its top one could see Jebel Musa, bare and gleaming as a lion's tooth, and much nearer, the yellow sands of Tarifa, beckoning travelers to make the shortest crossing from Africa to Europe. Below us to the northwest stood the Cap Spartel lighthouse, silhouetted against the Atlantic—which was as deep green as a cat's eye, the whipped gray of the strait, and the deep blue of the Mediterranean.

It was hard to turn one's back on this scene. To the southwest Dr. Nahon indicated a broken beach that ran to a flat-topped headland built of green grass over gray rock, and beyond the headland another beach of silvery sand stretched as far as the eye could reach. Pointing to the headland, he said, "There are the caves."

Perched on this lofty lookout, surveying one of the most strategic corners of the world—so strategic that Britain holds a rock on the edge of Spain, and Spain a fortified mountain on the opposite coast, and that a city of Morocco had to be governed by a committee of seven sometimes mutually hostile powers—it was easy to realize how important this spot had been in early times. The Phoenician fleet that an Egyptian pharaoh had hired to sail around Africa had had to wait for a westerly wind to sail through the strait, past the Neolithic farmers who had pecked and ground the axe on Mr. Doolittle's desk.

Rolling through the canopied forest of umbrellalike Atlantic pines that covers the high land above Cap Spartel, we descended in Dr.

Nahon's Hillman to the Atlantic coast road and soon reached the run-around on the headland over the caves—Ras Ashagar, it is called: Bald Head, the same word as Akshar (Scabhead) in Riffian. A few hundreds of thousands of years ago the limestone of which the headland is formed was battered and scoured by the sea, opening up some of the lower-lying caverns to the long tongues of its waves. One cave, as large as a small cathedral, is still entered and abandoned twice each day by its tides. Others are tiny cracks tempting the visitor to get out his flashlight and crawl to see what lies ahead.

The limestone of which the headland is built is of two kinds: the original rock of the promontory of Early Pleistocene date, and a secondary, gritty deposit formed later in its cracks and bearing the fossil bones of many animals. Parts of the first kind, being both porous and hard, are perfectly suited for grinding grain. Some of the depressions from which millstones had been cut were square, and what American archaeologists call metates were cut from them in Phoenician times. Circular pockmarks indicate places from which rotary querns were cut, from Roman times to the present.

Most of the stonecutting at the time of our visit was done inside the caves, by the light of kerosene lamps, by men who looked like gnomes. Clad in cotton shirts and baggy knickerbockers, their roundish heads protected by brimless knitted caps, they pecked out circles with small, sharp hammers, the sound of which could be heard from cave to cave. These men lived in the nearby village of Mediouna, and some of them claimed Riffian ancestry, particularly from Beni Tuzin.

The cave that Doolittle and Nahon had told me about stood high above the tide level; it had been formed by water seepage in the kind of limestone the millstone cutters did not like, hence they had left it alone. Before I reached it, Doolittle and Nahon had both told me that they had virtually cleaned it out, down to bedrock, removing many Neolithic artifacts and one skeleton. This gave me little hope. We reached it over a tortuous path, in some places having to leap from stone to stone. This was a good thing, for it kept tourists away.

The cave had been more extensive at one time, and erosion had exposed a face a few yards back from what had once been its mouth. Doolittle and Nahon had removed most of the soft, black Neolithic soil, down to a hard Red layer. They had not reached the bottom of the cave at all, only a calcified crust of Red earth. I picked at it with my knife and found that it could be excavated without too much difficulty. I asked Dr. Nahon if he minded if I should dig through this Red layer and on downward. "Not at all," he replied, and we did.

Our rented car was now ready, but instead of driving it southward we drove it backward and forward between El Farhar and the cave. I hired the two workmen that the former excavators had employed, both named Absalem (really Abd es-Salem in proper Arabic). As they came in two sizes, they were called Big Absalem and Little Absalem, although the latter was not a small man, just a few inches shorter than his partner. They both lived in Jbila, an agricultural village a short distance to the east, and not in Mediouna. When I asked them the name of the cave, they said, "Mugharet Mistadoolit." After we had been working there a while they tactfully changed its name to Mugharet Mistacoon, but as neither Hooker nor I wanted such an honor we all finally agreed on Mugharet el-Aliya, which it really was: the High Cave.

As such it appears in the literature, in either its Arabic or English form, but tour conductors who have been there in recent years say it is still called Mugharet Mistacoon by the local guides who lead visitors around, and who are either our old workmen or their sons or grandsons.

We slept, breakfasted, and dined at El Farhar, and we usually ate lunch in a Spanish café conveniently located a hundred yards or so in back of the High Cave, and could go for a swim on the beach below and to the right. Our chief problem was money. Not only had I to increase our staff, but also to buy excavating tools and to ship the finds home, including those previously dug up by Doolittle and Nahon. I wired Donald Scott, director of the Peabody Museum, and he promptly sent me what was needed. He was a retired publisher, and he judged us strictly on our merits. He never failed to back me.

Before the funds arrived I started work with the two Absalems; after, I immediately added two more workmen and others as needed. First we laid out a trench one meter wide and eighteen meters long, running west-southwest so as to cover the part of the cave floor on which its Stone Age inhabitants would be most likely to have sat and left their debris because it received the maximum afternoon sunlight, unimpeded because it shone straight off the Atlantic Ocean. I planned to leave a straight vertical face on the southern side of the trench for the sake of future archaeologists who with it might check my stratigraphy. At the back of my trench, where the top of the Neolithic black soil reached the roof, Nahon and Doolittle had left some of this soil and we took it out first, finding a few more celts, some sherds of channeled-ware pottery, also found in western Europe, and a few animal bones.

Two or three men were usually excavating and others carrying baskets of earth to a siever in the front of the cave, where one or both of the Absalems, and sometimes myself, searched for small objects that had evaded the eyes of the pick men. The Red crust was thin and soon turned into a gritty red soil. Red crusts and soils usually mean wet weather, oxidation, and Pleistocene.

THE EVOLUTION OF FLINT TOOLS IN WEST ASIA, EUROPE, AND
NORTH AFRICA.

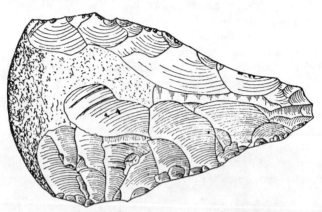

*A hand axe: the tool par excellence of the Lower Paleolithic, all the way from London
to Capetown to Bombay. A pointed tool flaked on both sides and retouched on both
edges, it is a splendid all-purpose cutter, as good as a steel knife for skinning and
butchering an animal, and adequate for felling sapling and fashioning poles and hafts.
(One half actual size.)*

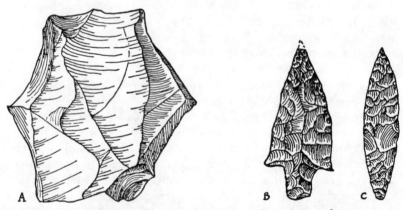

A   B   C

*A crude flint core (A) found at the bottom of the deposit in the High Cave of Tangier
shows scars where crude flakes were struck off more or less at random. (One-half
actual size.) In the same cave and elsewhere in North Africa the art of flaking fine
projectile points was brought close to perfection during the time span of the Upper
Paleolithic in Europe. B is barbed and tanged, C is shaped to penetrate deeply.
B and C are from the Middle Paleolithic.*

In the Red soil we found many beautiful flint points, made on flakes, not blades, and usually retouched on one side only. Below the Red soil was a layer of brown loam, very fine and easy to excavate. Besides the implement types of the Red soil, we found a large number of much more elegant implements. These were points, pressure-flaked on both sides, others tanged or with barblike wings at the butt end. They could hardly have been anything else than arrowheads, and closely resembled some of the specimens of American Indian arrow points made before the Indians got iron. Their workmanship was about the same as that of the famous Solutrean points found in Europe, particularly Spain, Portugal, and France; the Solutrean levels came between the Aurignacian and Magdalenian. This industry is called Aterian, and was presumably the North African equivalent of the European Upper Paleolithic.

This Brown soil and its implements reached to the rear wall of the cave in the area covered by our trench, but once we had begun to clean the face of the wall it suddenly ended. There was an inner cave beyond, which the Red-soil and Neolithic people had not known about. This inner cave was steep-walled and high, like an exaggerated dome. The three new workmen were not as blasé as the Absalems. They became excited, and there was much talk down below about jinns. They kept leaving the cave, supposedly to relieve themselves, and stayed out of the trench as much as possible.

"You know what this is?" said Big Absalem in Spanish. "Mistacoon, it is a jinn's office." So jinn's office it became, and that name remained.

Obviously something had to be done about this situation if the work was to proceed. As soon as a crawling space had been made, I entered it on my belly, and sat down inside. Then I commenced a two-way conversation with the jinn, in two voices, as loud as I could. First I used the usual phrases for exorcizing jinns: "*Alaikazik ya Shaitan! Alainka el-jnun!* (Get out of here, you shaitan; beat it, jinns)" Then the jinn replied in my best falsetto: "Please, Mistacoon, don't disturb me. This is just my place of business, I won't harm anybody."

"But it is not your office any more. You must get out. This is no longer your office. The whole cave belongs to me."

The jinn's voice grew fainter and fainter, and soon died out. I crawled out again and announced: "You see, the jinn has disappeared through a hole in the hoof, and will never dare come back again. Don't worry about him. He will soon set up a new office somewhere else, with a table and telephone and everything."

The Absalems began to laugh, and soon the others were laughing, too. My performance could not possibly have destroyed their belief in jinns, just in the presence of that particular jinn in that particular place. The tension had been relieved, and work went on as before.

In the Brown soil in which we had been digging at the time of the discovery of the jinn's office, we found the only complete skull of an animal that turned up in the same excavation. It was a lion's skull, and red all over, although the soil was brown. In retrospect I surmise that it must have been painted with red ocher. The poor creature had broken off its upper right canine tooth during its youth, and the jaw muscles on the right side of its head must have atrophied to such an extent that the crest of bone that separates the two temporal muscle attachments on the top of its skull had deviated to the right. I carefully took the skull home and presented it to Dr. Glover Allen, curator of mammals at the Museum of Comparative Zoology at Harvard, and he noted this malleability of bone due to muscular use or disuse with considerable interest.

Big Absalem, who had never heard of Charles Darwin, also rediscovered the law of natural selection. He told me one day that the men in his village were mostly tall because they worked out of doors, and there was no advantage to being short. The Mediouna men were all short because they worked in caves. Whenever a tall man appeared in the Mediouna population, he hit his head so many times that he killed himself, and only the short ones survived to beget offspring.

By the first of June the weather is likely to change in that part of the world, and instead of blowing steadily off the ocean the wind became temperamental. One day as I was standing near the mouth of the cave, near the sieves, a zephyr from the south moved up along the beach like a testy jinn and hit our sifting platform a quick, hard blow. It picked up the dried grit left over from the top Red soil, and drove it into my left eye. The pain blinded me. Full of solicitude, the men leaped out of the trench and tried to help. One of them, named Hamidu, reached in his scrip and pulled out a small bag containing kif—a mixture of hashish and tobacco—rammed it into his pipe, lit it, and inhaled a deep lungful. He put his mouth over my left eye and blew the smoke over the affected eyeball. Waiting a few seconds for the drug to have its anesthetic effect, he seized my head in his hands and ran his tongue over my eyeball, under the lids, licking the entire surface, and then spat.

While he may have removed the grit, the pain returned, and my vision was still blurred. It seemed best for me to have Dr. Nahon look at it. Unfortunately I had no transportation because Mary had deposited me at the cave early in the morning, and was not to return until the end of the working day.

I left the cave and made my way to the turnaround. Several

taxiloads of French tourists and/or prospective colons had debarked at Tangier on their way to Casablanca. They had seen the caves that the guides had shown them, and were about to return. I approached a middle-aged couple and said, in my best French, "Excuse me, *msieu-dame*, I have just suffered an accident and need to see a doctor. May I have your permission to share your taxi to town? I will pay my share."

The woman let out a little scream and placed a plump hand over her mouth. The man raised his fist and growled: "*Va-t'en*, you dirty dog of an Arab! Filthy beast!" I turned to the next group and recognized a pretty Jewish prostitute who habitually sat around a café-restaurant in the Socco Chico where I sometimes ate lunch. She was accompanied by a young Frenchman.

"Come with me, *monsieur*," said she. "I will take you to the doctor." Once we were in the cab together, she asked, "What is that on your head?" and giggled.

I put my hand to my head and found I was still wearing one of the knitted caps worn by the Mediouna men to keep from hitting their heads while cutting millstones in the caves. The little point on top is a tactile antenna, like a cat's whiskers. This marked me as a Muslim. Dirty dog of an Arab, indeed! At that time I predicted to myself that this kind of treatment could not last forever, and that sometime Morocco would again be free. It took no crystal ball to make this prediction, only seventeen years in advance of the actual event, but a little personal experience imprinted it, as with Pavlov's—and more recently B. F. Skinner's—dogs.

The next day, with a patch over my eye like the man in the shirt advertisement and Moshe Dayan, I resumed work. At the bottom of the Brown earth we found a thin white crust, completely unbroken. It was a seal formed during a spell of wet weather, making that part of the deposit below it as inviolable as if in a bonded warehouse. Nahon and Doolittle had found a similar crust between the Neolithic and the gray earth above it containing Roman and later artifacts. They had left a little of this higher crust in a small tunnel, which I had excavated, and I knew it showed that some time had passed between underlying and over-lying deposits.

Before breaking the crust, we took great pains to clear our trench of all other soils and to clean the faces, lest anything else fall in from the sides. When we broke it, we found that it overlay orange-gray sand which had either blown or been washed in. It was absolutely sterile, without artifacts or animal bones, and it reached to within three meters of the back wall of the jinn's office. This last three meters was composed of a second layer of red grit, which we called Red #2, making the first one Red #1. Its surface curved under the bottom of the sterile sand, presumably to conform to the shape of the floor of the cave, which we had not yet reached.

This level was a thin one and contained few implements, which were like those of Red #1 without as high a proportion of finely finished pieces. Bones there were in plenty, including those of dog, jackal, fox, cave hyena (plus his droppings), wild ass, hippopotamus, gazelle, wild sheep, wild cattle, water buffalo, rhinoceros, elephant, crested porcupine, and hare. Both the European wild boar (*Sus scrofa*) and the African warthog could have rooted and snorted in the forest outside.

Two things were notable about this list of fauna, identified by the indefatigable Glover Allen: Not a single beast was present in any level which is not alive today, and animals of both Western Palearctic (European and West Asian) species and those common to other parts of Africa were living together, with one exception, the extinct cave hyena. Water-loving forms such as the hippo coexisted with desert types such as the wild ass and the gazelle. The climate was obviously favorable for many kinds of life,and connections were open with the Sahara and the parts of Africa south of it, and with the Sahara and the parts of Africa south of it, and with the Palestine-Syria part of Asia, if not with Spain, Italy, or both. As all but one species are still alive somewhere, the time was not extremely remote. The latter part of the Pleistocene was indicated.

It interested me to see that the people who lived while Red #2 was being deposited had knocked off a stalagmite about six inches from their own floor. Its broken surface lay flush with the crust that sealed the layer. While scraping around that area one day, I came upon a small, light yellowish piece of bone which looked like nothing that had turned up before. As I turned it over in my hand, I realized that it was human.

Before we left that day, I saw that it was a piece of the left maxilla (upper jaw) of a child about nine years old whose permanent incisors and first molars had erupted but had fallen out after death. The permanent canines and premolars, which had not yet erupted, were still there, sunk in the bone. These teeth were very large. For a child of the age indicated by the stage of eruption of the teeth, the bone was very heavy and thick. The edge of the nasal sill was grooved, somewhat like that of an ape, although this feature is still present in some modern skulls. Obviously I had found something of extreme interest. Carefully padding it with cotton, I put it in a Player's cigarette tin and tucked it in a pocket of my jacket, and then looked around for more. Before long I came upon a very much worn human molar that must have come from a second, and adult, individual.

I honestly could not say that I had found either *in situ*, but they did not come from the sieve, as some publications have stated. How they got where they did was a mystery, for neither specimen had any trace of Red earth on it, only Brown. I therefore concluded, temporarily, that they had fallen down from the Brown layer, loosened during the excitement of the discovery of the jinn's office, and that they belonged with the Brown soil.

I put the tooth with the piece of maxilla, and Hooker Doolittle sent them to Earnest Hooton by diplomatic pouch. They are still in the Peabody Museum at Harvard.

The next day I found a third crust under Red #2, and under that a layer of sand that had turned to breccia. It was full of bones as clean and white as they were the day the animals had died. There were no implements, and the bones had not been broken by the hand of man. But still I had not reached bottom. George Reisner, the Egyptologist, impressed on me his admonition: "Never quit until you have gotten down to *gebel*." Gebel is Egyptian Arabic for *jebel* (mountain), in this case meaning bedrock. So I kept chiseling on, until at the very bottom I found a Mousterian core, a lump of flint with many scars from which flakes had been removed.

At that point I deposited a twenty-five-centime French-Moroccan coin on the spot from which the core had come after kissing it and saying, "O jinn, here is the rent for the use of your office." That was the end of the dig at the High Cave for 1939, but I swore that when the impending war was over, I would come back to finish the job—and I kept my word. The coin was secure under several stones and a layer of earth. No eyes but the jinn's could see it, and we found it again eight years later. The jinn had protected it well.

Just before we were to leave El Farhar, two obviously wealthy Arab gentlemen, immaculately dressed, appeared on the terrace and asked for Mistacoon. When I appeared they drew me to one side so that no one else might overhear our conversation. Then they told me in lowered voices that they had heard of my success as an expeller of jinns. On the property of one of them was buried a box of gold coins, but they could not dig it up because it was guarded by a most ferocious jinn. If I would drive the jinn away, they would pay me well for my services. I thanked them very much and told them that unfortunately we were leaving the city for the southland at dawn the next day.

So we did. We had a fine time in Mogador watching potters make their famous glazed ware, and when we reached Taroudant in the Sous, Carl Jr. chased his brother around the top of the city walls from gate to gate. I sat below, horrified, for it reminded me of Tom Scudder chasing Pat Putnam around the edge of the museum roof, although this seemed more dangerous because there might have been loose bricks to slip on. But like Tom and Pat they came down, panting and unscathed.

At Taroudant we saw our first blue men, camel nomads who had come in off the Sahara. Their skins were blue from indigo dye sweated out of their clothing. We also saw one very black Negro with pale blue eyes. I decided that I would visit the Sahara after the war, but I had to wait almost thirty years to do so.

As the clouds of war were darkening to the north of us, we rode a Danish cargo ship home from Casablanca.

The only incident possibly worthy of note happened one day when our sons entered the galley while the cook was absent and spied an open crate of raw eggs. They began throwing them at each other and finally smeared them at close range over each other's faces. The cook arrived, grabbed them both, locked them in the freezer, and kept them there until they were well chilled.

During the next two years Nahon and Doolittle continued excavating in the High Cave, under the guidance of Movius and me talking with Dr. Nahon over ham radio stations. Eventually all the specimens removed from the cave before Dr. Nahon left Tangier to join the U.S. Navy were shipped to the Peabody, where Bruce Howe and Hallam L. Movius, Jr., authored *A Stone Age Site in Tangier* (Papers of the Peabody Museum, etc. [PMP] Vol. 28, No. 1, 1947), following *Fossil Man in Tangier* by a Turkish Harvard Ph.D., Muzaffer Süleyman Şenyürek (PMP Vol. 16 No. 3, 1940). The author was killed shortly afterward in an airplane crash in Turkey. Both the artifacts and the human remains showed that the dwellers of the High Cave were not Caucasoid, and possibly not fully sapiens, on an evolutionary level with but not identical to the Neanderthals. Their flint-knapping techniques were different from those used in Europe.

I bear no grudge against Bruce and Hallam for stealing my show, but my lip curls a bit when I read French critics blaming these two men who were not there because the maxilla and tooth were not found *in situ*. If blame there be, let them vent it where it belongs—on me.

14. *The Uneasy Calm*

In the fall of 1939, after returning from the High Cave in Morocco, I joined Eliot D. Chapple in writing a book called *Principles of Anthropology*, a rather grandiose title as it had little to do with physical anthropology or archaeology. It was based on work done over several years by Conrad M. Arensberg, whose office at the museum had been to the right of mine, and Eliot, who worked in the one just beyond. They had jointly written a monograph entitled *Measuring Human Relations: An Introduction to the Study of the Interaction of Individuals.** Before my return, Conrad had moved on to MIT.

Besides my usual duties of teaching and tutoring, before Conrad had left I had been too busy with my own work to pay much attention to what these two younger men had been doing. But now things had changed. I could hardly avoid hearing the grunts and other human noises wafting out of Eliot's office when his door was ajar—just background music for his experiments with his own students and colleagues, until they included me.

Then I found that the field being studied was social anthropology—neither ethnography, which is the study of individual whole cultures, nor ethnology, the comparative study of cultures in general, trait by trait, as in canoe building or girls' puberty ceremonies all over the so-called primitive world.

Social anthropology was supposed to be divided into two schools: the historical, which traced the spread and growth of cultures; and the functional, which grew out of Durkheim and other sociologists into the studies of how living cultures worked. The functional school was headed by two great leaders: Bronislaw Malinowski, whom we met at the Harvard Tercentenary; and A. Radcliffe Brown, sometimes known as A. R. Brown, or simply Rex. Rex had taught W. Lloyd Warner at Chicago, and he had taught both Arensberg and Chapple at Harvard, but these two had gone a great step further.

The older three had analyzed their material on general terms. The younger two had decided that such studies could be quantified to warrant mathematical studies like those performed by physicists and

---

Genetic Society Monographs, Vol. 22, No. 1, Provincetown, Mass., The Journal Press, 1940. Chapple was the senior author.

chemists, and to make a real science out of what had been a sociological game.

After Conrad's departure Eliot had taken over his ex-partner's office as a secret annex to his own. In that small cubicle now sat a Chinese graduate student, Mr. Yue-Hwa Lin, who was watching Eliot and his guinea pigs covertly through a one-way screen. Eliot would ask his proband, usually a student or colleague, questions that the latter would answer either immediately, after some delay, or by interrupting. The proband might respond speechlessly by nods or manual gestures, shoulder shrugging, or even falling asleep. Eliot would vary his own interaction rate to see how his proband would change his in return.

This was a lot of fun for Eliot, but a lot of work for Mr. Lin, who had to record the beginning and end of each item of interaction, verbal or otherwise, by pressing a key on Eliot's wonderful machine, later called the interaction chronograph, a piece of sheer Yankee invention. It was an old typewriter frame which did not write, but traced moving tapes in different colors when Mr. Lin pressed the appropriate keys. Its motor had to be so rigged that the tapes flowed across the platen at an even speed. Afterward Eliot measured and plotted the data from the tapes on graphs, and analyzed them by a special formula devised by a friend of all three of us, the now famous Harvard mathematician and philosopher Willard Van Orman Quine.

Thus Eliot documented in detail how one person was overly aggressive, another hesitant to respond, who interacted in short bursts, who was long-winded, and, most important of all, who was likeliest to become a leader, and who a born follower. In order to check out his findings, he had the most interesting of his subjects return several times, and they always performed the same, no matter how Eliot varied his act. Then he tried them in groups of two or even three (which gave Mr. Lin the heebie-jeebies) to check out the leader-follower syndrome, and that worked too.

When my turn on the hot seat came, I was a troublesome guinea pig, but still the best potential collaborator for the *Principles* because I had already taught the cultures of the world several times, could write fast enough and probably well enough, and had traveled fairly widely, while Eliot—a Salemite—had, by his own admission, not yet ventured west of the Hudson River. Men from Salem go to China and India, but they travel only by sea.

So from Eliot's point of view I venture to say that we made a well-balanced team—he brains, me brawn, or maestro and scribe. Or even Hall and Nordhoff—although on my paternal grandmother's side

I had a little Hall in me too, and my Halls were clockmakers and inventors.

Also our working patterns were somewhat different. He may have done a lot of silent thinking, but to the outside world he seemed lazier than I. Sometimes he drove out to Sudbury, where we conferred in my unheated harness-room study in our barn. One other time I drove way east to Annisquam, where I found him itching to go sailing in his sloop, but we got the work done, on our own land and on the Atlantic Ocean, although the book was published in New York.

The object of our study was to explain how equilibrium was vigorously maintained in different kinds and combinations of human groups, just as it is also maintained between the particles in an atom, between the sun and its planets and their satellites, and between the stars and galaxies in the infinity of the universe. It was a bold and awesome goal for a pair of north-of-Boston Yankees in their early thirties even to dream that they could do (really a triumvirate, counting Connie Arensberg's earlier contribution).

As we wrote on page 43 of the *Principles*, "A state of equilibrium may be defined as follows: *If a small force is impressed upon a system, a change or adjustment takes place within the system, and once this force is removed, the system returns to approximately its previous state.*"

Our next concern was how to define a system in terms of our own field of work—human relations. Despite our vaunted "intelligence," which places us at the top of the animal kingdom in our own minds, human relations make our behavior just as predictable, especially in a crisis, as that of lemmings, and as blind as that of moles. For all that we cared, the millions of watts of verbiage spieled out on television nowadays are just as much blah-blah-blah as the words spoken in Eliot's office that Mr. Lin did not record.

Mr. Lin's records revealed that each of us has a private interaction rate almost as individual and invariable as his fingerprints. While sorting out the usual gamut of personalities, one may also turn up an oddball who disturbs others so much that he may be killed or confined. In some cases it turns out, after he has died, that he was a genius.

Predictable disturbances to a human system may come from births, puberties, marriages, illnesses, accidents, and deaths. These individual crises disturb others, who calm themselves down by the well-known *rites of passage*. Other disturbances may be cyclical or seasonal, like midsummer, the equinoxes, and the winter solstice, which mark the times that the reindeer migrate, the honeybees swarm, the salmon swim upstream to spawn, the monsoon begins to blow, or sudden eclipses come. A monstrous snake in the sky is swallowing the sun. Will it vomit it back again? Such events that affect everyone evoke mass performances, including rainmaking ceremonies, which we named *rites of intensification.* The fact that both these kinds of rites are universal suggests that they are just as automatic as the restoration of equilibrium in lifeless systems.

The human systems are *institutions,* not in the sense of notable men (e.g., Mr. So-and-so was an institution), or even customs, like the Sacrament, but rather, in social-anthropological jargon, a group of people who interact with (nowadays *relate to*) each other in pairs or in sets of three or more, more often with each other than they do with other persons outside their group. The amount of interaction among these people is judged not necessarily in terms of each person's total interaction, but of his interaction for some particular purpose—or in some special activity, as in the complicated age and sex relationships with and between families, and extensions thereof; in making things singly and in teams; trading; worshiping and performing rituals; playing games instead of fighting; producing almost every kind of art, from body painting to dancing out dramatic legends, decorating implements, poetry creatable only by illiterates, and soul-stirring music. Healing and trance visions require special personalities, as does governing. The first exercises gifted men's imaginations, the latter their judgment and punch.

When I said that the content of speech of Eliot's guinea pigs' interaction could be disregarded for his special purpose, I did not mean that it could be tossed away like the wrapper off a stick of gum. Speech is made of symbols. Some may be just filler, like "Have a good day," "Sleep tight," "Salaam alaikum" or "Shalom aleichem," or a monosyllable. Speech is built of symbols, as is art. Symbols are as real as things and animals, including people; a poem unwritten is as solid as the Taj Mahal. Faith may not visibly move mountains, but a faith like Islam could send Arabs on horses, camels, and sailing ships, with no weapons but their swords and lances, to Tours and Mindanao. Now we move mountains with explosives and bulldozers, utilizing physical energy from outside our bodies, but the Arabs needed only that of fire, their own bodies, their horses, and the wind. The energy they drew on was of low voltage, really chemical, their motors silent and frictionless, inside their probably not anatomically unusual brains.

When Eliot and I came to deal with the relative complexity of institutions, we found order spinning and winding around inside the inscrutable chaos of cultures which Franz Boas, high pontiff of Columbia Heights, told his students and disciples—by word of mouth and in numerous books—could never be solved. In fact, to find it might somehow be indecent, because it might imply that some cultures might be "higher" than others, instead of just more complicated.

Now in the most simply organized of living societies, the system and the institution are synonymous because they have no divisions of labor beyond those based on sex and age. Everyone in the system belongs to a family, which may extend beyond the simple marital household to include all sorts of cousins and other kin to the nth degree—the limits of human memory—and if a stranger happens along, he and the persons he meets may count back generations of ancestors' names until they find a common forebear; but it is easier if such kin are lumped in groups—like eagle hawks and crows, or bears and willow trees.

But once food has become so abundant that all hands are not needed to hunt it and collect it, some men may find more time to make weapons and women to plait baskets. Others may be traders, as when one people's country has good spear wood and another's abounds in fine-grained stone for knives. Among most part-time specializers the family may remain the system, with decisions made by the heads of families, with the help of healers and prophets; instead of simply the best hunter as decision maker, there may have to be what outsiders would call a chief.

As food grows more abundant—among groups of people living in bounteous lands teeming with game, fruit, and fish—some specialists may become full-timers, and thus other institutions begin to wax as the roster of kinds of basic institutions, depending on their functions, remains the same or atrophies. A critical threshold is reached when a culture moves from handmade to machine-fabricated goods produced by energy furnished by animals, water flow, wind, steam, or cosmic or solar forces, and by modern techniques of instantaneous communication.

We are passing the principal bounds of Eliot's or my ideas. His greatest discovery was not so much that order can be made out of social chaos, but in determining that differences in interaction rates are dependent on individual combinations of the inheritance of special parts of the nervous system and the secretions of the endocrine glands. Eliot has been following this line since, in medical school and a mental hospital, and has been generous in giving me references useful to me in my own research on inherent racial aptitudes.

Before, during, and after my half sabbatical in 1939, the office to my left was occupied by William H. Sheldon, M.D., Ph.D., the somatotyper. Hippocrates had noticed differences between body types and temperament. During the Middle Ages aristocrats were shown as long and lean; peasants broad-shouldered and broad-hipped; while sly, self-indulgent merchants were thin-nosed and thin-fingered, and fat of paunch and jowl.

Several German workers had documented the existence of such types statistically, and in America, after he had viewed the bodies of American soldiers killed by the influenza epidemic of 1918, Dr. George Draper noted that they were all constitutionally alike. My next-door neighbor was well aware of Draper's work.

Sheldon realized that "pure" endomorphs, mesomorphs, and ectomorphs (fat, solid, and lean) were virtually nonexistent. Everyone apparently was a composite of the three components, which he numbered, in that order, on a scale from 1 to 7. Because one man might have solid legs and a skinny chest, Sheldon rated the different parts of the body separately, noting sixty variables per subject. These he reduced to between one and seven overall values for his three components.* Thus Jesus Christ (according to early paintings) and Earnest A. Hooton rated as 2-3-5's.

Both Draper and Sheldon, as well as the European somatotypists, attributed mental and behavioral characteristics to their somatotypes. Sheldon's work was drawn into fine focus when he teamed up with S. Smith Stevens, the Harvard psychologist whose life work was a completely objective mathematical study of the human reception and tolerance of tones and decibels of sound.

Sheldon traced his components though an evolutionary cycle from gut to bone plus muscle to brain. Endomorphs may be relaxed and deliberate; mesomorphs fly into instant action; and ectomorphs are shy and sensitive. Not one is very competent in an extreme state.

With Stevens he showed that temperament is hereditary. So are patterns of behavior—while external influences can work failure or success, they cannot erase the blueprints of the genes.† While their initial research was on white Americans, Sheldon and Stevens also recognized somatotypic differences within and between other races, including those of temperament and styles of art.

Sheldon served in the U.S. Army Medical Corps during World War II, and resumed his work at Harvard afterward. One of his products was a study of one hundred delinquent youths sheltered in

---

*W. H. Sheldon, The Varieties of Human Physique, Harpers, New York, 1940.
†W. H. Sheldon and S. S. Stevens, The Varieties of Temperament, Harpers, New York, 1942.

the Hayden Goodwill Inn in Boston, taking into full account their life histories, psychiatric diagnoses, and somatotypes. He published this in *Varieties of Delinquent Youth*, two volumes published in 1970. It documented his finding fully, but was, as expected, ignored.

William H. Sheldon died in Cambridge, Massachusetts, in September 1977. Much earlier, his somatotyping with its special jargon had become a parlor game, great for after dinner and with drinks. Nothing is more ephemeral than a fad. This treatment with levity of a serious and important cross-discipline subject may have contributed to the general academic disapproval of Sheldon's work, which haunted him the rest of his life, as well as to the unavailability of many of his works.

It was my good fortune to have been allotted the corner office of the fifth floor of the Peabody Museum, between Sheldon and Chapple, shaping much of my later work. Mr. Yueh-Hwa Lin had not been joking when he painted the Chinese ideogram for Coon under *C. S. Coon* on my office door, for that ideogram is also Confucius's name. It brought me luck, at least in coming back alive from my overseas mission in the war about to begin.

15. OSS and World War II, North Africa*

In 1941, while I was still helping Eliot Chapple put *The Principles of Anthropology* to bed, Gordon Browne had already begun to offer his and my services to various government agencies in preparing for the probable invasion of Morocco by American forces, well before our country declared war on its Axis enemies.

Our first step was to tackle G-2 (Army Intelligence) through its Boston office. We received a polite brush-off. Then my classmate Patrick T. L. Putnam, who had left his home in the Ituri Forest of the Belgian Congo where he lived with the Pygmies, got in touch with Colonel Sharp of the New York G-2 office, and through Pat first Gordon and then I made the colonel's acquaintance.

Until I left for Morocco in May 1942, under other auspices, I worked unofficially for Colonel Sharp, digging out maps and documents, assembling photographs, locating people who spoke Japanese, finding local people whom he wanted investigated, etc. Although he appreciated this work, Colonel Sharp was unable to find a way to send either Gordon or me to North Africa.

In the early spring of 1941 Gordon had the idea of preparing a handbook and dictionary of local Arabic phrases to be used by American troops landing in North Africa. We wrote it and sent it to the Military Dictionary Committee. It was printed in modified form and used at the landing, along with fliers dropped from covering aircraft which read that we were there as friends, not foes.

While I was working on the handbook-dictionary in Cambridge, Gordon was going back and forth to New York conferring with

---

This chapter was first written from sheer memory in 1970, twenty-five years after its final episode. I rewrote parts of it in 1972, and again in 1980 after I had discovered a carbon copy of two reports I wrote to General William A. Donovan in 1943. These reports have been published in my book A North Africa Story (Gambit, Ipswich, Mass., 1980). This chapter and that book are not identical: One fills in where the other leaves gaps, and vice versa.

various persons about our problem of how to be sent to North Africa. He missed out on becoming one of the vice-consuls sent to Casablanca in February 1941 by G-2 and ONI to supervise the distribution of food shipments from America to the needy, because they were forbidden to take part in either intelligence or operations.

A British representative made him an offer, which he refused, to work for his government in Casablanca. They had no overt agencies in French West Africa, which was ruled by the Vichy government, a puppet of the Germans. The Vichyites had barred the British on the face-saving excuse that the Royal Navy had shelled the French naval bases at Mers el Kebir, near Oran in Algeria, and at Dakar, in Senegal, during 1940, to keep them from being used by the Germans.

Gordon also made contact with two men who belonged to the then-nascent COI (Coordination of Information), the parent of the OSS (Office of Strategic Services) and grandparent of the CIA (Central Intelligence Agency). They were Colonel Solberg and Mr. Wallace Phillips, a retired American businessman from London.

Before the year was out I was to meet both these men, to my advantage, but before continuing my narrative let me anticipate it by explaining what kind of outfit I was getting into.

Early in 1941 Colonel—soon raised to Major General—William A. (Wild Bill) Donovan, conceived of and created the COI. He had once served as a bouncer in his father's Buffalo saloon. Although I have seen him hold a glass of amber-tinted liquid in his hand, he never drank it, nor did he smoke. In World War I he became a hero rivaling Douglas MacArthur. Although the latter stayed in the army, Donovan became a very successful lawyer. He knew every man in his outfit by name; he also knew all he needed to know about each one. A peerless judge of character, he had no trouble drawing the cream of our land into his fold.

Once the need was felt for a central pool of information to replace the Byzantine bureaucracy of rival services, he fought as he had fought in World War I to create such an office, which would recruit the kind of men who could not only collect intelligence in the field but also conduct guerrilla warfare behind enemy lines. I am proud to say that the first place that both kinds of work were done by Americans was North Africa, where our results made a critical difference in the course of the war.

The COI was founded under Franklin Roosevelt's order on July 11, 1941. On June 13, 1942, it became the OSS, which was dissolved by Harry Truman as of October 1, 1945. Truman seems to have been no hero-worshiper—he disposed of both Donovan and

MacArthur, themselves bitter rivals, with his usual and equal aplomb with or without personal satisfaction.

My own employment in Bill Donovan's short-lived but glorious agency began about five months after its birth and ended seven before its demise. During these four years of excitement, boredom, good companionship, and the rare ecstasy of being on my own, I feel that I went through an ancient and fabulous rite of passage and maintained the tradition of service to my country that my then-blind grandfather taught me when I was very young.

My father died on the fourth of October, 1941. I'm sure he smelled a rat about my plans, but he never let on. My mother took my involvement stoically, even when my brother Maurice joined the outfit later; and when he was sent to Assam and Burma his wife Katya, Hooker Doolittle's daughter, kept Mother company in Wakefield. Jack, who wanted to be sent to Alsace to sabotage some foundries, was turned down because he had flat feet and his French was not Parisian.

The culmination of Gordon's machinations befell me on the day before the Harvard-Yale game in November 1941. It was to be played in the stadium, and many loyal alumni were swarming around Cambridge and Boston, mixed with Yalies. A tall, dignified, elderly gentleman wearing a blue serge suit and black shoes would be unnoticed in that multitude.

Such a man knocked on my office door and introduced himself. He was Wallace Phillips, USN, who had been a businessman for many years in London. First he swore me to utter secrecy, then he told me more about myself than I had dreamed anyone else could know. He asked me if I wanted to serve my country. I told him that I was already in the Massachusetts State Guard at Sudbury, but that was not enough. He then informed me that I had been chosen to be the Lawrence of Morocco. He did not mention Gordon's and my efforts about the projected American landings on the Atlantic coast, but told me that the Germans planned to drive through Spain from Vichy France and then to conquer Morocco, reinforcing Rommel and taking over the whole Middle East.

Aside from direct American participation, the only force that could stop the Germans was a rejuvenated Riffian army, still smarting from the loss of their freedom in 1926. I was to offer the Riffians hope, to unite them, and to arm them. Would I do it? I could not breathe a word of this to anyone, particularly to my wife, sons, or mother. I thanked God my father had died the preceding October. I thought a moment, then said yes.

At home in Sudbury, I told Mary that I had to disappear for a while, but that she had to trust me. She eventually found out where I was going, but not until the war had started.

I went to Washington, where I was given an office in a three-quarters empty building, with very little to do. After what seemed an eternity I was sent home for a few days and told to go to a city in Canada, where I would meet others of my kind in a hotel lobby. We were to identify ourselves by secret gestures and apparently innocent greetings. We were driven out to a secret camp surrounded by barbed-wire fences and put in our quarters. We were given Canadian army privates' uniforms, and assigned false names. No one was supposed to know who anyone else was. Long afterward I found out that the others all knew each other, being regular army men ranking as high as colonels, while I was the only civilian—in their esteem the titman of the litter. One was called Carl (his real name), while I was given another moniker, which I had trouble remembering.

We went through courses in unarmed combat, street fighting, and particularly demolition. In Washington I had been trained in signals.

One of my fellow students, a beefy braggart and bully, said that he was going to shave my mustache off by force. I replied, "If you do, I'll kill you."

A few days later he buried a charge under a mound of earth, with an activated timing device set to go off in a few minutes. He invited me to sit on the mound with him, and we chatted in a friendly fashion until he said, "Excuse me, I've got to go take a leak. I'll be right back."

As soon as he was out of sight I got up and walked away. Before I had moved very far the mound blew up with a deafening explosion, and dirt fell on my head.

When that course was over I returned to Washington, and was sent home to see my friends and to act normally. I lunched at the Harvard Faculty Club, where my tablemates remarked that I had grown thin and tanned.

"You must have been in the West Indies or someplace," they said.

I didn't say I hadn't. Another reason for being home was to get Rocky Mountain spotted fever shots along with Gordon, who was also being sent to Morocco, where there was a similar but not identical disease for which no serum existed. Dr. George Shattuck of the Harvard Medical School, who had been let in on some part, at least, of the secret, injected these shots into our arms. The bugs' legs were still visible in the serum. Dr. Shattuck thought this great fun. It got us closer to our destination.

Gordon went to Casablanca as a vice-consul distributing food donations, but I had trouble getting a cover. I was told to get a commission in the Navy, but in Boston the Naval medical officers rejected me as being too fat. The next idea was to make me special assistant to the American minister to Morocco at Tangier. The State Department turned this down because in 1933 Mr. Addison Southard, then American minister to Ethiopia, had sent in a disparaging report about my behavior.

When Bill Donovan heard of this he sent a special messenger, whose identity I do not know, straight to Franklin Roosevelt, who ordered the State Department to destroy that report. That is how I came to be special assistant to Mr. J. Rives Childs, although I was really working for the naval attaché, Marine Colonel William A. Eddy, who had been born in Sidon to missionary parents and who spoke perfect Arabic and could think like an Arab.

I was sent to Lisbon via Bermuda and Horta, where we refueled. At Horta one of my British friends from the cable station told me that he had known I was coming. What security! In Lisbon I had a long wait. Mr. Childs didn't want me. After several weeks I was loaded aboard a small plane destined for Tangier. Its pilot was José Cabral, chief of the Portuguese Naval Air Force, who was pleased that no Japanese were aboard, for he was afraid that his plane would be blown up.

In Tangier I registered in the Minza Hotel, where Colonel Eddy lived, and reported to him in the naval attaché's office in the Calle de America. That was a narrow alley directly opposite the American Embassy, given to the American government in President Washington's first term by the then reigning sultan of Morocco, the first nation to acknowledge our country's independence.

Bill Eddy took us to a cottage he had rented, where he fed me lunch. His cook fried up a batch of eggs. Although I have been allergic to eggs since the age of twelve, I ate them, vomited violently, and nearly choked. My meeting with Mr. Childs was less friendly and less violent. He ordered Mohammed Riffi, a red-headed Riffian doorman and guard whom I had known since the Doolittle days and earlier, to bring in an Arabic newspaper. Then Mr. Childs asked me to translate it. So that was why a Harvard professor had given up his job to come to Tangier! My Arabic reading was confined to the classical, my spoken Arabic to the colloquial. Had the newspaper been printed in the latter, I might have made out, but from Iraq to Morocco journalese Arabic is a single, synthetic jargon which I have never mastered—nor do I see any reason why I should. Mohammed Riffi tried to help me, sweating and putting ideas in my mouth, until I pushed him away. From that time on my relationship with Mr. Childs lacked cordiality, but he did not send me home. I was perhaps the first secret agent to be given diplomatic cover. It was hard on both of us, but we managed to live through the misalliance.

Gordon Browne had been sent to Casablanca earlier as one of Ambassador Murphy's vice-consuls. When I arrived Murphy released him to Eddy. Gordon was a member of SIS (Secret Intelligence Service), while I was SOE (Secret Operations Executive). Eddy was in charge of both. This duality distressed the British, who kept their intelligence and operations apart. They had two intelligence agencies, that of the "Sleeper," who lived in Tangier continuously, and that of the wartime agency, headed by a Canadian. Each had his staff, including one or more "blonde lures" whose job was to seduce enemy agents and to get secrets from them in the usual fashion.

One of Gordon's first jobs was to get Randolph Mohammed Guesus, whom we met in Chapter 10, away from the British Sleeper and into our camp. It was Guesus who arranged our interviews and negotiations with the Riffian leaders to set up the rebellion that Mr. Phillips had chosen me to rouse, got us in touch with a holy man who led thousands of followers who would die at his command, helped us in many other ways, and was decorated by the American government after the war.

Our SOE contact was a meek-looking clerk in the British Embassy whom we passed without recognition in the streets but was a fiend. We called him Stripes. One of the first missions he gave us was to drive over the French Zone looking for stones in the road ballast to serve as models for explosives to be placed on the highways to blow off the treads of German tanks, should they arrive. This was a British scheme, but because Britain did not recognize Vichy France and the United States did, such jobs were delegated to Gordon and me. Although we had been forbidden by Mr. Childs to attach CD (*Corps Diplomatique*) plates to our cars, we did so as soon as we had left the city limits. We cruised around over many roads in the French Zone, and found that the kinds and colors of stones in each region were different from the others, depending on the local geological formations. We also learned that most of them had been broken by road gangs into too small pieces for the intended purpose.

Suddenly one or both of us observed that the one constant factor on all roads was mule turds, large enough for our purpose, uniform in size, fat and greenish brown, depending on the animal's feed—but the color differences were of little importance because they fade. Gordon and I picked up as many as we could without being observed, for why should two Christians in an American car be picking up mule turds?

Carefully wrapped, these turds made their way to London in a British diplomatic pouch, and were returned via Gibraltar in plastic facsimile, the mule's revenge on the motor vehicle. The plastic turds were used in at least one battle. They were not camel turds, as has been reported in several books and *Time* magazine. In 1942 there weren't enough camels on the roads in northern Morocco.

Our principal reason for being in Morocco was the impending Torch operation, the projected and supersecret landings of American troops on the Moroccan and Algerian coasts. Both Eddy's OSS men and Robert Murphy's vice-consuls in Casablanca knew it was coming, but until almost the end we were not told when, nor did we want to know. One of our jobs was to keep open the clandestine radio stations in Vichy-governed North Africa, particularly those in Casablanca and Oran, and the main station in Tangier, to which the others reported. The Casablanca station had to be mobile because the Germans there, as supervisors of the Vichy French, had triangulation units that could zero in on the station's location. Its operator, using a code name, called us every day.

At first we received the messages in the naval attaché's office across the narrow street from the American Embassy. Soon Mrs. Childs, a White Russian lady who had no knowledge of what we were doing, complained that the buzzing and crackling of our radio transmitter spoiled her sleep, and it had to go. Colonel Eddy then installed the station in the cottage on The Mountain where he had fed me fried eggs. There we stationed Stork, a British signals man who was on duty only in the daytime, so someone had to guard it at night, lest the Germans blow it up.

The guarding duty fell to three men: Gordon Browne, Captain Franklin Holcombe (son of the commandant of the Marine Corps), and myself. This meant that, with full daytime duties, we could sleep only two nights out of three. This got to be too much. Holcombe was relieved because of a stiff knee left over from a schoolboy injury; Gordon and I alternated with a tough, dedicated local Sephardic Jew, Ishak Cohen, who had been through the British Commando school at Haifa. He was the brother-in-law of Henry Perkins, an elderly American Negro who had been the leader of a jazz band, and at the time in question ran Uncle Tom's bathhouse and restaurant on the beach. Uncle Tom was one of our men.

One night when Ishak was on duty, he dozed off on the couch

with the door open. Suddenly he awoke when something heavy landed on his chest. He looked up and saw gazing at him two huge, luminous wide-set eyes. He reached up and grabbed the thing about its broad, cold, slimy neck. The thing jumped off. Ishak switched on a light—the thing was a giant bullfrog.

D day, whenever it was to be, was approaching. Tension was high. On one of my smuggling visits to Gibraltar I saw both General Eisenhower's and General Mark Clark's baggage being carried about, Eisenhower's under the "deceptive" name of General Howe, Clark's under General Mark.

The next major job, perhaps the most important of all, was Gordon's. It was to exfiltrate Malverne, the chief pilot of Casablanca and Fedhala harbors, to Tangier, whence he could be taken to Gibraltar and put aboard the American invasion fleet to land on the beaches of these ports. Because he did not think Gordon should make this trip alone, Bill Eddy ordered Frank Holcombe to go with him.

They set forth with a car plus trailer on the guise of getting kuskus semolina for the local Tangierian Arabs to eat during a forthcoming religious feast, because this cereal was in short supply in the International Zone. They had no trouble going down. André Bourgoin, the local Dodge and national Vacuum Oil Co. dealer—an ardent de Gaullist who had delivered a busloadful of other de Gaullists onto a ship in the harbor, which had straightaway weighed anchor and departed without clearance—had also recruited Malverne and delivered him to the safekeeping of Colonel David King, our head vice-consul. When Gordon knocked at Dave's door the latter greeted him with a Colt .45 in hand, and then they stowed Malverne between the semolina sacks.

Ensconced between the dusty bags and subject to the car's exhaust fumes, the pilot, like Paul Revere, had no easy ride. When they reached the frontier of the Spanish Zone, they were halted. Although their vehicles bore CD plates, they had not counted on the Spaniards' dogs. Smelling something gamier than semolina, they began to sniff at the tailboard. Gordon threw stones at them. (In an earlier version I had written that he threw pieces of bully beef; in 1979 he assured me that he and Frank ate the bully beef and threw stones.)

Once Malverne had been delivered to a hideout that Stripes had chosen near the shore in Tangier, another problem arose. Someone had leaked word of the pilot's presence there to the British Sleeper, who was the only one of us agents who had a good smuggling boat capable of carrying such a living prize to Gibraltar. But we had the pilot guarded. It was a stalemate.

So the Sleeper invited Gordon and me, among others, to his villa for drinks. When we went he fed us both mickeys. I did not like the metallic sheen or the taste of mine, took a tiny sip, and poured the rest into a potted plant. My vision began to dim, but I soon got over it. Gordon drank none of his, apparently, and was unaffected. We found another way to carry Malverne to Gibraltar, and he guided the American fleet into Fedhala harbor on November 8, 1942, complete with the phrase books that Gordon and I had compiled for Colonel Sharpe more than a year earlier. That our landing parties were attacked by Vichyites was due to a leak that I think I have traced, but I shall not mention it here because I am not sure.

Meanwhile we received an urgent request from Casablanca for some explosives with which to blow up the Germans who were bugging our local radio operator. I got two gunnysacks full of hand grenades from our loyal religious leader, who had been saving them for some future conflict. At five o'clock in the morning—before Win Buckingham had arisen, between dawn and sunrise—two Arabs leading mules loaded with baskets arrived in the courtyard of the El Farhar Hotel on The Mountain. Under the tea trays and other picnic paraphernalia atop the load were the gunnysacks. They loaded them into the luggage compartment of my car, and we all were off. Before reaching the Spanish border, I stopped and attached my unauthorized CD plates, as usual. My chief worry was that the pins on the grenades, being rusty, would break and blow up the car, but they didn't. Five minutes after my departure Spanish soldiers arrived at our rendezvous and found no one there. Because Bob Murphy had forbidden us to kill Germans in Casablanca, Dave King's secretary and I took a few of the grenades to the harbor and threw them in. They were duds, and sank like rocks.

While all these other operations were going on, I still had my main job to do: to make contact with the Riffian leaders and arrange for an arms drop, which I would accompany in Riffian clothes that I carried to Gibraltar. This meant hiding under hedges, picking up bearded men disguised as veiled Arab women, and transporting them to secret meeting places, mostly Mrs. Bertram Thomas's house. I had to get them the money to buy bulls to sacrifice before the various tribal chiefs and councils, and to provide them with fluid funds for other expenses needed to raise their mehallas (units of one hundred men).

Getting the money was simple. I presented myself before the undistinguished door of a Jewish banker, which bore his name on a copper plate little larger than a calling card. Inside I faced a shabbily dressed clerk behind a grille. He led me into the inner quarters, to a huge, sumptuous room fitted with antique oak furniture. These were, I found out, the fittings of the wardroom of Admiral Nelson's *Victory*, given by the British government to one of the banker's ancestors, along with British citizenship, as a reward for having financed the battle of Trafalgar. After World War II, the banker moved to Switzerland.

Another problem was how to let the Riffians, especially the Urriaghlis, know that I was on deck and still meant business, without revealing myself to the Spanish. During the tense lull of late October, shortly before the landings, Gordon and I drove from Tangier to Melilla and back in order to deliver a message from Stripes to a British colleague in the latter city that he could leave only by sea.

It was a clear, crisp day. We bypassed Tetuan, still deep in its Spanish slumber, then climbed to the walls of Sheshawen, their masonry pockmarked from rebel gunfire, and on to the cedar forest of Ktama, where Mary and I had ridden on horseback in 1927. Here a Moroccan soldier stopped us in front of the Army post. "Are you going through Targuist?" he asked.

When we said yes, he brought out a large package of sealed envelopes and put them in Gordon's lap.

"Deliver these to the commandant at Targuist," he said and disappeared back into the building.

All the way to Targuist, Gordon wrestled with temptation. He looked at the package, turning it this way and that, but in the end judgment prevailed. When we arrived we presented the package to the soldier on duty at the commandant's office. He accepted it without comment and we drove on, over Abd el-Krim's old motor road to Ajdir, out onto the plain of Nekor, my supposed landing place, and across it to the western hills where the road serpentined into Beni Tuzin. This road was critical, because all depended on whether or not it would take tracked vehicles. It would, but perhaps not the biggest ones.

On across the rolling wheatland of Beni Said, we reached the arm of the desert that almost touches the Mediterranean and stopped at a market held by nomadic Riffians. From a beautiful blonde nomad girl I bought a flat basket in which a succession of family cats have curled themselves. Then on to Melilla, a part of metropolitan Spain, to visit our British colleague, then back again over the same road we went the next day, double-checking.

At Nador the tribal elders were gathered for the market, and we stopped to greet them. Some of them remembered me from when I had measured them fifteen years earlier, and my mission was completed.

About that time Uncle Tom provided our command with a piece of cheerful information. Catering at the Tangerina Hotel down the beach from his "cabin," he heard the Spanish plan an invasion of the French Zone to regain territory lost to them in the partition of Morocco, and he knew their D day. It fell later than ours. After our troops had landed, Spain called off its invasion.

Meanwhile someone leaked our own D day to the Vichy French. In our service we believed it to be a double agent whose phony name was Maurice Despax. Others have claimed we accused him unjustly. We called him Pinkeye. He was a small, lithe man, as quick as a mongoose, with albinotic blond hair and one pink eye and one blue one. Having no chance of disguising himself, he made himself more conspicuous by leading about with him a towering French wife and two miniature dachshunds on a leash. His cover lay in thus seeming eccentric as well as in a facile way of flattering everyone.

Pinkeye could glide into anyone's office and photograph the contents of a sheet of paper on a desk, upside down, from a distance of four or five feet, with one or both of his eyes, and remember its contents verbatim. He carried the tiniest automatic pistol I have ever seen, and I have no idea how many others were hidden on his body. He could hardly have gotten the date of D day in this way, because none of us whom he visited had it written down. If he got it he did so orally, from whom I have no idea. Whoever got it sold or leaked it to the Vichy French, who slaughtered many Americans wading ashore through the surf at Fedhala. The last I heard of Pinkeye placed him in jail in Italy, but that was thirty years ago.

Writing nearly half a century after the event, it occurs to me that Gibraltar may somehow have been involved. Dozens of Spanish subjects walked into the fortress to work and out again every day. The presence of two American generals there must have been noted, and Mark Clark's submarine trip to Algeria to rendezvous with Bob Murphy and return might have been noted there or in Algiers. Colonel Eddy's and my frequent trips across the strait in the British tug *Mascotte* might also have been reported to the German agents in Tangier by any little Arab shoeshine boy, at least one of whom was always on the dock.

Three or four days before D day I made my last trip to Gibraltar to relieve Colonel Eddy for running the message center connecting Tangier and points east with London; it was my job to decipher, encipher, coordinate, and relay the messages that were coming in at all hours from Tangier, Casablanca, Oran, and London. I did not sleep for three nights and went into a state of mental exaltation comparable to that of prophets receiving divine messages. One signal concerned the proposed paratrooper landings on the airfield at Oran. The question was, should I give the London operator the words for peace plan or those for war plan—meaning, should the paratroopers be prepared to land or jump? I thought I told London what I had received from Oran, and London told the paratroopers to land. As the subsequent events will relate, that message was wrong. Someone muffed it along the line. Was I that someone? I have never been told, but would like to know before I die.

The subsequent event was the climax of Gordon's trip to Oran, carrying with him a small black box with a telescoping antenna. This device was called Rebecca. Gordon spent his first night in the Palais Jamai in Fez, where he was Heil Hitlered by two Germans; he Heil Hitlered them back. With the help of our man in Oran, Gordon posted himself in a slight depression in a field outside the city near where the paratroopers were supposed to land if the peace plan were adopted, or where they would jump if the opposite.

The Vichy French troops appeared and some of them began shooting at Gordon, who killed several of them and kept Rebecca signaling until the planes came in sight. The planes landed, and the Vichy French engaged the paratroopers, who won after some losses. When I first saw Gordon after this battle, he told me that he bagged five Vichyites. Nowadays he is more modest, cocks his head, and says, "Maybe two."

Whatever the head count, for this deed of valor Gordon was awarded a richly deserved Silver Star.

Over in Gibraltar, when I was packing up to leave, Gordon's triumph was balanced by my own disappointment. Among my belongings I had packed a complete Riffian warrior's costume, which I had been prepared to wear when parachuted into the Suk el-Khemis of Nador in Beni Urriaghel. My Lawrence mission was off—either because Bob Murphy, who disapproved the use of natives, had won out over Bill Eddy, who championed it, or merely because the Germans had not yet even begun to enter Spain.

Back in Tangier, the Americans and British celebrated the landings from dusk to daylight, in the ways victorious warriors and their womenfolk have done since before the dawn of history.

Life suddenly grew dull after the landings. I drove back and forth to Casablanca, mainly, it seems to me in retrospect, to smuggle Famous Grouse Scotch, which I got from the British Sleeper in his cover shop, across the two borders for General George Patton, Jr. He was a very warmhearted and sensitive man, beloved by his men, but he hid his sensitivity under a shell of braggadocio and profanity.

One day while I was in his office he said: "Christ, Doc, I have a dirty job today. I've got to hang two niggers for raping an Arab girl on a bicycle. How the hell could they have raped her on a bicycle?"

I knew exactly how he felt about it, and I don't believe he would have said this to me if he hadn't known I knew.

During this letdown period I also had to go to Sheshawen (*Xauen* in Spanish spelling, a Berber word for chickens), a beautiful old city in the mountains back of Tetuan. It is almost entirely inhabited by Andalusian Moors, whose ancestors had left Spain involuntarily in A.D. 1492. I had measured some of them there in 1928.

I went because several of the paratroop planes headed for Oran had gotten off the beam and landed there, where the Spanish Army had interned them. Although treated well enough, with old-fashioned Andalusian courtesy, their size and equipment made the Spanish soldiers jealous, and they were badly needed elsewhere. There were two ways for me to spring them. One was by a clandestine operation through our holy man in Tangier, or by simple negotiation. I laid on the first, but a gentlemen's agreement with the Spanish command rendered it unnecessary. In obtaining this release I acted in my cover job, as special assistant to Mr. Childs.

Meanwhile Colonel Eddy had been transferred to Algiers, where he occupied the Villa Rose, a small but sumptuous residence in the lee of General Eisenhower's HQ, the St. George's Hotel. I lived in the Villa Rose too. We worked and ate at first in a small villa, the name of which I have forgotten, but soon moved to the Villa Magniol, which was almost palatial. Here Bill Eddy had a large staff, including my student L. Cabot Briggs of Boston as security officer, and Frank Schoonmaker, the well-known wine expert, as wine steward.

But I was not to enjoy this villa's delicate provender for long. Colonel Crawford of the British Army was running a training school at Cap Matifou across the harbor for the Corps Franc d'Afrique, a group of Gaullist or at least anti-Vichy volunteers of mixed origin: French royalists, colons, some Arabs, Jews, Spaniards, and others. They were young, enthusiastic, and eager to learn. My job was to teach them all sorts of paramilitary activities, including tossing hand grenades and tying up prisoners. I taught in French, and in Arabic when needed. Being a professional teacher who missed his audience, I enjoyed it thoroughly.

But I did not enjoy what befell me on a day when I was off duty. I drove to Algiers to visit my superior officer, finding him in such a state of gloom that I dared not leave him until the time came for me to return to Cap Matifou for dinner. His gloom involved his sacred honor. As I well knew, what had disturbed him would soon blow over. Only when I had convinced him of this did I dare leave him.

On my way back, so great had the strain on my nervous system been that I drove like a zombie. When I reached the gateway of the Presidential Palace I saw a crowd milling about, and paused to ask a splendidly uniformed Berber guard what had happened.

"Darlan is dead," he said. "Move on."

On my return Colonel Crawford quizzed me on the events of my day. I was still a zombie.

"Did you see or hear anything of importance?" asked the colonel.

"Not much," I answered, and finally my wits unscrambled and I added, "Oh yes, when I passed the Presidential Palace a goum told me that someone had killed Darlan."

My local popularity level now plummeted close to zero. Colonel Crawford rightly quizzed me to explain my reticence, but I said nothing and continued silent until a French captain of the Corps Franc d'Afrique burst in and declared that not only had Darlan been assassinated, but that the killer was one of my students, to my view a harmless titled young French aristocrat named Fernand de la Chapelle, who had shot the admiral with a pistol and been summarily executed. The pistol was a Colt Woodsman, like the one in my possession; but he could not have used mine, because I still had it.

Being obviously implicated by circumstantial evidence, Colonel Crawford sent me out at once in civilian clothes to drive eastward to join the British SOE contingent, which consisted mainly of remnants of the kilted Scottish commando that had raided the German heavy water plant in Norway. Their headquarters was at Guelma, on the Algero-Tunisian frontier. I set out in my ancient and somewhat decrepit Oldsmobile over the high plateaus, and soon reached snow. Plowing through this, I nearly ran out of gasoline, and stopped at an American post to refuel.

There I was ordered into the post by an American major with an Italian name who took a dim view of me. As I was unable to tell him my mission, he became very suspicious. I showed him my calling card, which identified me as a special assistant to the American minister to Morocco at Tangier, but it was not enough. He demanded my passport. It was special, not diplomatic. The major thumbed it over and looked me in the eye. "It expired yesterday," he said, and added, "I will have to put you in jail."

Thinking almost as fast as Pinkeye, I remembered in a flash that Hooker Doolittle, my brother Maurice's father-in-law and American consul general at Tunis, was living in exile in Constantine, on the coast, not far away. I told the major this, and while he was pondering this news, in walked his superior, Colonel Charles Saltzman, who quizzed me some more, found out that I was a Harvard professor on leave, and asked me my class. I told him it was 1925. He then asked me if I knew Mason Hammond, Harvard professor of Latin. I proved that I did and that I also knew his maternal uncle, who lived across the street from my parents in Wakefield, Massachusetts.

That did the trick. Colonel Saltzman sprang me. He became a general, is still alive, and has recently confirmed my account of our meeting.

Once sprung, I continued through the snow and night to Constantine, where I found Hooker in a cold room with his wife Vecka, two Basque maids, and two Pekingese dogs in attendance. Hooker renewed my passport, and must have communicated with Colonel Eddy, or his OSS vice-consul Springs did, because the next morning Springy drove me back to Algiers, where we found Bill Eddy completely recovered from what had bothered him.

Springs then drove Eddy and me back to Constantine, where I recovered my car, and we three entered Guelma together. It has taken me many years to realize why Bill Eddy snapped out of his condition and made this trip. In view of what happened later, the cure must have been to let him assert his authority; to keep me as his man, whom he could recall when he needed me; and to save me from dissolving into the ranks of the British SOE. Colonel Eddy left me at a requisitioned civilian house in Guelma, in which Colonel Anstruthers, who ran the show, lived, along with the house's French owner and the latter's wife.

From there I was passed on to a place called Jebel Halluf (Pig Mountain), our quarters. As I was still in civilian clothing there was some doubt about my rank, although I said I had none. Colonel Eddy had told the staff there that I too was a colonel, although I did not know it. Captain Hamish Torrance, master of the billet, vacated his bed and gave it to me, over my protest. When he finally was persuaded that I really was a civilian, he said that he could make me a captain, but could give me no rank higher than his own.

It was easy enough to find me British battle dress and trousers, for some of the Scots were of my size or bigger, but the insignia was a problem. There were no captain's pips around. So the Guelma house owner's wife cut six diamond-shaped pieces of green felt from the cover of her billiard table, and sewed them on my shoulder straps.

Next was a hat. I had an old gray felt fedora from the Harvard Coop, but that seemed inappropriate. All the helmets were too small for me. The only headpiece big enough was an officer's peaked cap bearing the insignia of the Royal Engineers. It had belonged to a Greek demolition officer who had tried to open a case of live shells with a hammer and another live shell, and blown himself up—case, shells, hat, and all. Luckily his hat had popped off his head intact. A spoon and a sponge removed the brains, and the hat was waiting for me—or so I was told. Later a real R. E. officer spotted it on my head and demanded that I give him the corps insignia on its band. To save an argument, this I did.

Although I could remember many details when I first put this chapter down on paper, the sequence of what happened to me after that is quite foggy in my mind, probably because some of the events in question happened before a roof tile fell on my head, and others later. Being allowed to keep no notes, I relied wholly on memory, in this case chronologically topsy-turvy. Only when I discovered my copy of my report to General Donovan dictated in Villa Rose, Algiers, dated February 23, 1943, and published as *A North Africa Story* in 1980, was I able to sort out the true sequence, if not the chronology.

A few days after my arrival and outfitting, Brigadier (later Major) General Gubbins, creator and head of the SOE—despite his surname, a Scot of the McBain clan of the Outer Hebrides—arrived in Guelma. He was very friendly and I was to see more of him in other places before the war was over. Gubbins took me with him to dine and spend a night at a shooting lodge in a cork forest full of wild boars. It was really a conference. Across the table from me sat a British admiral. Knowing me to be an American, he took the chance of asking me if I knew who one other American was whom he was thinking about, without stating sex or age. I happened to know that Evelyn Cole, a classmate of my wife Mary at Wellesley, had married a British admiral living at Alexandria, Egypt, her second husband.

It was too easy. I pretended to ponder a minute or two, then named her, much to the admiral's surprise and Colin Gubbins's amusement.

Two chairs down from me at the right sat Randolph Churchill, Sir Winston's son. He seemed to be running a private show of his own. He announced that he had a truck full of explosives parked out back, and planned to drive it to the German ammunition dump near Bizerte, to leave it with a time switch set and then lope away. In the early morning hours we were wakened by an explosion. A large hole gaped in the earth where Randolph's truck had been parked.

Before receiving a major assignment, my first job was to teach some Arabs to blow up railroad tracks, a form of academic instruction of which the French took an exceedingly dim view, for they were thinking of the postwar future. I managed to teach two men adequately, and to sew the needed explosives and other equipment into an

Arab packsaddle. Off they went with a load of grain, fruit, or something equally innocent, to the railroad track between Bizerte and Tunis. At a place where it ran over an embankment between two bodies of water, they set it, assuring the Germans of a salty bath. I was told that it worked, but received no official confirmation, and my Arabs had not returned before I left.

My next assignment was to join a small garrison guarding the lighthouse at Cap Serrat on the Mediterranean coast. We were the only Allied force between the sea and the Tabarka-Mateur road. We faced unknown numbers of Germans and Italians, and the Italians were more dangerous than the Germans because while the Germans fought only in the daytime and at predictable hours, the Italians were not only night raiders, but also a militia of Tunisian-born colons who were fighting for their own territory. They also carried percussion grenades, the size and shape of baseballs, that could kill from the shock of an explosion without even touching the victim.

I forget how many we were, and the number was not constant. At first we were three British and two American officers, and thirteen to fifteen men, mostly from the Corps Franc d'Afrique. We were of various ethnic origins but with uniform enthusiasm.

Oddly enough, the officers were mostly Cornishmen, Scots, or a combination of both. Among the latter was an Australian-born British Naval surgeon, Dr. Paul Chin, who had come ashore on a wrecked ship. Johnny Warren, the other American, had a Cornish mother. Later on we were joined by Captain Michael Gubbins, the general's son. He and I had been demolitions instructors together at Cap Matifou.

We lived in the lighthouse, which had ceased to flash its light; hence the wreck that brought the commandos, including Dr. Chin. When there was nothing else to do, I told my companions tales or answered questions within my range of academic competence. It was there that I stumbled on an idea that I could use later—that in any evolving society, quantity turns into quality at a certain level. A division of labor gives rise to guilds; craftsmen improve their products and make new inventions; and skills give rise to arts. I could think of many examples, from cave painters in the Pyrenees to the point where too much technology began to take over. I put this on my brain's back shelf for future use, should I come out alive.

If these sessions took place in the morning, by 10:55 A.M. we would change our positions away from the windows, because at 11:00 A.M. on the dot a German Messerschmitt flew past the lighthouse, dipping low, and machine-gunned the building. It was like catching the 7:58 train to Boston. But we had a Bren gun, and we made it fast on the

The author, temporarily in command at Cap Serrat, wearing a phoney British uniform, with phoney captain' pips from the green felt of a billiard table, and a Greek officer's Royal Engineer's cap which had been blown off with his head inside, at Pig Hill. With me were eight men, of whom six at least were members of the Corps Fran d'Afrique, and two more were Arabs, probably hostages.

lighthouse roof. One morning at 10:45 we stationed a young Frenchman from the Corps Franc d'Afrique who had volunteered to man it. On his first burst he knocked the Messerschmitt down, but the pilot escaped. A homeless Arab boy took the plastic blister to live in as his house, and I took the red aluminum sign that read *Notwürf für Bomben* off the instrument panel for another purpose.

We were, in effect, the guardians of the coast as far inland as the Mateur road. With fewer than twenty men we were all the Allied forces had to keep the Germans directly east of us from encircling our own contingents and establishments farther south, and we could not move in or out with vehicles by road.

We sent out night patrols. I led one of them. We were lying on our bellies at one edge of an open glade when we saw branches moving, apparently coming toward us, from the other edge. The temptation to fire was great, but if we were witnessing an optical illusion we would reveal our position and risk being wiped out anyhow. It took me a bit of whispering and pressing arms, but we held our fire, the branches stopped moving, and we went on. It was like old-fashioned Indian fighting, in the days of General Israel Putnam of the American Revolution and the French and Indian Wars.

My principal personal job was setting booby traps. Any foe that approached the lighthouse by night was likely to blow himself up, and I had to make my rounds like a trapper every morning to spring the traps and then to reset them again before nightfall. Remembering where they all were taxed my memory, and I acquired a phobia against taking my trousers down and defecating in the woods lest I hoist myself by one of my own petards.

The only person I know that I nicked was a friendly Arab on his way to visit us early in the morning. He tripped a wire under a cork-oak branch, releasing a hand grenade, a piece of which hit his head, but did not prevent him from walking to the lighthouse, where Dr. Paul Chin operated successfully without professional equipment. The Arab walked home unaided and I saw him several times later. He had been on the way to give me the latest news. He was one of the former prisoners of the French from whom we had taken over the lighthouse. We had freed these prisoners and treated them well, and I debriefed them regularly about enemy movements.

Later on a night patrol Johnny Warren was hit in the head by a piece of piano wire from the inside of an Italian percussion grenade. The wire went into his brain, and Dr. Chin took it out, God knows how.

We were not sure that Johnny would survive, so we radioed staff headquarters at Jebel Halluf. Soon an expedition of Scots headed by Colonel Jaimie Young arrived in a half-track, having decontaminated the road, and took Johnny away. The last I heard, around 1960, Johnny was still alive, in England.

With the road cleared we could move again on wheels. Once we captured three or four German prisoners and had to take them to some headquarters, the name of which I disremember. I was one of those charged with delivering them intact. On our way we came to a hamlet called Jebel Abiodh (White Mountain in Arabic, although I saw none there) on the east bank of a river, just before a wide steel bridge. The buildings at Jebel Abiodh had been constructed mostly of mud brick, with large red tiles on their roofs. Most of them had been knocked down by a tank battle a few days earlier.

Without warning a flight of Messerschmitts swooped down, machine-gunning us. Some of us hit the road flat, others darted into the ruined houses. I was one of the latter. Once the Messerschmitts had gone, a Stuka followed, dropping bombs at the bridge, but missing it. One bomb dug deep into the jellylike alluvial soil between the house I was in and the river.

The soil shook. A red roof tile fell from above the second floor and hit my head. I was dazed, but still conscious. My Harvard Coop fedora had broken the blow enough to keep the edge of the tile from cutting my scalp, but that edge had landed smack over my left parietal bone over Broca's speech center. I made it back to the lighthouse, but my memory began to fog out, and my night vision was minimal. I forgot words in English, but did better in French and Arabic, which I had learned later—a classic syndrome. I simply sweated it out.

It was not long after that that a signal came through from Colonel Anstruthers ordering me back for reassignment. There being no vehicle handy, I reached the road riding bareback on a mule, and then hitched rides to Jebel Halluf and thence to Guelma, where I reported to Colonel Anstruthers. By then my English had come back, and I said nothing about my mishap.

From the urgency of his signal, I had supposed that Colonel Eddy had asked for my withdrawal to handle some more purely American mission, but before Anstruthers could bring himself to mention what it was, Brigadier General Colin Gubbins appeared and took me with him to meet the American command at the Roman ruins of Thelepte, near Kassarine Pass, before the woeful battle in the latter place. Not understanding British insignia, the colonel in command mistook Gubbins for another colonel, and Gubbins introduced me as a colonel too. Because of my accent, the Americans asked me if I were a Canadian, and I said that I came from just over the border east of Calais, Maine. Gubbins could hardly contain his mirth, but burst out laughing when we left.

When the disaster of Kassarine fell, and thousands of untrained American recruits panicked in front of the tiger tanks, our outfit was out there with plastic grenades, Coon-Browne mule turds, and other equipment, to try to stop the tanks, the high-pitched singing of whose treads reminded me of that of the bronze tires of the heroes' chariots on the pebbly ground in the battle of Troy as sung in the *Iliad*.

We stayed on in this battle, shifting around and arguing about whether or not to stay behind the German lines, as noble sacrifices, until Lieutenant Colonel Jaimie Young came out and ordered us in, on the grounds that we were highly trained personnel and not just soldiers of the line. Jaimie Young was a noted bagpiper and Highland dancer, a large, handsome man whom everyone respected. He drove me back to Jebel Halluf in my car, although he had never driven on the right before. It was at night and during a blackout. I was supposed to give him directions, but I was somewhat blacked out myself. Somehow we got there.

The whole operation took nine days. After I had rested a bit I returned to Algiers, where I relaxed in Villa Rose and dictated to Colonel Eddy's British secretary, whom he had brought from Tangier, my report to him and General Donovan printed in the first part of *A North Africa Story*.

Colonel Anstruthers was supposed to tell me to come back, but it was Jaimie Young who sent me. Neither knew the reason why, but I soon did. I was to be transferred to General Mark Clark's command in Oujda, to help police the railroad track just below the Spanish border. Over this track moved the bulk of the military supplies headed for Tunisia. Between Taza and Oujda was the weakest stretch. In addition, Operation Lawrence might again be in order.

My service with the Fifth Army began on March 6, 1943, and ended on May 9. Gordon was also in it, until July, working out of Tangier. Another prime participant was André Bourgoin, the Vacuum Oil Co. agent in Casablanca who had helped in the exfiltration of the pilot Malverne, and was a captain in the Cinquième Bureau of the French army, their equivalent of the OSS. Incidentally, his son later married Gordon's daughter, as my brother wed Hooker Doolittle's.

After joining General Clark at Oujda, I was placed on the staff of Colonel Edwin Howard of G-2. First I went to Tangier and thence to Casablanca, where I joined Stripes, and we drove to Oujda together. There we conferred with General Clark, and as usual the Americans and British reached a perfect agreement as to who should do what in case such-and-such should happen.

Instead of narrating what happened during the rest of my Fifth Army tenure chronologically, I shall do it by subjects, because it will be the simpler way.

First comes my original mission, arousing the Riffians in case of a German invasion through Spain via the Bay of Alhucemas. General Clark wanted to know whether heavy tanks, which would have trouble moving eastward over the tight curves in the motor road through Beni Tuzin, could cross the Riffian mountains more easily via Targuist, Beni Amart, and Bu Red in the Gzennaya, over which Mary and I had ridden horseback in 1927. To find out I was driven to Bu Zineb by a lieutenant in a jeep. Bu Zineb is a French outpost and lookout station on a mesa at the edge of the Spanish Zone, in the northeast corner of the tribe of Gzennaya. We went there, were well received by the French officers, and could see for ourselves that heavy tanks could indeed pass over the open slope and thence down the military road to Taza.

The native-affairs man there had the courtesy to send a runner down the Vale of Iherrushen to tell Zarkan I was there, and he soon arrived, and we had a tearful meeting. On the way back I stopped at Si Moh's house along the motor road, and was greeted emotionally there also. He was then kaid of the Gzennaya, as Midboh used to be. He excused himself for hastening our departure, but the stream below his house that we had to ford would soon rise in flood, and we might be trapped there for a week.

General Clark's next idea was to fly over the border in his small private plane and then, circling the Thursday market of Nekor, address the assembled Urriaghlis below in Arabic, assuring them of America's continued interest in them. My job was to translate what he wanted to say into Arabic and coach him in it. I regretted that I couldn't do it in Riffian—if only I had brought Zarkan down with me. The general learned the speech and gave it.

As the small plane, circled low over the crowd, his voice boomed out the following: "I am General Clark. I have come to set you free."

The crowd waved. They knew that it was neither my landing signal nor a false alarm. They had had one of the latter on D day when a parachute plane had landed there, mistaking it for Oran. The Spaniards had gotten the Americans out quickly, because the comparison with their own troops was obvious and invidious.

The Lawrence job received its coup de grace when Hamid, a known German agent, admitted to one of our group that the rumor of a German invasion was being spread to keep us busy and to sap our manpower, which was needed in other fronts. When confirmed by our agents in Spain, we dropped the plan and concentrated on the other problem: guarding the railroad track from the mouths of the Moulouya River to the Algerian border.

The first thing we wanted to know was who were the German toy makers in Melilla and the Spanish Zone? (A toy maker is a bomb and booby-trap maker.) We found out that Kramer was the sleeper-toy maker in Melilla, joined from time to time by Karl Frick, alias Carlos Frique, who alternated between that fortress and Oviedo in Spain. The other was a Moslem convert, Abdallah Richter, in Alcazar Alquivir (Al-Ksar el Kebir) just above the bridge over the Loukkos River on the Franco-Spanish border. Richter was said to have had enough explosives in a building near the river to blow up the bridge. Bourgoin's fingers itched to get at them.

Our next objective was to find out whom the toy makers trained, supplied, and tried to send to the railroad track. This required the use of many agents. It also caused us much chagrin when Vichyite officials, including judges, let the ones we caught go, and also necessitated innumerable patrols by Bourgoin and myself along the French-Spanish border. The Riffians being natural smugglers, more Spanish brandy was smuggled than explosives. One saboteur got through and attached a device to the side of a rail, but when we found it, it was a simple amateur apparatus, not to be compared to the ones I had sent out in Tunisia.

It would be easy to elaborate on this phase of my service during the war, but it ended without being finished. I was called back to Algiers to be sent home to get a military commission, which would be needed so that I could serve in other theaters.

16. *More War,* *at Home and Abroad*

In Washington I was taken directly from the airport to General Donovan's office, where he was sitting up waiting for me, although it was at night. He debriefed me, asking me many pertinent questions.

The next day, when I was asked what branch of the service I wished to join, I opted for the Marines, but all they would give me was a captaincy and even that would take a long time. The Army would make me a major, and almost at once. The medical examiner made a little trouble over my having a short left leg, the result of a breech delivery; it might, he said, prevent me from marching smartly in parades. I told him that my duties would not include parading. I did not mention my egg allergy or the roof tile on my skull at Jebel Abiodh.

While waiting for my commission I was sent to a special school run by Harry Murray, a Harvard psychology professor. Its purpose was to test officers who had been in heavy combat situations to see what they would do under stress. We students all had false names, as in the demolition camp. Although no one was supposed to know who anyone else was, it did not take me long to recognize the tall, gaunt frame and face of James Harvey Gaul, another Harvard archaeologist who had been digging in the Balkans. Although we told no one that we knew each other, the mutual kidding we indulged in may have raised a few suspicions. Jim was dropped onto a baronial estate in rural Czechoslovakia, where he was almost immediately picked up by the SS. Instead of becoming meekly subservient, he gave them a bit of lip, and they shot him on the spot, to the deep grief of his British-born father, the organist at the Cathedral in Pittsburgh.

Among the various ordeals we had to undergo was the following. I was sent out to a brook where a "sergeant" and a "corporal" were sitting on some lumber, including a couple of barrels. I was supposed to direct them to bridge the brook, and they to appear lazy and to resist my orders by procrastination. Every time I told them to do something I received: "Oh now, Major, isn't it getting a little late?" or "We are tired," or "Can't we do it an easier way?"

Finally I lost my temper and said: "You do thus and so; that is an order!"

When they still delayed, I said, "If I had a gun I would shoot you."

They still did nothing, so I hit one of them with a two-by-four and rolled a barrel over the other one. These two men were professional psychologists. Other combat officers beat them up too, and the experiment had to be discontinued. In 1964 I met the "sergeant" in the corridor of a Moscow hotel, where we were going to different conferences. We recognized each other and had a hilarious laugh. If the corridor was bugged, I wonder what the Russians thought?

Albania was my next target. With Allied troops in the south of Italy, won with great sacrifice, the plan was to send an invading force across the Strait of Otranto, a mere forty-five miles at the narrowest point, then up the course of the Shkumbi River and on to Lake Ohrid on the Yugoslav border, then eastward to the Aegean, Black Sea, or both. This was a splendid idea, supposedly Winston Churchill's brain-child, but I will not deny that I too had thought of it many times, a good reason why it appealed to me. So had probably many other people.

The first part of my job was to go home to visit Mary and the boys, and then to Brockton, Massachusetts, and Boston, to recruit young and patriotic Albanians to send in ahead of the troops to collect and send back intelligence. I found Mary living in her grandmother's house in Wakefield, having given up our Sudbury home. She seemed thin and nervous, and the boys put on a brave front. I was wearing my new uniform, a handy topic of conversation.

I also located some Albanian volunteers, and arranged for them to be trained and sent to Bari.

The second part of my job was to go to Cairo to prepare for Albania in concert with the British. Our route was scenic—it would have cost a mint if hosted by a modern travel agency. In small propeller planes we flew to Bermuda; to a camp in the jungle outside Georgetown, British Guiana; to Belém and Recife in Brazil; to Ascension Island in the mid-Atlantic, where there was danger of submarines shooting us down; to Lagos in Nigeria; to an airfield outside an unidentified walled city; to Khartoum in the Sudan, where we came down in a torrential rainstorm; and up the Nile to Cairo. For an anthropologist, it was a fruitful journey, that for a few days took my mind off the war.

One of my principal collaborators in Cairo was Mrs. Hasluck, who had written widely about Albanian culture. She was a very vigorous Englishwoman—so vigorous that some of her less energetic male military associates referred to her as Fanny Freelove, a name I deemed inaccurate because she never tried to freelove me.

She was on cordial terms with the Bektashi monks, Albanian anchorites who lived in extensive quarries on the outskirts of Cairo. Being Sh'ia, they had photographs and printed pictures on their walls, and drank whatever they chose to. They had been brought there during the reign of Muhammad Ali, early in the nineteenth century, and had remained through the span of his dynasty, which terminated with Farouk, who lasted through World War II. Visiting the monks was a pleasant diversion from the then-hectic social life in Cairo.

Just before my time had drawn near for the parachute course at Haifa, I was rescued by Bill Eddy. I say "rescued" because although I was willing and mentally prepared to jump, at my age and in my unadvertised physical condition, it was not my favorite cup of tea.

Bill Eddy ordered me back to Algiers, and back I went. Now I was supposed to go into Albania by torpedo boat. After a day or two of comparative rest, Bill Eddy called me into his office, and there, in his shirt sleeves, sat Bill Donovan.

"Carl," asked the general, "how would you like to go to Corsica?"

"Well, Bill, I replied, "I thought I was supposed to go to Albania."

Those pale blue Irish eyes snapped, and Bill said, "That is for me to decide. I repeat, how would you like to go to Corsica?"

"Fine, I'd love to," I said, and I did.

Later I learned that Roosevelt had talked Churchill out of the invasion of Albania in favor of ANVIL, an invasion of southern France that would please de Gaulle but do us less good in the end. It was to take off from Algiers and had been leaked along the waterfront, because of which we somewhat vulgarly called its day of landing "Bidet."

The reason for our smaller invasion of Corsica, at more or less the same time, was that the Germans had a panzer division of heavy tanks on Sardinia and had to get these tanks up to Corsica, along that island's narrow east road to Bastia, and over to Leghorn via Elba before the Allies could cut them off at Leghorn.

To his infinite credit, Prince Serge Obolensky, who was ten years my senior, did not mind jumping, and he parachuted into Sardinia where he did a job recorded elsewhere. I was to go to Corsica by sea. A British mission took off by submarine and was landed at Calvi in the northwest. The men in this mission were few in number and not concerned with combat.

I was given one single night to round up my crew, which included an outstanding demolition officer, Elmer (Pinky) Harris, an American of Norwegian parentage; John Ffolke, a Corsican-American whose born name was Levie; and a whole OG (Operation Group) of tough American-Italians, most of whom were the sons of Abruzzi mountaineers settled along the Main Line outside Philadelphia. These were the first troops I ever commanded, and the best I can imagine.

After considerable delay we boarded a fast French cruiser in the harbor with our gear and were carried on the deck. The antiaircraft guns were manned by Breton crews. This comforted me because the Bretons are transplanted Cornishmen, who still speak my ancestors' language, and while on the watch for German planes they played small bagpipes. No planes appeared, and it was easy to fancy that Merlin's magic was holding Odin's hawk men at bay.

It was a sleepless night. When we docked at Ajaccio the next morning, it was clear that someone had broken security because a crowd awaited us with a brass band. I had been wrong about not having to march. That day I did, with the mayor, up to the hotel annex that was to be our headquarters. Children who had theoretically never seen American soldiers held out their hands and cried, "Gimme candy please, gimme chocolate." Other hands waved American flags.

Next on the agenda was transportation, for we had come without wheels. John Levie soon brought in a man whom I called Shirt, because he wore flamboyant ones. Faced with confiscation by the Italians and the Germans, the citizens of Ajaccio and neighboring places had dismembered their automobiles and trucks, hiding a wheel in one attic and a battery in a wine cellar, so that nobody else could assemble and confiscate a working vehicle. Shirt knew where all the parts and pieces were. He and his confederates assembled them for us, and our thousand-franc notes flew out of my coffer like rice at a wedding.

This arrangement was fine while it lasted. Before long General Henri Martin of the French Army came over, theoretically in full command of all of us. His men did not bother to bring or to buy vehicles, they simply pinched ours. Within a week or two we got a shipment of jeeps and other military vehicles that the French could not inconspicuously steal.

It was also due to General Martin that I was forbidden to use our explosive mule turds, which would have untracked tiger tanks rolling up the narrow coast road from the tip of Corsica facing Sardinia to Bastia. In my audience with him I used the word *merde*. He pretended he did not understand it and dismissed me haughtily. Had I used the explosive turds without asking him, he might not have known it.

We did not give up. Other means were found. John Levie had

already posted an agent in Bastia, a local schoolmaster who walked by nights through the mountains and maquis to pass on his messages, which we sent on to Algiers to tell our air force there when tanks were being loaded on ships for transport to Leghorn. American bombers, which we saw gliding between clouds, then knocked them down.

We fought in two battles of sorts before the Germans quit Corsica. One was north of Corte near Ponte Leccia, where the Germans were trying to break through the mountain spine of the island to cover their retreat. My men leapt in front of the tanks, hurling plastic grenades at them, and some of the hurlers were killed by their own grenades because they had rushed in too close. If we had only had batteries for our bazookas, some of these men might or might not have survived the war, but we had left in a terrible hurry. Pinkie and I had combed Ajaccio for suitable batteries, and the ones we asked for later did not arrive in time. For want of a nail, etc., but the battle was not lost.

The other battle was the troublesome business of the German 88-mm (3½ inches) long-barreled gun on the Col (Pass) de Tighime, blasting Saint Florent on the northwestern coast. This, too, was a holding station. Colonel de la Tour—later a general, and fittingly the last French governor general of Morocco—was there, with a tabor (drum) of anti-Atlas goums, from the tribe of Ait Atta, the last to submit to the French regime, and afterward their most loyal soldiers. The colonel's goums and my Italo-Americans cleaned out the defenders of the 88-mm post at night with knives.

Early in the morning the colonel and I rode up in my jeep to the Pass of Tighime, called by the Berbers Tizi n Tighime in their own language. Before we had been there long a flight of German jet fighters flew over us and then back again, firing. Their chief target was a mass of Italian soldiers who had already surrendered to the Allies and wanted only to help us fight the Germans. Some of them were wearing "Lily Daché" branches and leaves on their green helmets, and the German pilots took apparent delight in their overkill, mowing them down like sheep.

After the first flight of jets, Colonel de la Tour sat down on a conspicuous rock, with his red-topped kepi the most visible object on the landscape, lit a cigarette, and waved it at the Germans, who gave him a wide berth on their next pass. Having no such tradition of chivalry behind me, and no distinctive uniform, I lay down between my jeep and a bank of earth, and got shot at. All I got was a slight crease in the skin of my right thigh that didn't even draw blood.

When the jets had left, Colonel de la Tour asked me to drive him back to Saint Florent with a wounded goumi (singular of goum). The two sat together. The goumi may have been mortally wounded, but he showed no fear. "*Awud afus inek,*" meaning "Stretch out [or give me] your hand," the colonel said softly in the wounded man's own language. The goumi did, and the colonel held it until we reached Saint Florent.

There was no use in my hanging on in Corsica once the action had ended. The two Bills, Donovan and Eddy, had other plans for me, but they overestimated my physical condition, especially that of my nervous system. I was sent to Bari in Italy to send off some of my volunteers to Albania by night in boats, for that operation had more or less been reopened; I had to persuade the Pope in German-held Rome to desanctify a putative parachute landing field located on papal property; and I was also supposed to oversee the shipment of arms and other supplies to the Yugoslav partisans on the island of Vis, close to the Yugoslav coast.

In order to compete in rank with the British, who could raise their officers from captain to brigadier in one jump, I was made a lieutenant colonel, a rank I had to give back when I was sent out in a hospital plane.

General Gubbins came to my requisitioned apartment one day and broke down in tears, not because his son Michael had been killed in action in northern Italy, for the general could take that blow like a Highlander and soldier, but because a MacLean had been quickly promoted and given the job of dealing with Tito over his head.

As for me, I began to lose consciousness at noon every day, and was soon taken to a Canadian hospital where many of their men were suffering from jaundice. Gordon Browne came down from London to see me, and told me later that he had walked through pools of blood (not mine) while I was lying there unconscious. Gordon arranged for me to be flown to Tunis, where Springy's chauffeur met me. There I began to feel better. I was sent on to Algiers in a twin-motored bomber with a catwalk between the rear compartment and the pilot's cabin. Two youthful Air Force pilots, one of whom had been my student at Harvard, ordered me to come forward along the catwalk and opened the bomb bays while I was en route. In the cabin he seated me in his seat and left me to fly the plane, which I did for quite a distance until I persuaded him to come back and to land it at Maison Carré. This was a great joke. At least it improved my circulation.

From there I was driven to Oran in a jeep to board a naval hospital ship. There were three of us—the driver, a civilian in uniform, and myself. We stopped at a place called Relizane to get a little food. When we sat down in a booth in a bar some of the locals cried out that we were dirty Americans and should be sold no bread. A French sergeant with a woolen scarf around his neck protested the protests, saying, "They are our allies and you must let them have bread."

While so stating, the sergeant, who had been holding a baby, set it down on the edge of the zinc bar. The chief protestor, a shaggy, redheaded, thin-nosed man, grabbed the baby and dashed it to the floor. As the sergeant looked on in horror the redhead grabbed his scarf and twisted it until the sergeant's eyes began to bulge. No one else seemed to have noticed these events. I stood up, crawled out of our booth, smacked the redhead with a karate shot on the back of his neck, and seized his jugular veins between the thumb and forefinger of my left hand, then threw him against a wall, which his head hit with a crunch. The civilian with me got me out of there fast, and once in Oran we tarried little before I boarded the ship, convinced that I was growing stronger, if not wiser.

Bill Donovan did not want me to go to Walter Reed, because once there I might be given a medical discharge and be no longer available. Instead I went home to Wakefield and was taken to a Boston hospital for a brain operation by Dr. Gilbert Horrox, unofficially and at my mother's expense. Dr. Horrox drilled a hole through each of my parietal bones, drained off my cerebrospinal fluid, took X rays, found adhesions, and blew compressed air in; at least that is what I believe he did.

While Dr. Horrox operated, I was having a delightful conversation with Dr. William Seagraves, the Burma surgeon, who was watching my reactions closely. He told me about the Naga tribes he had lived with, and among whom my brother Maurice was then stationed. The time passed so rapidly that I felt let down when the operation was over. But the cure did not stick. As I have discovered rather recently, what Dr. Horrox was looking for was a tumor of the brain, and he found none.

Despite my elegant surgery, I still had spasms and spells. Dr. Horrox operated again, this time by cutting some of nerves on the back of my neck. This helped, but also not permanently. I returned to Washington with a cap of plaster of paris on my head, and was lying in my bed when the telephone rang. It was a lawyer in Newton, Massachusetts, telling me that my wife was suing for a divorce.

From that moment on the war unwound, as far as I was concerned. General MacArthur, who had heard of me as a rouser of rebel Moslem tribes, demanded that I be released to him to be dropped among the Moros. He and Donovan had been great rivals in the First World War, and three stars stood between them. But Bill kept me out of it.

He gave me easy jobs to do, like training frogmen on Catalina

Island how to limpet Chinese junks, lecturing in the congressional golf club on various subjects, and finally joining a staff of about twenty civilians in writing the history of the OSS, to be printed in a limited edition to be shown to the congressional committee from whom he had to beg for funds. He even sent me on a short trip back to North Africa to collect data, but few of the old-timers were still there. It was sad and almost fruitless.The history was never finished or published, despite the fact that the historian Crane Brinton of Harvard and Geoffrey Hellman and Saul Steinberg of *The New Yorker* were working on it.

Before this project ended, I collapsed again and was sent to Walter Reed Hospital, where I was given a medical discharge: "Psychoneurosis, anxiety, and hysteria, severe." Unable ever to earn a living. No pension because when hit on the head I had been a civilian.

Shortly after this condemnation to limbo, I received a summons from Cambridge. Paul Buck, the provost of Harvard, running the show during President Conant's leave of absence, told me: "Harvard needs you more than the government does. Please return promptly for the spring term."

Return I did, with a new wife—Lisa Dougherty, the daughter of Paul Dougherty, a well-known marine and landscape painter. Vivian Katz, wife of Milton Katz, also of the OSS, U.S. ambassador to NATO, and later head of the School of International Law at Harvard, served as matchmaker, unknown to either of us. We met at a party at Frederick Wulsin's apartment. I had known him first as a fellow anthropology tutor at Harvard, as an explorer in the Mongolian desert and Africa, and also as an archaeologist in Iran and in Chad—to the latter dig he had taken Milton with him. I mention him here because Lisa worked as a cartographer in his outfit—the Arctic, Desert, and Tropics branch of the Quartermaster Corps—and also because after the war my son Carl Jr. married Freddy's daughter Janet, who gave us six grandchildren.* One meeting between Lisa and me was enough. Lisa obtained a reluctant release from the Army.

We were married quickly and informally by a Lutheran minister (Lisa's deceased mother had been Swedish). Just before the ceremony Whitney Shepardson, General Donovan's chief of staff, debriefed me at the airport because, as Whitney said, we could be spotted there but not overheard or bugged over the whir of propellers.

In a letter to me from his Wall Street office dated August 10,

---

*To keep our text as simple as possible I save for a footnote the news that Freddy's last wife was Gordon Browne's older sister.

1960, Whitney wrote: "Please give my best wishes to your wife. It was a race by the stopwatch to get you back from the airport in time, but we (you) made it:

CC: "What time is it? I haven't got a watch with me."

WHS: "Twenty-five minutes past two."

CC: "That's all right."

WHD: "Have you an engagement?"

CC: "Yes, I'm to be married at three o'clock."

Thanks to Whitney and his watch, I not only made it, but even stopped at a florist's to pick up an order of roses.

The spring term found me back at Harvard, teaching Anthropology 1. A little later I was given a Legion of Merit, and my uniforms went into mothballs, including the British battle dress with the billiard-table pips on each shoulder. I still wear my officer's trousers, both pinks and greens, because they were made of better cloth than can be bought today.

17. Back to the Cave

Lisa and I bought a three-storied Victorian house at about one twentieth of its present asking price. It stood close to the highest point of land in Cambridge, Gallows Hill, at 92 Washington Avenue, just three houses away from the Crazy House on Upland Avenue, the one-time abode of Limnibhy, Pat Putnam, Chimpo, and Gordon Bowles and his owl.

Anthropology 1, which I was supposed to teach, was attended by a small clutch of conscientious objectors and minority students whose allegiance was more to other lands than to the United States. In the spring of 1947, when the G.I.'s were coming home and going to Harvard on their bill of rights, the quality of my audience improved sharply. Lisa and I were also busy helping Hugh O'Neill Hencken, an Iron Age archaeologist, plan a summer expedition back to the High Cave, where there wasn't any Iron Age except for a few Phoenician tombs, and Roman material directly overlaid the Mesolithic.

During the war I could not visit the cave because the Spanish government had declared Ras Ashagar out of bounds. Yet they did not stop Big Absalem, who lived within sight of the promontory, from knowing everything that was going on and reporting it, most of the time, to one of our agents in the city. We did not want him to be seen too often going in and out of the consulate or the hotel in which we lived. Only in the case of a tight emergency did he come to us in person.

He told us that the Spanish soldiers had set up antiaircraft guns directly over some of the caves, which might cause rockfall from the cave roofs when the guns were fired, and that the Spaniards had also converted the High Cave into a mule stable, which was not propitious for our stratigraphy. His prize report, however, was that a fuel depot had been set up in the large, tide-washed cave below, to refuel German submarines bound through the Strait of Gibraltar. As soon as we got one of these reports, we relayed it to Gibraltar, and a number of submarines were sunk as a result of Big Absalem's diligence. For this he was rewarded by the American government with an official commendation, of which he was, and may still be, enormously proud.

Despite Big Absalem's gloomy reports, Dr. Hugh O'Neill Hencken, the director of prehistoric studies of the American School of Prehistoric Research, based in the Peabody Museum (and Thalassa Cruso's husband), decided to take an expedition to Tangier in the summer of 1947 to salvage as much as possible of the contents of the High Cave and to dig elsewhere in the neighborhood as needed. He took along Dr. Bruce Howe of the Peabody; Dr. Charles Stearns of the geology department of Tufts, a former student of Kirk Bryan's and later dean of Tufts; two graduate students, William Schorger and Charlene Kraft; as well as four Coons: Lisa, Carl Jr., Charles, and me. This was quite a large party for El Farhar, and caused the Buckinghams, Tayeb the cook, and everyone else there a lot of work. But Ellen Buckingham, our hostess, was always happy and gay, ready for all emergencies.

One day when we were all seated at table, Tayeb was having some trouble with his cutlets. He beckoned to the proprietress, and she went into the kitchen to find water dripping through the ceiling onto Tayeb's hot stove.

"Oh, dear, the bathroom must be leaking," said Ellen, and she dashed up the stairs. Pinned to the bathroom door was a neatly written sign, *Je jure que je suis innocente* (I swear that I am innocent).

Ellen walked in and found a plump, blonde, Tangierian Jewish lady lying naked in the bathtub, like some bath salts advertisement, except that she was not smiling and was apparently unconscious. Ellen, although not a large woman, is very strong. She hauled the would-be suicide out of the tub, shut off the water and pulled the plug for Tayeb's sake, slapped the woman a little until she opened her eyes, dried her, and helped her dress. She then led her by the hand down to the dinner room and seated her between the Buckinghams' early-teenaged twin daughters, at the same table with us Coons. The cutlets finally appeared. Lisa and the twins chatted nonchalantly with the Lady Godiva of the Bathtub. We never found out what she was innocent of, and no one at El Farhar cared.

Bill Schorger was not an archaeologist but a social anthropologist, and still is, besides being chairman of the department of anthropology at the University of Michigan. He was fascinated by the gnomes of Mediouna and their quern-making activities. Bill made them his special study, and later on built a house there and lived with them. In June 1972 I received a postcard from him in Tangier. He was back again at Mediouna to see what changes had been made since his last trip. Thus he has a time span of a quarter of a century to work with.

It may have been through his agency, or vice versa, that we recruited one of the Mediouna stonecutters, a blue-eyed, merry-faced, gray-haired man whom we immediately dubbed Mr. Stone. As soon as he knew what it meant, he liked that name. It was prestigious, like Mistadoolit, Mistacoon, and Mistahencken. As the other workers also called him Mistastone, I cannot remember his real name.

Stone was a wizard with a pick, teasing bones out of breccia and breaking nothing. It was he who recovered the twenty-five-centime piece that I had left in 1939 in payment to the jinn, who had not even bothered to come back and get it. Lisa keeps it in her purse, along with my World War II dog tag. Once Mistastone had found the coin, he dug down a little farther in the breccia and opened up an ancient hole in the roof of the lower cave, where he could see some of his villagemates pecking out millstones. He put his head down to the hole and called out to them; they dropped their picks in astonishment, and were soon laughing. As far as I know, this was the greatest joke in the cave since my expulsion of the jinn eight years previously.

As I had expected from Big Absalem's report during the war, the Spanish soldiers had spoiled our 1939 face in an attempt to level off the floor of the cave for their mules. Although some artifacts and bones remained, they were scrambled. Nevertheless, the soldiers had not cleaned the cave walls, and enough material still adhered to them to allow Charlie Stearns to obtain soil and crust samples for a geological study. Lisa usually sat in the cave with him over a drafting board, for she had graduated from the School of Landscape Architecture at Smith College, and had worked on cartography in the Quartermaster's Corps during the war.

Hugh Hencken's special concern was the Horse Caves (Mugharet el-Khail) in the Wed el-Khail, a dry stream just north of the headland near which Hooker Doolittle had had a summer house. Part of the time Bruce Howe worked on artifacts on some portable tables set out in a patio behind the kitchen in El Farhar; part of the time he joined Charlie Stearns in the cave, and the two of them went down the beach a kilometer or so to the tomb of Sidi Qasem, a local saint. Near it they found Mesolithic implements in shell middens. So there had been Mouillians—Mesolithic people—within a short walk of the High Cave— why they didn't occupy the big cave, I do not know.

Digging near the saint's tomb was apparently all right as long as the tomb itself wasn't desecrated. But once a year any Christian that went near there would have risked death. This was during the feast of Sidi Qasem, almost as violent as the head chopping of the Hamadcha in Marrakesh, from whose axes Tom Scudder had rescued me in 1925. It was a real Dionysian rite. Several hundred devotees attended, smoked kif, beat drums, played flutes, chanted, and danced themselves into a *hal,* a trancelike state caused mainly by hyperventilation. Some professors who are forced to lecture to classes of five hundred or so students without amplifiers get into a hal and tell their students things that they would not dream of mentioning to a class of thirty. In ancient

Greek depictions of Dionysian rites we see men, or satyrs, prancing around holding up forequarters and other anatomical portions of sheep. At Sidi Qasem they did more. They sheared several sheep closely, threw them up in the air, caught them on their massed heads, and bit them, before they butchered them.

Despite the danger if caught, Bill Schorger attended one session of this festival. Bill is tall, lean, and dark. He was the only one in our group who could pass for an Arab, and he could easily. Big Absalem made sure that he was properly dressed and briefed, and took him along. No one paid much attention to him, and he observed everything carefully. If he had started to get into trouble, Big Absalem was keeping a close eye on him and would have tried to get him out if needed—incidentally at the risk of his own life—but Bill was not detected. After a while the two of them nonchalantly strolled away. Naturally Bill did not tell any of us about this until afterward.

My own assignment was rather dull. It was to excavate a narrow ledge known as the Summer Cave (Mugharet es-Saifiya). Its contents were entirely Neolithic. The cave lay right next to another smaller one known as the Grotte des Idoles, excavated in pre-Nahon-Doolittle times by a pair of Franciscan monks, who seemed perfectly harmless to the locals because not only were they holy men, but also the Franciscan garb is also identical to a brown jellaba. Their cave was called the Grotte des Idoles because they were alleged to have found some Neolithic phallic symbols in it. Apparently this did not please their superiors, so there has been a lot of secrecy and rumor about this shocking discovery ever since. Personally I thought that it was very funny, for they had published some grooved celts, like American Indian stone tomahawks, the only ones—as far as I know—in North Africa.

It was easy to fancy the sex-starved minds of two monks thinking the grooved celts were phallic symbols—some people have seen phallic symbols in many objects that look much less like the real thing. But I have just recently learned from a graduate student at Harvard who had been on the spot and had perused the literature more carefully than I had that the monks really did find some phallic symbols, not of stone, but of clay, but their superiors would not let them publish these, only the grooved celts.

While I was on the Summer Cave project we were visited by the late journalist Robert Ruark and his wife. He wrote about the dig in his column, which was then almost as widely circulated as "Dear Abby" is today. He depicted Lisa sitting in the cave excavating while I sat outside, and she allegedly said to me: "Goody, goody, gumdrop, Pappy, I think I've found a bone."

Not only was the episode a complete fabrication, but Lisa could not conceivably have said "goody, goody gumdrop." When Lisa saw a clipping of this, she was as furious as I have ever seen her—and I didn't care much for it either. Unfortunately, Mr. Stone had improved the path to the cave, or Mr. Ruark might have broken his neck. Journalists should not be allowed on digs until after they have been dug.

Toward the end, Carl Jr. found a perfect Acheulean cleaver sticking out of a road cut a few hundred yards from the turnaround on the road to Jbila. Weathering had completely transformed it from flint to chalk. This find interested Hugh Hencken very much, and he dug a trench at right angles to the find, but discovered no more Lower Paleolithic artifacts.

Shortly afterward Little Absalem invited us to his house for dinner. This meant sitting around on the floor and drinking cups of sugary mint tea while the food was being prepared, which might well take over an hour. My two sons were bored, as most of the conversation was in Arabic and did not interest them anyhow, so they did something I have never seen done before or since. I should have written "heard" instead of "seen" because there was nothing in it to see. They actually played a complete game of chess in their heads, saying: "I move the white queen's pawn to such and such a square," and so on. Before the food was on, one of them had checkmated the other.

One day we had a pleasant visit from an old friend. It was Colonel Sanchez Perez, the commander at Tétouan. He had been Captain Sanchez Perez in 1926, in charge of the dangerous post of Beni Amart in the Rif. We had a fine time reminiscing about those already ancient days, and he was just as pleasant and friendly as ever. It was a wonderful reunion.

Shortly before our field trip was over, everyone in our party was away somewhere one weekend, except for Charlie Stearns and the four Coons. I believe that most of the others had gone down the coast a way to look for new sites. And that had to be the weekend when we had trouble with George Martin.

I had known George during World War II. He was a Swedish clockmaker and watch repairer who had run a shop in the main business block of Tangier. I had bought watches from him myself, and I knew one thing about him that he may not have been aware I knew: He was alleged to be the man who had made the clockwork timing device that had blown up the British pouches from Gibraltar on the Tangier dock, killing several Englishmen and more Arabs. He was of middle stature, solid as a barrel, and had one wooden leg—the left one, as I remember. He was a very serious man with no fun in him, and spoke English with a strong Swedish accent.

Some time between the end of the war and our arrival, Win Buckingham had given George permission to set up a bar on one edge of the famous terrace at El Farhar. George himself inhabited a small addition to the main building, just below and slightly to the rear of our second-floor room. In that small room George not only slept, but he stored his liquor for safekeeping, at the same time enabling himself to take a nip without getting out of bed, a hard thing for a man with a wooden leg to do.

The bartender was named Absalem, along with Mohammed the commonest name in Tangier. He was a very good bartender, but he sometimes made mistakes when faced with unfamiliar situations. That Sunday afternoon was one of those occasions.

Now the worst thing that could happen in George's oft-stated opinion was for children to come into the bar and order soft drinks. That, he said, was not only unprofitable in itself, but it also drove hard-drinking customers away, for they were ashamed to be seen with children sucking pop through straws.

Lisa and I were sitting in there when in hopped the two youngest Buckingham girls. They plopped themselves down and said in turn, "Absalem, I want a lemon squash," in healthy, piping, schoolgirl voices, except that the second one added, "As well."

George, who was already quite drunk, became furious and ordered the girls out of there. They ran to fetch their father. Meanwhile Absalem had just made George his nth martini, and I slipped Absalem a couple of phenobarbital pills to put into George's drink. As George was still distracted by the episode of the girls, there was time for Absalem to have crushed the pills first, but he did not know that, and simply popped them in. They did not dissolve, and when George saw two white pills in the bottom of his glass, he went berserk. He blamed me, and quite rightly, but I escaped his vengeance momentarily by the quick arrival of Win Buckingham, who was pretty angry himself, for he had already put up with a lot of nonsense from George.

Win, then still in his prime, was a good six feet four and a lean 190 pounds. George was six inches shorter and would have weighed well over 200 had he had both his legs. Win picked George up like a thrashing baby and threw him in his room, slamming the door behind him. But it did not take George long to regain his footing, and out he dashed again. Win put him back in again and pinned him to the floor, but he couldn't keep George's wooden leg from waving in the air.

Guests were moiling about and calling for the firemen: "*Les*

198 / Back to the Cave

pompiers, les pompiers!" for the police were not considered worth calling at
that time. But it was Sunday and the firemen were off duty. Anything in
Tangier that could burn would have burned to the ground.

Win was getting exhausted, for he had expended much strenu-
ous energy, and he was older than I. Ellen was standing in the doorway,
crying, "Winkie, come out, he will kill you." There was an element of
truth in what she said, because George had a pistol on his desk, just out
of reach of his right hand. He must not be allowed to stand up again.

So I replaced Win, pinning George to the ground and trying to
avoid his powerful hands, while Charlie Stearns rode his wooden leg
like, to use his own words, "a small boat in a high sea." Actually
Charlie, though game as a fighting cock, was doing no good, and I
asked him to leave me alone with the monster. He left, and Lisa and
Ellen watched the following scene anxiously.

Noticing that the floor was bare concrete, and that George was
bald, I grabbed his nose with my left hand and kept lifting his head and
banging it on the floor until he was quite groggy. Then he tried to stand
up and I hit him over the head with his own chair as hard as I could,
felling him—at least long enough for me to grab his gun and make an
exit.

Upstairs, my sons had taken a number of specimens out of
their canvas bags. They were lumps of breccia from the cave, each one
surrounding an animal bone. No one had had time to clean them yet.
My boys lined them up on the windowsill in the right position to drop
them on George should he come out again.

George remained holed up until Wednesday afternoon. I was
sitting on the terrace with a priest. George was dressed completely in
black, from homburg hat to polished toe, and he wore dark glasses. He
held out his right hand, saying: "I am sorry, Professor, I apologize. I
did not know vat I was doink."

But he certainly knew vat he vas doink now. He held out his
massive right hand, and I gambled with myself whether or not the
baraka of the holy man beside me would save me, for unless I could
kick George's left leg out at once, he would have me. Taking a chance, I
shook George's hand, which was surprisingly limp, and forgave him for
what had happened on Sunday, but not for what had happened six
years earlier. That handshake ended my last battle of the war.

George was still there when we left Tangier, but I doubt if he
stayed much longer. Clocks are clocks, and some are needed almost
everywhere.

Shortly after the season's work had ended, I paid a last visit to the caves with my family and Big Absalem. Assuming an air of con-spiratorial secrecy, and looking around to see if he were being observed, Big Absalem led us to a certain place not far away, where he dug a bit of soil that covered an opening. "Look in there," he said. I did. It was a huge cave, lighted somehow from the other side. It was loaded with pay dirt like a bitch full of pups. A few slabs of limestone had fallen in from the roof as a result of antiaircraft fire, but they could be broken up and removed.

"Why didn't you show me this before?" I asked.

Big Absalem looked both sly and embarrassed at the same time, which is quite a feat, particularly for a man with buck teeth. Glancing about in all directions, he bent his mouth close to my ear, and said, in a lowered voice: "I am saving it for you, for your next trip."

P.S. Gordon attended Winthrop Buckingham's funeral in Tangier on July 22, 1975. Mr. Buckingham was buried near Hooker Doolittle's grave.

18. Good-bye to Harvard

This chapter begins where the previous one did, but it covers other subjects and ends a year later. When I began teaching Anthropology 1 again, I also began writing a new book in the Chapple-Coon manner. (Eliot had left his office and had opened one in Boston, where he was serving as a consultant to industry as to whom to hire or not to hire in terms of their performance on his interaction chronograph.) This book was called *A Reader in General Anthropology,* also to be published by Henry Holt & Co. in New York. I did not do this behind Eliot's back. He knew full well what I was up to. There was room for both *The Principles* and *The Reader* in the postwar college boom.

I avoided the word *culture* in the title because Eliot said it was incapable of definition. Be that as it may, I edited synopses of twenty societies, or ways of life, in 561 two-column pages, starting with the gibbons—the apes which, while anatomically least related to man, behave the most like us—and ending with Imperial Rome, described by Edward Gibbon.

These twenty ways of life were divided into seven levels of complexity: Level Zero, Subhuman Society; Level One, Simple Family Bands; Level Two, The Band Contains Several Families; Level Three, The Rise of Specialists and Multiple Institutions; Level Four, The Numbers of Institutions per Individual Increases, and Hierarchies Begin; Level Five, Hierarchies and Compound Institutions; Level Six, One Complex Political Institution.

After these twenty societies in seven levels of complexity I placed an appendix of fifty-one pages, in which I explained, in simple language, everything I had been writing about. The information is just as true today as it was when it was first printed.

When the book appeared it met the competition of rival texts as well as the *Statement on Human Rights* of the executive board of the American Anthropological Association sent to the Commission of Rights of the United Nations. Principle Two of that communication states: "Respect for differences between cultures is validated by the scientific fact that no technique of qualitatively evaluating cultures has been discovered."

This statement is a logical fallacy. It is like saying that before it had been proven that the earth is a globe it had to have been flat. By assigning cultures to levels of comparative complexity I had by inference compared them in quality in the sense that quantity makes quality when a guild of craftsmen arises in a city. As stated in Chapter 15, this idea had first come to me in the lighthouse at Cap Serrat. So neither the United Nations nor the executive board of AAA could scare me out of it. Nor did they frighten Mrs. Martha Dick, a bright young woman from Colorado who helped me edit the texts of the twenty societies into reasonable lengths.

For 624 pages of the book Holt charged a mere five dollars, and it was reviewed in many newspapers as well as in academic periodicals. The *Herald Tribune,* San Francisco *Chronicle,* and Oklahoma City *Oklahoman* showed a wider range of public interest than most textbooks receive today.

During the much too busy period between my return to Harvard and my leaving it I wrote another book—*Races, A Study of the Problems of Race Formation in Man,* by myself Ph.D., Stanley M. Garn, Ph.D., and Joseph B. Birdsell, Ph.D., and published by Charles C. Thomas of Springfield, Illinois, as a monograph in the American Lectures in Physical Anthropology, edited by T. D. Stewart, Adolph A. Schultz, and W. W. Howells.

Stanley Garn was an ex-tutee of mine who had studied teeth during the war and was, at the time in question, a candidate for a Ph.D. in anthropology, which he got in 1948. Birdsell was another Harvard Ph.D. then teaching in Los Angeles, and an expert on Australian aborigines. His contribution was to let us use some of his ideas and photographs. Stanley begged me to put Joe on the masthead because multiple authorship looked prestigious. Stanley also worked hard on this book, and had a slightly moderating influence on my natural exuberance. Instead of stating what we knew, he specified what we had to learn in the future, more like a clinician than an anthropologist.

We encapsulated the subjects of the meaning of race; genetics; mutation and selection; human breeding habits; social selection; isolation and incorporation; class and race; environmental influences on the sizes and shapes of peoples' bodies; geology; minerals; and meat diets; adaptations to altitude, damp heat, dry heat, extreme cold; skin color and ultraviolet penetration; eye color and intensity of light; but we missed the discoveries I have made in the late 1970s on skin and eye color, physiology, and behavior, which I shall discuss when I come to them chronologically.

We then pursued the distributions of different major races

through time and space, and their special adaptations to heat and cold, followed by a brief and cautious ramble in the field of human evolution. A chapter on disease selection comes next, and we wound up with a list and photographs of some thirty geographical "races," as of the present, with little reference to their basic relationships.

This book was a compromise between what Stanley and I each wanted, but it must have filled a need because it soon fell out of print. I suggest that most teachers of general anthropology courses who gave a few lectures on race out of old textbooks had firmly believed that the dimensions and surface features of all races were immutable. *Races* awakened them to a new idea. Professional reviews were not unbounded in enthusiasm. Marshall Newman, a Harvard Ph.D. and son of a famous biologist at the University of Chicago, politely informed us that all we had discovered about people had long been known about other animals. We had rediscovered the Rules of Allen, Bergmann, and Rensch. If I had had a tail it would have been between my legs.

Races was soon sold out. Mr. Thomas, the publisher, called me and invited me to breakfast with him in New York City. I declined. He then demanded that I write a second edition. Apparently he had printed it from hand-set type, and pied it, or so I guessed. He then turned to Stanley, who produced *Readings on Race* in 1960, *Human Races* in 1961, and a second edition of the same in 1965, three years after the appearance of my *The Origin of Races* (Knopf, 1962). Stanley was also given the honor of being invited to write the article "Races, Human," in the latest edition of the *Encyclopaedia Brittanica,* while I was given the same job under the cryptic title "Populations, Human." My assignment was made over the telephone by a junior editor, and apparently only discovered by the editor in chief after it was too late. At a huge luncheon in a Boston hotel after the encyclopedia's publication, to which all the New England contributors had been invited, I tried to speak to both the editors involved, but both ignored me—the higher one by turning waxen and not speaking to me, the lower one by hushing me and shooing me away. Such are the wages of truth, under whose crimson seal—VERITAS—dear Harvard was founded, and I was reared.

But let us return from that thirty-year leap forward to 1947, when we came back from the cave, and I had to face Anthropology 1 again. The soldiers were there. Harvard and Radcliffe students were combined. At first the class was held in the Geographical Institute, a legacy from Alexander Hamilton Rice. The auditorium was modern and acoustically perfect. It was also equipped with a microphone and amplifiers. The students numbered nearly five hundred, far too big a class for comfort. I could not remember anyone's face, let alone his or her name. This made paired interaction, so necessary for proper teaching, virtually impossible.

One morning when I was lecturing there a secretary from the anthropology department came in and interrupted my lecture, an unpardonable deed. Paul Buck had just phoned her. I must take my class out of there at once because Hamilton Rice's will forbade the presence of Radcliffe girls. I told her to inform Paul Buck that as the provision had already been violated I would finish my lecture, come hell or high water, and then would find another hall for the next one. The students heard this and responded with loud cheers.

After that we had to be crowded into the main hall of the Semitic Museum across the street from the Peabody. The former building was periodically bombed by the Weathermen about 1966, but in 1948 the students weren't even throwing spitballs. There the acoustics were abominable, as I knew from long experience, and I had to shout at the top of my lungs, with the result that I became hyperventilated before the class was over, grew dizzy, and began to pass out, whereupon my assistants drove me home.

I went to the Massachusetts General Hospital to consult Dr. Stanley Cobb, the rightly recognized crown prince of psychoneurologists, who told me that I should hold a paper cone over my nose in order to reinhale my exhaled breath to prevent too much loss of carbon dioxide. He added that being a drone at Harvard was not the proper life for a man of my constitution and experience, that I should live out-of-doors. I agreed to leave at the first feasible moment.

In fact, I was utterly bored, particularly at faculty meetings, where I did two things: drew caricatures of the others, and sat next to Marshall Stone to keep him from assaulting Mr. Conant or Mr. Buck, for he worked himself up, on those occasions, to a white heat. He quit Harvard a year before I did. As for the caricatures, I gave them all to the poet Ted Spencer, and after he died I do not know what became of them.

Being past forty when Dr. Cobb gave me his wise opinion, I dreaded the idea of spending a quarter of a century more being a character actor like Hooton or Friskie Merriman, the History 1 star, or even Copey. The future seemed pretty bleak.

Hooton didn't like it much either, although his wisecracks were appearing regularly in *Time* magazine, via his friend Ilka Chase. When I was in Afghanistan in 1954, he died, shortly before his retirement birthday of sixty-five. He had written science fiction stories under a pen name for several years, and had painted some humorous and, for the time, somewhat lascivious watercolors. He gave me a few of the latter, which I prize. He had started out in Wisconsin as a cartoonist, and perhaps he should have kept on, had he not been given a Rhodes Scholarship to Oxford. One of his last expressed wishes was that he should not be succeeded by Sherwood L. Washburn, who had oedipally criticized him. William W. Howells got the job and held it most competently until his retirement in 1974.

Among other things that I did in those three years was to demolish successfully the Dixionian idea that the "races and cultures of" courses should be given by continents. Dixon himself had never mentioned Iran or Arabia under Asia, nor had he any notes on them. He had confined himself almost entirely to Siberia. My idea was that the division should be made by genuine culture areas, such as the Middle East, from Morocco to Afghanistan; Black Africa; circumpolar regions; and the like. This made much better sense, and caught on.

The idea was in the air. It was followed by the rise of area studies in American universities, which provided one of my justifications for leaving Harvard, much as I loved the place. Mine was not a simple departure, but a second divorce.

One night in the Columbia Faculty Club in New York, a big meeting was held to discuss the problem of area-study programs, not just in anthropology, but in all pertinent disciplines. The idea was that no one university could afford to cover the world. One would take Black Africa, another China, another India, and still another the Middle East. The finger was pointed at me for the Middle East, although Philip Hitti already had a functioning Middle Eastern program in Princeton.

Paul Buck, who had arrived late, eaten hastily, and was toying with a spoon, offered to trade me like a baseball player to Princeton. Philip Hitti very correctly replied that he had neither a place nor an adequate salary for me, for which I was grateful, for I did not want to have to turn Princeton down. Then Ephraim A. Speiser of the University of Pennsylvania approached me on behalf of that institution. I didn't really want to run a Middle Eastern program at all, for that would be even more confining than Anthropology 1, and away from home to boot.

I told Dean Buck that I didn't so much mind leaving Harvard as I did being treated like a piece of merchandise; that I would pick my own destination when it suited me, and not when he wished. After all, I was a full professor and didn't have to go before reaching sixty-five except by my own choice.

At this point, the Philadelphia plot thickened quickly. While I was still dickering with Speiser, Froelich G. Rainey, the new director of the University Museum, smelled Speiser's plot, which seems to have been to make me a North African expert in a Middle Eastern program under himself. Rainey made me a substantial counteroffer much more to my liking. I could become a curator of the University Museum; go on field trips whenever I chose, to interesting and relatively unknown countries; and lead the kind of life that Dr. Cobb had said I should. Speiser's idea of a Middle East program died aborning, and in the fall of 1948 Lisa and I were off for Nippur and points east.

Despite our departure, Lisa and I still kept one foothold in the holy soil of New England, within commuting distance of Cambridge. It was a lot on Concord Street, West Gloucester, Massachusetts, including both wooded upland and tidal marshland that drains into Crooked Creek and the Essex River not far from its mouth. We bought it in 1947 and planned to build on it the following year, before the Philadelphia decision had come up. We still own it, but it has grown from two to almost fifty acres, counting marshland, upland, granite outcrops reminding us of the recent Pleistocene, and a few modest buildings.

Despite its trials, 1947 had a few light moments, at least for me. One of them was a banquet in a Boston hotel hosted by the Eastern States division of the Syro-Lebanese Association of America. At the head table, to the right of the club's president, sat Faris Bey el-Khoury, the prime minister of Syria, and beyond him Professor William Thomson (a dry Thompson, as he used to say) who had taught me Arabic at Harvard. To the president's left sat James Michael Curley, mayor of Boston, and beyond him, me.

I found Curley a fine conversationalist, asking me the proper questions and seeming most relaxed and urbane. When the time for introductions came, the mayor arose, and greeted Faris Bey by saying: "In the name of the city of Boston I greet the honorable prime minister of Syria. In ancient times it had one of the two most brilliant civilizations of the world, the other being Ireland, my ancestors' home."

To this Faris Bey replied: "I thank the honorable mayor of Boston for his greeting and for his remarks about the ancient civilization of Syria, but I must correct one of his statements. Syria had a brilliant civilization before Ireland had risen from the sea."

This bothered Mr. Curley in no perceptible way. He kept on chatting at a lively pace with me. When the moment came to leave, he shook hands with Faris Bey, bowed, and walked out with a springy step—not to another meeting but to jail.

For many years I have thought of this story, and called it "Erin Go Bragh and Syria Go Bragher." When I have been in the dumps it has cheered me up. Courage is the key to life.

19. *The Most Highly Paid Water Boy*

One year after we had finished our second season at the High Cave in Morocco, Lisa and I passed Cap Spartel, almost in sight of that sea cave on our way eastward. We were clutching the rail of an inelegant, flounder-paced freighter bound for Trieste, Alexandria, and finally Beirut.

This time we were supposed to re-excavate the city site of ancient Nippur, first unearthed by a joint mission of the University Museum, Philadelphia, and the Oriental Institute, Chicago. Our predecessors had found cartloads of cuneiform tablets, and now—our sponsors hoped—we might bring back more, as well as to excavate parts of the city previously untouched.

Lisa and I and Francis Steele, a biblical scholar, were the Pennsylvania team, while Don and Garnet McCown and Joe Collins (a veteran Indian-mound digger) represented Chicago. Our quarters aboard were one stateroom and a steerage, full of pipe beds in tiers of three.

Because we were the oldest, the captain put Lisa and me in the stateroom, but until we got to Trieste we didn't know whether the leader was to be Don or me. It was Don. In a sense this made me very happy. I no more wished to command a city-site dig than I had yearned to run a Middle East area-studies department; but on the other hand, I had made up my mind to give up measuring people and to search for the bones of their ancestors in the moist soil of caves. Mud-pie cities were not my cup of tea. Sumerian art looked cute, or like Disneyland, and cuneiform inscriptions were less enticing than the curvaceous Egyptian hieroglyphs and Arabic script.

But the decision held minor disadvantages. Don and Garnet ousted the Coons from their cabin, and in the steerage, Francis Steele (bless him) prayed rather loudly at odd hours while we were trying to sleep.

The preceding paragraphs are written from memory. Once docked at Alexandria, before debarking at Beirut, I began writing a diary of 135 pages, from October 31, 1948, through February 4, 1949.

The first 66 pages take us through our stay on the Nippur dig. Of the whole brief expedition I wrote on the flyleaf:

This is the record of 80 exciting, boring, breath-taking, nauseating, sand-blasting, kidney-freezing days, from Alex to Amsterdam, written without inhibitions at the times things happened. Any references to living (or recently murdered) persons is deliberate and intentional. If anyone is interested it can be published on the backs of bully-beef labels after my death.

Unfortunately, in this sense, I am currently alive; and bully-beef labels can be obtained only by buying whole tins at $1.39 apiece. With four labels to a page, 135 pages would cost $750.60 just for the paper. For both reasons I shall have to abbreviate and somewhat mollify its content, skipping Alexandria, Beirut, a night in a broken-down jeep in the middle of the desert, Baghdad, and our life in the expedition house in Afej, the nearest village to the site.

On the dig, Lisa and I excavated a ṣmall, early Muslim-Arab cemetery so that the bones could be moved, because their mourning kinsmen had buried them right over the royal library, from part of which the earlier expedition had removed the world's largest collection of Sumerian tablets discovered, in situ, to our date. Naturally I measured each skeleton, taking special pains with the skulls, and Lisa recorded my numbers as I called them out.

Once when I had finished with one skeleton and was moving to the next one, Lisa stood up to change her position too, but her left leg fell through the soil, up to her knee. After I had lifted her out, we enlarged the hole a little and saw that the whole library had been gutted by robbers, who had had time enough in fifty years to remove every tablet, then either closed their tunnel mouth behind them or left it to be plugged by wind-borne dust.

After this I was reduced to driving my jeep back and forth from the riverbank to the dig, to slake the thirsts of hundreds of workmen, whose intestinal tracts could tolerate this contaminated fluid after generations of natural selection, and the only light moment in it was on December 10. While I was getting water the usual crowd had collected. I noticed a five-year-old blonde girl, and said, "She looks like an English girl." Then a woman standing nearby said, "Yes, an Englishman made her."

But a few days later, Lisa's and my cloud began to lift. On the fifth, Thorkild Jacobsen, Don's boss at the Oriental Institute, came through. He said to me, "You are the most highly paid water boy in the

Middle East." Then he recommended the more salubrious climate of the Iranian plateau, adding that we might leave on the thirteenth or, at latest, the fourteenth. On the eighth a second visitor from Chicago arrived. He was George Cameron, a cuneiform man, who had just come from Iran. In fact he was still trembling a little from having just copied, with quick-drying latex, the world-famous Bisitun stone on a shaky painter's ladder hanging from the lip of the cliff, some 150 feet above the stony ground. It was the cuneiform Rosetta stone, giving the key to the decipherment of Assyrian, Babylonian, and Sumerian. Sir George Rawlinson had first copied it in 1835, but he had made a few mistakes which George was correcting by a modern technique.

When George heard that I was interested in caves, he said, "There is a beauty right under the inscription at Bisitun. It is right beside the road."

After the two visitors had departed, Don agreed that I might go, but that Lisa and the Pennsylvania museum jeep must stay behind. I leave to the reader's imagination the conversations that followed, happily without muscular action, but in any case, Lisa and I rode to Baghdad in a railroad coach, while the jeep crossed the flooded plain on a flatcar, with a chilled soldier dozing fitfully at the wheel.

We remained in Baghdad for a few days while I measured some Sumerian skulls for Naji Bey, the director of antiquities, and found them to have been Nordic, totally unlike the Arabs buried over the library; they were invaders from the healthy uplands into the stone-less river-valley plain. It occurred to me then that that might explain why the irises of the eyes of the Sumerian statues had been colored blue. And this would also fit the theory of some audacious linguists that Sumerian, a non-Semitic language, was related to Finno-Ugrian.

My diary for this period also contains the rudiments of a study of the local Arab tribes, particularly the Shammar, and the mysterious water-buffalo people who were suddenly in one place, then vanished overnight. The region was full of ethnographic problems more vital to me than the architecture of Bronze Age settlers on a plain so devoid of stone that they had had to fashion sickles out of clay. Bronze, which had to be imported, was too precious to be cast into agricultural tools. It was reserved for weapons, palaces, temples, and the trappings of onager-drawn royal wagons.

My hurried, synoptic study of the living scene led me to write in my diary, on the Muslim Sabbath, Friday, December 17: "As I see it, a competent study of the ethnography of the Afej area is essential for the interpretation of the Nippur archaeological material, since point by point the two are alike. Even the bricks of the floors of the government building have exactly the same dimensions as those of the Parthians and the Sumerians.

"Archaeology is a technique, but a technique is only a method of learning. Who the Sumerians were and how they lived is what we wanted to know. Archaeology is merely one of the ways of finding out."

In Sumer, Mexico, China, and in caves, the opinion I expressed on that Sabbath is one that many others, quite independently, have discovered and put into practice. It is the "new archaeology," or one kind of it. It was only new to me on my first and last city-site expedition, from which it is my pleasure to move on.

When I had finished with the Sumerian skeletons, Lisa and I were ready to leave for Iran, except for one drawback. Much of our equipment, needed for the winter, had been left in storage in the Afej expedition house because the Chicago vehicle blocked the entrance. Now that the roads were dry enough to warrant it, I asked Don for the keys to the storage room so that we could drive down there, pick up our gear, and then move on. His answer was that the keys would stay in his pocket until his return to the site on April 1.

So with the trailer lightly loaded, Lisa and I left Baghdad for Iran. We made two false starts, one over an unmarked road, the other at whose entrance its signs had been switched. We drove ever upward in cooler, cleaner air, over ever-rising ground and through orange groves, their trees bowed down like domes with loads of brightly colored, sweet-smelling fruit. Already we had begun to find ourselves in a more familiar-looking—and more relaxing—world.

As I had learned before the war, real Arabs rarely laugh. Persians, like Berbers, do. Both have keen minds, but the Arabs run as straight as a railroad track over a prairie, while the Persians twist and loop like the hairpin turns on a mountain road. I could usually predict what an Arab would say or do, but with Persians my crystal ball had turned to basalt. I admire them both, but being with Persians is more like living at home.

As I was to write a few years later in *Caravan,* the real boundaries between Muslim states are marked, not sharply, but in depth. Boundaries seen on maps are mostly the products of European pressure, and that is why we got confused crossing from Iraq to Iran.

First we drove by the Iraqi customs house without seeing it. When we reached the Iraqi passport building we were told to turn back and go through the customs. On our second pass toward the passport house we picked up a teeth-chattering hitchhiker, inadequately clothed.

We loaned him a blanket, in which he wrapped his body, just leaving his face exposed, propped up over the trailer's tailboard.

Lisa remained in the jeep. I carried the passports inside. No one checked the occupants of our two-piece vehicle, and heads were averted when they spied Lisa's unveiled face. I could have crossed the border with a junior-grade harem, and the hitchhiker could have been my servant for all the Iraqis cared—or the Persians either, at their ornate building a mile or two up the road. Their officials were snappily dressed in more or less Balkan style, and they were most polite.

But the Persian customs officers were the sharper, as we learned when we pulled in behind a closed gate a mile or two higher up. Their principal concern was cameras. "Have you any?" they asked.

"Yes, two."

"Let me see them, please."

They were a Rolleiflex and a Leica, and I showed them a letter from the Persian Embassy in Baghdad, directing them to let me take the cameras through.

"Yes," said the officer, "they can go through, but I will send them to Tehran for you, and you can pick them up there when you arrive."

This conversation took place in French, but sensing a bit of trouble, a second officer wearing a beret moved in. He spoke perfect English.

"Let me see the cameras," he said. "Oh, but they are only little cameras."

Then he buttonholed a slick-haired youth who had just walked up, and the two conversed rapidly in Persian.

"He is the chief of customs," said Beret, who stamped the cases and let us through.

It was just as well that he did. During the next two weeks Lisa and I were to drive to the Caspian shore, across the eastern tail of the Elburz Mountains, then westward over the bumpy, muddy Mashhad pilgrim road to Tehran, where we placed our jeep on cement blocks in the National Museum parking lot, just in time to catch the next plane home, where I had to teach the spring course.

On our first day in Iran we left the Persian customs at 4:00 P.M. with 110 miles to go to Kermanshah, our sleeping place. George Cameron had given us a letter to The Reverend John Watson, an evangelist who knew where the cave of Bisitun was. This was a rather exciting mission we were on, because as far as prehistoric caves were concerned, we were broaching terra incognita, except for one Neolithic find by the French archaeologist Ghirshman just a few years before. We were seeking older stuff, Neanderthal living floors, Cro-Magnons (to use a popular term for Upper Paleolithic folk in general). Was it here that our European ancestors had originated?

It would have been hard to hold the steering wheel on course with such thoughts milling around in my head, had it not been for the scenery, lit by the slanting winter sun. Thirty-five miles from the customs we passed a proto-condominium of caves in the limestone wall to the left. At eight thousand feet we crossed a pass in the dark and saw, in the glare of our headlights, a pack of five wolves cross the road, their gray bodies clear against the white of newly fallen snow. Among the highroad fauna we also identified a jackal, an Asiatic porcupine, several hares, and paused to let a herd of white-tailed deer go past, but couldn't name any of the many kinds of ground-running birds except for grouse.

At 10:00 P.M. we arrived in Kermanshah, where a policeman led us to John Watson's house. He and Mrs. Watson welcomed us, fed us a fine supper, and we had our first hot bath since leaving Beirut.

Next morning the view outside the American-style house was like a winter scene in New England, rolling fields covered with snow, except that the trees were mostly poplars, planted in straight rows—a bit of Normandy thrown in.

The next morning the Coons and Watsons drove to Bisitun, where Darius's inscription loomed high overhead, visible if we craned our necks enough; under it was another inscription in Arabic. This was the road of conquerors, between the cliff and the swift-flowing, unfordable Gamas-i-Ab River, with a stream of pure water flowing from a hole in the cliff so fast that it never froze, even in winter—water enough to slake the thirsts of any army and its horses in the ancient or the almost-modern world.

We poked around in the snowdrifts at the foot of the inscription, but found no cave. "It's not here," said John Watson, "but I know where it is," and Ali Akbar, George's companion on the painter's ladder, who had joined us, agreed. While Inez Watson, clad in a snowsuit, sat in the teahouse across from the cliff, the rest of us rode a mile or so down the road. Now we knew why Inez had stayed behind. Her husband led us up over seven hundred feet of tumbling blocks of stone; it was like climbing out of a granite quarry after an ice storm.

Then he disappeared into a black opening, and we followed. It was a beautiful, cozy cave, just the right size for a small team to dig, with an undisturbed, fine-grained dirt floor, warm, unfrozen—ready to be trenched in winter had it not been for that super-Alpine climb. [Rather than describe it in detail, I present my crude, original sketch, copied directly from my diary.] It was 27.0 meters long (88½ feet), by 6.4 meters wide (21 feet), and with an average headroom of seven or eight feet. The ceiling was fire-blackened, and the cave had been used by shepherds, as witnessed not only by their sleeping place, but also by their flocks' matted dung, which gave the floor a comfortable, springy feeling underfoot.

As shown by the profile, the walls sloped inward on the left side and ran almost straight down on the right. These contours prognosticated that the cave would be deep, possibly deeper than its present width. John Watson had shown me the perfect cave, less than twenty-four hours after our arrival in Iran. I dug down about 40 to 60 cm, through sterile earth, as I had expected, until I had hit a small hearth. I did not collect a sample of it because radiocarbon dating had not yet been invented, but it looked old to me, and I decided to dig it as soon as I had finished my spring-term lecturing in Philadelphia.

The cave's name, I learned later, was Ghar-i-Khar: the Cave of the Ass. As future events showed, the ass was me.

Our next stop was Hamadan, a modern provincial capital built on the ruins of an older one: Ecbatana, the royal city of the Medes. Besides the Jewish sanctuary of Esther's tomb, it also contained a Presbyterian mission complex, including a hospital, and a spacious house inhabited by the widow of an evangelist, Dr. Marie Zoeckler. Before we left Kermanshah, John Watson sent her a telegram advising her of our arrival that evening, and asking her to put us up.

So we said good-bye to the Watsons, with many thanks, at 10:30 A.M. Soon we passed an oval enclosure, some eight miles long by two miles wide, surrounded by a dyke and wall. Because we drove straight across it, we saw sections of the wall. It had a solid core of molded, unbaked brick, ten feet high and of the same width, and was covered with earth thrown out of the dyke. Although it was called Darius's racecourse, it looked like a military camping ground to me.

A few miles farther on we approached what might have been called one of the wonders of the world, in beauty but not in size. It is Taq-i-Bustan, another cliff carving, with a facade above and beside a man-hewn vault, lined with carvings in high relief, and dating from the reign of Khosrau II to the recent dynasty of the Khazars. It tells more of Iranian history than a dozen books, showing not only the animals ridden (horses, elephants, camels) and those hunted (deer, wild boar, and birds), but all the trappings of rank: the weapons, the boats, and the positions and functions of the different kinds of people, all alive and in motion.

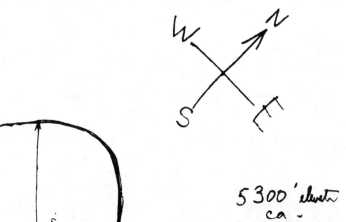

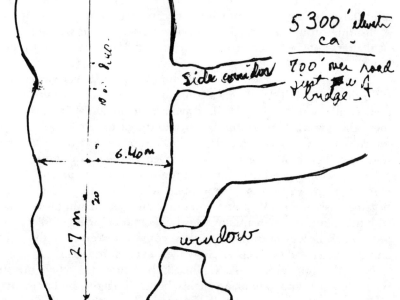

A sketch of the Cave of the Ass at Bisitun, the one we didn't dig. (Page 81 of my diary, Thursday, December 30, 1948.)

The panel that intrigued me most was the emperor himself, who first appears in the upper right-hand corner mounted on a huge charger, armed with a sword and a short, double-arched bow, surveying the scene, while a flunky holds a parasol over his head on a long pole. As one's eye moves downward and toward the center, His Majesty rides his horse at full gallop, his own torso leaning forward, one hand holding a double-arched bow outstretched, while fingers of the other clamp the notched arrow butt in its cord.

In the middle, near the bottom, the king who temporarily demolished the Byzantine Empire, was defeated at Nineveh, and murdered by his son, is seen quietly taking his leave.* He was born in A.D. 589, and died in A.D. 682, eleven hundred and seventy-seven years after Darius, whose aerial craftsmen had carved the trilingual inscription at Bisitun, through which village we now passed on our way to Hamadan, after shooting several rolls of pictures, thanks to the man I called Beret.*

My concentration on the continuity of royal Persian culture from the time of the Aryan invasions out of the north until the eve of their conversion to Islam, while driving past the Ass's Cave, did not mean that I was fickle—for the cave would still be there when we should return, while a new vista had been opened to me, one that I had not noticed earlier, in my eagerness to find George Cameron's cave.

As we crossed the plain and mounted the escarpment toward Hamadan, the snow grew deeper, and with the failing light, the air became crisp and cold. At one point in a curve of the unplowed road, with the transmission in all four wheels, we suddenly came radiator-to-nose with a heavily laden ass. To avoid contact, I swerved to the right, and the trailer and the jeep's right wheels went off the road.

Lisa's right foot was stiff. She climbed out to try to help me put the trailer back, and to hook on chains, but my fingers would not move. As I blew on them to thaw them, a downward bus nearly collided with us, and halted. Out jumped some passengers, who helped me, but a man in a gray uniform with three stars on his shoulder bands seized Lisa's arm and tried to throw her into the bus. When he turned to me, I pulled Lisa out.

It was well below zero degrees Fahrenheit, but we made it.

At 8:30 we drove up to Dr. Zoeckler's house, to her astonishment. John Watson's wire had not arrived. For about three seconds her firm and handsome face looked grim.

The scene described above may be seen as Plate XX of The Story of Man. *Full photographic coverage of the Taq-i-Bustan sanctuary is given, with English captions, in a deluxe album,* Taq-i-Bostan, *Volume II, Tokyo, The Institute of Oriental Culture, University of Tokyo, 1969. Volume 1 contains the text, in Japanese.*

"You are welcome," she said. "Come in. I will show you to your room, and when you are ready, come on downstairs. I am having a New Year's party. Come join my friends."

Her friends were little Persian girls, all sitting cross-legged in a circle on a rug, surrounding plates of pilaf, dried fruits, and sweet-meats. We had a lovely time, much to our hostess's relief. What she had expected when she first saw us, I will never know, because the brave and dedicated lady is long since dead.

Beside visiting the hospital and meeting the rest of the small American mission colony, we achieved two things in Hamadan. Because the snow had blocked the road to Tehran, the governor gave us a paper to go down, if we could make it, to the warmer and snowless Caspian shore. This trip we started two days later; but the night before, I left Lisa with Marie Zoeckler while the Reverend Arthur Muller, son of the chief of mission at Tabriz, took me to a *zurkhané*, meaning "strength house."

We could hear the drum some distance up the alley, and on the way Art Muller explained that there were four of these clubs in Hamadan, patronized by sedentary businessmen trying to keep in shape. That was a monument of understatement, as I realized once we had been seated in the spectators' chairs.

We saw a singer on the corner pulpit holding a corset-shaped drum on his lap so that he could beat it with both hands. He could get three tones from it, as well as a raspberry scraping sound.

There were twenty-one men in the pit, including the master of ceremonies in its center. They wore tight plaid knee breeches. The pit itself was about twenty feet square, with corners cut to make it octagonal; under the earth floor was said to be a 20 cm layer of thorns to make it elastic. The floor around the pit was flagged with octagonal stones. At the left was the wrestling platform, at the right another platform with two Ping-Pong tables and two shields leaning against the wall.

When we arrived, the men were already in the pit dancing to the beat of the three-toned drum, while the drummer sang—in a scale like the Riffian one—the *Shahnameh*, Firdusi's epic of the wondrous deeds of the ancient Persian kings, and of Rustem and his magic steed.

Health club, hell! This was a revival of an ancient Aryan ritual, and the singer on the pulpit might have been Homer with his lyre, and me back in Andover translating the *Iliad* at sight.

When the men in the pit finished dancing they did pushups, holding short-legged pi-shaped pieces of wood, then danced again waving these props aloft. Then they twirled heavy Indian clubs, first all together, and then fewer and fewer as the exhausted men dropped out, until only three or four were throwing their clubs into the air and catching them. Then they began whirling like dervishes, the worst ones first, then better and better until the best of all spun a solo. He was a fifteen-year-old boy; the others were grown men.

To go through the program would take almost as long as the performance. The master of the pitmen clasped his hands behind his neck and sang verses from the Shahnameh in Appalachian "Barbara Allen" style, his fine muscles knotted. Then he whirled until he lost his footing and fell on the floor, rubbing dust on his forehead, and made a speech to his students, to which they responded.

Now comes the *kapardé*, or bow dance. Having caught his breath, the master seizes a heavy iron replica of an old Persian bow, its string festooned with metal jangles, the whole rig weighing thirty-three pounds. He dances with it, moving it back and forth over his head and pretending to draw it. Then another dancer takes it from him, and another, until the moment has come to do the shield dance. By this time the master has changed back to his business clothes and joined us. As tea is forbidden in a strength house, we have been drinking hot milk and eating cakes.

Past the Ping-Pong tables walks a very muscular man. He lifts the two shields from the wall. Each one weighs 150 pounds. The bard steps down from his pulpit and stands over the hero, who now is lying on the floor, and sings special verses from the chronicles of kings.

First the hero lies on his back. Then he picks up both shields, protecting both sides of his body, and writhes from side to side to protect himself from imaginary blows.

This triumph of nerves and muscles couldn't last long. When two other men began lifting weights, the master said to Art and me: "You've seen it now. It's time to go home."

What, if anything, happened after that, is not for me to guess. I had been carried in a time capsule back almost two thousand years. Tomorrow Lisa and I must rise before dawn to start searching for more caves wherein still earlier men had held their rites. Outside it felt as cold as Greenland, and the frost clung like a persistent ghost upon my breath.

On the next morning—Sunday, January 2, 1949—the thermometer read 5° F, compared the 2° the day before, but mist hung over the mountains, which spelled more snow. Before we had left the city limits the jeep broke down, and an Armenian truck driver fixed it for nothing, provided that I would speak to the surgeon at the hospital, Dr.

Frame. Why? Because his mother had an appendix that wanted out.

We bought a sheepskin blanket at the bazaar, and a piece of felt to cover the radiator, then made a second start. We were three on this leg of our journey, the odd man being a convert son of a convert, named Ahmad Haq-Guyan, meaning Ahmad Truth-teller, which must have been a Persian joke. His father had been a colporteur, a dangerous job—a seller of Bibles in Persian, as George Borrow had done in *The Bible in Spain.*

Once Haq-Guyan, Sr., was held up by two bandits, for his money or his life. He happened to have a wristwatch, a rare accouterment in his day, so—anticipating Dick Tracy by several decades—he pretended it was a telephone, and carried on a two-way ventriloquistic conversation with the police at Hamadan.

Once when we were badly stuck, Haq-Guyan, Jr., waded through the drifts to a village near the road and returned leading a dozen or more men carrying one-piece wooden shovels, who immediately dug us out. When I asked him how he had managed this, he said, "I told them that my master was a very ferocious man, and they must not say a word lest he get angry and jump out and shoot them with his gun."

Whether this is what he really said or not, I shall never know, for he was his father's son.

Qazvin was the junction point between three roads leading to four cities. The railroad tracks and motor road from Tabriz to Tehran passed through it, and the road from Hamadan eastward joined the Tabriz route about thirty miles west of Qazvin. From Qazvin also began a steep, winding mountain track, built by the Russians and well graded, down to Rasht, the seaport at the western end of the south Caspian shore.

When we finally reached Qazvin in the later afternoon, we found the Grand Hotel crammed to the windowsills with pilgrims bound for Najafabad and stranded; but a smaller, less impressive Armenian inn had room for us because no Shi'a pilgrim would sleep under a Christian roof. There we were fed well on shish kebabs and other Armenian delicacies. We met many Armenians who had kinfolk in the United States, and one civil engineer who knew the locations of several, in his opinion, promising caves.

In the morning new snow was falling in large, soft flakes. Getting through to Rasht with jeep and trailer would be impossible, and there was no place else to go. So we packed the trailer with all our nonessential belongings and left it with the innkeeper, to guard until we should come back. Even the jeep alone would surely get stuck because of the depth of the truck ruts in the road, and the fact that—like the Russian-built railroad tracks—the truck ruts were broad gauge, and the jeep narrow. So we would be hung up, as we had been at times the previous day, like a short-legged man trying to straddle a waist-high padlocked gate.

There was only one solution, the huge, bearlike Armenian truck drivers said. One of them was about to drive an empty truck to Rasht anyway, so why shouldn't we mount the jeep on his truck piggyback, for only a thousand rials? We did, at a spot less than a mile outside the city, where the truck was driven into a convenient pit. I drove the jeep directly over the tailboard, and then the driver lashed our jeep down tight to keep it from tipping off on the hairpin curves that lay ahead.

This was wonderful fun for Lisa and me, but Ahmad Truthteller in the back seat was scared almost to death—such a sky ride lay beyond the bounds of his fertile imagination. The sky was clear except for some higher-riding cumulus clouds, and the air was as heady as Chateau Mouton-Rothschild of a special vintage that I remember not by year, but by its bouquet and taste.

Through stratified limestone, I thought Jurassic, the road had been cut by two agencies—the Russian engineers and the tumbling, somersaulting Sefid Rud. The latter's stony banks were pitted by many caves, some large enough for human habitation, some with and others lacking earthen floors. I plotted them feverishly in my notebook, without marking their distances along the road, because our odometer, of course, was not recording the miles (or kilometers) of the truck's travels. Here I thought might be another Dordogne as it had been in the days before the French prehistorians had begun their work. A whole new version of the origin of Caucasoid man might be lying there within my sight but beyond my reach.

The country was now forested, with beeches and rare species such as boxwood, and the smoke of charcoal burners desecrating this precious botanical garden sharpened the air. Stocky men in brown woolen trousers and tunics, shod in buskins laced up their stout calves, stood looking at us. They had round caps on their heads like Albanian mountaineers, and also carried lethally sharp billhooks casually over their shoulders. These men were Gilakis, forest men and water men, a hardy stock from which the late Reza Shah was drawn—his surname, Pahlevi, was the name of a seacoast town west of Rasht.

Some other people who did not look at us very much, if at all, were passengers on several buses grinding up the grade. To let them by, our truckman had to pull over as far as he could to the right. Some of them were officers in uniform, one with three stars—but of what importance to them could be two figures almost out of sight, huddled in blankets on a roof, and a third one, obviously Persian and patently frightened, perched behind?

At 4:10 P.M. we arrived at a hamlet called Ab Tosh (Sour Water), where the snow was thin enough to unload the jeep, but here there was no convenient pit. In front of a *chai-khané* our truckman lowered his tailgate and some men brought up two planks for me to back down over, at a steep angle. Lisa stood outside agonizing while the men kept changing their minds and the positions of the planks.

When I was about to back out into empty space on the left side, she pushed the men apart with her hands and grabbed one misplaced plank, sliding it over into its proper place. Like the Swede that she half is, she took this calmly, and didn't begin to tremble for about four days.

About one day before her reaction, it occurred to me that it had been far safer on mules and among feuders and bandits than now on trucks and among civil servants. Wheels made me no longer an explorer, except in the sense of searching for yet-to-be discovered caves. People and places rushed by us too fast. Soon afterward I thought that if he who had invented the wheel had been stillborn, we might be living in caves, saving the trouble of having to reconstruct our less-satisfying lives.

But it was not the Paleolithic that we were riding into, but something akin to the European Neolithic, with high-gabled, thatched-roofed houses, sheep and cattle, fenced-in gardens with stiles to jump over. Soon the light failed, and we rode by headlights into Rasht. Our shelter for the night was to be with the Reverend Lynn* Browning, senior evangelist, whose house our guide-interpreter had so much trouble finding that when at length we were greeted by our kindly host well after his bedtime, the Truth-teller's son threw up on the minister's doorstep and hied himself back to Hamadan on the next bus.

The Reverend and Mrs. Browning were charming people. He was a little lonely, being close to retirement, and he talked to me a bit about the past, as I in my own septuagenarian state am apt to do. After all these years I hope it will not be deemed a breach of confidence if I repeat what he said was his chief regret.

Once while he was chatting with a member of the British Council (their equivalent of the USIA), and the latter was telling him

---

As noted in my diary. On page 132 of The Seven Caves *I called him John. Sorry about that.*

about how carefully King George V had been educated, the slightly bored reverend asked: "Did he learn his ABC's at his mother's knee, or some other low joint?"

The Councilman never spoke to Mr. Browning again. He regretted this conversation stopper deeply, and told me that as far as he knew it was his only sin.

In my diary Thursday, January 6, is labeled British Day. The jeep was in the shop. Bob Browning, our hosts' precocious fifteen-year-old son, guided me on foot. The first stop was at the Bank of Iran, to cash a check. Its proprietor, a Scot, told me of a wonderful site, but it was situated on a back road, where we would not have time to go. He then passed me on to the manager of the Iran Hotel, a Caledonian fellow-countryman of his, who told me the story of his life, but nothing about caves.

Then Donald Wallace, Mr. Browning's understudy, relieved Bob and led me to the chief of police, a colonel, who spoke French perfectly and loaned us his own jeep and driver to take us to the governor-general, who also spoke French perfectly. He had been in charge at Dāmghān on the plateau when Erich Schmidt of Chicago, whom I knew, had dug the Bronze Age site of Tepe Hissar before the war. The governor knew my old friend Ted Lockard, who had also been on the dig. After a few minutes the governor was telling me about cave sites all along the Caspian shore, and hoping that I would dig some while he was still there.

He then promised to telephone the governors of Mazanderan and Gurgan provinces that we were to pass through, asking them to honor our papers and to show us every courtesy.

We left his office in high spirits, early enough to pay a routine visit to the British Council. There we found a Mr. Micklethwaite in residence, but in a bathrobe and somewhat shaken from his journey down from Qazvin in a bus. He had almost just arrived.

He had been from Qazvin to Tehran and back again, over the same route, because the governor-general had denied him a permit to travel via Gurgan, although he had made it clear to the governor-general that *His own Majesty's ambassador had ordered him to come to Tehran by that road.* So busy was Mr. Micklethwaite telling me about his troubles that he asked me no questions, which I didn't mind at all.

On the way to the Wallaces for luncheon Don told me that Micklethwaite was the man whom Mr. Browning had asked the question of the knee.

Shortly after returning to the Brownings after lunch the other

British Councilman appeared. He was Mr. Owens. He had studied social anthropology under Darryl Ford in London, and he was drafting a city plan and layout of Rasht and its environs, plotting in their various locations the different ethnic elements, the shops of tradesmen, etc., and to do this properly he needed a copy of my *Reader,* not only for its way of organizing cultures, but especially for its chapter on an Indian village by Morris Opler and Rudra Datt Singh. I told him that I would order a copy to be sent him from Jonathan Cape in London, and he expressed his gratitude, but then he asked me a question: Why had the governor-general granted me a permit to travel to Tehran via Gurgan after he turned down Mr. Micklethwaite's request?

While wondering who in hell had given Mr. Owens that information, I replied, "Apparently the floods had washed out a bridge when Mr. Micklethwaite applied—Mr. Micklethwaite told me that himself—but in the week or so before I appeared, the flood must have subsided, and the bridge been repaired. This is just my supposition. The governor-general never mentioned this to me at all."

On Friday, January 7, we arose to a bright sun and a dry, beautiful day, already growing warm, for the soil on which the Brownings' house was built lay eighty-six feet below sea level, in an exotic strandline climate that might have been a fine wintering place for bands of early men.

When we had been seated at the breakfast table, Mr. Browning delivered a stirring grace, sincere and beautifully phrased, wishing us success on our adventure—a parting prayer powerful enough to launch a Crusader in chain armor into his saddle, to gallop off to slay a hundred Saracens.

Let no one fancy for a moment that I write these words in mockery. Had I felt that way I wouldn't have written it. My diary says I wept. To me, this is what religion is, for a fighting man. The governor-general might have sensed this, for he was a Kurd, like Saladin. And the governor of Hamadan Province, who let us go to Rasht on the way to Tehran, was a member of the ruling family of the powerful nomadic tribes of Bakhtiars.

What we had glimpsed by narrow headlight beam two nights before, now appeared 3-D in balanced color as Lisa and I rode eastward. The men in brown caps and buskins were still there, their billhook blades glinting in the sun's rays as only freshly sharpened steel can, their cheeks as red as those of men from Devonshire. Some were driving teams of oxen dragging summer sleds, as still was done in the princedoms of the Caucasus, in Basque lands, in Flores of the Azores, and in Madeira. Others were lopping branches from poplars to feed their cattle, and some women were drying flax on racks to spin and to weave into linen, as in Portugal and Ireland.

Before we emerged from the forest we passed through a watery landscape, where some men were adzing out dugout canoes and others lacing together three-plank skiffs with thongs. Fowlers were carrying flintlocks for duck shooting. Then we rode past rice paddies in terraces, tea plantations, and orange groves. We also saw, and bought, a kind of giant lemon called *badrang*. They were eight inches long by six inches wide, with a warty skin so thick that there was little pulp inside. They were grown just for their skin, which was candied.

Then the road ran along the sea—one long, pebbly beach with not a ship in sight, but only three rowboats out fishing, most of which was done in weirs at the rivers' mouths, with fenced-in caviar-packing plants nearby.

At Chālus we registered with the police and spent the night in a modern hotel run by a Russian woman. We saw two Russian men eating at the table next to us who spoke to one another in German, just as—before servants—English gentry conversed in self-styled French. They had good reason to take this precaution if they were discussing anything confidential, because during their recent occupation many of the Persians had learned Russian, and might possibly have need of it again.

On the next day we drove all the way to Gurgan, some two hundred-odd miles. It was not because the road was pitted, rutted, bumpy, or because bridges had been toppled by streams in spate that we drove slowly, but because there was so much to see. The road was smooth and fine, the bridges in perfect shape, with no signs of fresh repairs. The only thing unusual was that the last sixty miles or more of the road was being metaled for heavy traffic, by Mongoloid-looking Kirghiz carrying crushed stones and pebbles in their two-wheeled high-hubbed carts. They looked as if they had just stepped out of Central Asia, which was not far from the truth. Having fled the Soviet dominion, they were helping the Iranians in order not to have to flee farther. When we got to Gurgan, Lisa and I visited their yurts, where some of the women were selling their precious jewelry. We still have some of it today.

Starting back along the road again in memory, we passed cotton fields, a cotton-goods factory, many villages with their well-fenced and neatly laid out gardens, and rows of pomegranate trees. The people dressed more or less like the Gilakis, but were a bit thinner, and men drove oxen pulling summer sleds and small carts of their own. On the right of the road all was Neolithic plus iron tools; on the left modern industry, as well as almost countless round and oval mounds of earth. Some of the mounds had imamzadehs, in English saints' tombs, perched on top; not a single one that we could see had been opened up.

What kind of men were buried there? Not Scythians, for they pastured farther west. Perhaps Masagetae, their kinsmen to the east. While looking at these mounds on the left of the road I was constantly turning my head to look for caves in the cliffs to the right. Had I, like a bird, had one eye on each side of my head, I might have seen more—several times I almost went off the road.

I dimly remember seeing some caves somewhere near Behshahr, where the Swiss-built railroad track that crossed the mountains from Tehran ran close to the road, and the shore was not far away. They looked quarried to me, for the House of Parliament in Tehran had been built from this limestone hauled up on flatcars, but some seemed more or less intact. When the pictures I had shot of them were developed and blown up, they looked even better—but that was not until after we had reached home.

The hotel where we slept in Gurgan was old and not as comfortable as the one in Qazvin, and Lisa tells me now what she didn't say before, that she slept badly because she felt something ominous and disquieting about it, as if it didn't make sense.

In the morning we braced ourselves for the ride over the eastern Elburz to Dāmghān, expecting to get stuck again in the snow, and this time without any truth-teller to lie our way out. But the road was clear. The army had seen to that. And in Dāmghān we found the army, with its vehicles and portable weapons which it is not my place to describe, because no ambassador had demanded that I should take that road to Tehran.

The road from Dāmghān to the capital was execrable, so bad that we almost shook our jeep to pieces. At one place we got stuck in the mud while fording a stream—bypassing a truck that had broken its driving shaft—so that it took fifteen men, who came at once to our rescue without our asking, to lift the jeep up bodily and carry it to the other side. While they did this they shouted, in unison, "Yo Ali," with the accent on the last syllable, thus seeking aid or giving thanks to the Messenger of Allah's cousin, and the father of his daughter Fatima's martyred sons, Hasan and Hosein. This was the Shi'a rallying cry, and it rallied well for two Christians, who drove on to Tehran, then back to Qazvin for our trailer, and back again to the Antiquities Museum in Tehran, where M. Godard, a Norman and the director of antiquities, let us put our rig on blocks in the building's parking lot to await our return.

20. *Life in Philadelphia*

When we first went to Philadelphia I had a horror of having to live in a crowded brick row house, but Lisa soon allayed my fears. She had a friend from Salem, Massachusetts, Mary Shreve Sims, with whom she had gone through the Smith College Landscape Architectural School of Church Street, Cambridge, a stone's throw from Farwell Place. Mary's husband, Lancelot F. Sims, an architect, had built for the two of them, their son Crombie, and their dog Billy-Guts, a one-story cinderblock house on Beaumont Road in Devon, on the Main Line, not far from the horse-show grounds. We bought the adjacent two-acre lot. Lance designed and built our house, similar to theirs, mostly while we were in Iraq and Iran.

Luckily for us, our Devon house stood in the middle of the orchard of the old estate which had been cut up. We had old-fashioned apple trees, even then hard to get, including one golden pippin; also pear trees; and we planted a cherry and a quince tree, both of which bore abundantly and soon, and were loaded with excellent fruit. We also put in a vegetable garden, which was very productive because the seasons were longer and the soil richer than in the glacier-scoured earth of eastern New England.

No sooner had we bought our land and before we had laid out the stakes for the house foundation, a police car drove up and an officer stepped out. He wore delicate, low-cut black pumps, and both his trousers and sox were short, so that a few inches of pink skin were exposed on each ankle. He informed me that our neighbor, Mrs. Fleer, had complained that we had thistles growing on our property. This was against an old Pennsylvania statute passed in the days when thistles were dangerous to neighbors' stray cattle. As no cattle were around, I could not see what difference this made, but the officer was all for enforcing the statute, and I might be facing arrest soon before our departure for Nippur.

I had seen no thistles but, wearing heavy boots and thorn-proof trousers, I led the officer through all our thickets and brambles until both his legs were bleeding. Then I found two thistles, cut them down with my jackknife, and the officer, poor man drove away. This was not the end of the Fleer business, which continued for several years at times when we were home. Mrs. Fleer's chief complaint was that we and the Simses lived in one-story houses, like frozen-food lockers, while any respectable Dutch people lived in two- or three-storied stone houses. Her real trouble was that she was lonely, particularly after her husband died. She was out of her ethnic territory, and her only way of interacting was by complaining.

At the other end of the Pennsylvania Dutch spectrum were food vendors who operated the farmers' market once a week in a huge old store in nearby Wayne. At 5:00 A.M., when it opened, I was usually there to get the best cuts of meat. As they were talking Pennsylvanish to each other, I once joined in with my version of regular German, which convinced them that I was just as German as they were and had simply changed the spelling of my name.

This misapprehension served to my advantage once when a truck driver who had been sleeping in his cab found my car blocking his exit (he could simply have backed out had he wanted to), and began to curse and threaten me. I stepped into the market, asked for help, and at once a half dozen burly Dutchmen, some attired in the costumes of their religious sects, brandishing the tools of their trades, rushed out and drove the driver away.

All of this happened, of course, after our return from our first trip to Iran, after we were installed in our house, while I was commuting to West Philadelphia on the famous school train, the Paoli local. My duties at the University Museum were not onerous. I was supposed to teach a half course one semester each year, if so doing did not interfere with my fieldwork. Such a course was a two-hour lecture one day a week, usually from 11:00 A.M. to 1:00 P.M. Someone else gave Anthropology 1. My classes were usually small and relatively informal, quite enjoyable except for the freight cars rattling and banging on a nearby trestle, but their noise gave me a chance to pause and to regain my breath.

At first I lectured right through both hours, but soon found that many of my students were nibbling crullers and sipping soft drinks out of bottles at the end of the first hour, making an untidy mess. Then I gave them a ten-minute break to go to the snack bar if they wished. One young man in the back row nipped frequently at a thermos bottle. This seemed an odd way to ingest coffee, but it turned out to be a flagon of martinis.

My favorite subject, and the easiest to prepare, was the peoples and cultures of the Middle East. It was also the one closest to the interest of the museum. One of my students in the spring of 1950 was Dr. Mahmud el-Amin, our inspector at Nippur. One day when I mentioned the theory that the Children of Israel might possibly have originated near the western bank of the Euphrates, he interrupted me to state: "You had better not say that, or the Jews will claim that country too."

Mahmud also objected to a small exhibit in the hallway that contained a Perry picture depicting Muhammad's flight from Mekka to al-Medina. Abu Bakr, the father of the Prophet's favorite wife, A'isha, and the first caliph, was shown walking barefoot. This disturbed Mahmud so much that he ripped the picture off and tore it into shreds. It was as if a devout Christian had seen a picture of Saint Peter wearing a pith helmet.

The course I gave was based on one I had worked out previously at Harvard with Richard Frye, now Aga Khan professor there. In the summer Lisa and I went to Cape Breton Island to attend the Gaelic *mōd*, where we heard long speeches in that language, heard the pipers pipe their pibrochs, saw the kilted dancers, and saw the caber tossed.

Back in our rented cabin I turned my typed lecture notes on the course I had just given into a book called *Caravan; The Story of the Middle East*. The whole job took me about two weeks, not counting the illustrations, which were copious, the glossary, and the index. Holt did a fine job of supplying special type for Arabic and other non-Indo-European words as needed, and gave it a beautiful cover. Jonathan Cape published it in England, and it was translated into both Arabic and Persian.

In the first chapter I specifically set the time of the Middle Eastern cultural level covered at the zenith of the Abbasid caliphates in Baghdad and of the caliphate of Córdoba in Spain, both having peaked around A.D. 800. My point, conveyed in the final chapter, was that modern Middle Easterners, however westernized, have their roots in the civilization of the period specified, and that we westerners must take this fact into consideration while dealing with them. This warning might have been heeded during the crises of the 1970s and 1980s had *Caravan* still been available.

One of the junior editors tried to insert a sentence in page proof, to wit, "When I was in Israel I noticed that . . ." I quickly removed it with the remark: "I have never been in Israel nor shall I go there. Were I to do so, I would be excluded from all the Arab states where I do my excavating." Also, there was no Israel in A.D. 800.

At about that time a venerable colleague of mine whom I hold in deep respect invited me to lunch with him at the cafeteria. Over our food he told me that Dr. Speiser had repeated to him word by word a conversation I had had in a Baghdad automobile-supply store with its proprietor while buying jeep tires on the way to Iran. The proprietor had said, "America is the enemy of all the Arab States because all Americans side with Israel." I had replied that this was not true, that both Christians and Jews in America were divided on the subject and cited Julius Rosenwald and Rabbi Elmer Berger as examples of sincere and honest anti-Zionist Jews.

At first I remembered how the Jews in San'a had been the most reliable source of information in the Yemen, and suspected that some secret underground system such as we had used during the war had relayed the message. Then I remembered that Fred Speiser had worked for the University Museum in Iraq, wherefrom he was barred at the time in question. Some friend may simply have written him a letter. Occam's razar?

As soon as he had delivered his message, my venerable colleague resumed eating his lunch, and so did I. Neither of us showed any sign of emotion, or ever mentioned the subject again.

When it first came out, *Caravan* received many fine reviews both at home and in Britain, from both scholars and lay reviewers, but it petered out in the sixties, when the publisher cancelled the trade edition and turned it over to a reprint house. One retired CIA man told me that during his tour of duty in the Middle East he carried with him only the Bible and *Caravan*. At least I tried to continue serving my country, which means more than any religious denomination does to me.

One of my first jobs at the University Museum was to set up a Hall of Man in the first room to the right of the entrance, where new visitors naturally went. It was occupied by glass cases full of local American Indian axe heads, arrowheads, and potsherds. The average visitor either walked right past these cases or went back to turn left. Although it annoyed some members of the American Department, I was supposed to set up an eye-catching show that would hold the visitors' attention. It was a graphic representation of the physical and cultural evolution of man, including how races had been formed in response to differences in climates. From one wall stuck out a pair of phony human hands like Cocteau's in the film *Beauty and the Beast,* but instead of lighting fixtures one hand held a hammer stone and the other a piece of half-worked flint. It was meant to show how stone tools were made.

I had five helpers: Jane C. Goodale, one of my Radcliffe students; Theressa A. Howard (later Carter), now an archaeologist in Kuwait; Dexter Perkins, my student, an expert at identifying animal bones; and two staff artists, William Beardsley and Richard Albany. To top it off Al Bendiner, a well-known Philadelphia painter and caricaturist, made us a hilarious lopsided painting of an owl hooting in a tree, while a monkey thumbed his nose at a lion from whom a herd of gazelle was silently fleeing. Al's point was that arboreal animals and birds, like man's ancestors, could afford to communicate vocally, while grounded grazers cannot.

The largest exhibit was a chart plotting time logarithmically against man's use of energy, from fire and simple manpower through oxen and horses to wind, steam, and hydroelectric energy to atomic energy, culminating with the familiar mushroom cloud. This chart showed that once he had begun to use energy obtained outside his own body, man had ceased to be his own master. His growing skills at technology outgrew his competence at ordering his own societies. This was a message floating in the air for anyone to pick up who understood the relationships of the components of time, energy, the divers workings of the human brain, and of our glands. If anyone else had published it, I did not know. I hit on it in the winter of 1949–50.

CBS asked me to do this as a show on TV in a series called *Summer School.* It took much condensation, and was good training. The show won a Peabody Prize, which was given to the CBS station, with none for me.

CBS might not have asked me to do *Summer School* had the University Museum not already embarked on its weekly quiz show, *What in the World?*, Froelich Rainey's brainchild. He was the M. C. (master of ceremonies), sitting at a separate desk at the right end of the podium. Behind a curved table sat three panelists: the straight man, the guest, and the heavy. The straight man was either Alfred Kidder II, who had followed me down from Harvard, or Schuyler van Rensselaer Cammann, one an American Indian archaeologist, like his father, the other a sinologist.

The middle chair held the guest. Sometimes it was Margaret Mead, sometimes the sculptor Jacques Lipchitz, the jolly Jesuit Father Franklin Ewing, the anthropologist Ralph Linton, or Ernest Dodge, director of the Peabody Museum at Salem, Massachusetts, from whom Geraldine Bruckner borrowed objects when our own collections were running low.

The third chair held the heavy, your author, when I was at home. Who replaced me when I was abroad I do not know. The show began in 1948 and ended in 1964, two years after I had left Penn; I commuted by air. At first the show was live and had to be performed once a week. When it was cut on tape, we could do as many as five in a day, and needed to come to the studio only ten or eleven times a year.

We had different ways of working. Lipchitz diagnosed his object by its style alone, and put on a wonderful ham performance. He had a vast collection of so-called primitive sculpture in his studio at Hastings-on-Hudson, New York, and drew many of his ideas from those pieces. I cannot remember his having made a mistake. My method was to identify the materials of which the object was composed—animal, vegetable, and/or mineral. Then I would search the

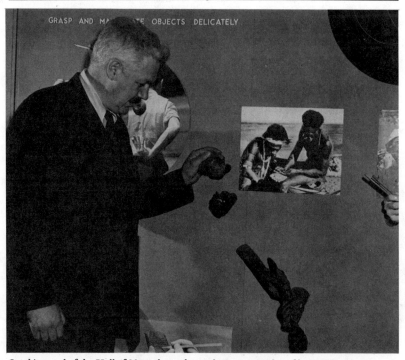

GRASP AND M▧▧▧▧E OBJECTS DELICATELY

On this panel of the Hall of Man, the author stole Cocteau's idea of having simulated human hands (in this case made of plaster) to show how different tools may be used for different purposes.

corners of my brain to think where those materials had come from and at what period. I made few mistakes either, especially when the guest was Jacques.

Among our overseas guests were Glyn Daniel, the British archaeologist, and Helge Larsen, a Danish one who had worked with Froelich in Alaska. Glyn started a similar show on the BBC called *Animal, Vegetable, Mineral,* and Helge did the same in Copenhagen. His show was called *What Is That?* in Danish.

Our show got CBS a Peabody Prize, but it never bagged a sponsor. Alpo tried it once, and the interruption was disturbing. We were told that we didn't sell enough dog food. If we had we wouldn't have received any more pay anyhow. *Tant pis, tant mieux.* Our academic purity was preserved.

During the intervals between expeditions when I was home I held two consulting jobs. One was with Scott, Foresman & Co. of Chicago, the giant grade-school textbook publishers. They had me

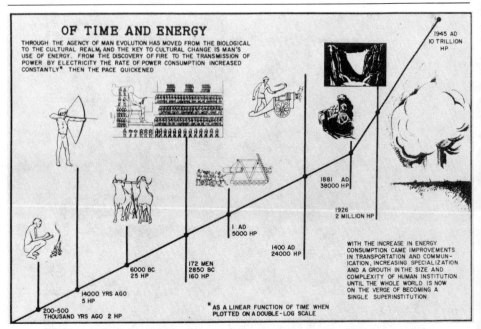

OF TIME AND ENERGY

THROUGH THE AGENCY OF MAN EVOLUTION HAS MOVED FROM THE BIOLOGICAL TO THE CULTURAL REALM, AND THE KEY TO CULTURAL CHANGE IS MAN'S USE OF ENERGY. FROM THE DISCOVERY OF FIRE TO THE TRANSMISSION OF POWER BY ELECTRICITY THE RATE OF POWER CONSUMPTION INCREASED CONSTANTLY* THEN THE PACE QUICKENED

1945 AD
10 TRILLION HP

1881 AD
38000 HP

1926
2 MILLION HP

1 AD
5000 HP

1400 AD
24000 HP

6000 BC
25 HP

172 MEN
2850 BC
160 HP

14000 YRS AGO
5 HP

200-500
THOUSAND YRS AGO 2 HP

WITH THE INCREASE IN ENERGY CONSUMPTION CAME IMPROVEMENTS IN TRANSPORTATION AND COMMUNICATION, INCREASING SPECIALIZATION AND A GROUTH IN THE SIZE AND COMPLEXITY OF HUMAN INSTITUTION UNTIL THE WHOLE WORLD IS NOW ON THE VERGE OF BECOMING A SINGLE SUPERINSTITUTION

* AS A LINEAR FUNCTION OF TIME WHEN PLOTTED ON A DOUBLE-LOG SCALE

Of Time and Energy: *The legend means that man is the creature of the machines that he has wrought. This drawing covered an entire panel of the Hall of Man.*

among other "educators," come to Chicago once a year, in January, to discuss their agenda and think of new ideas. They produced the well-known Dick and Jane books, which carried these healthy model children almost from diapers to puberty.

Their progress from grade to grade, as I recall it, advanced as the children enlarged the circles of their acquaintances. First Dick and Jane went to a neighborhood rural school, and what they learned to read about were their parents, relatives, farmyard animals, and other things they were likely to see and to know about. Then they went to a township school, and their geographical coverage widened, then to their county school, and so on to a rounded education.

This scheme was fine for the era of its introduction, but two other factors threatened it. Giant corporations moved their families from state to state, and busing began to break up the local primary schools. The other factor was race. Under egalitarian pressure black faces began to appear among the illustrations, and these books were unacceptable in the South. How the publishers solved the problem I do not know, because by that time I had ceased to be a consultant. Aside from advice, I wrote some chapters in some of their texts, mostly about the peoples and cultures of the world. I cannot give their dates or titles, because I cannot find them. Possibly some of my grandchildren swiped them.

My other consulting job was with Life, Inc. It was more lucrative than the Dick-and-Jane job, more time consuming, and more amusing. It had several aspects. For a fixed annual fee, I laid myself open to answer telephone calls on any subject, day and night, from the fabulous Life research girls, including Nancy Genet, Peggy Bushong, Marion Steinman, Valerie Von der Muhl, and Josefa Stewart (Bronislaw Malinowski's daughter). A second aspect was directing the composition of at least one of the magazine's picture books. That one traced human evolution. In it I had the Neanderthals painted blond, because they lived in a foggy subglacial climate. A third aspect of the job was that my employers paid our way to East Africa to attend the Third International Congress on Prehistory. In New Delhi in February 1957, Jim Greenfield, then the *Time-Life* chief, financed a trip to Katmandhu to investigate an investment made in New York concerning a dubious Yeti-hunting expedition. My relationship with *Life* was felicitous from start to finish, when the magazine suspended operations.

21. *Five Persian Caves*

At 3:00 PM on June 16, 1949, we arrived at the Tehran airport, to find the blue Pennsylvania jeep where we had left it, and the yellow Chicago one beside it. Don and Garnet McCown had apparently driven it up for a bit of rest and recreation at the Park Hotel. M. Godard said that we might use it if we would return it to Baghdad in October. We were lucky to have it, as our numbers had increased.

Charles Coon had come with Lisa and me. David Elder, a youth of Charles's age, son of the Reverend John Elder, head of the Presbyterian mission in Tehran, would ride with us to Bisitun; and Paul Schuhmacher, my former student, would arrive later, bringing the yellow jeep.

M. Godard had assigned to me an inspector, Mr. Habibullah Samadie, a native of Khorasan, next to the Afghan border. Like some others from his province, he was pink-skinned and light-brown-haired. His pigmentation made him nervous because his father had been captured by the Russians, who would not believe that he was Persian. They sent him to Siberia, where he must have died.

Mr. Samadie was also the most polite man that I have ever met. His French was flawless, his English nil.

When he called me Monsieur CarLÉton, or Monsieur CoWWan during introductions, I thought at first that it might be because of his French, but since he blushed each time he mentioned my name I suspected that he might be avoiding it; but I only suspected this dimly, for it was but a slight annoyance.

The truth was revealed one day while I was trying to get Mr. Payne, the business manager of the Presbyterian mission in Tehran, on the phone, usually a time-consuming procedure. When I said that Mr. Coon wished to speak with Mr. Payne, the wires were instantly open and the call went through at once. The operators were speechless, for in vulgar Persian, Coon means—in equally vulgar English—arse-hole, and Payne means what comes out of it.

Ten days it took us to get to Bisitun, our first target, and this was almost a record for the course. Mr. Samadie had hired us a broker who darted to the heads of queues, where he pushed our papers under grilles, and he was a fiend with the airport customs. But I will take my share of credit in getting our red cards, those documents vitally needed for travel in sensitive areas, particularly near boundaries or in tribes.

Instead of taking Samadie with me, I went alone, and right after lunch. The commander of the red cards was a major who lived in a miniature palace behind gardens of roses and fruit trees, and he saw me at once. Inside his office the floor was strewn with some of the most beautiful Persian rugs I had even seen.

He was seated at a polished desk, in full uniform, and after I had introduced myself he asked me, "You are an anthropologist. What race am I?"

I inspected his head and face professionally, and replied, "Your head is too wide and your teeth too big for you to be a Persian. You are a Turk."

Before he answered I thought, My God, what if I was wrong? But I wasn't. Allah had been good to me.

He broke into a great smile and said, "You're right. I am a prince of the Khajar dynasty. My family ruled this country before Reza Shah was born."

Then he promised us our red cards as soon as we had received our residence permits, and we picked up both on my birthday, June 23; then, except for a few more minor nuisances, we were really off.

At Hamadan we paused at Dr. Zoeckler's and other houses to buy excavating equipment, for Hamadan metal was better than Kermanshah's, and to hire a cook, Nosrat Allah (Rescued of God), the son of a convert who was the lady doctor's own *chef de cuisine*. The youth was a college student on vacation who could use a summer's job. He was tall and handsome, with ruddy cheeks and shiny brown hair, as well as good manners and good spoken English. Just what the doctor ordered, and a little more.

The jeep, with loaded trailer, could not hold six, so two of us went ahead by bus, not including me. When we arrived we found ourselves lodged in the village schoolhouse along with an old janitor and a widow, and a Rubaiyat-style pool and garden in the backyard.

As I pulled up in front, I looked at the cliff wall below the inscription. There, in the right-hand lower corner, was the mouth of a small cave.

George Cameron had been right, John Watson wrong. This was the Bisitun cave. I lost immediate interest in the hard-to-get-to Cave of the Ass, and started to work at once. The local villagers, who were what I would call defused Kurds, were sedentary sharecroppers working in fief to three landlords—two absentee, while the third one was Dr. Zanguineh, an English-speaking staff member of the Kermanshah Hospital. He was not a greedy landlord, like those who bartered in human flesh by putting their villages at stake with roulette chips at the casinos along the Caspian shore, but a hard-working, friendly man. In fact he offered us the use of his own house in Bisitun. Samadie had refused this on the grounds that, as the museum was part of the Ministry of Education, we had to be lodged in educational buildings, and I may add that our presence there was an education in an unscheduled way to the locals and travelers concerned.

Dr. Zanguineh may also have been happy that we were able to pay some of his hungry tenants for working in the cave. At first, some demanded to be paid at noon and again when quitting work. Eventually once a day was enough. Had I made them wait two weeks, as had been done at Nippur, some might have been too weak to lift a trowel, or to wash a flint.

While money was important and food vital, my workmen were not toil-numbed serfs, but intelligent and aesthetically emotional men. The flints they tenderly removed from the soil were mostly of chalcedony, some with several colors to a piece, and others, rich, shiny sepia, elegant to the eye and smooth to the touch. They placed them reverently in their cloth caps as they handed them to me, and when the animal bones came out, they knew what species they belonged to, often sooner than I did. This cave and these men held more wisdom than all the books in Widener Library, and I felt like an exile when we got through.

But we felt even worse one day in the middle of the dig. Our cook drowned. He, Mr. Samadie, and the schoolmaster, along with the telegraph operator, had formed an impromptu intellectual club of Bisitun. They discussed literature, read poetry together, and otherwise made up for their lack of city life by each others' company.

The first three (for the telegraph operator could not leave his key) walked across the fields to the bank of the turbulent, unfordable Gamas-i-Ab to bathe, for none of them could swim. Nosrat Allah stepped in too far, and vanished from sight. Later his body washed up on a bank farther down, and Charles Coon drove the jeep, with the body in the trailer, to the gendarmerie. The dead boy's uncle, Ali Askar, took his place as cook. Ali Askar had been on opium, but was now (we hoped) forever cured.*

My sources on the dig at Bisitun, as in the other caves noted in this chapter and the next one, are four: my copious diaries; my book *The*

This drowning incident consumed eleven pages of The Seven Caves. *The disturbance it caused in the village and among the officials, missionaries, and especially the deceased's kinfolk, was a classic example of what happens when an outside force strikes a system in equilibrium, as stated in* Principles of Anthropology.

Seven Caves; my monographs, in the case of Bisitun, Tamtama, Khunik, and the first season at Belt—*Cave Explorations in Iran, 1949,* Museum Monographs, The University Museum, Philadelphia, 1951; and my memory, which is perhaps more emotional than factual, tempered by Lisa's own.

Both my diaries are too verbose and fussy, my "popular" book too pop-science and too gussied up. But the monograph is brief and down-to-earth. From it I shall quote a little because it applies to my other caves in Asia and not just to Bisitun.

> *These four [Iranian caves—Bisitun, Tamtama, Khunik, and Belt] will have to serve as an attempt at geographical coverage. Being pioneer work, their excavation can only be regarded as a thin set of pins in a very obscure map. I would like to see these pins pieced in like a fence from the Karun River to Zahidan. For the moment, this is all we have. What it is has meaning. Negative evidence is ruled out.*
>
> *. . . I must be sure to excavate with the utmost care and mathematical precision, so that the flints, sherds, and bones that [other experts] identify can be properly related to one another.*
>
> *The Persian workmen use by preference a curved iron pick called the* kolang. *The bit of this implement is a little over 20 cm long. Hence it is easy to teach excavators to remove the soil within a designated area in 20 centimeter levels. As soon as they learn that they are being paid for precision work, and for their ability to excavate objects without breaking them, instead of by the cubic meter of earth removed, many of them, especially the older men, develop sufficient skill for the purpose. Those who do not can be assigned to the bucket line, and the sharp-eyed youngsters to the sieves.*
>
> *In [the soil within the cave one finds] a succession of layers of different kinds of soil, each deposited over a long period, more by geological than by ecological means. In this soil are to be found all sorts of objects, capable of preservation under local conditions, which the inhabitants of the cave have discarded, lost, or buried, at various times. The gross unit of stratigraphy is a special kind of soil. This layer, sometimes half a meter in depth may, however, represent a thousand years or more. Within the upper and lower zones of this layer important changes may be found in artifact types and the species of animals represented by bones. Hence it is profitable to excavate such a site by the smallest practical units, which amount to about twenty centimeters. Some will be thicker, others thinner. When a break is found between two kinds of soil, it is advisable to make the dividing line the bottom of one excavated level and the top of the next. But in the dim light of a cave it is not always possible to see such a break when it is reached. Small lenses [of different colored or textured soils] often lead to false alarms. Sometimes the change can only be determined from the section left on the wall of a trench. In such a case, the strict*

Lisa and I crawl out of the back part of Bisitun Cave.

adherence to the 20 cm rule permits at least the designation of zones of mixture, and all is far from lost. Every piece that comes out of a 20 cm strip is kept strictly with its fellows, and these pieces are bagged in strip units.

Before they are bagged, however, all of the subjects, whether handed out of the trench by workmen or recovered by the crew at the sieves, must be washed. In the case of flints, a count is made, by cores, unused blanks, and implements. If this count runs into the thousands, as it does in the more fruitful caves, many of the cores and most of the flake and blade scrap can be thrown away after enumeration. So can the uncharred bone scraps, hopeless from the standpoint of identification and useless as Carbon-14 material, and most of the pebbles, flat stones, and other alien bits of stone which could only have entered the cave in the hands of men.

This type of excavation ... is time-consuming and tedious [but] it permits an amateur like myself to make an original contribution, that of a statistical analysis. Were it not for a number of quantitative physico-chemical changes in inorganic substances, life would never have arisen, nor the human mind, nor archaeology.

Bisitun was dug over thirty years ago. I was working on a shoestring, with no "experts" along but myself. Carbon-14 was in its swaddling clothes, and thermolucent dating of pottery not yet a dream. I was more like a plant explorer than like a gardener. Later users of mathematical analysis save all the scrap; I had not the means to take it home. Anyhow, like it or leave it, that's the way I worked.

The deposit at Bisitun was twenty-two and a half feet deep. It started with twenty centimeters of grayish rubbish over sixty centimeters of disturbed black earth with some pottery, then sixty centimeters more of gritty red Pleistocene soil as at The High Cave, overlaying rich Brown soil, and finally clay, which is usually found at the bottom of caves. When you reach it this means you are "getting down to gebel" as George Reisner did at his pyramid.

In the gray we found everything from a broken triangle of a green beer bottle, stamped NO DEPOSIT NO RE (break), to bits of water vessels made of clay tempered with chaff to make the walls porous and the water cool; underneath were some painted, handmade sherds identified as somewhere in the Fertile-Crescent Neolithic sequence, and through it all the pathetic eggshell-like fragments of an unfortunate baby had been buried.

Geologically also this was a no-deposit period, unless Darius's inscription carvers, hewing their stone steps down behind them, had scraped off whatever it had been. The Red soil underneath was peppered with slivers of limestone, as if they had been broken off by water freezing and swelling in the cracks overhead. The browner earth below the fallen stones was smoother and slicker.

After we came home I made a plasticene model of the soil we had removed, from its pointed bottom to the flat surface where we had begun. Then the museum's caster made a negative replica of it, and I filled it with water, which was measured, to scale.

We had removed 39.26 cubic meters, or 1402.14 cubic feet, which had contained 22,792 artifacts: 6,500 pieces of flint, 12,542 of bone, and 3,750 of potsherds and brickbats. The ceramic materials were in or near the topmost layer, and the greatest concentration of flints and bones was in the Brown layer between the 3.5- and 4.0-meter depths. There we found 1,887 pieces of flint and 4,226 of bone, making a total density of 2,967.5 objects per cubic meter, or 16.26 per cubic foot. They were packed like Coronas in a cigar box, with hardly any soil at all between the pieces. Picks were lying on the platform, bucket men just lifted the flints reverently out of the excavators' caps, and the sieve men yawned or smoked cigarettes.

Such a sight I have never seen in any cave before or since. Nor had passerby spectators, including some Seventh-Day Adventist missionaries in air-conditioned limousines and panama hats.

How could I explain this squirreling of artifacts? There were four kinds of flints: discarded cores, from which the flakes to be processed further had been struck; scraps discarded like carpenter's chips; perfect or almost perfect points, scrapers, or knife blades, which had been retouched by snapping tiny flakelets off the edge, either to serrate them or to eliminate a nick; and the magnificent finished tools, of which we had found 1,151 in that 39-cubic-meter cave.

Having found all four kinds in one place, each in its proper ratio to the others, meant that it must have been a factory site where hunters carried in flint nodules with their chalky crusts already broken off to reduce weight—also a cache?

The bones meant that they had eaten there too, mostly the flesh of wild horses and of the red deer (*Cervus elaphus*) that North Americans call elk. Below the rockfall, at 2.5 to 3.0 meters, their meat was more horse than venison; while during and after ice had chipped the cliff above, the latter headed the list. In the absence of good dating, one can only suppose that that earliest tool knappers in that cave lived in a relatively mild, dry—or both—climate, which grew colder and wetter as time went on, perhaps to the end of the Pleistocene, who knows?

No trace of fire was found in the cave. Either the knappers had roasted their meat outside it and brought in cold snacks to nibble on, or they ate it raw. Knowing that other Neanderthals elsewhere cooked their meat, we figured that it must have been roasted, but not very

FLAKES STRUCK FROM PREPARED CORES, MIDDLE PALEOLITHIC

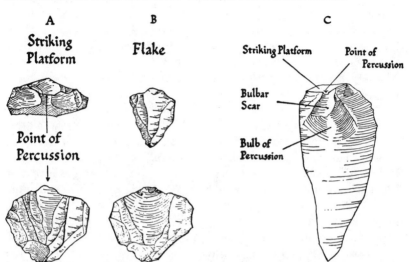

Making a flake on a prepared core. (A) The upper drawing represents the butt or top end of a prepared core. Its entire surface is a striking platform. Lower view shows the front of the prepared core. In both, the outline of the flake to be detached is marked by a heavy line. (B) The core has been struck by a hammer blow at the point of percussion and the flake, shown above, removed. The front of the remaining core is shown below. (After H. Kelly) (One-fourth actual size.) (C) Anatomy of a flake. Rear view of a typical flake removed from a prepared core. The butt end is the remains of the striking platform. Note that most of the work and forethought went into preparing the core, otherwise a useless lump of stone. (One-half actual size.)

much, and certainly not boiled. The clue was that every piece of shaft bone had been crushed to extract the marrow.

After we came home, one of my staff, Theressa Howard Carter, bought a goat at the Italian market in Philadelphia. She boiled one of its hindquarters behind the museum, and roasted the other. The boiled bone broke with a snap and its marrow slid loosely out of its shaft. The other, which had been only lightly roasted, had to be crushed, because the marrow clung tightly to its moorings; all the marrow bones at Bisitun had thus been smashed to splinters.

Twelve bones, omitted from the menus, were ornaments or tools. Two perforated seal's teeth, and one of a wild ass, indicate far wanderings or trade, because the nearest seals swam in the Caspian Sea, and the identified fauna contained no ass. Two shaft bones were spokeshaves and one a flesher, showing that they worked both wood and hides. Two others were spatulas, suggesting some cosmetic use with pigments, and two were deliberately broken horses' molars, which might have been used as fine retouching tools in sharpening the edges of flint blades. There were even two bone needles, one broken at the lower border of its eye. The men or women were sewing skins, most likely although not certainly into robes, as worn by some of the southern Australian aborigines and the Fuegian Indians into modern times.

The important thing about these bone tools is that they all came from the Red earth above the rockfall, laid down in cold weather. I can recall no needles from Neanderthal sites in Europe, or in Palestine; only the Upper Paleolithic men made them. But the Upper Paleolithic men made great use of staghorn, both as implements and as media on which to carve and etch mobiliary art. We found none of this at Bisitun.

When we study the tables in my 1951 report, we see that progress was being made throughout the levels of the Pleistocene deposits. True blades—struck from more or less cylindrical cores with flat bases, not with a stone hammer directly, but with a more or less elastic dowel like one of the accompanying horse's teeth—began with the rockfall and persisted through to the end. But they did not replace the flake tools, which were made throughout the occupation of the cave. The proportion of flakes made on faceted butts to those struck off cores quite randomly increased arithmetically, as did the regularity of the trimming along the cutting edges.

The spear points—in the form of triangles, struck off as flakes—ran through the entire sequence, for they were needed to provide meat. While horsehide is thicker and tougher than elkhide, in both species a wounded animal is likely to thrash about, and if a shallowly inserted spear point is too thin it may snap, and the shaft will fall out. With this in mind, I measured the thicknesses of all such points and found that their optimum thickness was lumped at 6 to 7 mm, with a range from 3 to 14, and the higher up in the soils we went, the more the range decreased.

On the whole their stone tools were more varied and fancier than those of many living marginal hunting peoples made during the last 150 years. These living peoples are all called *Homo sapiens sapiens,* by the current trend of thought, but what kind of men were the Bisitun flint knappers and hunters?

All we found to answer this question were one broken radius (thumb-side lower arm bone) and one upper right lateral incisor tooth. Both came from the lower Brown earth between 3.5 and 4.0 meters from the top. Both were clearly and exaggeratedly Neanderthal, as

PERFECTION IN THE MIDDLE PALEOLITHIC

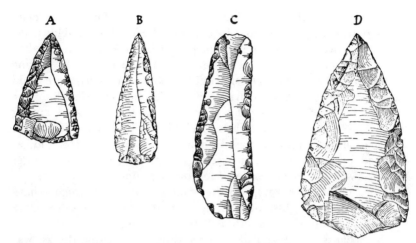

As at Tangier, the Middle Paleolithic flint-workers of Bisitun approached perfection
in the fabrication of flake tools. Their principal types were points (A) and knives (C).
Equally perfect were large, 1½-inch wide spear-points with butts narrowed for hafting,
as (D), from the Cave of the Heifer's Outwash in the Syrian Desert. (All four specimens
one-half full size.)

SMALL TOOLS OF THE MESOLITHIC

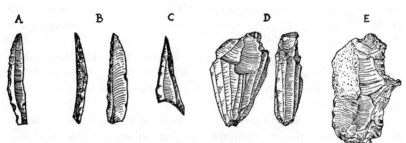

Among the caves we dug the richest in Mesolithic tools (ca. 9500–6600 B.C.) were from
Belt and Hotu on the Caspian shore. We named the levels for the principal animal
bones found with them—seal Mesolithic from both. (A) A small blade blunted to be
held in the curve of the index finger; (B) another one from Hotu; (C) a geometric
form from Belt, probably used as a barb in a missile head. Mesolithic Vole-Eaters of
Hotu: (D) a microlithic blade core; (E) a flake retouched in the form of a narrow
beak or drill. (All one-half actual size.)

careful comparisons with European and Palestinian bones and teeth revealed.

But were they living in a time when horses roamed the plain down to the bank of the Gamas-i-Ab, before the ice above had loosened the rocks above them, and before the people in the Red-earth time had either invented or, more likely, borrowed the technique of making blades? With the solid progression of blade-knapping skills, there could hardly have been an abrupt change of peoples, but had something else been added to the local gene pool, or had they mutated among themselves? Or had their children's children simply used the brains they had inherited to increased advantage, as people later did, as depicted in my chart of time versus energy at the end of Chapter Twenty-Two? The eyed needle came from the upper soil.

No further digging on the Iranian plateau of which I have heard has answered this question, not even the excavation of the Cave of the Ass by Philip L. K. Smith of Toronto in 1965.

That is why I said in the preceding chapter that the ass was myself, for I had measured it and photographed it, but had done nothing about it until I received a letter from Dr. Smith asking me if I would please send him a flash photograph that I had shot inside it in December 1948. He needed it for the report of his dig. In his trenching he had found a thin layer of microliths, pierced teeth, and other transitional artifacts, insecurely dated, but probably covering the demise of the Pleistocene and the birth of the Mesolithic, which preceded agriculture in many parts of the Northern Hemisphere.* It has been given the name Zarzian locally.

If Philip Smith had never found it, nor dug other Iranian sites as well, I would not be able to offer a solution to the Bisitun problem, which I have been wondering about in odd moments for the last quarter of a century.

What we had on top of the Red soil had been a mixture of the Zarzian, painted-pottery Neolithic, and metal-age Persian. The time that passed between the infant burial and our Pleistocene stuff underneath ran into tens of thousands of years. What Philip Smith had found in the Cave of the Ass was two other industries, separated from each other by a band of sterile soil. One was an older Mousterian than what

---

Smith, P. E. L., "Survey of Excavation of Ghar-i-Khar and Ganjj-i-Dareh," Iran, Vol. V (1967), pp. 138–9. Young, T. Cuyler, Jr., and Philip E. L. Smith, "Research in the Prehistory of Central Western Iran," Science, Vol. 153, No. 3734, July 22, 1966, pp. 386–396. Smith, Philip E. L., The Paleolithic of Iran, in "Mélanges . . . offerts à André Varagnac." École Practiques des Hautes Etudes—VIe Section, Centre des Recherches Prehistoriques, Paris, 1971, pp. 682–695.

we had taken from our bottom layer, and the other was a "Baradostian," a local Upper Paleolithic industry which ran from about 37,000 years ago to about 25,000 B.C., a duration of only (as far as we know) 10,000 years. It was a generalized Upper Paleolithic, with the burin (a thick, narrow chisel) as its principal instrument, and it was not likely to have been ancestral to the full-blown Upper Paleolithic of Europe and the Asian lands farther west.

The overall sequence of the industries of Bisitun and the Cave of the Ass are, from bottom to top (1) a rather crude Mousterian lacking fancy flakes struck from prepared, faceted, cores (Levalloisio-Mousterian), or blades, which may have begun 100,000 years ago (this from the Cave of the Ass); (2) a later Levalloisio-Mousterian with blades in its later phase, and one burin in the lower Brown earth (Bisitun); it may have ended between 49,000 and 40,000 years ago. Then (3) probably after another gap, the Baradostian, which was apparently not derived from its Bisitun predecessor, then another gap; and (4) the Zarzian, followed by the painted-pottery Neolithic, without an intervening phase of unpainted pottery.

Before I state my probably obvious conclusions, please let me pose one unsolved mystery: Why did hunters, Neanderthal or otherwise, occupy these two caves alternately, instead of, just for a little while, both at once? Obviously it never crossed their minds that it would be a help to Philip Smith and me. But they did it just the same—I thank them all in retrospect—and helped us solve our mystery.

As of late in 1975 it would seem that Dorothy Garrod, who had dug Hazer Merd (One Hundred Men) on the other side of the Zagros, was probably wrong: Our wonderful Nordic ancestors did not evolve on the Iranian plateau, but Neanderthals and later men walked in and out of the wings like actors on a two-set stage, in a play that took a near-eternity. In 1980 I am not so sure. Evolution on the spot may have been a possibility.

On July 19, 1949, we left Bisitun at nine o'clock in the morning with the jeep and trailer loaded to the gills. We arrived at Hamadan at one o'clock for lunch in Marie Zoeckler's house. There we lost David Elder and greeted Paul Schuhmacher, who had driven up from Tehran in the Chicago yellow jeep and trailer. During our stay there we met the governor, who was a burly Bakhtiari nomad chief. Paul had left his jacket-coat in Tehran, anticipating no formalities; but I had two, and I loaned him one, which, being very muscular, he nearly split. The governor had seen his own picture in Cooper and Schoedsack's documentary movie *Grass*. Everyone laughed at Schoedsack, he said, because his name meant "He became a dog." He told me there were lots of caves in *his* country, just ripe for us to dig, but we had other plans—

to see what we might find in other caves in the northwest corner of the country, higher up and even colder than Bisitun and the Ass.

We left quite early on Sunday, July 24, with a curious seating plan. Paul refused to let Samadie into his jeep because the latter, who had spent a few days in Tehran arranging things, had ridden up with Paul, who spoke French almost as well as Samadie did, but in a different accent and in an even more different frame of mind. Lisa too, to my surprise, refused to ride with Samadie, because he had shoved his nose into our bedroom just before six o'clock and caught her unawares. So Lisa and the cook rode with Paul, and Charles and Samadie with me.

This double arrangement had one advantage—I could keep my eye on Charles, sitting beside me on the front seat. He had been running a mild fever of a little above 100°F, but that morning it was normal, so the doctors agreed to let him come.

It also had one disadvantage. In the haste of who sits where and trailer packing. Ali Askar, the cook, had prepared a surprise for us. It was a two-gallon pail of gooseberry jam that he had just made, and he stowed it in the yellow trailer without a proper lid. As we jostled over the bumpy road toward the Tabriz junction, what happened next had one bored-looking spectator—Mr. Habibullah Samadie, our inspector.

Having passed two no-vacancy inns in the gloaming, we tented that night in a dry river bed, with Ali Askar and me sleeping near the vehicles, on guard. At 3:15 A.M. we heard a clump, clump of galloping hoofs approaching us down the draw. In a flash and with a torch Ali Askar was on his feet, a few seconds before me. It was just a herd of donkeys, but my fellow guardsman stayed awake to cook us all a belly-warming breakfast over firewood, and we were off at seven.

It was still cool and crisp as we rumbled down a twelve-turn mountain road flanking the torrential Aji Chai, or Bitter River, toward the outskirts of Tabriz, which stood at 4,400 feet. Tabriz then had a population of possibly a quarter of a million, almost as many as Tehran, and was once the nation's largest city.

The Aji Chai provided it with enough water for an even larger population, but before it reached the city walls it was put to another use—grinding flour. We passed a millstone-cutters' quarry, and then a row of fifteen or more gearless turbine gristmills. Along the banks of a tributary to the right stood a line of many more.

Tabriz was the plum in the middle of a ragged-edged ethnic pie, with slices of Armenians, Assyrians (Nestorian Aramaic-speaking Christians), Azari Turks, Shah-Sevans (Turkish-speaking, horse-breeding cavalrymen, the Shah's most loyal border guards against the Russians), and, along the Iraqi border and spilling over into Turkey and the

COMPARATIVE CHRONOLOGY OF BISITUN AND THE CAVE OF THE ASS

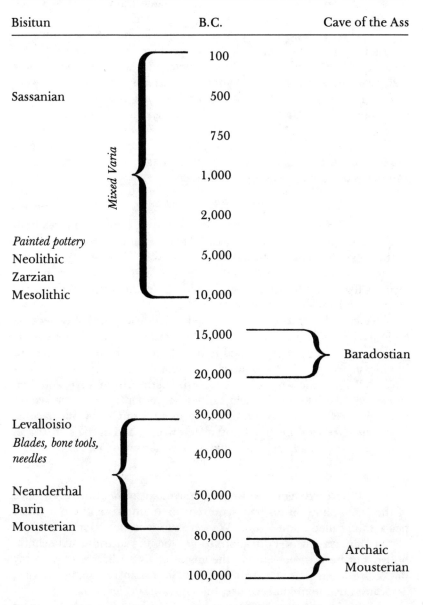

Bisitun	B.C.	Cave of the Ass
	100	
Sassanian	500	
	750	
Mixed Varia	1,000	
	2,000	
Painted pottery Neolithic Zarzian Mesolithic	5,000	
	10,000	
	15,000	
	20,000	Baradostian
Levalloisio *Blades, bone tools, needles*	30,000	
	40,000	
Neanderthal Burin Mousterian	50,000	
	80,000	
	100,000	Archaic Mousterian

Russian Transcaucasia, a slice of bitter lemon, the ancient, fundamentalist, sunni, Aryan Kurds, who called water *0* and man *merd*, which is what they seemed to think of most of the outside world.

Their ancestors had rolled boulders down on Xenophon's ten thousand Greeks, as every schoolboy used to know. When we were there their rebellion had just been squelched; their president, a holy man, was hanged in Mahabad Square, and his mourning followers were chanting, when alone: "Mullah Mohammed our King will rise again!" and it sounded to me like: "They're hanging men and women for the wearing of the green."

In a sense, the comparison was apt, for of twenty-five of a single tribe that I measured later (the Shikak), one had blue eyes, another brown, and all the rest had green.

The atmosphere was as taut as a frayed fiddle string ready to snap at the touch of the bow. When Lisa and I came down to breakfast at the Reverend Hugo Muller's house (he was Art's father), we were about a minute late, and our host said a six-syllable grace in two seconds flat: "God bless our food Amen." Then he turned the knob of his radio to hear the news from the BBC.

Samadie, who had been tossed in jail twice, probably because he looked so nervous, and who felt the presence of his father's murderers across the border, dashed in to tell me that he had arranged to broadcast over the local radio station, easily audible in Soviet Azerbaijan, all about our wonderful discoveries in the Bisitun cave, and then where we planned to go next, and what other marvels we would uncover—but before I could open my mouth, our savvy and laconic host squelched this idea in almost as few words, and at the same pace, in Persian, as he had used an hour or so earlier saying grace.

Where we went next was to Rizaiyeh, near the shore of the lake of the same name. Both had acquired that name recently, but many people still called them Urmia. We were supposed to visit the secretary of the Department of Education, to get lodging in the usual schoolhouse, but he was out. So was the governor. But I had a letter in my pocket from our host at Tabriz to Rabbi Shimshan Talyan, not Jewish, as almost anyone might suppose, but an Assyrian clergyman.

We went there at once, were all warmly greeted and most hospitably treated, and there began what might be called our Assyrian Connection, for as with other frowned-upon minorities, they claimed us and coddled us as their own.

Among them we met a most remarkable man, named Isaac Emmanual Shavel, who said of himself, in the third person: "Isaac is six men. He speaks six languages, and can do the work of six."

Part one of this statement was true. Part two was exaggerated twofold. Before morning he had written out a list of about a dozen caves, as well as the names of several Christian landlords within a few hours' jeep ride, but before we could start Samadie had darted out to see the education man and we had to move to a large, spacious, and empty normal school in which we camped like Gypsies in a rented grocery shop, carefully attended by its Turkish janitor.

While we were there Lisa missed her wristwatch. The janitor's son, aged twelve or so, had stolen it, as his father soon found out, and he heated a length of wire red hot and poked it through the skin and muscle of his son's right hand until it came out, with a horrid stench, on the other side. He had picked the adductor muscle between the meta-carpal bones of the index finger and the thumb. The boy was sent to live with kinfolk in the country. Lisa wished that she had never had a watch.

One day when we had returned early from our usual fruitless search, Paul and Charles proposed a swim in Lake Rizaiyeh, which is said to be the saltiest in the world. Samadie tried to stop us, saying that it was very dangerous—we might be shot. But we went anyway, with a dozen or so others, mostly young men. After a long wade out we jumped in, only to find ourselves lifted immediately to the surface, and then to stand like losers in a pie-throwing contest, encrusted in salt.

What the local young men had come there for, and what Samadie had tried to keep us from, was seeing the fat wives of wealthy Turkish merchants taking their beauty dips. Swathed in black robes with one eye peeking out, they were led by servants out to about navel depth. There the servants whisked off their ladies' robes and left them without bathing suits, to float on their backs on the brine, like lady customers on the tables of masseuses.

On Thursday, August 2, Six-Man Emmanuel led us to our cave, Tamtama. As I wrote in my report:

Tamtama is the local name of a cave. Today it means nothing, although phil-ologically it falls close to an old Semitic word for the sea. From its mouth Lake Urmiya is visible. It is situated at about 44° 57' East Longitude and 37° 36' North Latitude, some 13 miles north of the city of Rezaiyeh, at an elevation of about 5,000 feet. It lies in a border region in many respects. Behind are the mountains, in front is the plain. Kurds own the land west of the cave while east of it the landlords are Azerbaijani Turks. . . . Azerbaijanis, Kurds, and Assyrians all meet in this neighborhood. . . . The grass is green all summer, and thunderstorms bring rain in late July and August. In winter it is snowed in for several months at a time. Even in summer the temperature is cool, and the Kurds wear heavy felt clothing. During any period colder than the present, Tamtama would be uninhabitable most of the year.

Tamtama was large enough so that all of us could sleep there, work there, and eat there. We began to unpack at once and set up our folding cots and table, when a noisy quarrel took place outside. One Shikak Kurd on horseback said the cave belonged to him, while an Azerbaijani landlord said it was his, and demanded an enormous price. Assyrian shepherds in conical felt cloaks, leaning on their crooks, stood looking on ominously.

Said Samadie, "We must go to the governor and get three hundred soldiers." "No," said Emmanuel, "we must go get the word of Amr Khan." He was the leader of the Shikak tribe, and to them his word was law. He was not at home.

I simply hired a team of workmen on the spot, half Assyrian and half Shikak, the Assyrians being tenants of the Turk. Ali Askar bought a fat goat, and butchered it outside so that its blood might dribble down the slope. Lisa stayed inside the cave, while Paul took a roll of Kodachrome of the butchering and Charles lay on his cot; finally, by Coleman lantern light, we ate the goat.

From this point on my diary is so full of hullabaloo that I shall only note here that we dug Tamtama until dusk on August 10, when we were through. What follows is from my cave report.

Tamtama is a forked cave. Therefore we laid out a square where the branches met. As expected, the deposit immediately underfoot was of sheep manure, too old and caked to be easily removed by the shepherds. This deposit went down for about 50–75 cms, after which we struck bedrock. At the bottom of the manure layer we found pieces of porcelain, made in Russia less than a century earlier. Therefore we shifted our excavation until we found a section where soil underlay the manure. This was a yellow, sandy soil, full of small flecks of limestone, and larger pieces which had fallen from the roof. In its puddinglike appearance it resembled the area of rockfall in Bisitun. It yielded few bones, and no flints.

Below it was an area of plain yellow, sandy soil, without flecks or fall, and hence comparable to the fine, soft brown soil in Bisitun. This contained most of the bones and of the "implement" material. It will not detract from what follows to reveal that Tamtama was a very poor cave, the home of a very poor people. It was probably too high and too cold to attract permanent occupants. What we found,

including a piece of a Neanderthaloid femur, was probably left there by an alter-
nation of human summer visitors and hyenas.

No attempt was made to divide the remains from Tamtama into levels.
The workmen, half . . . Shikak Kurds and . . . half . . . Assyrians, were more
interested in their mutual rivalries, in singing warlike songs, and in turning out
vast quantities of earth, than in learning stratigraphy. A separation of the white-
flecked [later] Pleistocene level from the lower, later one might have been pertinent,
but this is dubious. The 24 pieces of "implement" material were all from the lower
yellow. None were really implements. . . . The ratios of articulating pieces of scrap
[bone] and of teeth and jaws to other pieces, remind one of the situation in the lowest
and highest levels at Bisitun, as does the number of bones per shaft fragments. Some
of these bones were gnawed by animals with pointed teeth and powerful jaws. The
identity of these culprits is easy to discover, since they left their calcareous calling
cards behind them. They were hyenas, who must have taken turns with human
beings as occupants of Tamtama.

There were 2,790 pieces of bone in our trenches, or 169.1 per
cubic meter, versus 1.45 pieces of flint. Obviously the hyenas were the
hardier of the inhabitants, but not necessarily the brainier. The almost-
implements were leftovers made by the same techniques as at Bisitun,
of which I wrote: ". . . Man does not think with his forearm, tooth, or
thighbone. If anyone is surprised that tools as excellent as those of
Bisitun were made by Neanderthal man, he should remember that no
braincase of these people has yet been discovered in Iran."

As far as I know at the time I am writing, that statement published thirty years ago is still true.

During the eleven days we stayed at Tamtama, the rest of us
were constantly worried by the health of my son, which varied alternately for the first few days, and then grew worse. I had received a letter
from Dr. John Frame of Hamadan telling me to bring Charles back as
soon as I could if and when certain symptoms appeared. One of these
was a drop in temperature, which fell to 97° just before we left.

The red tape we cut in leaving would fill a room of moderate
size, and to make a long and frightening story short, we took him back
to the schoolhouse at Rizaiyeh, and then down an otherwise forbidden
military road along the Iraqi border almost to Hamadan. I did it by
telling the guard the simple truth: Lisa's thermometer read 95°. The
surface of the road was as smooth as Route 128. But when we reached
the Hamadan highway, all was bumpety-bump. Paul shed the yellow
trailer without knowing it, and had to backtrack fifteen miles.

We got Charles into the Presbyterian Hospital, where he was
diagnosed as having either Malta or undulant fever from unpasteurized
milk. There happened to be a Persian lady patient there with the same

disease, and John Frame made some serum that saved both their lives.

When he was able to travel alone, I drove Charles to Tehran and put him on a plane, among scores of Persian students bound for stateside colleges, and he got back just in time to enter Harvard.

After Charles's departure we dined that evening with Dr. and Mrs. Elder, at whose house we met a Swiss Pleistocene geologist named Dr. I. Rieben. He had written his Ph.D. thesis at the Université de Neuchâtel on the geology of that age in Persian Azerbaijan. He placed the cave of Tamtama on the lowest of three terraces. Had it then been inhabited, it might have contained the bones and artifacts of pre-Neanderthal men, and we might have made a major discovery in human evolution. But it apparently hadn't been inhabited at that time.

He then told me that during the glacial maxima, when the climate was colder than at present, there was too little precipitation to form an ice cap, and the lower Brown soil that we had excavated was from such a period, whereas our Red soil was moister, with winter freezing that would account for the chips of stone. So, on the sequences of cultures chart for Bisitun and the Cave of the Ass, as I just now realize (Figure 17), the position of the lower left-hand box may have been substantially correct, ending before the 32,000 or so mark, when the Upper Paleolithic began elsewhere.

In the last week of August it was still too early to revisit the Caspian shore, where the summers were too wet and hot for comfortable excavation. So we set the caves we had almost seen in January in the second-class compartments of our minds. We had been shooting too high, I thought, in altitude. Why not try the lower lands near the Afghan border—the Sarrakhs Corridor, where the Arabs had swept northward from the Indian Ocean toward Merv and Bukhara, whence Ibn Fadhlan had traveled westward among the still-heathen Turks to write about the equally heathen Northmen, as told in Chapter 14 of my *Reader*.

We left on August 28, with Lisa and Mannie (Six-Man Emmanuel) with me, and Samadie and Ali Askar with Paul. That night we camped in the garden of the governor of Shāhrūd (Samadie still insisted that we use government property and keep out of hotels). It was pilgrim time, time for pious Shi'a to visit the holy shrine of Imam Riza in Mashhad. Many of them, including whole families, were bravely shuffling along on foot, crossing a stretch of desert without water, and suffering from thirst.

They were begging for water from every passing vehicle. One

old woman very pathetically held out her bottom-up clay cup, sticking her parched tongue out at the same time. I stopped the jeep, and filled her cup from my own canteen. This could not go on. Had Paul and I been driving water-sprinkling tankers instead of jeeps, we might still have run dry before Mashhad.

To save ourselves the shame and agony of riding callously past these conscience-torturing simulacra of rational human beings, we turned left off the main drag to Mashhad and followed a northern route. The road saved us eight farsakhs (the parasangs of Xenophon), or forty-eight miles. The road was so corduroyed and full of pits and holes that the windshield stanchions of our jeep snapped right off, leaving us to face the wind and dust without goggles, leather caps, or scarves.

But we rolled into Mashhad through a little-used gate where no one asked us for our red cards. When Paul caught up we found that his windshield had snapped off too. Thanks to Manny's nose for directions, we went straight to the house of the missionary, Dr. Mark Irwin, whom we had already met at Tehran, possibly the least inhibited of his brethren, and always fun to be with.

Wednesday, August 31, was a busy, busy day. I met almost everyone I should have, including the chiefs of police and gendarmerie, and a landowner who is also a judge. Number One gave us permits, Number Three told us of a surefire cave he owned, and Two volunteered to send us a sergeant to go with us, at the crack of dawn.

The next morning we were awakened at five to loud drumming and the shrill of shawms. The drums were on the five-beat, and the shawms on slightly different notes, like drones. The musicians sat on the top of a gate, greeting the rising sun, as their ancestors had done before the Arabs came.

Beth Irwin, our host and hostess's daughter, was awakened at the same time—not by the music, for she was used to it, but by something else. Running to her mother, she tremulously said, "Mother, there's a great big man with mustaches and a gun outside my window!"

She was right. He was Sergeant Brahim the Baluchi, a bit ahead of time. He was not really a Baluchi, who are related to the Kurds, but a Brahui, who live among them. Their language is Dravidian, like Tamil of southern India, and possibly that of the builders of the Indus Valley civilization.

He looked like a Sikh—those tall, burly, heavily bearded soldiers of the Indian Empire, who fought for the emperor in London for three hundred years before Indian independence reduced them to becoming taxi drivers, airplane pilots, and decorative doormen in Hong Kong hotels.

He and Six-Man Mannie made a stalwart team, along with

equally burly Paul, a fitting bodyguard for quaking Sammie, who was being driven to the scene of his father's abduction.

The place we were looking for was Bizangan, twelve miles off the Sarrakhs road. All the way the sergeant had been shooting out of the moving jeep at coveys of quail, and once at a distant mountain goat which, luckily, he missed. Bizangan was a village of 110 families, completely isolated and ruled by a six-feet-two youth of twenty who was as fair as Samadie, but powerfully built, vigorous, decisive, and unmarried. He didn't really need a wife, the sergeant said, because he had *jus primae noctis* over every village girl on her wedding night, thus saving possible embarrassment and producing what modern social anthropologists call "the founder effect"—what, in simpler-speaking days, was plain old eugenics. Remember that?

Off we went to seek the cave, about one mile on horses, which the others took, but nearly nine miles in a jeep, taken by me. When I got there and found the others rested, and my back nearly broken, I asked why had I not also been given a horse? It was Samadie who had arranged things. I was too important for a saddle and hooves; I had to ride over wheels. (Any expletive that comes to the reader's mind may be inserted here).

It was huge cave, entered through a small mouth, fifteen feet long by nine high at the peak. Inside, its chamber was over three hundred feet long, sixty to seventy feet wide, and fifty to sixty feet high. It was full of rockfall, which would have to be smashed and moved outside, and two curved pools of water, like dentist's spittoons, which would have to be drained. And squashed atop the fallen rocks were tons and tons of creamy-gray pigeon shit, which would have to be barrowed out before the rocks could be struck; the cooing and gurgling overhead meant that our workers would have to wear rubber turbans.

And who would these workers be? Not the men of the 110 families, for the harvest was just ripening, and the next month or so would be their reaping time. And there was no one else around. It was too big a project; Samadie was too shell-shocked; and we had not enough time, money, or staff to handle it. Some other time, perhaps, or some other archaeologist. I could have wept.

When we got back to Mashhad, three things happened. Without consultation or warning, Paul made the pilgrimage. Looking like any robust Persian in western clothes, he walked in line through the holy mosque of Imam Riza, kissed the golden doors, and walked out again undetected.

As soon as the missionaries, mission hospital doctors, and the

British and American consular officers heard of this they neither laughed nor gasped. They just looked grim. I should get Paul out of there before he was recognized, or every Christian in the city might be killed.

At almost the same moment word leaked through from border crossers that the Russians had exploded their first atomic bomb in nearby Turkmenistan, almost within earshot of the bazaar, through whose labyrinthine alleys the message wriggled and slithered like a snake.

The third thing was that Emmanuel had to leave us at once to resume his teaching at Rizaiyeh, and he had missed the bus. So I bought him an airplane ticket to Tehran, but before he left he found me a reliable Armenian, six feet six and English speaking, to drive my jeep, because Samadie was getting too gaga to interpret correctly, and at age forty-eight, I was growing a little too weak to handle a vehicle over the rough tracks that lay ahead and to think of all our problems too.

After Emmanuel had left, the Armenian changed his mind. He turned the job over to a blue-eyed mechanic named Alexander Davidian, half Assyrian and half Armenian—but, as events turned out, just half ass, the rest being supreme egoist, of Iran or of the world. He had been a driver for the American forces supplying Iran with motorized equipment just a year before, and held a certificate saying so; he had also acquired a G.I. way of speech, less elegant than what the missionaries taught, and his general point of view was also catch-as-catch-can G.I.—a reminder that we had not quite left home.

To me Alex was "Yes, sir! If you please, sir!" snap and click, as if I still wore my major's leaf on each shoulder. To Paul he was "Yeah, buddy," for Paul had been a noncom, and from Paul I got the poop.

Alex's mother had been the most beautiful woman ever born. Three suitors had committed suicide when she rejected them. He himself had won the national male beauty contest, and was Mister Iran. His chief worry was his beautiful legs, which he had to wash all the time.

This information dribbled through from Paul, one piece at a time, but I did not see anything wrong with Alex until, when we were leaving the outskirts of the city, he jammed on the brakes of the blue jeep, which Paul was hugging close behind, and smash! went the blue tail hitch, and the yellow radiator and headlights as well.

We got these things fixed, after a fashion, and rattled on from the fourth of September to the sixteenth, when we found a diggable cave. Meanwhile, we had viewed and photographed enough scenery, desert architecture, with windmills powered by sails on grinding shafts—like the turbine mills outside Tabriz—for a *National Geographic* article.

We also made two false stops for inappropriate caves. One was a chamber at the end of a crawl tunnel that held some remains of coffins and several dehydrated bodies with their skin and hair still on. The other was Pir-i-Asp—either the Holy Man of the Horse, or the Holy Horse (reader's choice), a keyhole-shaped aperture cut through two layers of some deposit turned to stone, with a stream of water trickling out. Local people sacrificed kids to it, and it was said to run many farsakhs underground. We went out to it on horses, for it was near the Afghan border, and men with rifles patrolled the ridge above.

We had spent the previous night in what we might call a ranch, where we were most hospitably treated, and where I first heard Samadie laugh. I had hit my head on a low-hung birdcage, and the birds' water spilled down the back of my neck. Accidentally he had once again played peeping Tom on Lisa, and he left us at Gunabad to see his mother.

Thence we drove across a corner of the Dasht-i-Lut (the Desert of Lot), one of the bleakest and hottest bits of unwanted real estate in the world. When we halted to pour our last tin of gasoline into our jeep tank, and had only a quarter of a canteenful of water left for all of us, Mr. Iran grabbed the canteen and poured about half of that over his hands and on a slice of freshly cut melon. I felt like leaving him there like Lot's wife, to turn into a pillar of salt with the world's most beautiful legs, a monument to envious posterity.

Our final truancy from archaeology was a short trip northeast of the road to Zabol, a small city on the western end of Lake Helmand, a pint-sized Caspian Sea. Its waters flow west out of Afghanistan, and evaporate into the air. Its swamps and creeks and open body remained fresh enough to feed vast schools of fish and flocks of waterfowl in their migrations, both to the advantage of an odd collection of swamp dwellers called Sayyads (Arabic for hunters), not to be confused with Sayyids, or Descendants of the Prophet.

The former set nets across the creeks to catch the ducks and geese by their necks, and the fish, in turn, by their gills. They also netted fish from reed boats when the winds were not too strong, and what they didn't eat they sold in the town. We found out all we could about them and their way of life, and I measured nineteen of them, against much official protest. The lieutenant in town had forbidden me to take their pictures because of an old, long-since-repealed law against foreigners photographing Persians in anything but modern dress. We were about to leave pictureless when a general who came to inspect the place invited us to dinner and said, in English, "What nonsense, go ahead and take any pictures you please."

From swampland fishers and fowlers we turn to Descendants of the Prophet, the inhabitants of Khunik Pai Godar, a free village that we had passed on our left after Samadie had disembarked, on our way south. A free village is a community whose members own it, and who choose their own leader. The difference was between serfs and free yeomen, in 1949, as it had been in Old England or in younger Russia before the serfs were freed.

The men of Khunik wore blue turbans, permitted only to descendants of Muhammad through Fatima and Ali; they stood straight; and they took no lip from any man. They and their wives and children were handsome, well-dressed people, their houses clean, their victuals adequate, their behavior correct and, as far as we could see, without noisy quarrels.

On wide, irrigated terraces they grew a precious crop—saffron—with consummate care, plucking the stamens and pistils from the small, tuliplike buds, and selling it at a fancy price in town. Paul wrote a master's thesis on the life of this village, still as unpublished as my measurements of the Sayyads.*

Across a little valley from the forty houses of Khunik rose a cliff, and under the cliff was a rock shelter named Lakh-i-Aspowr. In it are two pits in which the villagers steam-bend plow beams. The shelter is named after horses, which are sacred, although the beams are used with oxen.

At once we found, lying on the earth's surface in the rock shelter, Mousterian implements, highly patinated. On page 20 of my 1951 monograph, is written:

We laid out a square and went down. The deeper we went the fewer became the flints. On the other hand, pottery, scarce or absent at the top, increased. We soon discovered that we were excavating a dump of the early Islamic period where . . . the [original] village of Khunik had been located. . . . We discovered that a groove in the cliff seemed to be the main channel by which the paleoliths had reached the surface. . . . Above this groove we found the remnants of a small cave, which must have been smashed by an earthquake at some time after the settlement had been established. Perhaps that is why they moved. This cave was roofless and empty. . . . The best implements were on the top, and the deeper one went, the less impressive the material became.

We bagged and brought home ninety-one Paleolithic implements, all Mousterian. Much to my surprise, working downward by our

---

For a summary of Paul's findings, see my Caravan, *pages 179–182.*

twenty-centimeter levels, they followed the same typological sequence as in Bisitun, with the finest ones on top and the crudest at the bottom. The old village ruin was in its proper order too. Why then, in this upside-down deposit, had the two not met face to face instead of face to back? I did not think of this question at the time, but now, I suspect, the earthquake may not have been the only factor in the flints' downward movement. Maybe it was the water seeping through the softer and lower part of the upper cave's fill that brought its burden down, during a relatively dry period, while when the climate was wetter it had finished its job with the more solid upper fill.

To me this makes sense, but I can't prove it. In any case, Bisitun and Khunik, like Sir Harry Lauder's crooked legs,* held Paleolithic Iran in parentheses, from west to east. With this discovery, the chances of our Upper Paleolithic ancestors having been born on the Iranian plateau grew dimmer and dimmer.

Samadie joined us, riding on an ass, just before we left, and he was cheerier than when last seen. My heart was not in the highlands, but beyond them, on the Caspian shore, where the pomegranates were now ripe, and thither we repaired, after leaving Mr. Iran in Mashhad to face his Mexican wife of Assyrian parentage, one of whose arms he had broken just before his own departure.

On Saturday, October 6, six of us left Tehran for the North. We were Lisa, myself, Paul, Samadie, Ali Askar, and Sohail Azari, who was editor of a Persian-language Christian newspaper. Dr. Elder had given him three weeks' leave to come with us, an assignment that he looked forward to eagerly.

We crossed the mountains by the shortest route, past the Shah's tunnel, which was closed, and over a pass where I chilled my left shoulder so in driving that my left hand—my writing hand—was useless for four more days, during which I drove with my right alone, and dictated to Lisa many pages in my diary.

For the second time we missed our cave, on account of two unfortunate circumstances. In deference to my arm, Paul drove both jeeps, one at a time, to the local filling station. When he was about to wheel the blue jeep into the pumping slot, a soldier in an army jeep smacked across his bow to get there first, almost wrecking both vehicles. Paul took the driver's name and number, as any good soldier should.

---

*For the benefit of readers under seventy, be it known that Sir Harry Lauder was a bowlegged Scottish singer who did much to bring the United States into World War I on the British side.

I found a rumpus in front of the hotel. Several reporters stood there, beside a Swedish United Nations officer and an Iranian lieutenant colonel, all part of a commission to investigate the latest border incident near Gurgan. The lieutenant colonel was shouting at Paul, in a rage, and in French: "You have insulted a soldier!"

In the same language I replied: "My colonel, what is this *blague* about insults?"

Apparently his French was not as colloquial as mine, because he didn't understand that *blague* means simply kidding, or a joke. But the Swede knew what it meant, as he showed with a little smile at the corners of his lips.

The lieutenant colonel went on with his hysterics, screaming, "You call me *blackie*! A Negro!" And he proceeded with a tedious tirade about how we white Americans still treated our more deeply pigmented fellow citizens as slaves, and were now treating the Persians in the same way.

Finally the Swede calmed him down, or he ran out of wattage, and they took off, proceeding very slowly. When I proposed to pass them on the road and stop eating their dust, Samadie panicked again, and lest he collapse, we followed them. Both their dust and the twilight kept us from seeing our caves. We spent a comfortable night in an inn at Behshahr, which had a young bear roaming in its courtyard, and in the morning kept straight on to Gurgan without seeing any caves.

Red-card trouble pinned us in that neighborhood, as well as jeep repairs, so to keep from wasting time we drove out in one vehicle to Turang Tepe, which Dr. Frederick R. Wulsin had excavated for the University Museum before the war. We had both been anthropology tutors at Harvard in the 1930s; my elder son had married his daughter, and we became co-grandfathers of a tribe of expected hellions. He had beat me to it on the Caspian shore, in a time when there had been less bureaucracy.

In the shadow of Freddy's mud-and-brick pyramid squatted the yurts of nomadic Turkomans, on some of whom we called. The insides of their Bucky Fuller dwellings were as neatly and functionally arranged as the captain's bridge on a ship. My notes on them, in Lisa's hand, are voluminous, but we had to leave. We had really come to Gurgan to get Paul's red card in order, which was done by a classmate of Samadie's at the university.

On the tenth I drove with both hands back to our cozy inn, the Hotel Tabaristan, in Behshahr, where we took over the whole top floor. Because my arm was worse, I spent the next day in bed, but on the twelfth I got up—it had stopped raining out—and we found our cave just six kilometers west of the town, in a complex of caves that dynamiters had partly destroyed fifteen years previously. There they had quarried blocks of Jurassic limestone to send by flatcars on the Swiss mountain railroad to Tehran, to build the walls of Parliament.

It was Ghar-i-Kamarband, or in English, Belt Cave—ten feet wide at the opening, twenty-eight long, and seventeen high at the peak: a perfect vault. Two families of dervishes from the southland, seeking shelter from the cold, were camping in it, along with two donkeys and one small dog. It was pitiful to evict them, but we had to, renting them an empty tobacco shed. In the same day in the afternoon I hired five men to clean and sweep the cave, where we started work at seven the next day.

Abbas, who had learned his trade from Erich Schmidt at Tepe Hissar, was the foreman. With his aid and that of others whom he chose from many applicants, we went down to a depth of seventy-five centimeters, through a fabulously rich early Neolithic deposit containing beautiful long, thin flint blades and various kinds of plain, handmade pottery which Samadie said fitted with several Neolithic levels found elsewhere, and were earlier than the painted pottery which pre-carbon-14 archaeologists still used as a calendar for dating Neolithic sites.

We also found three somewhat flattened globes of limestone, about six inches wide and perforated with one-and-a-half-inch holes. What could they be? I had little time to think of it then, and toyed with mace heads (too early), loom weights, and fishnet weights, but none of these rang true. Later on at home I remembered—the Bushmen in South Africa had used such stones as digging-stick weights, for turning heavy soil. The patina around their holes showed that they had been pressed many times by bare, wet feet.

On the fourteenth we finished the Neolithic, and went into a layer of disheveled cow horns and masses of scraps of flint of indeterminate cultural affiliation, and, at the bottom, clay—first mixed with limestone flakes, as in the Upper Red at Bisitun; under that, the clay was varved. This means that it had been laid down in layers, as in a vanilla and chocolate cake. Varves had been found in lake beds in Sweden, and had been counted for dating, one laid down by sedimentation each year.

I shall postpone the rest of this narrative and the interpretation of our finds until later, because it was only our first season (if such a short working period may be so called) at Belt Cave. We kept digging until October 25, and stopped because Froelich Rainey had cabled that he wanted the blue jeep in Baghdad on November 5.

Just packing and hardening bones with alvar, a solvent made expressly for this purpose, and looking for more caves (we found two beauties) took all our time until the twentieth, when we left for Tehran.

We were tired not just from the work, but from being kept awake all night by noisy parties on the floor below. It was election time, and candidates were buying votes.

Their noise also kept the bear in the courtyard awake, which did not improve his disposition. As he was fast approaching puberty, he was beginning to lose his playful, cublike ways. As the deep-pit john stood in the rear corner opposite both the foot of the staircase and the inn's entrance, the bear became a holdup man, exacting toll from hurried passersby, particularly at night. Lisa paid him off with sheets of bread, water in tins, and later, more simply, with a pomegranate. One afternoon when no one else was around, I caught a man beating the bear with a stick and getting badly clawed in return. I took his stick away from him and pushed him out the gate, followed by his stick. If anyone had cared, it would have been easy to follow his trail, for his blood dripped on the road.

On the twenty-third we got back to Tehran, and arrived at Baghdad on November third. Froelich followed on the eighth. Between the fourth and the twelfth Naji Bey, the director of antiquities of Iraq, kept me busy measuring skulls. He also had me test a false-lead hole in the Kurdish hills, right next to Dorothy Garrod's cave, Hazer Merd (One Thousand Men, who could stand in it, as in a subway car), and I found out that her "Aurignacian" from that monumental excavation was little different from the upper Red earth industry in Bisitun. That pushed my westward parenthesis farther west.

Home we flew via Basra and Europe, sleeping most of the way.

Seven hundred and forty-four days later we landed at the Tehran Airport, to be greeted by Mr. Samadie. He not only was wreathed with smiles, but also carried in his hands a bouquet of flowers for Lisa and an enormous cake. It was Tuesday, February 6, 1951. We were itching to get back to our Caspian cave.

Also awaiting us was the yellow jeep, looking as if it had just rolled out of a showroom, for it had been completely renovated in the new garage of an old Lebanese friend of mine, Alfred Kittaneh. Samadie also told me, with justifiable pride, that all the permits were in order.

Only one element was lacking: the combination of the Duprees and our Dodge Power Wagon. Louis and Annie Dupree had both been my students at Harvard-Radcliffe. Both had been on an American Museum Expedition led by Walter Fairservis, Jr., who had been loaned our P.W. for use in Pakistan. The Duprees and the P.W. should have been waiting for us, but we found instead a telegram stating that the P.W. had been creamed and that the Duprees were proceeding by slow train from Quetta to Zahedan, just inside the triple boundary of Iran, Afghanistan, and Pakistan. Thence they would work their way to Tehran by bus.

This news somewhat wilted the bouquet and spoiled the cake, because I had been counting on the competent and amiable Duprees and the vehicle, which we had planned to use in exploring the Hazer Jerib* (One Thousand Fields) behind Behshahr, where there are said to be large caves with carvings in them above the maximum Caspian high-water level. Both Duprees spoke Farsi, the pure Persian of Afghanistan, without the Iranian Persian's Arabic loan words.

Leaving the yellow jeep for them, I bought an old G.I. ambulance, and took Sohail Azari back again. To drive the ambulance I hired a young Tehrani named Yedallah (Allah's Hand). Samadie had opted to come to Behshahr by train—a wise decision. We got stuck in the snow at the mountain pass, behind a line of laden trucks. Sohail, Lisa, and I slept in the body of the ambulance, Yedallah in one of our sleeping bags, and to put it mildly, we almost froze. And our food was nothing to brag about, because Ali Askar had been left behind. He had spent a night in an opium den in Tehran and had been stoned and rolled. In the morning he was walking stark naked in the streets, still in a daze. He had to stay behind to take the cure.

Finally, the next day, we broke through. An American snow-plow moving south faced us head-on, with a line of trucks behind. Like a city cabdriver, Yedallah wheeled into a field where the snow was thin, and was about to keep on when the motor stopped. As he got out to see what was wrong, the angry drivers closed in on him. They had run out of opium, and could brook no more delay. All they got from his hide was one square inch of skin, for Sohail and I had jumped out too to repel the attackers. But we were soon off, and we slept in the Hotel Tabistan in Behshahr, in our old beds, that night.

When we awoke it was February 26, twenty days after our arrival at Tehran. Between Fairservis and the Power Wagon and Ali Askar and one thing and another, we were beginning to learn that time and space were both variable. Patience, of which I was born with a minimum, is hard to learn, or it was in those days in the Middle East.

The Duprees and Samadie eventually arrived. Yedallah returned to Tehran, to be replaced by one Bizar, and we hired a cook named Musa, who minced all our food too fine because (as we learned later) he was pampering Yedallah's sore tooth. We were visited,

---

*A jerib *is a measure of land, I am not sure how large.*

bothered, heckled by communist demonstrators, disturbed by quarrels between villagers who lived beside the cave and townies, and so on, which is narrated in *The Seven Caves*. Throughout it all we worked, worked, worked.

First we continued where we had left off in Belt Cave, but when it was clear that the job would come to an end in no more than a week, one of the workmen asked me, "Who don't you dig that much larger cave next door?"

Then I remembered, with a start, something that had happened on October 21, 1949. In my diary for that day I had written, among other things of more immediate importance, "A.M. Found two new high caves, Kollareh and Flatiron—may be above clay level— Wonderful walk in cool country lanes with stiles."

In my 1952 report:*

On October 21, after the trench at Belt Cave was finished the workmen, wishing to ensure our return, told of a much larger cave, Hotu, the narrow mouth of which had been completely buried by the activities of dynamiters some fifteen years previously. Over the scene grass had grown, and no indication remained that such a cave had existed, other than a crack in the front of the roof, formed also by dynamite. With their help I was lowered into the body of the cave and found myself knee-deep in bat dung. Since this cave was higher than Belt, it seemed likely that it might contain deeper and thus older deposits, and I was determined to dig it the next season.

When I first entered Hotu I saw that it was the top of a beautifully vaulted cave like Belt, but larger, about twelve feet wide by forty long. A small fan of daylight shone through a crack in the front, over a pile of fill, behind which I had little headroom. As we dug downward Hotu became magnificent.

These two architecturally impressive vaulted caves, with their walls straight as plumb lines, courses of sedimentary layers as distinct as those in the walls of preconcrete government buildings, and nautilus shells gracefully ornamenting their surfaces, didn't look like any limestone caves I had seen before in Morocco, Bisitun, or the south of France.

They were too stately, too elegant, to have been carved out during the life span of that upstart sequence of precocious garrulous mammals, from ape to man. I knew this because the nautilus casts told me that the limestone was Jurassic—a period during which dinosaurs

---

*Excavations in Hotu Cave, Iran, 1951, a Preliminary Report *(Read November 8, 1951)*. Proceedings of the American Philosophical Society, Philadelphia, Vol. 96 No. 3, 1952, pp. 231–249.*

had trodden the earth—and the caves had been hewn in the Eocene, before even monkeys had peered bright-eyed from between the forest leaves.

I had a hunch that some of these caves might have sheltered very early men, but I had not yet done my homework on the aberrant rises and falls of the Caspian Sea, which remained an open question to Louis Dupree and me in 1951.

Skipping the balderdash and flap of the moment as recounted vulgarly in my diary and more politely in *The Seven Caves*, let us concentrate on the soberer record of my 1952 *Report*, first for Belt and then for Hotu.

> *Belt Cave contained four cultural horizons, reading from top to bottom: (1) a mixed deposit containing Neolithic remains along with Iron Age, Islamic, and Modern materials; (2) a true Neolithic horizon divided into an upper (2a) which contained pottery and domestic animals, and a lower (2b) which contained domestic sheep and goats but no pottery; (3) a Mesolithic culture in which the principal food was supplied by a grassland or desert animal,* Gazella subgutturosa jacovlew, *still found on the Turkoman plain; (4) an earlier Mesolithic during which time the cave was a flint factory, and the workmen lunched off a small species of Caspian seal and many water birds. Under this was sterile clay, and under the clay the limestone bottom of the cave. . . .*
>
> *In February 1951 Mrs. Coon and I returned to Behshahr, followed by Mr. and Mrs. [Louis A.] Dupree, and set to work finishing the trench in Belt Cave, carrying it out into the open, and particularly trying to trace the bottom forward, to see how the deposit could have been made. The presence of the levels previously noted was confirmed, particularly the preceramic Neolithic. Also the remains of a young family of four individuals were found buried at the threshold of the ceramic and preceramic Neolithic, with a beautiful bone fork under the skeleton of the oldest female. Then we moved over to Hotu [which we excavated between March 14 and April 21]. First Trench A, a 5- by 3-meter square near the back of the cave, was dug to 7 meters until gravel was struck.*
>
> *Since by this time the depth of the trench was over twice its width or length, and . . . the cave deposit was wet and shaky, we stopped out of consideration for the lives of our workmen. Then a contiguous section seven meters in length, called Trench B, was laid out. This, also, was carried down to the gravel. Realizing that the working space was still dangerous, we started to dig a third section, Trench C, outside the mouth, to let in light and to provide an avenue of escape should the face fall.*
>
> *Fall, unfortunately, it did, during the lunch hour on April 12, temporarily trapping three workmen in the rear of the cave. Luckily no one was hurt. Several days' work was needed to clear the debris. There was no question of continuing Trench C; time was growing short, the workmen were tired, and they were*

needed to plant tobacco. Very fortunately the soil that fell in from the south side of the cave, and thus escaped stratigraphic study, was nearly sterile. The cave dwellers preferred the north, or better-lighted, side of the cave.

On April 15 we were ready to excavate the small part of the Pleistocene gravel surface previously exposed on Trenches A and B. It seemed reasonably safe as long as nobody kicked anything down from above. Hence the small trench . . . D was made to the bottom of the Pleistocene gravel by a deposit of soft, wet kaolin, at 12.40 m from the surface. At this point the walls of the cave were sloping in, and the bottom seemed near.

On the reasonable grounds that it seemed too dangerous, the workmen refused to dig deeper, and there was too little time or energy left to broaden the base by clearing the whole cave to proceed downward. This task must be left to another season, at which time the mystery of what, if anything, lies under the kaolin, may be solved. [I didn't get down to gebel, damn it, but gebel almost got up to me].

Work was complicated by the discovery in the fourth gravels of three skeletons along the edges of Trench D, so situated that supplementary trenches had to be dug to get them out, thus narrowing the free area above to below the margin of safety. On April 20, the last two skeletons came out, and the dig was over.

The dig was over, in a sense, but the shouting and toting up the score had just begun.

Froelich Rainey had had a great idea. He sent a professional photographer, Bob Stevens, to all the University Museum's expeditions in the eastern Mediterranean and Middle East, and Bob did his job extremely well. While I was down in the bottom of Trench Four, Bob was right above me, shooting away by the light of an acetylene lantern, click, click, click, particularly when Abbas, Erich Schmidt's man, and I were teasing out skeletons 2 and 3.

After a while the lack of oxygen made me dizzy. I climbed one ladder and then another, totaling about forty feet, to collapse on the floor above. My heart was pounding. After another while I stood up.

Then, or probably later, Louis Dupree handed me a piece of flint without any comment. I hefted it and looked it over. It looked like a core implement, possibly a hand axe, to me.

Back in Tehran we returned to the mission compound. Bob went to the Park Hotel, full of international reporters covering the current oil crisis and the disturbed political situation as well.

There was a lull in the news. Something earthshaking had to be reported, and Jim Bell of *Life* came to interview me. I had had no time to look over the implements from the cave, for they were still bagged, nor to recover my physical equilibrium, let alone report on my finds to Henry Luce's magazine.

Bob had mentioned to Jim that we had found something really old, perhaps going back a quarter of a million years. That would involve not merely the bifacial implement but also the skeletons, which I had alvared and mended in my bedroom in Behshahr.

If I had only the cool to say, "I will tell you after I get home," everything would have been fine. But so many things were whirling through the neurons, axons, and dendrites of that soft thing inside my skull that I flunked the test. *Life* said that I had said that if the skull (Number 2, the most complete) wasn't a quarter of a million years old, I'd eat it, with ketchup. I probably said it, because Jim swears I did, and he is an honest man.

When news of this reached the shah, he invited me to bring it to his palace to show it to him. This very much excited Samadie, who fussed about my only suit of clothes. It was out of press, and I was carrying some implements in my pockets to show His Majesty. I drove with Samadie in the yellow jeep, but he was crushed when he was not allowed inside the gates. When I entered I was led first to a small office, where a small man was busy rapidly signing a pile of documents. When he looked up and asked me what my business with the shah was, I told him, and showed him the skull I was carrying in a box.

He nodded and sent me on across a courtyard into a medium-sized two-story building faced with marble. There I was met by the shah's first secretary, a tall, elegantly dressed and groomed man with impeccable manners. In British English, this man asked me what I wanted to talk to His Majesty about, and I repeated what I had said to the small man downstairs, adding, "I have heard that you have here a pair of Caspian tigers [a small local subspecies], and wonder if he might be willing to exchange a cub for some other animal from the Philadelphia Zoo."

At this suggestion the secretary drew back as if I had asked for the crown jewels. "Don't mention the two tigers to His Majesty!" he said.

Only after I had reassured the secretary would he let me in the next room. It was about twenty feet square and ten feet high, walled in marble, with a single desk in the middle, behind which sat the shah, a rather handsome youngish man in good physical fit. He spoke to me and I to him without formality, with well-matched interaction rates, as if we had known each other before. I showed him the skull, and he looked at it with interest. When I told him what a wonderful excavator Abbas, who had been a barber, was, the shah warmed visibly, and said: "I am of Mazandari stock myself." His emotional response showed that he really loved these people, more than he did the landlords, his chief obstructors.

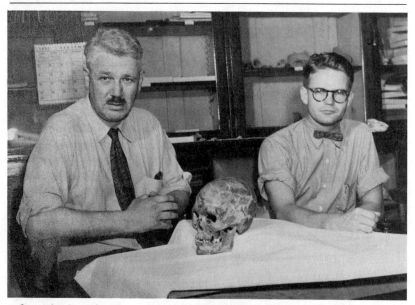

Left to right, the author, the reconstructed skull of Hotu No. 2 (completed by Dr. J. Lawrence Angel), and Dr. Louis Dupree, in the author's office in the University Museum.

On Sunday night, May 7, 1951, Lisa and I flew to Frankfurt am Main, where we arrived at nine the next morning, to be greeted by my son Carl Jr., who drove us to his house in Büdingen, Hesse, where he was resident commissioner for the Occupation Forces, on loan from the State Department. The following morning I had my first heart attack. A German doctor gave me what I needed, and there I passed a week.

But the week was not spent just in resting. Still thinking of my interview for *Life*, I wired Dr. Kenneth Oakley of the British Museum (Natural History) in London. He flew over; looked through the bags cf Trench D flints I had brought along, then told me, gently, that they could be no older than about 11,000 B.C., and were epipaleolithic, transitional between Upper Paleolithic and Mesolithic.

Kenneth bought some beautiful steaks in Büdingen, and said as he left: "Isn't it odd that we who won the war have to eat expensive rationed meat, while the losers . . . ."

After we had come home to the U.S. and relaxed a little, the rest of the work began. Beth Ralph, in her carbon-14 laboratory at the

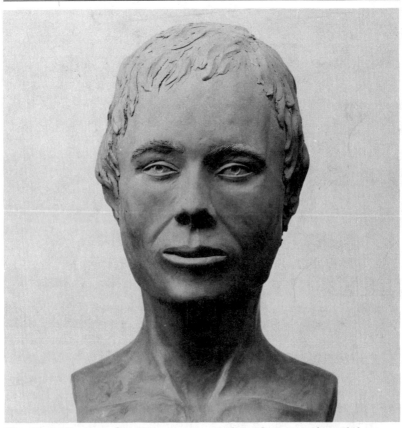

Hotu No. 2, Miss Hotu of 11,000 years ago, a Nordic on the Caspian shore. Flesh reconstruction by the author.

University of Pennsylvania, gave us a whole list of dates for both caves. Those charcoal samples from Belt had been taken at the same time as those from Hotu, because the technique had not been available in 1949.

As in the matched sequences of Bisitun and the Cave of the Ass, those from Belt and Hotu tell another story, and with greater certainty. The deposits in both caves began at about the same time, just about when Kenneth Oakley had predicted. Belt, the lower of the two caves, began higher up because its bottom was more elevated. It ended with the software Neolithic. Hotu had the painted pottery, a few sherds of which we had found at Bisitun. There was no trace of the Bronze Age in Hotu, but a gap of about two thousand years until the Iron Age began, which lasted into Parthian times. So, with a single gap, Hotu spanned the history of that part of the Caspian shore from the last flooding until the heroic events sung in the *Shahnameh*.

We know that the Bronze Age gap was not caused because the cave flooded, for the Harvard geology professor, John Miller, who examined the soil samples from each layer reported that all of them had been formed by the natural processes of deposition from within the cave, nor was any loess blown in. Possibly the Bronze Age folk, well known from their upland sites, had left some of the mounds along the shore and not used the cave, even as a garbage dump, or they had avoided that highly malarial country, perhaps then swampy. Perhaps Rustem the old Persian Hero had killed the mythical White Monster (*Diva Sefid*) that kept people out, before the beginning of the Iron Age deposit. Perhaps the White Monster was malaria.

In my rooms in the University Museum, between telephone calls and students, I worked over the animal bones. I found out two principal things—one was how to tell sheep from goats (the gazelles were easy); the other, to tell the domesticated from the wild.

The front cannon bone (a fused metacarpal) is long and graceful in the gazelle, as befits a grazer on the plain; those of the sheep and goat are stockier, as mountaineering requires, but the goat's cannon bones are shorter than the sheep's because wild goats climb higher and steeper cliffs than do wild sheep, and goats of any kind can climb the lower limbs of trees.

The bones of domestic animals and of domestic people are mostly spongy and white. The bones of wild animals and their wild hunters are glossy, tough, and brown.

The prehistory of the Iranian plateau is far from being written, but the chances of its having been the cradle of modern European man are floating out the mouths of caves. Maybe the Hazer Jerib, over 656 feet above sea level, will tell a different story.

Six hundred and fifty-six feet is the 200-meter contour height of the Manych Depression in southeastern Russia. This depression is a 330-mile stretch of saline lakes and rivulets, a series of canals, and a railroad track connecting the northeastern shore of the Caspian Sea with the Sea of Azov. At times when the continental ice cap was melting, the whole Aralo-Caspian basin was flooded to the height of the Manych Depression, through which the Caspian floodwaters flowed into the Sea of Azov and then into the Black Sea and the Mediterranean. The Hazer

Jerib caves, with their alleged sculptures, were a prime target that had to be postponed not only because of the lack of equipment and money, but because I wanted to follow my intuitions and my luck farther east before I grew too old. Hazer Jerib was therefore pushed to the back of the stove.

Instead we laid plans to search for caves in Afghanistan, the country Waldo Forbes and I had not been allowed to explore.

The last time I saw Mr. Samadie was in, more or less, 1960. He was on a guided tour of American museums led by the well-known authority on Persian architecture and art, Arthur Upham Pope. Although Mr. Pope rode close herd on his charges, this one had momentarily escaped.

Mr. Samadie dashed into my inner office in the University Museum, out of breath from climbing stairs. He was trembling from excitement, but also, poor man, because he was suffering from some kind of ague.

When he clasped my hand in both of his he almost wept. Then, after peering at my aging phiz like an entomologist squinting through a microscope, he shook his head and said, *"Monsieur Carléton, votre figure est tombé."*

That evening when I looked into my mirror, I saw that Habibullah had been right. My face really had fallen. I only wished that I might have brought him home with me, not only for a square meal, but also to let him see that Lisa's *figure* was still OK.

The last time I heard from him was in a letter he wrote me in the early 1970s, asking me to find him a job in the United States. If he is still alive I hope that he weathered the shattering recent events, wherever he may be.

22. *Afghanistan and the Syrian Desert*

On Friday, March 12, 1954, Lisa, Dr. Henry Coulter of the U. S. Geological Survey, and yours truly rode through Khyber Pass in a couple of ramshackle owner-driven Pakistani taxis, one full of people, the other full of gasoline. The reason for this arrangement was that the Afghanistanis would not sell the Pakistanis any of their own precious fuel for the latter's return trip. And just to complicate matters a little more the Paks drove on the left, the Afghans on the right.

But everyone was friendly and courteous. We passed both customs without inspection. The road was a little scruffy in the river bottoms, but beautifully graded on the flanks of the mountains. According to Hank Coulter's altimeter, the highest elevation we reached was 6,900 feet. As I wrote in my diary,

Scenery was incomparable, vast panoramas of mountains no camera could catch, snow-capped peaks, and fine-quilted valleys green with terraced rice and wheat, the pale dust of almond blossoms and the naked branches of walnut trees like the arthritic fingers of hundreds of witches.

Above the tree line, which is the walnut line, we met snow, and soon left it below as well as above us; out onto the vast plain with snow still on the ground, and flooded fields, floating ducks, and Afghan gentlemen stalking out of parked jeeps, with mufflers and shotguns. A wintry, even Muscovite, scene.

Into the gray dusk of Kabul, the dreary streets, Mongoloid faces of Hazara (a mountain people left behind by Somebody Khan), to the Embassy— mail! and our own house cold with the chill of winter emptiness. Poor Shirindel the cook, our Afghan sweetheart—that is what his name means—had not been warned. Fire in a dummy fireplace and smoke through the house, choking the Embassy bearer who had misdirected us. Omelette for Lisa and Henry and sardines for me, and to a glacial bed and a deep sleep.

The reason we had a house and a cook and a couple of vehicles in the garage was that I had said, "After you, Rodney" to Rodney Ballantyne Young, the classical archaeologist who had cut the Gordian knot when he had discovered and excavated Croesus' tomb. Froelich Rainey had previously visited Afghanistan, and he and the antiquities director, Ahmad Ali Kohzad, had agreed that the landlocked kingdom would be a splendid country in which the University Museum archaeologists should work.

In 1963, at a meeting in our director's office, it was proposed that Rodney and I should go out at once, he to look for ruins left behind by Alexander the Great and his followers, and I to look for caves. Once there, I had a feeling that Afghanistan was not wide enough for the two of us, and he probably felt the same. Then when Froelich said that he would turn over all the money to Rodney, whom I should have to ask for it, and I demurred, Rodney said, "You can take your damned money and throw it in the Kabul River," whereupon the Cornishman answered the Scot, "And then I will throw you in, too."

I could hardly have lifted Rodney, let alone toss him like a caber, and Froelich looked on in mock astonishment and probably internal glee.

So that is why we found a house, cook, and vehicles awaiting us, and no chance of Rodney's return, because the Alexandrian period was several centuries too late for him, while my much longer period had been finished before gold had ever entered this money-grabbing world.

In this part of this chapter there is no excuse for me to grouse about the bureaucracy and the eccentric behavior of some of the people we met and had dealings with, because everyone was square, truthful, honest, and helpful, as far as we could tell. One reason for this happy condition was, in my opinion, that they had not yet found the need to erect a top-heavy bureaucracy.

In their technological revolution they had gone straight from camel caravans to trucks. Being ingenious mechanics, they had cut their truck frames in two and stretched them by adding cannibalized pieces, thus overloading them so that they cut deep ruts in the roads leading over the Hindu Kush to the fertile plain to the north, where cotton, sugar beets, and other valuable crops were grown, and some factories were run, by Colorado-trained sons of local chiefs.*

The roads were so poor that a centralized government could not function in bothersome detail, and the old system of leaving the governors of provinces virtual autonomy was working like a railroad conductor's watch. And the roads were also narrow enough, where they followed the contour lines of cliffs, to thwart any invading vehicles,

---

*The most recent, detailed, and accurate book about Afghanistan is: Louis Dupree, Afghanistan, *Princeton University Press, 1973.*

particularly tanks (the tankable roads were built some twenty years later).

Even before we had left the United States, Henry Coulter had pored over geological maps to find the most likely place in Afghanistan to look for limestone caves. It turned out to be the northern foothills of the Hindu Kush, in the Mazar-i-Sharif province, which borders on the Oxus River. Beyond that feeder of water to the Aral Sea stood Soviet Uzbekistan. A mere sixty miles north of the Oxus, in 1938, the Siberian archaeologist A. P. Okladnikov had made a remarkable discovery in a similar limestone cave.

The cave's name was Teshik Tash. In it Okladnikov found a Levalloisio-Mousterian sequence similar to that of Bisitun, and in a small grave near the top was the skeleton of a nine-year-old boy that he had called Neanderthal, although it had a remarkably large braincase (even for a Neanderthal), and features that were intermediate between those of the western Neanderthals and those of modern Caucasoid man.

At the time we left for Afghanistan, the usual arguments over the child's geological age were going on, there having been no carbon-14 analysis anywhere in 1938. Okladnikov said that the skull belonged to the Riss-Würm interstadial, which would have made it over one hundred thousand years old, more than twice as old as the cave's comparable industry that we had found later, in Bisitun.

Hallam Movius, from his nest near my own old office on the fifth floor rear of the Peabody Museum at Harvard, stated that it was probably the Würm I–II interstadial, the heyday of our famous ancestor, Cro-Magnon man. Hallam based his clock reading on the fauna, all of which was still alive today, except for one bone-crunching hyena, now passed away.

Eighty percent of the animal bones were parts of the mountain goat, *Capra sibirica*, which only modern hunters equipped with binoculars and long-range telescopic rifles can bring down today. Whoever fed this short-lived boy must have been a better hunter than most men still alive. But Hallam did not refute the possibility that it might have been older.

Teshik Tash lay sixty miles north of the Oxus River and our target only thirty-five miles south of it. Men clever enough to kill mountain goats could surely raft over that river, even when the Aralo-Caspian Basin was in flood, because the river bed between Teshik Tash and the caves we were seeking was higher than the Manych Depression.

At last I was on a well-planned expedition, not a seek-and-find, hit-or-miss one. We all felt happy when we left Kabul, Hank at the wheel of a jeep and trailer, and myself at that of a jeep station wagon.

This was early in the morning of March 22, 1954. We had a pair of deadlines to weasel ourselves between: the opening of Shebar Pass, which had been blocked by snow, and the end of work at the beginning of Ramazan (Ramadhan in proper Arabic), which was slated, that year, for May 3, providing that the moon could be seen the previous night. If not, the pious sky-watchers would keep looking, night after night, until someone saw it and passed the word around.*

Because the Afghans were extremely strict Muslims, work would be impossible, or at best inefficient, after the fast had gotten well underway. Having only six weeks or so in which to find and dig a cave, we had no time to lose. When we crossed Shebar Pass, at some thirteen thousand feet, men were still removing snow with one-piece wooden shovels. We were six persons: Hank; Lisa; myself; Shirindel, our bearer; Alif Beg; and our inevitable inspector, Mohammed Nader Khan, whose English was unpredictable. He would say *hind* for *hand,* and *poopy* for *poppy.* On account of this second mispronunciation Rodney had nick-named him Poopy, a name that he admired because of his favorite flower. Although he wanted me to call him Poopy, I refused at first, mostly on general principles, and partly because Shirindel spoke English too, as did an American-schooled interpreter named Mo-hammed Nader Sawweri. The inspector had a Sawweri parked between his other names, too.

The real Mr. Sawweri was an almost incredibly blond Pathan with a face and sense of humor like Mickey Rooney's. We needed him both as interpreter and tension breaker, but he did not arrive until several days after we reached Haibak (or Aibak), a rather small town with a state-built hotel. Mr. Sawweri had been held up on his permits, and followed by bus. We took over nearly all of the hotel's rooms, had to share the john with busloads of passengers, and put Shirindel in the kitchen, where he boiled all our drinking water and cooked our food so carefully that we got no dysentery during our entire trip.

On Friday, March 26, at 2:30 P.M., we were greeted by the mayor and the governor's deputy in front of the Haibak Hotel. They fed us abundantly on rice and shish kebabs wrapped in mutton fat. As soon as we had finished, the mayor guided us out to a valley with limestone walls on either side, to see a wonderful cave. But we were too late to reach it. My diary reads: ". . . like Dordogne, a series of valleys scoured out. Many shelters, no real caves. Will go back in A.M. to see more. This *may* be the place."

---

*For more details, see my **Caravan,** pp. 112–115.*

We did. We managed to drive the station wagon as far as the lonely, rock-girt village where we had stopped the previous afternoon. Then we continued with the jeep to a place where a ten-foot boulder had fallen across the trail. From there we walked—with the mayor in the lead, still wearing his pin-striped suit with tails flapping behind him—at a mountaineer's pace. There, four hundred and fifty feet above a tiny village called Sar-i-Kunda, he pointed to the large mouth of a reputedly huge cave, to which we had to climb, if only to save our faces. It had a flint-strewn floor, but also large blocks of stone that had to be broken and removed, and it was too inaccessible to be practical.

I found this out dramatically on the way down, setting one foot in front of the other on a narrow trail, with the smooth cliff wall to my left and empty air to the right. My eyes went out of focus. I could no longer see my feet. I sat down. Hank appeared, handing me a piece of chocolate and a cigarette. After a few minutes he led me down.

What humiliation, in front of the mayor. I had quite honestly never been afraid of people, because they were variable, but air was air and a rock a rock. In three months I would be fifty. God! I was getting old.

Later on, Shirindel told us about that rock and road. He had driven over it several years earlier, when it was the truck route to Kabul, before it had been replaced. Below Sar-i-Kunda, where I had goofed, lay many caves. But Hank had meanwhile spotted another one, called Kok Jar, that he thought was in older stone than the Alpo-Himalayan rock we had just seen. Kok Jar means Blue Gulch in Turkish, a propitious name.

So at 7:30 A.M. on the following day we were off for the provincial capital, Mazar-i-Sharif, to call on the governor and get his permission to dig. On the way we saw more caves than all the archaeologists in the world could dig without rubbing each others' elbows. All very confusing. Much too much.

The governor spoke English, and had a son at Cornell. He fed us a fabulous lunch, topping it off with last summer's melons, coated with wax and kept in a cellar full of snow. Miraculously, he sent a messenger to the bazaar to fetch us a brand-new rear tire for the station wagon, in a land where no such tires were supposed to exist, and he told us of many beautiful caves to the west in the Maimana country, where he would like to have us go.

There were too many caves for us to choose from, and too little time to do it in. It was like a tanker-fleet owner's mistress trying to select a diamond in five minutes. We had opted for Kok Jar, so let's play it safe, we decided. It was easily approached by vehicle, and a whole village full of youthful labor was immediately available.

We had an awful time with our inspector. As soon as we had started to work he ran up to me waving a roll of toilet paper in one hand, and shouting incomprehensible words, which Mohammed Nader Sawweri blushingly translated. According to department regulations I had to build a wooden privy for the workmen, or work would stop.

But we went right on, from March 28 to the morning of April 4, when a workman named Abd el-Krim found a cartridge case at 3.8 meters, and a wise old man said, "That is where the bottom was, forty years ago, when I was young."

The rest of that day we dashed around looking for another cave called Kara Kamar, or Black Belly—the first word was Turkish, the second Persian, a reflection of the ethnic checkerboard thereabouts.

We had passed and rejected it several times, but now we took a closer look. It was a black gash just under the lip of a tall mesa, concave, like a smiling mouth. We had called it Smiling Boy, in honor of Oliver La Farge and the nation of Navajos.

Its rounded roof was black because it was a signal station where fires were lit to warn of invasions. It was not a cave, but a rock shelter, and we could drive halfway up to it, then walk—or climb—the rest. Having once been fooled by the Cave of the Ass (although I had not heard of my folly then, but felt it, like a weather change, in the holes drilled through my skull), I could not afford to reject another high site just because it was difficult of access. If the hunters could climb up there to count the herds of game miles and miles away from and below them, so could we, to hunt the hunters' own bones (if any), tools, and what was left of their kills.

We hired a team of Tajiks and Uzbeks, local Persian-speaking and Turkish-speaking villagers, both having kinfolk over the liquid curtain of the Oxus. Their masters were Pathans from the south—darker, hawk-beaked men who came to see us now and then as visitors, but never to jump into a trench to work. They had been moved north only a decade or so ago, as guardians of the border, and they looked the part. The Tajiks were European racially, some of them fair-skinned and blue-eyed, with heads flattened like those of Albanians. They were model workmen, as were the partly Mongoloid Uzbeks. The Tajiks talked a little with each other, the Uzbeks less. Their interaction rates were more like those of Kurds and Assyrians, and far lower than the Mazanderanis of Belt and Hotu, who were always fooling around, boasting, and playing tricks on one another, like American kids on the school's playground during recess.

This doesn't mean that the Tajiks and the Uzbeks didn't fight, only that they did so less often, after graver provocation, and with more visible results. There was little or no humor in their fighting, and the Uzbeks would break out in a rage suddenly after holding it in, as Tibetans also do, I found out later. There seems to be a racial hierarchy in wit and violence (subject postponed here).

Locally, our inspector started most of the trouble by ordering men in and out of Trenches A, B, and C, mostly when I was out squatting on the bare, windy hillside. When I got back I gave him proper hell. By that time Rodney had my sympathy, but there was nothing to do but slap his Poopy down and sweat it out. I was the boss; he was the inspector. Any complaints could be saved for Ahmad Ali Kohzad's consideration, once—and if—we both should return to Kabul, simultaneously and each in one piece.

We laid out Trenches A, B, C, and D in alphabetical order, from right to left. We started on the right because that seemed to be the shallowest. Should it be rich, we could go deeper in B without worrying about an earth wall on two sides. Trench A ended abruptly with a New England-style stone wall. Had these rocks, over millenia, fallen precisely on top of each other, or had some chilled people set them up as a shelter against the wind? If robins and gorillas built nests, why not?

The floor of Trench A sloped to the left. So did that of Trench B. So we kept on to the rock wall of Trench C, which bottomed out and began to slope up again. Trench K was Hank's attempt to see if the habitation area had stretched forward beyond the present overhang, but it had not. That soil was sterile.

In the section, *chalk* means the same as the chalks used on blackboards in schoolrooms. Once loosened, the wind carried it off in swirls, into the pick men's faces. It had been formed from the alternate lighting and slaking of signal fires set on a limey floor, at least from the Bronze Age, for we found some Bronze Age sherds in it, and also one heat-pocked piece of flint. It was these fires that had blackened the belly of our site.

As we went down in Trench B, and later also in C, we saw that the sequence of soils was different in the latter two from that in A. B and C had been more exposed to the prevailing westerly wind. In A the chalk was thickest, because most of the fires had been built there for draft; the loess, blown in by the westerlies, was thinner behind the wall than it was in B and C.

Loess is a fine yellow powder found in many parts of the world just below the toes of glaciers, lifted and carried by unbridled winds into every nook and crevice in their path, and in some places, as in China, simply dumped in dunes on the land. It is almost as coherent as cheese, and a trench hewn in it will not fall in. Furthermore, we know that it was deposited during successive periods of the Pleistocene—which ones, in Afghanistan, we did not know.

In Kara Kamar there were three layers of loess, deposited at three different times with gaps in between them. We know this for two reasons. The top loess had the coarsest grains, the lowest the finest grains, with the middle layer intermediate. In the section, each layer slanted in its own direction, from left to right, and there were marked disconformities—meaning old floor levels—between each, marked on the section drawing by dashed lines.

Between the chalk and the upper loess lay Brown I, a fairly loose, mealy soil laid down in weather as mild as that today. Between the lower loess and the bottom lay Brown II, a thin deposit with the same kind of soil as Brown I. In both these browns the occupants' favorite meats were wild mountain mutton and the flesh of our old friend *Gazella subgutterosa,* both of which exist in that faunal region today. The loess men in between preferred horseflesh. Periglacial loess is rich soil, first-class for grazing and for growing grain, as in Central Europe and in China.

Brown I yielded fifty-eight implements, excluding a small amount of scrap. Most of them were small blades from 15 to 30 mm long, some unretouched, others fashioned into different kinds of scrapers, including two "thumbnail" scrapers familiar to American Indian implement collectors. Three pointed ones could have been arrowheads, at least two were burins (narrow gravers made by removing single spalls from the corners or tips of blades), and one was a triangle, obviously meant to be set in glue or gum in a row in a wooden staff, to make a composite tool. Three were microcores, 10 to 15 mm high, from which tiny bladelets (which were not found) had been struck.

This was patently a Mesolithic industry, different from that of Hotu, somewhat like Bisitun's. But the bag was too light for definite comparisons. There is no reason why all Mesolithic tool kits should be alike from France to Central Asia, as well as in North America. At a certain stage of technological development, different peoples must have discovered some things independently, just as Roland Dixon had said, and as I have believed ever since.

In the bottom of the upper loess and the top of the loess below it, we found forty-three implements, or worked pieces of flint, of an entirely different character. They were flake cores and flakes, not brown on the surface, but milky white. Where broken, their insides were brown. In 1939, outside the High Cave, my older son had found a beautiful Lower Paleolithic cleaver, which had turned completely to chalk and lost its weight. In Kara Kamar Industry II, as I called it, the process had not gone as far, but it had begun. These flints had been exposed to wind and weather, just as the chalk above had been to fire. Someone had been sitting on the top of the loess and scuffing some of their implements into it between its last phase of deposition and post-glacial Mesolithic. Who might these people have been?

The implements were full-sized, and mostly flakes, some re-touched into scrapers like those at Bisitun, but without the latter's points. And it was more like those in the reddish earth at Bisitun than like those in the upper Red. The Neanderthal bones had been found among more highly evolved implements of the same nature. The finger pointed at Neanderthal in Kara Kamar, but it wobbled as it poked.

Toward the bottom of the middle loess and right on through the lower loess a much more advanced tool kit was found, along with hearths and animal bones.

In it we unearthed eighty-two implements plus scrap. These were blades, not flakes, reversing the usual order of deposition in Pleistocene caves. These were sophisticated implements, comparable to but different from the Aurignacian of western Europe, particularly France. Forty-three of them were specialized steep scrapers, with flat undersides and finely faceted, curved front edges. They were obviously woodworking planes. Because the deposit contained no hunting spear-heads, the hunters must have fashioned their spears wholly of wood, no doubt fire-hardened, as the Tasmanian aborigines did with theirs up to A.D. 1820 or so. And whatever else the lower loess people made from wood is anybody's guess.

In its five cubic meters of soil (140 cubic feet) we removed only nine implements, which indicated an intermittent and infrequent occu-pancy by a people who knapped simple, rather awkward flakes, coarsely retouched. If they were early Mousterian, they looked like none of it that I had seen.

Who were these people, anyway? What could be made out of this crazy sequence? It wasn't just the same old play where the same actors walked in and out of the wings. Had the scenes been scrambled, or had two or several companies of actors, some hairier than others, shambled on and off to what seemed to each a brand-new cave? We didn't know.

We arrived in Kabul close to midnight on Wednesday, April 21. My diary reads: "To narrate the events of this day is a big job. It beggars (or buggers) description. The simple fact is that we drove from Do Ab [Two Waters] to Kabul. The details make *Pilgrim's Progress,*

PRECOCIOUS TOOLS FROM KARA KAMAR, AFGHANISTAN

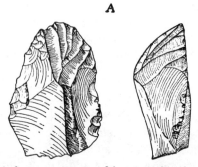

(A) Two views of a typical steep scraper, one of the principal implements in the rich cultural deposit of the lower loess at Kara Kamar. Suited for working wood, bone, and other hard materials, this tool was fluted by the removal of a row of small blades around the working edge, by means of a punch. This procedure anticipated the microlithic technique in which the product sought was not the core but the small blades themselves, and the tool itself adumbrated the Upper Paleolithic that have arisen independently from the fusion of two technologies at the same time a little later in the caves we dug in the Syrian Desert.

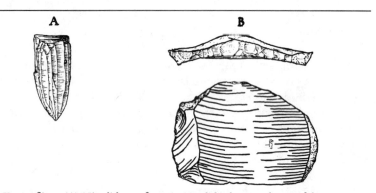

Kara Kamar flints: (A) Microlith core from the Mesolithic layer at the top of the deposit. (B) From the upper loess, a piece struck off the top of a prepared core to level the surface of its striking-platform. In the upper view, note the elaborate faceting on the edge, done to control the direction of the line of fracture. This control made possible the invention of the tubular blade core of the Upper Paleolithic. (All three specimens shown are reduced one-half actual size.)

Dante's *Inferno,* and *The Road To The Land of Osiris* look like a trip through a love tunnel."

The rest takes two-and-a-half pages. The result was that both vehicles were as dead as mice that had fallen into the bottom of a pickle jar. So, almost, were we.

Upon my arrival I found a letter from Froelich Rainey requesting me to drive the blue jeep to Baghdad again for him to use. Yes, it was the same old blue jeep that Lisa and I had driven from Beirut across the desert to Baghdad in 1948. I sold the two vehicles for cannibalization to another American. More letters discussed finances. It had been a ten-thousand-dollar expedition. Lesser forays in recent years have received ten times that much from national foundations.

I divided the spoils with Ahmad Ali Kohzad after his return from Italy at a United Nations conference, "accidentally" held during Ramadhan, and when he saw that I had brought in only flints, he took what I had set on one side on his table, plus a few others that I had called unique. Then I glanced at the felt-covered case where Rodney's gold coins were supposed to be—all of them being unique—and saw the impressions they had left there. And I learned that Poopy was, as I had suspected, the oddball son of a prominent Shi'a family (they have the money there), who had been given a government post to keep him happy while driving others outside the capital crazy.

The last time I talked with anyone about Poopy was in Washington, with Rodney. We were both members of the Smithsonian Committee on Soft Money. How Americans might find ways to spend American money that we had loaned to foreign countries, in those very countries, without having to tax the museum's finances, intrigued him. He was very pleasant and affable with me, and vice versa. I am glad that we met that way, because shortly after, Rodney died.

One of our chief memories about Rodney, which endeared him to the University Museum staff, was the following incident. In the backyard of his home, on the periphery of the Radnor Hunt, he was working one afternoon repairing his motorcycle, on which he commuted. His companions were his two Turkish sheepdogs, huge and energetic and shaggy.

Suddenly several horses ridden by fox hunters, fully clothed and equipped in old-country style, burst in upon him. His dogs leapt up barking. "Call your dogs, my good man," a rider said.

Rodney answered, "Don't be afraid of them. They are just laughing at you, for your silly clothing."

We got the charcoal samples out one way or another, and Hank flew to Bahrain Island on one of Peter Baldwin's Terry-and-the-Pirates airplanes (Peter was a close relative of a lady friend of ours). Before Lisa and I left, I read proof of my *The Story of Man*. In a copy of a letter from Brandon Barringer to Percy Madeira (a member of the museum's overseers to its president), I see: "If anybody can straighten out the Afghan mess . . . it is Carl with his reputation among the Moslems and his knowledge of them. He is planning to come back by way of Australia. . . . It would seem most important for our Paleolithic expert to see the only people still living the hunting-gathering life."

Thank you, Brandon. Lisa and I flew in a small Indian Airlines plane, piloted by a sick Sikh who had had one too many the night before. As he flew over the Golden Temple of all the Sikhs in Amritsar, the emergency door to my right opened, and I was partly sucked out, but a healthy Sikh grabbed my legs and pulled me back.

On the way to see the Australian aborigines we stopped off in Bangkok for a rare reunion with Gordon and Eleanor Browne, and also with Bill Donovan, our ambassador, in his usual ticklish spot. Unfortunately, Bill's infant grandson had cut one of his grandfather's eyeballs with the coated-paper edge of Brandon Barringer's magazine, *The Saturday Evening Post*.

Gordon had arranged for the Donovans, Coons, and Brownes to go cave hunting on elephants, but Bill sent his aide, Jim Raferty, instead. This may have been the only dashing expedition that Bill ever missed, because the cave we meant to visit had been slept in by four other people the night before, and all but one of them had been eaten by tigers. The sole survivor crawled down the trail to warn others before he too died.

Our aborigines were the Tiwi of Melville Island, off Darwin. Jane Goodale was there studying the women, on a *National Geographic* expedition run by the late Charles Mountfort, and greatly aided by the also late Bill Harney, the anthropologist's anthropologist, whose books are gems. The Tiwi were still hunting and performing their ceremonies, including the Pokomoni, which we attended. They danced in and around painted poles carved à la Brancusi (or vice versa?). The women carried branches, with which they brushed the men. Lisa, not knowing the significance of this part of the rite, was given a branch and brushed Allee, a young man who had danced before the queen. This brought on much mirth. I measured and photographed them. Each one was quite different from the others in looks and personality. Lucky people, they had not been homogenized.

We then flew counterclockwise across the wide Pacific, and over America the Beautiful from sea to shining sea, so to speak, with happy memories of how our distant ancestors might have lived and played.

And our faces were shining too, on the seventh of December, 1954, when Beth Ralph, director of our radiocarbon laboratory, brought in the carbon-14 dates. Eighty centimeters down in the Brown I soil, right near the bottom of it, the count read 10,580 ± 720 B.P. (Before Present), meaning 8630 ± 720 B.C., making our Mesolithic comparable in age to the quite different Seal Mesolithic of Belt and Hotu.

Separate samples from five hearths of the blade industry in the lower loess ran over the edge of the counter. Each one was older than 34,000 years old,* but how much older we do not know. From the purely competitive standpoint this does not matter much, because 32,000 B.C. alone was the oldest blade-culture date found anywhere in the world at that time, if not later.

In the rush of bone sorting and bagging in our house in Kabul, I noted one faunal item that seemed odd, but only now begins to intrigue me. In every layer where evidences of human occupation were found, pieces of tortoiseshell were always present. What can this mean? Could these dome-shaped, cold-blooded reptiles have lived through the periglacial winters as well as those like the present? Or were they carried in, or traded, used as ornaments, or for divination? Or for different purposes in each level? Who knows?

During periods with climates like the present one, tortoises may very well have lived in the valleys below Kara Kamar, down to the Oxus. I know this because near Bisitun I once stopped my jeep to pick one up and carry him from the middle of the road to the side toward which his head was pointing. That would take care of the bits of carapace in Browns II and I. But as for those in the loess? Again, who knows?

While keeping office hours, teaching, and doing various other things for nearly a year, it occurred to me that Afghanistan could wait a bit until I had tested the western boundary that I had theoretically set around the less, from my special viewpoint, interesting Iranian plateau. Where, then, would be the best hunting grounds in the Pleistocene world, or that part of it in which Caucasoid man might have evolved into his present physical and mental state?

---

*These dates were determined by Dr. Hans E. Suess in the laboratory of the U.S. Geological Survey in Washington. Our equipment, at that time, would not go back that far. (C.S. Coon & E. K. Ralph, Science, Vol. 122, No. 3176 [Nov. 11, 1955] pp. 921–2.)

Not the mountains, where I had previously searched, but on the open or savanna-covered plain—like East Africa into the present century. It had to be what now were deserts, after the northward shift of the westerly winds, plus the soil erosion brought on by overgrazing, first by domestic cattle, then by sheep, camels, and goats.

In 1952 I had spent the month of February in Saudi Arabia as a consultant to the oil companies on another matter concerned with human relations, but that had not kept me from knowing that a young man named Peter Cornwall had found a hand axe in the desert, nor from finding an open-air site near Turaif, on the Tapline, just south of the Jordanian border (the ubiquitous Henry Field had seen it first). It contained a curious kind of implements, which fitted no excavated category and had no date.

Partly because my older son was in Damascus, serving as second secretary at our embassy, Lisa, Hank, and I had gone there first on our way out to Afghanistan, hoping to fly directly from Amman to Kabul, but Air Jordan failed financially after we had bought tickets, and that is why we opened this chapter with a taxi ride from Peshawar to Kabul.

While we were waiting around for Air Jordan not to take us out, we tackled Turaif from the Jordanian side, thus seeing, in two years, the whole site. And we had also visited several other sites from Damascus to Aleppo, through Homs and Hama with their high-wheeled irrigation machines, and dozens of town and city mounds as succulent as newly raised loaves of bread.

My son, who had cut his teeth on the flints of the High Cave of Tangier, knew all about these things, just whom and what to see, and where to go. Hank Coulter had also done his homework on the geology of Syria. He told me that there was limestone in two principal regions, the western mountains and in the middle of the desert. The first had already been sampled by a previous archaeologist, the second lay untouched.

So when we returned at the Damascus Airport on February 22, 1955, we knew that we would go, if we could, to Palmyra, where a city of nouveaux riches Nabataeans had built temples and palaces out of pink limestone. Their baths were drawn and thirsts were slaked by a great spring of bubbling water, but when the water turned sulfurous, they abandoned it, like a Nevada ghost town.

Enough ordinary water remained to permit a little agriculture and to sport a hotel. We knew all this because Jannie (our daughter-in-law) told us that her grandmother had ridden out there and back on a camel. If her grandmother could have done that, said Jannie, we could surely get there in a station wagon with her, of course, and William, Howard, Katharine, and Lizzie, who was minus six months old at the time. My son, also of course, would be driving.

This children's crusade did not take place immediately, for other things needed doing first, like throwing a party for us, conferring with Dr. Selim Abd el-Haqq, the director of antiquities (under, as usual, the minister of education, a system imitated from the inimitable French). There were plans and counterplans; too many departments of the government had to be consulted, each of which overlapped the others. The normal, postcolonial tangle: Every time you did something you had been told you could do, you had broken some other department's law. On top of this hovered paranoia about Israel, or was it justifiable fear? In view of what has happened since, a cosmic viewer from on high might say both. It was mostly a ritual fear of being contaminated by an enemy's breath. An Arab taxi driver born in Jerusalem was as untouchable and as suspect as a genuine Jew.

It didn't help our expedition much, but neither did it wholly prevent it—nor did baby Katharine's sticking her head out the window of my son's automobile and screaming in Arabic at a fender-clipping taxi driver: "*Ma fi mokh!*" (literally, "not in marrow"; colloquially, "you have no brains"). Could she have been an Israeli *agente-provocateuse,* disguised as a talking doll?

During the sixteen days following our arrival we made one trip to Beirut and two to Palmyra. In Beirut I was examined at the American University Hospital for a mild heart attack, and pronounced OK. Then I went to the Tapline wing of the Aramco Hospital, to call on Bill Eddy, then head of Tapline. He expressed to me his indignation about the behavior of a fellow missionary grandchild who, for his personal advancement, had considered softening his attitude toward Israel publicly. Bill said to me that he told his friend, "Our grandparents are buried in this soil. They devoted their lives to the welfare of these people. If you do what you plan, they will rise up in their graves. *Don't do it!*"

Bill did not die from that attack, but from another. And he was buried near his parents and his grandparents in a hillside graveyard in Saida (ancient Sidon). After his, the smaller, leaner body of another great Arabia man was lowered into the earth beside him. It was the remains of Harry St. John Philby, the courageous explorer of the Empty Quarter, a convert to Islam and mentor to His late Majesty, King Abd ul-Aziz ibn Sa'ud.

I saw both these men before they died. This is just a pre-obituary. A real one would be too long.

The two trips to Palmyra were Jannie's children's crusade, and another with my son alone, to unsnarl the spaghetti of bureaucracy. Fortunately there was one Syrian strong man who could untangle it himself. He was Colonel Adnan Malki, a giant both physically and in personality. I called on him. He saw my point. He ordered all the other bureau chiefs to let us work with a minimum of harassment. While he lived, his word was law.

Our third trip to Palmyra was in a World War II British weapons carrier, driven by an Armenian named Garabed, with Lisa in the front seat and myself viewing the scenery on both sides and above from the open rear. I could see that this land would still have ground cover had it not been overgrazed, and my point was driven home by a cloudburst that soaked me to the skin.

We found our first undisturbed cave on March 13, 1955, after having made a tour of several valley bottoms beyond the Palmyra quarrying line, at the crest of a pass beside the abandoned Palmyra-Aleppo road. It was called Taniat al-Baidha, the White Pass. Its breadth was thirty-five feet, and its height from zero to crawling space, but when we got inside the next day to work on it, we found that it ran into the mountainside a longer distance than we needed to dig, for all the fill was in the front, as is usual in deep caves.

We went down through three soils: black, which contained Palmyro-Roman pottery and metal objects and the bones of domestic animals; a sterile yellow, not loess, but coarser, as if water-borne; and a bottom yellow that resembled the lowest yellow in the High Cave of Tangier. It contained flints and animal bones. The flints were flakes and flake blades of yellowish chert, worn out from sharpening and re-sharpening, as if the material of which they were made was scarce and from a distant source.

This puzzled me because the flints that had been thrown out of the caves ruined by the quarriers of pink limestone to build Palmyra had all been of finest quality—a rich, shiny deep brown. The eroded surface over which we had driven was covered with sheets of that very flint—sheets, not lumps or nodules. They made it easy for the knapper to strike off blades. Blademaking may have been invented in this barren, once-fertile land, or in some other place or places like it.

But the yellow-flint misers could not have found the sheets of flint we saw. Why not? Only because the present soil had been covered. And that must have been long ago. So must have been the flints on the Jordanian-Saudi border at Turaif on the Tapline, which were of similar types. Neither could be dated by carbon 14, because neither had hearths.

PRECOCIOUSLY EARLY BLADES FROM THE ARABIAN DESERT

Tel es-Suwaish: Several hundred flints, highly polished and deeply patinated by the sun, were found on the eroded surface of this open-site in the Arabian desert. The series forms a cultural unit of which broad flakes (A) and course blades (B) are characteristic. These are shown in two views. (One-half actual size.)

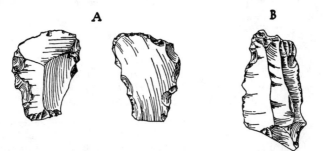

Like the material from the desert site of Tel es-Suwaish, the flints excavated in the Cave of the White Pass form a nondescript assemblage of broad flakes (A) and coarse blades (B). In both types the bulb ends were removed, and the flints retouched on several or all edges and either or both sides. (One-half actual size.)

We do not know the age of either site, only that the White Pass is patently older than its neighbor, the Heifer's Outwash, wherein a transition apparently took place between Middle Paleolithic flake and Upper Paleolithic blade industries.

AN UPPER PALEOLITHIC BLADE CORE AND BLADES FROM KARA KAMAR

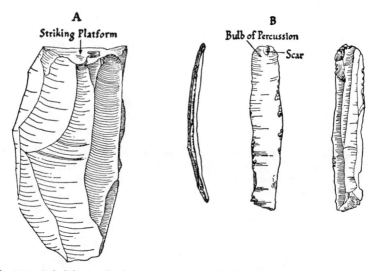

The Upper Paleolithic people also prepared cores for blades as shown in A. The result was an all-purpose thin and narrow blade struck off with a bone or antler punch as in a specimen from Kara Kamar (B). (Both one-half natural size.)

The animal bones were our only available dating material. They included an extinct *Bubalus*, a wide-horned buffalo, while most were the bones of camels and half-asses (*Equus hemippus*), not to be mistaken for the cold-adapted hook-nosed horses (*Equus przewalskii*) of the Kara Kamar loesses. Another hefty member of the yellow-soil fauna was the wild ox. If wild oxen, buffalo, and half-asses had grazed there, while wild camels browsed on trees, the climate could have been mild and fairly dry, more or less as it is now. This would not mean the last or next to last Würm glacial period, but sometime in between, or the great Riss-Würm Interglacial—which one we didn't know.

As usual in cave-bearing country, before we had finished the first cave our scouts had located another, a mile or two down the valley. It was as full as a barrel of russet apples in the late harvest, its brown mouth yawning. "Dig me," it almost said.

Its name was Jerf Ajla, the Outwash of the Heifer. The last word meant that there must have been cattle there within fairly recent times; the first word described a fan of mixed gravel and soil piled up in front of it by a tributary of the Wadi el-Abioh (White River) dead ahead. What was now a seasonally dry riverbed had been a lake at some time in the past.

TWO BURINS MADE ON BLADES FROM THE CAVE OF THE HEIFER'S OUTWASH IN THE SYRIAN DESERT

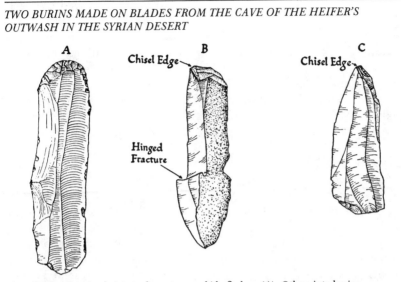

Some blades were made into end-scrapers, or hide-fleshers (A). Others into burins (gravers or narrow chisels, B and C), all found in the Heifer's Outwash. (One-half actual size.)

From the cave's lower lip hunters could see and count game almost to the horizon, just as we could see the dust rise from a Damascus bus. It was a perfect place for a family of hunters to live in, as part of a band, I suspected, because it was only one of a row of such caves, the most inviting and the easiest to excavate. A band of, say, thirty to one hundred hunters, their wives and children, with more food than they needed, could easily support a few specialists such as a shaman and one or two older men who were at least semiprofessional flint knappers.

This idea was not just speculation, but was based on what we had seen on the family tour. We had been limited to a radius of seven kilometers from the Hotel Palmyra, with a soldier aboard to stop us from going farther. He did not know our speedometer registered miles, so our radius grew to ten kilometers. This limit was just right to let us observe what had happened to the original contents of the caves the Palmyrean quarriers had destroyed. They had simply tossed the fills, and the sun and the rain had cleaned the flints so that they shone like polished agates. Among them was everything from a plain, unfaceted flake tool, through the whole Levalloisio-Mousterian sequence, to fancy blade tools and microliths.

That was the menu I hoped to find in Jerf Ajla, and we found it, although in a different fashion than I had expected. I had expected these different industries to have been laid down in separate soils, without overlap. That would have meant the usual after-you-please shuttle of different peoples moving in and out as the climate changed. What we really found was a gradual evolution of a single industry in time but not in space.

We went through seven different soil colors, from black to Yellow 2. The black on top was matted sheep dung, which contained one recently deposited sheep bone with its meat still on it, and some crudely serrated raw-flint flakes made by bedawins in place of their knives. Whether they had, incredibly, left their knives behind, or saved them for stabbing each other, is inconsequential.

From Brown 1 through to the bottom was one soil, despite its differences in color. I found this out later in Damascus when a Dutch geologist, Dr. W. J. van Liere, studied the samples I had brought from each layer. He said that they were all rock meal, the product of wind action on the limestone of the region, powdered and blown into crevices like Jerf Ajla. The different colors may have represented either differences in the intensity of occupancy, the darker colors having been produced by the decay of organic materials brought in by people; differences in mean annual rainfall, with the rainiest the darkest; or both.

The Brown soils were actually pousse-cafés, with lenses (thin, discontinuous layers) the color of leaf compost, as they probably had been used as bedding against the hardness and dampness of the earthen floor. Many of them didn't cover the whole floor at all, but only parts of it, as my diplomat son found when he excavated them with a spatula and brush on weekends. Others were the remains of fires, from which we carefully extracted bits of charcoal, and which had also left small lenses of white ash.

In Damascus I also identified the animal bones as best I could without comparative material.

The bottom Yellow soil contained some kind of horse (*Hemippus,* I was told later), gazelle, and wild goat or sheep. The gazelle was probably the same as ones still there today, the sheep-goats were sheep. Thus the lowest Yellow of Jerf Ajla resembled that of Taniat el-Baidha, except for the latter's extinct buffalo, ox, and hyena.

So Jerf Ajla, fauna-wise, may have begun where the White Pass had left off. And in the layers above the bottom Yellow in Jerf Ajla, horses and gazelles alternated in proportion as one went up: more horses in the Browns and more gazelles in the Yellows. In the white level we found fragments of ostrich shell. Ostriches had only recently been killed off there. So the climate of that period may have been like today's.

Unlike the fauna, which alternated with changes in the weather, the implements themselves followed definite gradual evolutionary changes from the bottom to the top. I could follow this clearly because I had identified 4,692 implements out of 67,850 pieces of flint.

One change was in the percentage of faceted butts found on flake tools, running from 94 percent down to 5 percent at the bottom. Another was in the percentage of special kinds of tools, meant to be used for different purposes. These ranged from 50 percent to 5 percent in the same direction. And most of the specialized tools were made on blades, probably because being relatively flat and rectangular, they were easier to alter into many shapes. Only in the bottom did we find a more ancient kind of tool, hand axes and cleavers, like the Lower Paleolithic all-purpose implements found in gravels from England to Capetown to India. These particular ones were thin and elegant, finely retouched, but made on large flakes instead of cores, and none of them showed any sign of use.

Had they been tucked away in a narrow crevice, like Australian churingas, where women and children couldn't see them? Were they used for scarring bodies in puberty ceremonies, amputating widow's fingers, or just prized as works of art, which they definitely were? If that is what they were, just think of the wooden wonders that we shall never see unless we go to museums to see the burial posts from Melville Island off Darwin, Australia, the Sepik masks from New Guinea, and the works of Brancusi—who sculpts stone as an Abo would have done had he the marble, the chisels, and someone to feed him and to warm his bed after work.

When we got home, atomic fallout was polluting the carbon-14 machines of North America and Europe, but not the crystal-clean air of New Zealand. We had only one good-sized charcoal sample from Jerf Ajla. It came from the level 8-A, in the top of the first Yellow, right under Brown 1. It was also in the earlier part of the full Upper Paleolithic. Dr. C. J. Fergusson, chief of the government station at Lower Hutt, near Wellington, radioed to Beth Ralph a date of 43,000 ± 2,000 B.P., or about 41,000 B.C. At that time, this date was the oldest yet found in the world, and a good fifteen thousand years older than any Upper Paleolithic date yet ticketed for Europe.

I couldn't call it Aurignacian, because the French don't want that name used for any industry found outside their country, any more than they like to hear "cognac" used for any foreign brandy. But I didn't need to call it Aurignacian, because it was older than that product. I haven't ventured to give it a name. Let someone else label it, if they choose—e.g., "Palmyrean" or "Ruwalian," for that land was the Rwala bedawin's summer pasture.

We had found not a scrap of human bone in Afghanistan nor in the Syrian Desert, but man is a toolmaker and his tools more or less identify the man—or at least they did so during the Upper Pleistocene. If our ancestors were popping out of the soil of caves in several places, what's wrong with that? Man was already an old species, and the Caucasoids not a new race.

After I had laid out the Jerf Ajla implements on tables in the Damascus Museum basement, the noted English convert, the Hajji Abdallah Philby, paid us a visit. Despite Ramadhan, the museum staff almost turned itself inside out to tidy up and to dress themselves properly for the great honor of this visit.

I had previously only spoken with Colonel Harry St. John Philby, but I had never seen him. On New Year's Day in 1934 I had rung his telephone, Mekka 6, to ask him about measuring people in Saudi Arabia. I was in Jidda—a few miles away by land, but as far away as Jupiter religiously. He had offered to come to Jidda for me to teach him anthropometry with my instruments, which he would take away.

Being en route to Aden and the Hadhramaut for the same purpose, I couldn't give them up. Our conversation had been amicable and regretful. During my month in Dhahran and elsewhere in 1952 the oil executives had kept me and Philby apart, although each of us wanted to meet the other. They did it because Bill Eddy had told them that I had punched Philby in the nose on that New Year's Eve party in Jidda. Bill had been mixed up. It wasn't Philby I had punched, for he had stayed in Mekka, but a fellow American. He had been arguing with Waldo Forbes about who had won the War of 1812, in front of Britishers. Some of them were on Waldo's side too.

Now that Hajji Abdallah and I had met, we had a lovely time, telling each other all sorts of things, both in the museum and in a mutual friend's house, where we toasted each other with scotch. He had left both his master's employ and his library, which he had been forbidden to take out of his master's country.

After Philby's visit, the Syrian ground on which I stood was cut out beneath my feet. At an international soccer game, some schismatic fanatic from the northern hills had shot Colonel Malki through the back of his head. The bullet knocked one eyeball out. I wasn't present at the time, but heard that the Russian diplomats jumped over the fence. I was in the parlor of the Honorable James Moose, the American ambassador, when the news came.

I turned to Mr. Moose and asked him, "Was it the colonel's right or his left eyeball?"

James Moore kept looking at me, then smiled a little.

"Does it really matter?" he said gently, as if speaking to a child.

I couldn't speak for choking and holding back tears. It mattered a hell of a lot to me, but I didn't know why.

Of course I knew what would happen, and it did when Dr. Abd el-Haqq, who had just returned from Europe (during Ramadhan, as usual), invited me to his office. He offered me a Turkish cigarette and said, "You have violated two rules. You were supposed to come here with an assistant director of excavations, an architect, a photographer, and an epigrapher. You have brought only your wife."

(I had been over this *ad nauseum, ad infinitum* in correspondence with him before we had left Philadelphia. Lisa had an architectural degree, I had sold photographs professionally, and the men who had lived in our caves had been illiterate. This had been agreed beforehand, and he knew it just as well as I did. Now that Malki was dead, Abd el-Haqq was being pressured from above. He was not that kind of a man.)

Then came the final blow. "You did not perform an excavation (fouille), you just dug a test pit (sondage). Therefore we will have no division. You may take nothing home."

Whew! I parlayed a loan of fifty flints and all the animal bones for one year's study under a ten-thousand-dollar bond if I should default by a single day.

Hallam Movius looked at the flints in Cambridge, Massachusetts, and John Waechter did the same in London. I sent the bones to Dr. Charles Reed in Chicago, who didn't have time to study all of them. He had his classes to teach and too much work of his own piled up already, so he had to send them back without a full report.

Bruce Schroeder of Columbia went out to Syria and found the flints back in Palmyra, where he identified them from my list of numbers painted on them by our inspector, Ahmad Tahir, who was as careful and slow as Mr. Samadie and Poopy had been the opposite. Bruce wrote his doctor's thesis on the cave, and came to the same general conclusions I stated earlier.

Bureaucracy, it seems, is its own reward. As far as I know, no foreign cave digger has tackled Syria since.

Jerf Ajla was the last cave I dug for twelve long years. Meanwhile, I devoted my prime attention to physical anthropology, especially the racial history of man. And that was the roughest thing I ever did, more harrowing than the war. It was easier for me to have fought the enemy abroad than to be drawn reluctantly into the racial tragedy going on here at home—a dead hero is more comfortable than a living martyr.

An odd thing happened while we were in Palmyra that had no perceptible bearing on our expedition or on our life at home. One day a cable was delivered to me at the hotel. It had been sent from New York, and its message contained two words: "Congratulations, Harry."

Lisa and I and my son Carl Jr. and Jannie puzzled over this, but no one could think of who Harry was or why he should be congratulating me. After we were home I discovered that it was my old friend Harry L. Shapiro, who had taken his Ph.D. at Harvard two years ahead of me, and was the head of the physical anthropology section at the American Museum of Natural History.

Harry was also the chairman of our section in the National Academy of Sciences. He was trying to tell me that I had just been elected to the academy, and he wanted to make sure I got the message, even if I didn't understand it.

23. No Gorillas in Russia

In the previous chapter I mentioned that I had read proof on my book *The Story of Man* in Kabul early in 1954, shortly before our departure homeward counterclockwise. This means that I had finished writing it before leaving for Afghanistan. It was easier to write than it was to sell. Having no prospect of ever lecturing from my Harvard Anthropology 1 notes again, I simply turned them into a book, but more simply than I had done with those for *Caravan*, because I had slanted the first toward sophomores rather than toward graduate students.

Instead of mentioning *Homo erectus*, I called the latter Half-Brained Men. It has taken me over twenty years to discover that this leap in the dark was right, in the sense that *erectus* had roughly half the cortical neurons of *sapiens*. I took care to offer no element in our population any grounds for even calling the book controversial, and I was especially kind to the Gaels in depicting their paradise, the *Tir nan Og* (Land of Youth), as a model.

It is dedicated "To HOMO SAPIENS, wishing him good luck on his next adventure." The next page contains what might be called an explanatory poem:

> *THIS is the story of man*
> *who alone of beasts mastered the wild-fire,*
> *became a skilled hunter and healer,*
> *a tiller of earth and a herdsman,*
> *who conquered the cold and the sea*
> *while the power of the sun altered him.*
> *Wheel-making, smelting, and writing,*
> *he hammered out empires with iron,*
> *circled his planet with cannon,*
> *found and took a new world—*
> *whence he challenges space with his atoms*
> *while facing the ultimate challenge*
>
> *—HIMSELF.*

One night at a ladies' club in Philadelphia I heard Bucky Fuller read these lines with great gusto. I had been supposed to introduce John P. Marquand, but he was ill, and Bucky was substituting for him. So I introduced Bucky instead, after a thoughtful lady who was a cousin of both these gentlemen had put a copy of my book in his hand.

After I had finished writing *The Story of Man*, it was turned down by Charles Madison of Holt and Ted Weeks of the Atlantic Press. Why they didn't want it I can only guess. Perhaps it was too close in date and title to Hendrik Van Loon's *Story of Mankind*, and possibly to H. G. Wells's *Outline of History*. When I was beginning to feel dejected by these rejections, I received an offer from Harold Strauss of Knopf for just the kind of book I had already written. Knopf spared no expense in typography or illustrations. Jonathan Cape, as usual, published it in England. It made *The New York Times* best-seller list for one week, and according to the jacket blurb of the third printing of the third edition, dated 1974, it had already been translated into eight foreign languages. From my own point of view, it was neither the fame nor the pelf that pleased me, but the calm that engulfed me—if only temporarily— because nobody had called me a racist, anti-Semite, or anything else horrid or pejorative because of it. I was Mr. Clean, just for once.

The second unrelated event that merits space in this chapter was Lisa's and my trip to the Rhodesias in July 1955, to attend a prehistoric conference at the expense of the Rhodesian governments, North and South, which were then still British. All expenses were paid except for travel to and from America. In our case, the Wenner-Gren foundation footed part of the bill, and *Life* the rest of it, thus putting me in a rather awkward position. I took many photographs, both for my use and for theirs. One sequence was of Louis Leakey making a hand axe and with it skinning and butchering a buck. Another was of a team of iron smelters creating a bloom of iron in a pit with charcoal, ore, and lime, the flames fed by pumping piston bellows. They chanted as they worked. One gained the impression that the chant was an ancient formula and if they made a mistake, puff! the bloom was spoiled. This must have been a great ordeal to these elderly men, not only because they had not done this magic deed for decades, but also because they were surrounded by a ring of sweating white skin and their chanting was interrupted by the clicks of cameras.

We made many excursions to see hand axes still imbedded in the faces of trenches; Louis Leakey's field of other hand axes still in place at Olorgesailie; and Zimbabwe itself, the enigmatic walled and towered fortress that Miss Gertrude Caton-Thompson had excavated, and she was there to explain it to us. On the way to Olorgesailie, whither Louis had taken us in a Land Rover, he stopped to give two Masai warriors a lift. I started taking pictures. Their women flopped to the ground. To help the warriors in, I offered to hold one's spear and hand it to him but Louis said, "If you touch that spear you'll get it through your belly."

Another excursion was by plane over the Caprivi Strip, that thin ribbon of Namibia separating Botswanaland from Angola and the two Rhodesias. This no-man's-land was an unspoiled game park, with wildebeeste and buffalos and elephants and giraffes and all the usual African animals in abundance. Click-clack went the shutters, and the tallest got the best shots, while some toes and feelings were probably hurt.

We missed one last excursion, a train ride into the Ituri Forest to see Pat Putnam's Pygmies. I could not go because I did not have the shot against yellow fever needed for a permit. I am allergic to egg yolk, which is contained in the serum, and thus missed my chance to see my grandfather's pygmy.

We went home early, for reasons of our own, but I cannot leave the narrative without a confession. By what seems to have been some mistake, I was the guest of honor on the trip, but didn't know it. No one told me. Miles Burkitt of Cambridge University wanted it and should have had it. He was the teacher of most of the British archaeologists present, and at least ten years my senior. I was seated beside the governor of Northern Rhodesia at the opening banquet; I was invited to make a radio speech, which was indiscreet; and we were lodged in the fanciest quarters, where I met a belted earl called Eddie, who recognized me at once from the war, and said, "Oh, yes, we called him the Boy from Boston."

Miles Burkitt took such deep umbrage at my presence that he tried to get ahead of me on every occasion, particularly in cars. I dismissed this as simply bad manners plus senility. One day after he had passed us we drove up a narrow road behind him to its end, where a bull elephant confronted Burkitt's car in a threatening manner. Burkitt's driver could not back out because we were right behind them, and someone else was close behind us.

By the time the way was clear, the elephant could have rolled the Burkitt car over with its tusks, but Tusker didn't have to. Never before or since have I seen such a frightened old man, but it was all my fault, as Miss Caton-Thompson told a friend of mine about five years ago. She was in the front car too, and still blamed me.

A third unrelated activity took place on December 28, 1955. Lisa and I signed the papers making us owners of a fourteen-acre property in West Gloucester, with a frontage on the Essex River marsh and a view across the river and Crane's Breach to the mountains of Maine, as seen on a clear day. Our land contained a rundown, unheated duck-shooting lodge, several hen houses, a toolshed, and a pigpen. It was almost contiguous to our original lot, which we had bought eight years before. A good place for retirement, now that our major expeditions were probably over.

The fourth activity was the International Anthropological Congress, held in Philadelphia in September 1956, before the college opened. It was hot and damp as only Philadelphia can be. Because the center of activity was the University Museum, and its trustees and directors were Proper Philadelphians, some of them left their cool havens on the coast of Maine to do a proper hosting job. The Russians who had arrived in heavy woolen suits were sweating and complaining bitterly. We should have told them that Philadelphia had a tropical climate.

One of them, their commissar, who kept track of the others, was constantly scribbling in a tiny notebook little more than an inch wide. We wondered where he put it when asleep. It was he that the most prestigious hostess bagged as her special guest. While dining at her mansion, he asked her: "Madame, please, what is the population of Philadelphia?"

She replied, "Alas, there are only five families left."

Prince Peter of Greece and Denmark hung out when possible in my office, because it was air-conditioned. My brother Jack, who had an office in Philadelphia, had given me the machine. Peter had much movie film that needed to be kept cool. He invited me to visit him in Kalimpong in the Himalayas. I accepted and we went there later on. Professor Ito from Tokyo, his wife and daughter, were assigned to us. We took them out to Valley Forge to see where the Americans had defeated the British, and Mrs. Ito gave Lisa some silk scarves. As will be told in the next chapter, the professor got us invitations to the holiest Japanese treasure, the Shoshoin.

I spent the most time with my old friend from Moscow, Gyorgi Debetz, who had been studying Eskimo skulls in Harry Shapiro's laboratory in the American Museum in New York. One morning he and I were sitting in my office looking over some bones when we heard a knock on my door. "Come in," I said.

In walked a friend of mine named Mickey, a retired naval surgeon and the husband of a famous lady biographer named Kitty. Unlike other Proper Philadelphians, they summered in Gloucester, my new home.

Mickey carried something very long and slender, draped in paper. He set it down on my desk gently and unveiled it. It was a walrus's penis bone, beautifully carved and etched by some Eskimo genius. It was a masterpiece.

"Kitty got tired of seeing it on the wall," he said, "and asked me to get rid of it. Do you want it?"

"*Want* it?" I replied, and made a call on the telephone. In a few minutes in strode David Crownover, the exhibitor, who said, "Froelich is setting up an Eskimo exhibit, and this will fit in beautifully."

Holding it up triumphantly, David carried it away.

That left Gyorgi, Mickey, and me becalmed.

"What would you like to do next?" I asked Gyorgi.

My guest wrinkled his brow, and said, "A gorilla. Do you have one in Philadelphia?"

"A beauty," I replied, "in the Philadelphia Zoo. Let's go."

Then Mickey said, stammering, for he was terribly polite and self-effacing, "M-m-m-may I c-c-come too?"

"Sure, come along," I said.

I drove Gyorgi in Lisa's red Saab, and Mickey followed in another rather small car, I believe it was orange. He rode just far enough from us to be unobtrusive, and for anyone who was watching us to be sure that Gyorgi and I were being followed. When we had parked, he followed us on foot with a gap of about sixty feet. I kept saying, "Come on up and join us, Mickey," but he would say "Shh!" This was beginning to give Gyorgi the collywobbles. Finally I persuaded Mickey, and Gyorgi relaxed.

Gyorgi sat in front of the gorilla, watching him with complete concentration, and the gorilla looked in Gyorgi's eyes with equal intensity. Mickey and I remained absolutely still. When the gorilla moved his head to the right, Gyorgi followed suit, and vice versa. Each seemed to have taken over the other's identity.

I forgot what broke this seance up, but soon Gyorgi and I were back at the rear entrance of the University Museum, to face a battery of cameramen and reporters. Among the usual clicks, they asked him questions like: "How does it feel to live in a free democracy rather than in a communist state?"

I did not translate this literally into French, and he replied with a few words in Russian. "What did he say?" the reporter asked.

I replied, "Professor Debetz said, 'Alas, we have no gorillas in Russia.' "

24. *Faces of Asia*

After the conference in Philadelphia was over in September 1956, Lisa and I were invited by the U.S. Air Force to take pictures of people and the places in which they lived in some parts of the world we had not visited. We were to travel by military aircraft (MATS) wherever such transport was available, and to be put up in military lodgings under the same conditions. Lisa's way was paid as well as mine because she had a certificate of service from the QMC's R & D branch (Climatology Unit, Military Planning Division). She was not a "dependent." The purpose of the pictures was to let downed pilots discover where they had landed.

When I had visited the Institute of Far Northern Peoples in Leningrad in 1930, I had been given pictures of the peoples living around the Arctic from the Lapps to the Chuckchi and Siberian Eskimo. Later I had made exchanges with Gyorgi Debetz to get pictures of the inland peoples of Central Asia. In return his museum had wanted pictures of American Indians located, oddly enough, on the sites of atomic plants in the west. It was hard to get such pictures because the Indians whose grandparents had lived there were decimated and scattered in reservations.

By these means we covered much of the Soviet Union's Asiatic territory, and could concentrate on the fringing peninsulas and islands from Japan to India (I already had Iran and Afghanistan). The only leg of the route on which we had to pay our own way was from Bangkok to Karachi, which did not leave us impoverished.

I did not consider this trip a proper expedition because it did not include any exploratory fieldwork, but rather as an overseas extension of academic life. It lasted from October 17, 1956, until March 26, 1957. During this period we visited eleven countries where we spent a maximum of eighty-eight days in India, the world's most complex nation geographically and ethnically, and twenty-nine days in Japan. Taiwan received ten days, and the others, including Korea, the Philippines, Ceylon, Nepal, Sikkim, Pakistan, and Saudi Arabia single numbers each. In these places I took hundreds of photographs of people, saw thousands of others of many races, visited many sites and museums, conversed at length with local authorities, and did some lecturing when necessary.

Lisa and I arrived in Tokyo on Friday, October 19, to be met by Gordon Bowles (remember the crazy house and the great horned owl). He was the associate director of International House and a professor at the University of Tokyo, lecturing in Japanese, which was just as much his native language as English. He drove us through the fiendish city traffic to International House, where we were very kindly put up in his and his wife Jane's own house.

After six days of sightseeing, conversations with Japanese anthropologists, and visits to museums, Gordon, Lisa, and I took a train northward on the twenty-fifth, spending the night in Sendai, and on the twenty-sixth we crossed the Tsugaru Strait from Honshu to Hokkaido on a ferry. Although this strait is not very wide, being only thirteen and a half miles at its narrowest point, the winds can be strong and the currents powerful and treacherous. The decks were almost clear of passengers, who were lying down inside as if expecting death, the women vomiting automatically. We went by rail from Hakodate to Noboribetsu on the south shore,and thence visited several Ainu villages—Shiraoi, Mukawa, Piratori, and Mibutani.

Originally, most of the Ainu had lived along the banks of nine major rivers, flowing spokewise from a central mountain core—the seat of the gods and the home of the owners of the bears—down to the sea. There the Ainu had trapped and speared salmon in season, and hunted bear and deer. When the Japanese forbade these activities, they moved most of the Ainu to seashore villages to become saltwater fishermen instead. A few remained on the shores of Lake Akan in the north, but we did not have a chance to visit them.

In 1944 the Ainu still numbered about sixteen thousand, and in 1956 the chances were that the numbers had not greatly decreased. Most of the ones we met in the southern shore villages wore western clothing and spoke Japanese, and many were mixing or had mixed with Japanese. An exception was a family headed by one man and his son who had become wealthy horse breeders. Another was the much photographed "Chief" Miyamoto, a professional Ainu who wore the traditional long hair and long beard, an elm-bark fillet about his head, and an elm-bark robe. His wife, along with several other elderly women, had blue "mustaches" tattooed around her mouth. These were not mustaches at all (a Japanese fantasy), but magical barriers to keep evil spirits out of the women's nostrils and mouths. The Reverend John Batchelor, an English missionary who wore a long beard and looked like an Ainu himself, had frowned on this tattooing, and the practice had been discontinued. These ancient crones shuffled around in a ring in what had once been a gay and youthful maiden's dance, to the clicking of 35-mm cameras held to eye level by busloads of Japanese tourists and schoolchildren.

From this pathetic scene we moved on to Sapporo, the capital of Hokkaido, where we visited Professor Kodama, a noted brain anatomist who had a collection of over one thousand Ainu skulls. He told us that although Ainu brains are larger than Japanese ones, they are simpler than the latter, particularly in the organization of the motor areas. We examined as many of these skulls as we could, but it would have taken a month to have gone over all of them. Many of them looked less European than the living Ainu do, with their light skins, an occasional green eye, and abundant brown hair. Professor Kodama also explained that the Japanese people must be 10 percent Ainu in origin because they have 3 percent of enamel pearls on the gingival borders of their upper molar teeth, while the Ainu have 33 percent, and this would partly account for the abundance of beards among the Japanese. We— that is mostly Gordon and Professor Kodama—fell into a discussion of the distribution of Ainu place names on the main island of Honshu, and it turned out that they occur as far south and west as Lake Biwa, just west of Kyoto, but no farther. So north and east of Lake Biwa must once have been Ainu country.

During this trip to the north Gordon spent much time lecturing to us, and I learned more than I could have done in several years of hard work, even if I had been able to read Japanese. Japanese scholars divided themselves rigidly into nonoverlapping disciplines and apparently considered it unethical to try to coordinate their fields. By talking about Ainu place names in Honshu, Professor Kodama had shown a freewheeling tendency in defiance of these canons.

In the same vein, Gordon told us about the composition of the Japanese language, which contained European, Chinese, Ainu, Turkish (Altaic), and Malayo-Polynesian elements. The European words were quite recent and could be discarded, from the research point of view. The Chinese had come in at various periods. These could be discarded, too. Of the words that remained, Malayo-Polynesian accounted for 42 percent, Ainu for 10 percent, and Altaic 48 percent. The Ainu words are mostly place names, but only north of Lake Biwa. The Malayo-Polynesian element was probably brought in by pre-Chinese seafaring people from the coast of southern China, related to those that sailed out into the Pacific, and probably centered mostly in southern Japan. The Altaic speech was most likely introduced from Central Asia via Korea by the Yayoi people, who brought horses and iron. Of the basic core words by means of which linguists seek the relationships between languages, all but one were Altaic. That one was *to*, meaning father; it was Malayo-Polynesian.*

---

*Some linguist or linguists reading this in 1981 or later may well dispute what I have written. Let it be clear that what I have stated above is not intended as gospel truth, only what I was told in 1956.

The favorite place for these lectures was the bedroom in Japanese inns, where the three of us lay on the floor on mattresses before we fell asleep.

On October 30 we flew from Sapporo to Tokyo, after the stewardess had announced: "We will now have a two-hour fright to Tokyo." It was a perfectly peaceful trip. The fright came later, in the tangled, breakneck Tokyo traffic.

On November 2 we were off for Kyoto on the famous express train, The Swallow. On the way we were cautioned not to lean out the windows on our side because it would offend the emperor, whom we were to pass. Being tall enough to see without leaning, I saw the miniature ruler all decked out in braid and medals on a station platform, surrounded by well-disciplined schoolchildren. As all the Kyoto hotels were full, Gordon had wangled us rooms and board in the mansion of a wealthy tobacco manufacturer who had begun to take in paying guests on a small and elite scale.

The next day we went to Nara, an even more ancient capital than Kyoto, dating back at least to the sixth century A.D. It now consists mostly of a deer park, with several temples and the residence of a bishop. We visited the latter in the company of Dr. and Mrs. Arnold Toynbee, whom Gordon now had to lead around, as well as ourselves, because the Toynbees' mentor, the director of International House, had collapsed with a so-called heart attack. It was probably an angina or he would not have been able to make it back to Tokyo alone; the next time we saw him he was fully ambulant and cheery.

I had never met a man aged sixty-seven with as great a store of inexhaustible energy as Arnold Toynbee, with whom anyone over twenty would have had a hard time keeping up. At any rate, it was a break for me because I enjoyed his company very much, especially as he had a new idea every thirty seconds.

Two things impressed me most at Nara. One was a stone monument to our late friend Langdon Warner of the Fogg Museum at Harvard, who had persuaded someone in Washington during World War II not to bomb Nara—the holiest place in Japan, with its priceless treasures—nor even Kyoto. The second was the repository of many of those treasures—the Shoshoin, a Finnish-style two-storied log building of rectangular shape, constructed around a court, and set on posts. It was made of cryptomeria logs, some as much as two feet in diameter, with dovetailed corners. Some of the logs had been replaced from time to time, but many if not most were original. It was said to be over 1,300 years old, or built about A.D. 600, the oldest wooden building in the world.

Once a year, in November, it was opened to a few select visitors by special invitation, and through our embassy, with Professor Ito's help, we had been lucky enough to get on the list. The Toynbees went with us. We padded around the cold wooden floors in stocking feet in the dark, peering into glass cases with flashlights. Included among the treasures were sixth- to eighth- century textiles; robes; screens; boxes; tables; backgammon boards; *go* boards (*go* was just becoming popular again with the youth of America as a new discovery); jewels; a glass pitcher, presumably from Syria; pottery; bronze and silver mirrors; swords; spears; pikes; Baltic amber; some inlaid tables that could have come from India; saddles and saddlecloths, the saddles with cowboy-style pommels; iron stirrups dating at least to the eighth century; and many kinds of beans, bits of ginger, cloves, and other botanical specimens in jars; as well as a box made of sixth- to eighth-century persimmon wood, thus permanently disposing of the thought that the Japanese persimmons had been a post-Columbian import from America. As far as art motifs were concerned, it was easy to see Finnish resemblances, Central Asian appliqué in felt, the Scythian flying gallop, and Northwest Coastlike faces in masks. Two hours were scarcely enough to assimilate all of this, but more than enough time for us all to come out coughing, and to have caught colds.

The next day we went to Tenri, a city on the outskirts of Nara, as new as Nara is old. There, in a dream, a woman saw the first people in the world issue from a hole in the ground, and from them everyone now living is descended. On this basis she founded a new cult, which spread widely among Japanese everywhere. Her son succeeded her, followed in turn by his own son. Her son was a large, jovial man known as the patriarch, who greeted us warmly and invited us to lunch. There I had the usual trouble finding a place to put my feet, for I could not double them under me as the Japanese do, and avoiding food with eggs in it; but the conversation was most amiable, assisted by a nisei girl from San Francisco, who was a convert. The patriarch assigned us quarters in his guest house, and let us witness a service in his huge and spotless temple and visit his museum.

At the service we had to sit outside an inner circle, in the middle of which was a hole in the floor, directly over the original hole from which the first people had emerged. Around the edges of this hole squatted special initiates who peered below to see what was going on. Certain unseen performers entered the space down below through an underground tunnel and produced mysterious noises indicating both physical and vocal activities of considerable intensity, marked by loud beats on gongs up above, and responses from the audience.

The members of the sect came from all over Japan and from countries overseas, even as far away as Manchuria, China, Peru, and

Brazil. It was their duty to spend a certain number of days each year laboring on the buildings and grounds at Tenri, as well as contributing funds, and the sect was obviously quite wealthy.

This wealth was even more manifest when we visited the museum, where we saw objects from all over the world sent or brought in by cult members. There before my eyes lay a large and very fine collection of Shang Dynasty bronze vessels from Anyang in China that were supposed to be Chinese national treasures, as well as Peruvian vases, Mexican sculptures, and even ancient Egyptian collections, and American Northwest Coast totem poles.

The Japanese Anthropological Association was holding its annual meeting there, and I had to show slides I had brought with me of my excavations at Belt and Hotu caves in Iran, in which the participants showed much interest. That evening, instead of the usual arguments and resolutions that mar the final sessions of comparable meetings in my own country, everyone relaxed. The patriarch served us a fine dinner, comely maidens kept filling everyone's cup with warm sake, and they all began wrestling. Curiously enough, warm sake did not seem to affect me as it did the others, all of whom, out of courtesy, challenged me to a bout. Being at that time almost in the sumo weight and size class, I had little trouble tipping each of them over in turn, much to everyone's satisfaction, and we all parted good friends.

During this trip to Japan, with constant travel, lectures from Gordon, consultations with Japanese anthropologists, and viewing thousands of people, I had been puzzled by the physical heterogeneity of the Japanese people and the partial resemblances between some of them and comparable elements in Europe and the Middle East, with which I was more familiar. For example, there were moon-faced Mongoloids; round-headed and round-faced Alpine-looking people; rather tall, gaunt, hatchet-faced aristocrats who lacked the Mongoloid eye folds and facial flatness; and smaller, narrow-faced, and narrow-nosed city people who looked more like a local version of urban Arabs or Jews.

It was impossible to ascribe all of these variations to a faithful maintenance of different racial elements brought in quite mysteriously from abroad. It made more sense to suppose that they had unscrambled themselves from a total population pool by selective forces so operating that some had remained countryfolk while others had become urban; some had risen on the social scale while others had not. In other words, what had happened in Europe and the Middle East had most likely also happened here, whatever the origins of the elements concerned, and if it could have happened in two parts of the world separated by the mass of Central Asia, it could have happened elsewhere, too. Thus, I was knee-deep in a somewhat sticky idea that contributed to my later theory of the origin of races, which was to be born into a partly hostile world, as all new ideas are.

On November 13 Lisa and I left Tokyo for Korea, this time flying in considerable luxury in a general's plane. As we stepped off at Kimpo Airport, a Jewish G.I. rushed up to me and asked: "Are you by any chance Rabbi Lipschitz?"

I had no idea what caused this misidentification except possibly that I was wearing a double-felt South African hat, the only one I owned except a derby that fitted me, but such hats are generally not part of any clerical outfits. The soldier seemed obviously disappointed, but withdrew to await the next plane and try again.

Meanwhile, our transportation had finally arrived. It was a jeep driven by another G.I. who had gone to the wrong airport. He took us through the city to an officers' billet on the outskirts, run by one Sergeant Snowball, with the able assistance of a beautiful Korean girl, where we were most hospitably lodged and fed.

In the following days we called on the president of the University of Korea, who introduced us to the head of the department of anatomy at the medical school, and the two took us to lunch at a restaurant where we ate broiled prawns six inches in diameter, so delicious that I have dreamed about that meal several times since.

The anatomist then led us to his laboratory, where he took great pains to explain to me the basic differences between Mongoloid and Caucasoid skulls. First of all, one difference lies in the relative positions of the upper attachments of the temporal and masseter muscles, which move the lower jaw up and down and give it a characteristically rotary grinding motion peculiar to human beings who have not lost it through overlapping bites, as many of us highly "civilized" people have through eating soft food. The temporal muscles run from the coronoid process of the lower jaw up under the zygomatic arches to attach themselves fanwise to the surfaces of the temporal, parietal, and frontal bones, while the masseters run from the outer surfaces of the gonial angles of the lower jaw over the temporal muscles to the outer surfaces of the zygomatic arches.

In Mongoloid skulls both pairs of muscles are set forward of their positions in Caucasoid skulls, necessitating a forward projection of the molars. These muscular positions give the Mongoloids relatively more strength to the biting power of the incisors, which are relatively large, and less chewing power to the molars, which are relatively small in proportion. In fact, third molars are frequently absent in Mongoloids. Another consequence of this anatomical peculiarity is that the mongoloid molars tend to mask parts of the nasal cavity and make the nasal bones look relatively low, while the cavity is just as capacious as those of other races, and the orbits are made shallower, with a consequent protrusion of the eyeballs.

While these details may seem technical to the general reader, they were of immense importance to me on theoretical grounds, particularly as they had some bearing on the controversial cold adaptation of the Mongoloid race. After having made these simple and lucid explanations to me, the head of the anatomy department then most graciously gave me a perfect Korean skull, which I packed and shipped back to Philadelphia.

Later we were driven about the countryside in jeeps, taking many photographs of people, and finally to a wonderful cave in Cambro-Devonian limestone. It was spacious, near the road, had a fine floor, a spring inside it, and its walls sloped downward and outward at floor level, a sign of considerable depth. I would have given almost anything to have been able to stay there and excavate that cave, but could not for two reasons. It was too close to the North Korean border for comfort, and President Syngman Rhee had forbidden all archaeological excavation on the grounds that it might disturb his ancestors. If that cave had, as I suspected, contained remains of *Sinanthropus pekinensis,* Syngman Rhee might well have been right.

The Koreans were larger and heavier than most Japanese, and less variable. Some of them had quite light skins, a few had mixed greenish and bluish eyes, but so had a few northern Japanese. Caught in front of the sunlight, as the sun was setting, many of the Koreans seemed to have red hair, but when they turned around again it was black.

Our flight back to Japan was quite different from the one over. We went in one of General Chennault's Flying Tigers—of World War II vintage, with bucket seats along the sides—and we all had to wear parachutes because of the proximity to the North Korean border.

On November 22, which was Thanksgiving Day, we flew in a Sixth Air Force bomber to Okinawa, where everyone in uniform deplaned to buy American liquor at the PX at exceptionally low prices, including several bottles of bourbon for me. Meanwhile, I sauntered about near the plane observing about forty Okinawans walking by. They are much smaller even than the Japanese, darker skinned, and quite hairy. Few had eye folds. They did not look particularly Mongoloid, nor did they resemble the Ainu as much as I had been told to expect. To my surprise, the pilot brought me six bottles of Harper's and four of Old Crow, some of which made excellent presents on Taiwan, where such beverages are hard to get.

We were driven to the Grand Hotel in Taipei, and grand it was indeed, most luxurious and expensive. At dinner we met an old friend, John Pope, a Chinese art expert, who was happy to get one of my bottles, while an officer took another, leaving me with a mere eight, and still feeling like a one-shelf liquor store proprietor. The hotel being beyond our means, we obviously could not stay there, so I phoned Bob Lindquist, a State Department friend of Carl Jr. and Jannie, to see if he knew of any place for us to stay. Bob was running a foreign-service training school for budding China hands at Taichung, in the central part of the island's coastal plain. He invited us to stay there, but we could not come at once because of a dilemma which reared its horns at 8:30 the next morning. I was supposed to report to my local boss, the local air force attaché of our embassy, Colonel Fish. We should have reported immediately upon arrival, but instead had been taken to the island's number-one post hotel.

At 8:30, when I was about to leave for Colonel Fish's office, who should appear but Dr. Li Chi, director of the Academia Sinica that stood outside the city, the discoverer, excavator, and remover of the world-renowned burial site of the Shang emperors and of their magnificent bronze vessels, of which I had seen a pilfered sample at Tenri. He was then the oldest Ph.D. in anthropology from Harvard, having taken his degree in 1923, when I was a beardless youth of twenty-three and third in line.

He explained that he had met every plane from Tokyo on the previous day and had no idea how I had gotten to Taipei, nor could I tell him either what plane I had taken, or that I had an imminent appointment with the U. S. Air Force attaché. Furthermore, he had broken an ankle and had been tracking me in considerable pain. He had another car waiting outside at the moment to whisk Lisa and me to the suburban buildings of Academia Sinica to begin my tour.

Feeling like a peck of lice, I managed to tell this dear old man that I had to go to Taichung for a few days and would do whatever he wanted me to do on my return. I then gave him a bottle of Harper's in full Christmas wrapping and left for Colonel Fish's office. There Colonel Fish informed me that I was in Dutch with the Chinese customs for not having checked in with them, although they were not around when we landed. His most efficient secretary, Lettie Wu, said that she would take care of that, as well as getting us red-card permits to visit aboriginal territory. Colonel Fish invited Lisa and myself to ride with him in his own plane to Clark Field, Luzon, our next destination, on December 2. This was an offer that we could hardly refuse, but one that left us very little time.

Arthur Prager, whose rank I forget because he was in plain clothes, was Colonel Fish's assistant air attaché. He volunteered to wait around until our permits to enter aboriginal territory had come in and then bring them down to us at Taichung. After that he would stay with us as guide and troubleshooter until our departure. To this Colonel Fish agreed. We rented a car and driver, and it was a long and beautiful drive, with many stops for picture taking and one for lunch.

On this ride we saw all three kinds of Chinese to be found on the coastal plain of the island. Five million (in 1956) were descended from settlers who had come before or during the Japanese occupation, and spoke Fukienese, the language of their ancestral province, as well—in many cases—as Japanese. They called themselves Taiwanese and resent later comers, in particular the four million Nationalists from North China who came over more recently with the Generalissimo Chiang Kai-shek. These were tall, bony-faced, light-skinned men, easy enough to distinguish from the others, and they spoke Mandarin. One million were Hakkas, the oldest of all, who wore blue clothing and lived mostly on the edges of the Central Mountains. They and other early settlers had absorbed some sixty thousand aborigines called Pingpu who had once lived on the plain, while about one hundred and ten thousand unassimilated aborigines still occupied the mountains and some of the eastern coast, as well as offshore islands. Their territory totaled well over half the land surface of the island. It was easy enough to tell these three elements apart, and just drinking in the human as well as the beautiful natural environmental scene was more than a day's work.

We arrived at Taichung at around 6 P.M.; I, at least, was exhausted. The next day we drove with the Lindquists down to the southernmost city of Tainan and back, passing both ways the monument marking the Tropic of Cancer. In the evening the Lindquists invited us to a banquet celebrating the graduation of one of the foreign service officers from the school. This was a rich feast of many courses, exquisitely cooked in Peking style, with many toasts and speeches in Mandarin Chinese, and imitations of animal noises. In the latter Lisa won first prize by quacking like a migrating duck. Before we were through the tablecloth was covered with the bones of birds and beasts, strewn about in good Peking style, and we wended our way back to the Lindquists for a sound sleep.

The next morning—Sunday, November 25—Art Prager arrived in an Air Force station wagon, bearing our permits. Bob Lindquist, Jwan (one of his teachers), Lisa, and I climbed aboard, and Art drove us to Pengyuan, and then up a mountain road through a more or less vertical region of almost incredible beauty. First we photographed a Hakka village and then, a little more than a mile before the pass, we came to a group of rock shelters and caves. One rock shelter and one cave had good floors and fire-blackened roofs. Both were promising sites. These were of considerable interest because Li Chi had told me that no one had yet excavated a cave site on the island.

Immediately ahead we were stopped at a control post, where the officials took a long time inspecting our new passes, then drove past a hydroelectric station, past plantations where tea was being grown on steep slopes, and on to Pwo Ai, the end of the road. There we crossed a suspension bridge on foot into our first Atayal village. The Atayals were the northernmost of the aboriginal tribes, numbering thirty-eight thousand, almost twice as many as any other tribe. They were also the most warlike, and had been inveterate headhunters right through the Japanese occupation. The Japanese had sealed them off with an electrified barbed-wire fence.

A mission building with a cross in front stood at the entrance to the village, but we saw no missionary. Beyond were the Atayal houses, of stone, wooden crib work, and thatch. Storehouses of log crib work, like miniature Shoshoins, perched on posts with wooden rat guards, and they were filled with red millet and, apparently, dry rice. The women were tattooed, some with "mustaches" like Ainu women, except that the tattooing reached up to their temples, and some of the men had it on their foreheads. One whole household was drunk, and one man had the shakes, apparently from bad liquor. A young Atayal named Sye Jun Jang guided us around until we were accosted by a Chinese major.

The latter went into hysterics, shouting and screaming at poor Jwan, and clapping his hands in front of his face, his eyes popping and his neck bulging, until finally Bob said, "You are insulting the professor." This quieted the major a little, but not enough, and finally Art pulled out his air attaché calling card, printed in Chinese on the back. This pricked the major's bubble. He shook hands with Bob and Jwan and explained that he had mistaken me for a missionary.

Theoretically the Atayal language is usually called Indonesian, but studies made since my visit suggest that Atayal is either extremely aberrant or possibly an isolated language all its own.* Physically the Atayals whom we saw in this village and elsewhere are extremely variable, especially the women. Some are Ainu-like, others could pass for Europeans facially, and one, at least, was a ringer for a light-skinned Maya Indian. Some had green-brown eyes, others light brown ones, and very few had epicanthic eye folds.

For a discussion of this question, and its documentation, see my book The Living Races of Man, *New York, Knopf, 1965, 169–70. Of course, new classifications may have arisen since 1965.*

.   On Monday the twenty-sixth we went back to the mountains, taking along Carol Lindquist and Bob Thomas, a foreign service officer who spoke Taiwanese. After a few wrong turns we arrived at Sun-Moon Lake, a vacation and honeymoon spot of great beauty, with a magnificent government-owned hotel. We crossed the lake to Pu Chi, a village of the decimated Thao tribe, numbering only two hundred persons, and led by Chief Mo, who looked like a big and portly Polynesian. For our benefit he dressed in his fancy regalia, which consisted mostly of squares of red cloth. He immediately took a fancy to my big brown South African hat, which exactly fitted his large head. I "loaned" it to him and "forgot" to ask for it back, it looked so good on him.

He and his large family of daughters by several wives, one Chinese, put on a tourist-style show of pounding pestles and hollow bamboo tubes of different lengths on the tightly tamped ground, thus issuing different tones, and dancing. I bought a local version of an Iroquois or Northwest Coast Indian twisted-face mask, then we returned to the hotel, to find it swarming with movie cameramen and tall, gaunt-faced North Chinese special police. We were politely denied admission on the grounds that the generalissimo was about to arrive, so we departed.

The next day, Tuesday the twenty-seventh, we visited another Atayal village and saw the same variety of physical types; finally, just before sunset, we reached a village of Bununs, the next tribe to the south, whose people are rather large and pronouncedly Mongoloid, with brown skins.

On Wednesday I lectured to the foreign-service school on Mongoloid racial problems, and Art Prager drove back to his house in Taipei, where we slept. On Thursday the twenty-ninth we reported to Li Chi at the university. We saw his An Yang bronzes, jades, and other treasures that he had moved fourteen times to keep them from the Japanese invaders. He was fascinated by the representation in bronze and jade of people with round, non-Mongoloid eyes and broad noses, probably the non-Chinese sea peoples of South China in the third millenium B.C.

That evening I received a cable from H. Otley Beyer, dean of archaeologists and anthropologists in the Philippines and also a Harvard alumnus. He was next on our travel list. He protested the brevity of our proposed stay in his bailiwick. He was right, but our schedule was set by MATS. The Air Force was being shortchanged between its own or MATS's timetable and the hunger of lonely overseas anthropologists. In a minor way, perhaps, I was their Bob Hope.

On Friday the thirtieth I reported at the university at 8:45, where Li Chi let me look at his precious An Yang skulls, of which he had about two hundred. All or nearly all were from sacrificial victims buried to accompany their emperor or emperors to the afterworld. I examined the forty that were in best repair, and at Li Chi's suggestion selected eight for careful measuring. From certain marks on the critical points, I had a feeling that these skulls had been measured before, and wanted to make sure that my measurements came out the same as the last ones. Li Chi finally admitted that they had been measured in Peking by Dr. T. L. Woo, than whom a more skilled craniometrist had probably never existed. After the Communist takeover Dr. Woo seemed to have disappeared, at least as far as Li Chi knew. Somewhere or other Li Chi had a copy of the earlier measurements, with which he compared mine, apparently favorably. This led to a subtle hint, never overtly stated, that he might want me to study the whole lot, but I did not pursue this further.

My observations led me to the tentative conclusion that the eight he had let me measure had not been drawn from a single population, and that it would be a statistical mistake to treat them as such. In the first place, they all seemed to be female. This implied that they were the deceased emperor's wives and concubines, taken from several peripheral and tributary populations. Despite shovel incisors, two were otherwise manifestly Caucasoid, and they were older when they died than the others, who fell into two categories. Some were heavy-boned, round-headed, and flat-faced, like Mongols, and the rest long-headed, more delicate, but still Mongoloid in facial features, particularly through the critical region of the orbits, malars, and nasal bones.

As An Yang is well inland on the Yellow River plain, it was quite possible that its monarch had taken women from Scythianlike people to the west and Mongols or Huns to the north, as well as from Chinese rivals in neighboring states. In my own time, Ibn Saud had married daughters of the chiefs of rival tribes to consolidate his power, a trick as old as kingdoms and empires. Li Chi added that all three physical types were still to be found in that part of China.

Li Chi then changed the subject to a statement by a disciple of Confucius who had referred to a creature that was not a man, but men ate him; he stood on two legs and was covered with hair. Also the philosopher Hsün-tzu, living a century after Confucius, said that an orang that walked on two legs was to be seen in the Yellow River valley in his time. These two references could easily be the earliest accounts of the yeti, or Snowman of the Himalayas. He then discussed hairiness in general, stating that in the early Chou dynasty, about 1130 B.C., there was a brain trust of ten men, one of whom was so hairy that no one could see his skin. At that time such hairiness was already rare. Li Chi opined that the Chinese had become less hairy over the millenia through a deliberate social selection on the theory that hairiness equals bestiality, partly on account of the hairy subhuman primate that walked like a man (and still did in 1976).*

From 11 to 12 A.M. I lectured to his class on the subject of Neanderthal man. After I had said a few sentences Li Chi would translate it into Mandarin in less than half the time I had taken in English, in contrast to a lecture I had given in Tokyo where the Japanese translator took at least twice my time. The same thing had happened in a lecture by Toynbee, much to the latter's annoyance, because the performance kept us up quite late. The Chinese students, with their little brushes held vertically, took verbatim notes without any trouble.

In the afternoon we visited a museum devoted entirely to the Formosan aborigines, under the guidance of Chen Chi-lou, a graduate of the University of New Mexico who had been studying the aborigines himself, and had excavated some prehistoric graves. There were models of aboriginal houses, their boats, and other artifacts, and hundreds of photographs of people. Some of these confirmed my impressions of the heterogeneity of the Atayals versus the internal homogeneity of the other tribes.

I mentioned the idea of cave hunting to Mr. Chen, who received it with much enthusiasm. The next morning Mr. Chen and a Mr. Pan, Art Prager, Lisa, and I set out for a cave in the north that Art knew about, but it was hard to get at and on the way Lisa sat down plunk on a rock in the middle of a stream. Only Mr. Pan made it to the cave, to report that it had no floor, only heaps of iridescent insect wings disgorged by bats. We drove on to the northeastern plain of the island, where most of the Pingpu aborigines had been absorbed. The people there were quite tall, some over six feet, and more nearly Caucasoid than any others we had seen.

We rode up a narrow-gauge railroad on pushcarts to visit a waterfall where a large rock shelter stood alongside. It had a lovely floor. Mr. Chen said that he would go back there when he had a chance, and no doubt did so. We rode back over the rails without brakes, at breakneck speed in the dark, propelled by gravity alone, and arrived in Taipei just in time for Messrs. Chen and Pan to attend an Academia Sinica wedding. In 1970, incidentally, Chen discovered a group of eleven caves in a cliff over the sea on the east coast of the island. He made soundings in two of them and found Bronze Age and then Neolithic deposits on top of Pleistocene gravels, with chopping tools and

---

*China Reconstructs, *Vol. XXVIII, No. 7, July 1979, pp. 56–59.*

many animal bones in perfect preservation, and I presume that this work is still going on. By June 1973 they had found there that the Neolithic began about 3500 B.C. and may have had something to do with the settlement of Polynesia and of southern Japan. How long the crude stone culture lasted we do not know, but it may have been quite late, with much use of bone tools.

The next day, December 2, we flew with Colonel Fish as planned to Clark Field, and were put up in the VIP officers' quarters and placed under the care of Captain (later Major) Si Simon, who could not have done a better job. He was the officer in charge of relations with the Negritos. A whole campful of them lived just outside the post, and were very much in evidence. The next day he flew us in a Cub plane to a Negrito village in Crow Valley, where he was very popular because he gave these ferocious little men five pesos apiece for the decapitated heads of Huks, Communist bandits whom only the Negritos seemed able to hold at bay.

One of the Negritos, whom I mistook for chief (this causing the real chief to sulk in his hut), was a pocket-sized replica of Tuki, a Snake Bay Tiwi. After I had made a mistake measuring Tuki and had tried again, he refused, calling my effort "proper humbug." This one was also recalcitrant in that he refused to remove a cigarette from his mouth while I photographed him. A few women looked like South African Bushmen in features and peppercorn hair, but not in other respects, while others ranged between these two extremes. Their weights, I estimated, varied between a little over fifty and a little under one hundred pounds.

During the next two days we commuted between Clark Field and Manila, where we visited Otley Beyer, who had been there since 1905 and had toured the islands thoroughly with Waldo's uncle, Governor General W. Cameron Forbes, and also with Leonard Wood. He had taken time out for a sojourn at Harvard with Li Chi; Biraj Guha (whom I was to see in India); Joe Spinden, the Maya scholar; and Vilhjalmur Stefansson.

He was the dean, founder, and global authority on Philippine anthropology and archaeology. He spent his days in his office-apartment-museum, a large expanse on the upper floor or floors of the government census building, and his evenings at his corner table in the Keg Club, betting, usually successfully, on jai alai games.

Dr. Beyer, who was then quite elderly and, perhaps deceptively, frail-looking, was extremely gracious and said no more about the brevity of my stay, but instead tried to condense his life's work into two days of lecturing and dictation, until my left hand grew limp and cramped from trying to take it all down. In his estimation he had seen about 50 percent of the populations of the islands on his incessant tours, had excavated many sites, and knew the entire gamut of insular geology, faunal history, and archaeology from the Pleistocene onward.

He had evolved what seemed to be sound theories about the origins of the Polynesians and the succession of racial and cultural influences coming from the mainland. He had collected textites—glass nodules of probably meteoritic origin—and apparently had realized before others their significance in archaeological and geological dating.

He had owned twenty-two volumes of five-by-seven-inch contact prints from glass negatives of peoples of all tribes, but nineteen of the albums had been burned during the Japanese occupation, and three thousand negatives had been lost. He said that copies of many of the pictures still existed on the back shelves of a certain Chicago library, presumably covered with dust, and that no one had looked for them for ages. He showed me two of the three remaining albums, which depicted hundreds of Negritos, and of these a few individuals were not dwarfed, but full-sized, like Tasmanians or curly-haired Australian aborigines. My fingers had time to get uncramped while I turned the pages of these albums and followed Dr. Beyer around his museum looking at his voluminous collections.

On Friday, December 7, we had trouble getting off on the MATS plane because some passengers were being bumped to make room for excess mail, and we barely escaped being left behind—two angry young "cartographers" were sacrificed instead. As soon as we had arrived at Clark Field I had cabled both the air attaché and Jim Thompson in Bangkok warning them of our arrival date, but neither received the message. All hotels were full because of an international fair, but Jim wangled us a room at the Arelan Hotel, where we had as fellow guests Senator Jacob Javits and Benny Goodman's entire orchestra.

Jim Thompson was an old OSS man who had stayed on to found the extremely profitable Thai Silk Company. One day, not long after we passed through, he suddenly vanished into thin air; as far as I am aware no one knows yet what happened to him. His disappearance remains one of the most fascinating mysteries of the East.

The next day we rode luxuriously on a BOAC plane to New Delhi, where we were greeted by Carl Jr., Janet, John and Barbara Waller (whom we had first met in Mashhad), and Major Brooks, the air attaché, and thus began eighty-eight days of dashing about from Nepal to Ceylon and Calcutta to Karachi, all of which I shall try to describe as briefly and simply as I can.

We rode in a Sikh-driven car to Rajasthan, as far out into the

Thar Desert as it was safe to go without four-wheel drive or a half-track. There we saw the most European-looking people in India—except for the Sikhs themselves and the Red Kafirs who bordered the Nuristanis of Afghanistan—as well as many Gypsies. Some of the Gypsy women, who were forging iron, wore jewels set in their incisor teeth.

With Carl Jr. and Janet, we then went by rail to Ranchi, a former British summering station in the Chota Nagpur Hills of Bihar State, to stay with Professor Biraj Guha. He had been section man in Anthropology 1 at Harvard when I took it, and had marked me severely. He had also written the anthropology volume of the *Census of India*. At the time of our visit, he was protector of aborigines for that region, and he took us around to see as many of them as possible: Birhors, Oraons, Asuras, Hos, Mundas, and Santals.

The Birhors were food gatherers who hunted monkeys in nets; once a year several bands would get together for a highly ritualized deer hunt. They practiced elaborate rites to assure success in the chase. The Orans were large, black, fully Australoid people, some of whom could pass for Australian aborigines. The Asuras were similar but part Mongoloid. They lived high up on a mountain where they smelted iron with bamboo ash, and forged springy, laminated steel by superimposing many small blooms. The Romans had obtained small amounts of it from the Asuras' ancestors, but only the invading Muslims had gone up to where the steel was made, learned the process, and carried it to Damascus and Toledo.

The Ho, Munda, and Santal aborigines were wet-paddy rice growers who spoke three related languages, in turn related to Cambodian. They are a blend of Australoid and Mongoloid, mostly with chocolate-brown skins, but two of them whom we met, who were members of Parliament, had light skins and green eyes.

Biraj led us to his birthplace, Gauhati on the Ganges, where Hindus occupied a very narrow and very sacred strip of land on either side of the river, and also seven holy islands, which we visited. Then we rode up to Shillong where we met his brother, B. S. Guha, a well-known eye surgeon, who told me that Mongoloid eyeballs are smaller than Caucasoid ones, a racial difference I confirmed later in a Japanese publication. He knew this because he had operated on many Khasis, the natives of the Khasi Hills, who are mainly Mongoloid.

They are an ancient people whose land has many massive stone monuments in which, until quite recently, they performed human sacrifices. Their language is related to Ho, Munda, and Santal, and they probably once had the same racial components, but were sorted out differently by living in a high, cool, cloudy climate. Most of them had become Christians. This is to be expected, because British evangelists tend to seek out the climates most similar to those of their native islands.

The man in charge of permits to move about in this part of India was Dr. Verrier Elwin, a young English anthropologist who had become an Indian subject. We found him on his back in a hospital following an umbilical hernia operation. He bristled at the sight of Biraj. To distract his attention I asked him if the doctors had sewn him up flat or put back his navel. He replied that they had sewn him up flat, and wanted to know why I asked.

I told him that I had undergone the same operation after lifting a heavy millstone onto a jeep at the High Cave of Tangier, and that I had asked for my navel back because of what had happened to a friend of mine, Walter Cline, in Siwa Oasis when word had gotten around that he had been born without a navel. (The oasis dwellers thought that he was supernatural and thronged to his hut to look at him). Dr. Elwin thought little of this conversation and told me bluntly that he had never heard of me, to which I replied that I had seen two of my books in his library. Clearly, I should have come alone.

As far as I could make out, no two Indian anthropologists, native or naturalized, had anything good to say of one another, and few would even speak to each other. When we asked Dr. Elwin for permits to go up to Nagaland, where my brother Maurice had been stationed in WW II, there was no refusal, only the tiresome runaround of no plane seats, no hotel reservations, and no chance to use the telephone in the foreseeable future.

Returning to the extreme academic jealousy in India, as an outsider, I spotted two principal, visible causes. One was the persistence of the caste system, which I predict will not disappear overnight. The Bengalis had a natural advantage over their endemic rivals, the Hindi speakers, because when the British Raj had been centered at Calcutta they had the best chances. On the other hand their skins were considerably darker, caste or no caste. The Dravidians, especially the Madrasis, seemed to speak English the most naturally, and had to use it in conversing with the Bengali and Hindi speakers, who could not be expected to learn Tamil.

In addition to caste, skin color, and language, the Indian anthropologists faced another hurdle. It was the Indian habit of aping British procedures other than retreating to the hills in the hottest weather. A British civil servant who had spent his working years up to the age of fifty was fully entitled to retire on a fine pension and to return to Kent, Peeblesshire, or wherever, and to seek out or be sought out by a succulent widow with a tidy income to spend his so-called golden days with; to open an inn on the Riviera, to play golf, or to do whatever else he chose. But that is no reason why the Indian Civil Service should kick out their employees at age fifty, in the prime of their lives, with scarcely two rupees to rub together, more work to do, and nowhere else to go.

Guha's case was a maddening (at least to him) example of this dry-run procedure. He had been professor at the University of Calcutta, in charge of the anthropological laboratory, when his magic number was rung up on the cosmic cash register. He was replaced by a young man, Datta Majamdar, who was not only a physical anthropologist, but who also hired Mrs. Guha as his assistant. It was too much. The two men would not speak to one another. One night when we were dining with Guha in the Grand Hotel in Calcutta and Dr. Majumdar was entertaining Dr. V. Gordon Childe, the famed writer on the Aryans and on Near Eastern archaeology, Majumdar left his table and walked over to ours, ignored Guha, and invited me to his house. I declined.

Before he left Calcutta I found a chance to talk with Gordon, who, incidentally, was one of the homeliest men I have ever seen, and one of the brightest. He told me that he was going home to his native Australia and would not return to England because he could pass through the tropical heat only once more. He kept his word. He climbed to a cliff over his birthplace, took off his hat and then his thick glasses, placed the glasses in the crease of his hat, and then plunged to his death.

Returning briefly to Guha's dilemma, he was partially replaced by a Dr. Mitra, who had charge of the Bronze Age skulls from Harappa on the Indus, which Biraj had helped excavate and then studied. After the partition between Pakistan and India, the skeletons had been partitioned too; the long bones stayed in Karachi and the skulls went to Benares, where they were damaged by floodwater. Then they were moved to Calcutta, where Guha had begun working on them when he was rusticated to Ranchi. I saw them. Like those from An Yang, they were not all alike. They represented at least three populations. One was a heavy-boned Nordic, like the Sumerians I had measured in Baghdad. Another was a big, round-headed, more or less Mongoloid group, relatively few in number, possibly representing traders from the north; and a third was Australoid, as shown on some of the bronze statuettes and found in living aborigines not far away—to wit, the Gonds.

One of my perennial ambitions had been to visit the Andaman Islands in the Bay of Bengal, where lived Pygmy-sized people with fat bottoms and curly hair. They were of three kinds: the Great Andamanese, who had been studied by E. H. Man and Radcliffe Brown, and were virtually extinct; the Jarawa, who remained in the forests of the southern part of Great Andaman and had never been subdued by the British, Japanese, or Indian governments; and the Önge of Little Andaman, who were peaceful but still intact. The Önges had been visited by a team of blood-group physicians, including Dr. Lehman of London, and by the Italian anthropologist-explorer, Lidio Cipriani, the only European to have crossed the island and who found its center uninhabited; all of the Önges lived on the beach.

The Indian government, without giving a clear reason, refused to let anyone else go to the islands. As soon as I got to New Delhi, I applied for permission; after some time it was granted, on one condition: that I take Professor Guha along with me. But at the same time they told him that he could not go because he could not leave his post as protector of aborigines at Ranchi. This seemed rather odd because he was already traipsing around many other parts of India as my guide and amanuensis without arousing any official comment or censure.

On one of these trips we took the express train from Ranchi Junction to Calcutta via the industrial center of Jamshedpur. Guha's servant, who wore a long green robe buttoned down the middle, brought his food in a brass stack of dishes, and tucked him into his bunk before leaving. Under Guha's instruction I locked the door from inside, and the three of us had the whole compartment to ourselves. At Jamshedpur what seemed like a squadron of passengers banged on the door and almost knocked it in, whereupon Biraj shouted, "Resarved, resarved."

Just after the train pulled out and the hubbub had subsided Biraj, who had been reading a paperback of P. G. Wodehouse, said: "Carl, Jeeves says that to be a gentleman you must have thirteen suits of clothes. How many have you?"

I counted them on my fingers, including dress clothes, summer cottons, and the like, and came up with exactly thirteen, and told him so.

"Then you are a gentleman," he said, "and so am I."

A few years later he was killed on that very same express train in a head-on collision.

A sticky matter that arose before we left India was the question of the Tom Slick expedition to chase down and capture the yeti. A member of the *Life* magazine staff had promised to give the late Tom Slick, of the Texas oil family, twenty-five thousand dollars for the first genuine photograph of a yeti, and to give him the money on spec, so to speak, assuming that he would get within camera shot of the animal. Certain other members of the *Life* staff considered this a rather hazardous venture.

Whereupon Jim Greenfield, the New Delhi representative of the Luce empire, employed me to investigate. This involved a trip to Darjeeling, along with Lisa and my daughter-in-law Janet. There I bought another big brown hat to replace the one I had given Chief Mo at Sun-Moon Lake. Thence we went to Kalimpong, where we had a magnificent view of Kachenjunga, and on to Gangtok in Sikkim, where I had a long chat with the Raj Kumar, who had just succeeded his late father. He could not keep us overnight because his guest quarters were already full to overflowing with the Dalai Lama and his entourage. So we had to return to Kalimpong in the dark, and the next day went to a fair at Pedong, which is ethnically Bhutanese but politically part of Assam.

Prince Peter of Greece and Denmark took us to Pedong fair in his Land Rover, and there we saw and photographed many Bhutanese, Lepchas (the natives of Sikkim), and tribespeople from western Nepal, as well as the man in charge of the livestock judging—one of the Dorjis, the royal family of Bhutan. On that trip I obtained a piece of alleged yeti skin which I sent home, where it was declared to be bear.

We later went to Katmandu on the same Slick investigating mission, and returned to New Delhi, where I found myself in the unenviable position of having to face poor (in one sense) Tom Slick, who seemed to be a very nice guy.

In my opinion he was inadequately staffed, despite the inclusion of Tensing, whom we had met in Calcutta, and I felt that his plans to use helicopters, bloodhounds, and the like, were impractical. Much to my relief he took all this with good grace, and I believe made another attempt later, with the expected results. A few years later he was killed in a small plane crash in the American Northwest while searching for the American counterpart of the yeti, called Sasquatch, Bigfoot, and other things.

It would have made me very happy if Tom had really found the yeti or the Sasquatch, for I am sure that both these bipedal primates exist. But their only connection with the Faces of Asia project was that the *Life* side mission gave me a chance to see and photograph some peoples that I might otherwise have missed.

Back in New Delhi, the naval attaché invited Lisa and me to fly with him in his plane to Cochin in Kerala State, the most Catholic and most Communist state in India. There we hired a car and driver to take us up over a new road into the Cardamom Hills to see the Kadar, a short-statured group of yam diggers with black skins and curly-to-frizzy hair, and ranging between the Australoid and Negrito poles. I managed to measure the stature of several of them and to snip off a lock of a woman's frizzy hair that she had not had time to straighten with palm oil. Back in Cochin we took a boat ride in the harbor, where we felt at home among Omani booms, from which muezzins intoned the call to prayer in impeccable Arabic at the prescribed intervals. Ashore we visited both the White Jews and the Black Jews, and an old synagogue decorated with centuries-old Dutch tiles.

Our final trip was to Ceylon (Sri Lanka), principally to photograph and to measure some of the Veddas. They are the aboriginal, Caucasoid bowmen who had lived in the mouths of caves and in rock shelters until the turn of the century. They marked out the floors of these shelters into individual compartments, with strict protocol about who should step in whose section, and their hunting territories were marked by arrow-shaped blazes on trees. They were monogamous, and married for life.

The authority on them and their protector was a Dutch burgher, Richard Spittle, M.D., who had written several books about them, had a collection of their skulls, and arranged for our visit to Maha Oya, near their camp. We slept in a government rest house at Maha Oya, to be awakened by the songs and cries of many birds. When we arose we found eight Veddas sitting on the lawn. They had come to us because the stream between their place and ours was in flood.

They were tiny people, perfectly shaped, with European facial features; long, wavy head hair; thin beards; and graceful movements. It was a wonderful journey backward in time. Lisa loved every moment of it, and begged me to write more about them here than I had done in my first draft. I am glad she did.

When this dream was broken, we rode back to Colombo, where I photographed Sinhalese with hairy ears, and we called on Paul (né Pieris) Deraniyagala, a Portuguese burgher who was director of museums, and a Harvard contemporary of Li Chi and Biraj Guha. Paul had discovered some fossil human cranial material and teeth, and had sent them to Harry Shapiro, who had not reported on them. Then we went to the famous botanical gardens at Kandy and on up the mountain to Nuwara Elia, about a mile high and cool. There we recognized some expatriate homosexuals and their Moroccan boyfriends, refugees from Tangier. Down again we climbed, to the Colombo Zoo, one of the finest in the world. There I heard a siamang howling out of its inflated neck sack, more or less like a gibbon. I had heard them in the St. Louis Zoo. Then the thought came to me: The siamang's call was more like a seagull's. I had heard plenty of them on the Massachusetts beaches. People who had heard the yeti's call said it sounded just like a seagull's. Siamangs, like gibbons, walk on their hind legs on the ground.

With these thoughts in my mind we flew back to New Delhi and then to Karachi, where we stayed with old friends at the embassy. From Karachi we MATSed to Dhahran in Saudi Arabia, where Bill and Mary Eddy met us and lodged us in ARAMCO's number-one guesthouse. Bill was top man for the Tapline. I spent two days in Dammam with the linguist Charles Matthews, who was recording the Mahri-Socotran language from a number of informants brought up from the Mahra country south of the Rub' al-Khali.

Years earlier Bertram Thomas, the explorer who had crossed the desert on a camel and written *Arabia Felix,* had measured some of these men and had found their heads impossibly short. I had discussed this with him while digging at the High Cave in Tangier in 1939, but had failed to persuade him that his technique was wrong. Now I measured Charles Matthews's informants and found their heads of normal size, but it was too late to tell Bertram. He had died long before of a stroke in Shepherd's Bar in Cairo.

From Dhahran we flew to Wheelus Field in Libya, where Arabs had sabotaged the plumbing, and thence to Rome, where we were put up and shown the local archaeological sites by the Baron and Baroness Blanc, whom we had hosted in Devon, Pennsylvania, earlier. We had found them huddled on our doorstep because Hallam Movius had told them that they could stay with us, but had forgotten to tell us. From Rome we taxied to Florence and stayed with the Italian explorer-photographer Lidio Cipriani and his widowed sister and nephew. At the Philadelphia International Congress I had given him one thousand dollars (an advance from Knopf) to use to go to Brazil and study the plight of the Negroes there. In return I would drop into Florence someday and pick up one thousand of his negatives of Bushmen, Andamanese, and other peoples I had not visited. When Henry Field heard of this he went to Florence and bought five thousand.

We took a night train to Paris, MATS to Maguire Field, and arrived home on March 26, 1957. In 1958 the University Museum published forty-one of my portraits from that trip in *Faces of Asia.* It soon sold out, and has been widely copied ever since.

25. *The Alakalufs*

My last field trip before retiring from the University of Pennsylvania took place in August and September of 1959. My job was to serve as anthropologist on a physiological expedition.

Like many others, I had often wondered how the Canoe Indians of the Magellanic Channels and Tierra del Fuego were able to endure a damp climate, hovering about the freezing point, with heavy winds and rains, not to mention some snow, with a minimum of clothing. These Indians were of two principal groups: the Yaghans or Yamana, who lived on the southern shores of Isla Grande and the smaller islands to its south; and the Alakalufs or Káweskár, whose territory ranged all the way from both shores of the Strait of Magellan on the Atlantic, through the strait, and up the Magellanic Channels to the Gulf of Penas on the Pacific, at about 47°S latitude, where they met their neighbors and linguistic kinsmen, the Chonos. The latter ranged as far north as the Island of Chiloé and the mainland.

The Yaghans had been well-studied ethnographically, but had been reduced to less than a dozen full bloods through disease and mixture, and had been considerably acculturated. At least forty-eight Alakalufs had survived. They lived mostly near the Chilean radio station on Wellington Island, about halfway down from Valparaíso to Punta Arenas, to avoid the Pacific storms. At one point east of Wellington Island was the so-called Angostura Inglese, or English Strait, where ships had to wait for high tide in order to proceed through.

The Alakaluf camp was located below this strait, and Indians swarmed up the rope ladders to squat on deck, begging and offering model canoes (Yaghan-style) for sale, or prostituting themselves. Their fee for everything was two of something—like two packs of cigarettes, or two shirts—for two was as high as they could count. Needless to say, these visits gave them many diseases, of which tuberculosis was probably the worst.

Although the Alakaluf had been the most numerous of the Canoe Indians in precontact times, and had survived the longest both physically and culturally, they had been studied the least. I would have liked very much to have had a chance to see more of them than I did, but what I did was far better than nothing at all.

Many years before this expedition materialized I had longed to go to Chile to find out how the Alakalufs could tolerate moderate cold while practically naked. I knew that they slept in domed huts covered with sea-lion skins and kept warm by fires of *Nothofagus,* an evergreen beech. It was only by day that they were exposed to the cold. Then they had fires in clay hearths amidship in their canoes, and smeared their bodies with sea-lion fat. They usually draped a skin over their shoulders with their fronts exposed, but these means of protection seemed hardly enough to preserve life on chilly waters in heavy rains carried by gusty winds of high velocity. Some internal physiological mechanism must also be involved, and it would take one or more professional physiologists to find out what this mechanism or mechanisms might be.

Similar thoughts had occurred to Dr. Theodore Hammel of the University of Pennsylvania Medical School and Dr. Robert Elsner of the University of Washington, Seattle. Both physiologists had come to the same conclusion independently of each other and of me. Both had worked under Dr. Per Scholander of the Scripps Institute of Oceanography at La Jolla, California, who was an M.D. as well as a Ph.D. Scholander and I were both invited to come along, although both of us were nearly twice the age of any of the others. The group included Kristian Lange-Andersen, M.D., of Oslo; Raymond J. Hock of the White Rock Research Station of the University of California; and Fred Milan of the Arctic Aeromedical Laboratory at Ladd Air Force Base, Fairbanks, Alaska. Chile was represented by Dr. Alberto Medina R. and Luis Strozzi, M.D., both of Santiago University, and both anthropologists.

Nine persons, some of whom had never met before, seemed to me an unwieldy number, until I remembered that scientific papers on physiology, genetics, and some other highly technical subjects often bear a long list of authors, such as: "Smith, J. W.; R. M. Sullivan; H. F. Hsiu . . . ," instead of simply "Smith, J. W. et al.," which would make life much easier for bibliographers, but would be unfair to most of the participants.

Anthropologists are lone wolves. They cannot work in teams because if they could they probably would not be anthropologists. Physiologists are gregarious folk who divide up segments of their job just as the organs of the body divide their functions. One handles the rectal thermometers, another watches the oxygen intake and CO_2 output of a subject lying on his back in a tent outside the field laboratory. Exactly what each one of our team did on this trip I do not know, because they worked all night and slept during the day, when I had to measure the Indians.

While the physiologists were at work, they had to maintain absolute discipline to avoid complete failure, but while they were not working they let off steam by horsing around and kidding each other, particularly picking on Ray Hock, who was almost a giant. The two

Chilean members of the expedition could not understand this Nordic humor and laid it simply to poor manners.

This misunderstanding was based partly on a paucity of communication. Of all the gringos, including the Scandinavians, I was the only one who could speak any Spanish. Of the two Latins, only Luis Strozzi could speak some English, and he understood the horseplay a little better than Alberto did.

Strozzi's job was principally to inform Alberto of what the others had in mind, or were doing, or vice versa, and I had to communicate mostly with the captain, the cook, and the Indians. It was somewhat like being the best-paid water boy in Iraq all over again. This was particularly true in the morning, because neither of the two Latins would get out of his bunk before 11:00 A.M.

The province of Magellanes, of which Punta Arenas is the capital, had a population of forty thousand, of whom 75 percent were Chilotes, that is, natives of the Island of Chiloé, just south of Puerto Montt, lying mostly between latitudes 42° and 43° S. Its area, less than four hundred square miles, is deeply indented, an ideal hunting ground for a maritime people.

The Chilotes began as a mixture between the Chono Indians, otherwise now extinct and related to the Alakalufs, with early Spanish settlers said to be from Castile and Aragon. To this blend were added Araucanian Indians, coming from the mainland at two different intervals. It took the Spaniards over 350 years to subdue the Araucanians, who are short, stocky, and extremely hardy. To dismiss the Chilotes as ordinary mestizos, intermediaries between whites and Indians, would be to miss the point. They are a very special people. Like the Irish, they had a population explosion due to a superabundance of white potatoes, and expanded everywhere that they could go south of their island. Now they furnish the bulk of the manpower in Magellanes Province and southern Argentina, both on land and in boats.

In Punta Arenas and on the estancias, the upper crust is provided mostly by English, Scots, Norwegians, and Yugoslavs, especially Dalmatians. The admiral in charge of the Chilean Naval Forces in Punta Arenas had a Polish father and an English mother and went to Eton. He seemed a little hurt that he had not been previously consulted about our expedition, as his fleet was responsible for the safety of all vessels in the channels in which we proposed to navigate and had aided several glacier-climbing and other kinds of expeditions before. In dealing with the admiral and other important persons, the two "old men," Pete Scholander and I, were given full charge, and we found this assignment most agreeable.

In Punta Arenas we were taken over, more or less, by the

Norwegian consul, a wealthy, generous, and most effective man. With him as sponsor we received several invitations, which two of our party could not attend because they had flown almost from pole to pole in sweaters without bringing any suit coats. The most important of these events was the Rotary Club luncheon, at which all top-ranking dignitaries were present in full regalia. One of them who sat next to me said that he had attended a Rotary International dinner in New York City at which they had been seated at the incredibly early hour of 6:30 P.M. and then given no wine.

At Punta Arenas, Alberto and I learned that an Alakaluf girl named Marghareta had been taken off a boat to the local hospital with tuberculosis of the spine, and we went to see her. She appeared to be about thirteen. One thing that I noticed most about her was that her hair grew down over her forehead, leaving but a narrow strip of skin exposed over the central parts of her eyebrows, and over her temples the head hair was continuous with the lateral portions of her eyebrows. Such hairiness I had seen before only among Ainu in Japan, and in one Czech.

On this trip to the hospital I saw my first Norfolk Island pine, which looked like a cross between a conifer and a fern. As I was looking at it, a sudden flurry of antipodal wind picked up a load of loose sand and deposited a grain in a corner of my right eye. There it remained until I got home, despite many attempts to get it out. I only wished that I had a Moroccan cave digger at hand with a lungful of hashish smoke and a nimble tongue.

To carry us to our destination, Ted Hammel had chartered the bark *Gloria,* sixty feet of stout Chilean pine, as broad and as tough as a Hudson River tug, and even capable of bucking small icebergs. She had two short, thick masts, a bowsprit, and a galley smokestack that could be telescoped to make room for the main boom when under sail. Below decks a brand-new diesel engine could drive her through stormy waters at seven knots, or eleven with the sails set to a following wind. The galley, the wheelhouse, and the head (nautical) were all three-quarters size—just right for Chilotes, but rough on gringos, who were always bumping their heads (anatomical).

At Punta Arenas, the first living thing any of us was likely to see was Bua, the ship's dog, a small, neat Scottish shepherd, friendly to man but unflinching foe to any other dog that tried to come aboard. Bua slept on a coil of rope or in any other shelter that was handy.

We seldom saw Captain Delgado, the skipper, for he had much business ashore and when he was not needed he kept to his quarters aft of the galley. Like his crew of five, the captain was a Chilote. So was

Luis, the expedition cook, who brought along his fourteen-year-old son Lucio to learn the trade.

At Ted Hammel's request, the captain had given over the entire hold to our expedition. In a space twenty by thirty feet, just under the deck, he had nine bunks built along the sides, plus one each for the cook and his son, plus a galley of our own, plus a mess table. A ladder let us climb up to get out on deck in the fresh air, because between the smells of the stove and oil lamps and eleven unwashed bodies of *Homo sapiens* plus their unchanged clothing, the atmosphere grew ripe enough in there at times to grow mushrooms. Any nooks and crannies were filled with physiological equipment, most conspicuously Dr. Andersen's special bicycle rig to measure caloric expenditure, with which he had flown all the way from Oslo.

At ten o'clock in the morning of Monday, August 24, we cast off. At our peak flew a Chilean, an American, and a Norwegian flag, snapping briskly in the breeze. A considerable crowd was there to cheer us off, as if they never expected to see us again. Overhead scores of seabirds, mostly gulls, wheeled and glided, with one eye cocked on the wake to see what delicacies we should cast overboard. I tried to write some hurried notes, but the motor made the ship jump and I gave up.

At 5:45 P.M. the engine had a fuel leak, so we anchored in Bougainville Bay near the tip end of the continent. Quiet water, steep cliffs, and a narrow shore with dense vegetation, *Nothophagus* trees in full leaf, and a true cedar related to the cedar of Lebanon but locally called cypress. This scene lay to the right. Astern and to the left were small islands with twisted trees and the snowy mountains of Isla Grande in the background. At the moment I thought this the most beautiful place I had ever seen, and felt as if I were a midget standing in the middle of a Japanese garden. Everyone was elated. Hundreds of cormorants flew over and past us, some black and white and some pure black; Ray Hock said that the black and white ones are not cormorants but loons. Down below deck our cook served us pea soup with a sheep's tail in it for flavor. The soup was delicious, and he ate the tail. For lunch he had given us filets of beef, as good as in the Plaza Hotel.

We didn't stay in Bougainville Bay very long. The skipper made his repairs and we proceeded at full speed all afternoon and night. On Wednesday I was up at seven, which was almost daylight, to find us in a channel flanked with bleak, snowy islands. The scenery remained the same all day. Finally the captain tried to get the ship through a narrow hole between two islands, but anchored instead to await the rising tide.

On Thursday morning the captain gave up this idea, which was to proceed up the quiet channel between Figueroa Island and the mainland. Instead he steered the ship to the west of Tamar Island into Smyth Channel, between Manuel Rodríguez Island and the mainland. Here we passed a lighthouse and saw its keeper waving frantically from the roof. A tanker passed us. We saw steamboat ducks which, being flightless, use both their wings and feet as paddles. Porpoises swam up to inspect us. Some of the younger men saw condors drifting motionlessly aloft, but they were too high up for my eyes to reach.

In late afternoon we anchored in a cove in Bahia Isthmus to take aboard fresh water. The beach was covered with limpets and mussels by the thousands, some of which were served for supper. We went ashore and saw the flimsy pole skeletons of Alakaluf domed huts, and their shell heaps. There was much botanizing and identification of holly, *Nothofagus,* magnolia, and a sort of tree cabbage. It was apparent that the first few feet of altitude along the shore, being below the frost line, constituted a narrow subtropical zone.

Ted Hammel, who was eager to get to Puerto Eden and begin work, expressed fear that the skipper was stalling, what with his waits for the tide and all, but we who had been born by the sea and knew the ways of boats assured him that this was not so. No man's strength or wits can match the power of the sea. Captain Delgado was only taking proper precautions in a very dangerous reach of the ocean, with great responsibility for his ship and for our lives.

On Friday we continued a tortuous route between islands until at 10:50 A.M. we had reached the Sarmiento Channel, whose shores were marked on our charts with many dashed lines, meaning "unknown." We passed two automatic lighthouses and saw two fires on shore. The second belonged to some cypress cutters from Punta Arenas. At 4:30 P.M. the sun broke out of its clouds for the first time since we had left Punta Arenas, and at 7:00 P.M. a larger ship passed us, so we knew that we were in the shipping lanes, although we saw two small icebergs, and this sight did not please the captain at all.

Yet he kept running all night, and at 5:00 P.M. it was bump-crunch, and everyone out of his bunk. We had hit a small iceberg, which had done the *Gloria* no harm. When dawn broke we could see that we were in a steep fjord, with sheer cliffs covered with ice all gleaming in the morning sun like a wall of diamonds. At the head of the fjord sprawled a glacier, calving into the sea, and many small bergs bobbed around us.

So upset was Captain Delgado at this sight that he openly wept. He had made a wrong turn during the blackness of night, and steered the ship into Eyre Fjord by mistake. Now he was in danger of losing his license. I could not see why. He had not lost, nor even damaged, his ship. No one aboard had been even scratched. He had given us the unexpected dividend of a free tour to a sea glacier, one that few people had seen. I proposed that we should all forget it unless asked, and if so, say that we had requested him to take us there. But that was not the end of the episode.

After we had left Eyre Fjord we proceeded to our destination, Puerto Eden on Wellington Island, where we arrived at 6:00 P.M. on August 30. From the *Gloria* we could see a two-story wooden house with a large wireless antenna, which was the Chilean Air Force radio station, and on the shore three or four sawn-board shacks in which the Alakaluf lived, plus two or three skeletons of domed huts, and a number of canoes and some dugouts, all in disrepair. There was a shaky dock, and behind the huts numerous drums of aviation fuel.

We went ashore and found there three adult male and three adult female Alakalufs, of whom all three males had one infirmity or another that had kept them from leaving the camp on the news of our impending arrival; there were several nubile girls, one of whom was pregnant by the corporal, who was half German and half Araucanian, and many children. In the house, besides the corporal were his sergeant, the radio operator, and a cook. The house was clean and well furnished but unheated. The rest of the Indians were out in their rowboats hunting sea otters.

The physiologists found the wooden house ideal for their purposes and would sleep as well as work there, but there was no room for Alberto, Luis Strozzi, or me, who had to sleep aboard the *Gloria*, although our hold would have benefited by being thoroughly aired and cleaned. After these arrangements had been made, Alberto began holding forth in angry tones, in Spanish, which had to be translated, the only non-Spanish-speaking audience being Fred Milan (who incidentally spoke Lapp, of little use where we were). All the other gringos had left to unload their gear from the *Gloria*.

First Alberto explained why the otter hunters had fled before our arrival. The sergeant in command at Puerto Eden took all their sea otter skins and sent them to the chief of the Air Force in Punta Arenas. The two split the loot fifty-fifty. The sergeant had sent them away to keep them from telling us.

Next he stated that Ted Hammel had persuaded Captain Delgado to run the ship all night, because he was in a hurry to study the Alakalufs. The captain had wanted to anchor in a sheltered cove until dawn. When I asked Alberto to prove this statement, he admitted that he couldn't. I knew this very well because Hammel could communicate with the captain only through me and, if he had communicated through Strozzi, I would have heard of it.

Before we went to bed, the captain came below and said that he had received radio permission from the admiral at Punta Arenas for us to sail north to seek the otter hunters and to bring them back to Puerto Eden to be studied. To me, at least, this news came as a great relief. But we did not get off until 8:30 A.M. on September 1. By then the tension between Alberto and the gringos had reached such a height that had we tried to stand it much longer something would have burst.

At 6:00 A.M. on August 31 I saw an unusual sight. Alberto, who usually kept Spanish sleeping and waking hours, was sitting bolt upright in his bunk, writing rapidly in a small notebook and mumbling a few words to himself, among which *gringo* and *yanqui* recurred frequently, and with some venom. During the ensuing day I measured the adult Alakalufs present for Bob Elsner, and also for myself, and tried to take down the rudiments of an Alakaluf vocabulary from Alessandri, who had been left behind because he had TB. From him I discovered and later confirmed that Alakaluf uses clicks, like the South African Bushman at the opposite end of the earth, and of the racial spectrum.

During this session Alberto shouted at me that I must *not* ask Alessandri the Alakaluf word for *abuelo* (grandfather), but I had not intended to. While Strossi diverted Alberto's attention, I asked Alessandri how to say father's father and mother's father, which he told me readily and without emotion. As I had suspected, they were two different words. There is no Alakaluf word for *abuelo*.

At dinner one of the physiologists asked Alberto how to say pisso-potto in Spanish, but as neither Strozzi nor I ventured to translate this request, it fell flat. This was just as well, because after dinner Alberto's and Luis's services were needed to explain what was going on to two of the three male Alakalufs, who were being wired to various recording devices in the control room upstairs, as the Indians lay under thin blankets on cots in a tent outside the house. Alberto's tender solicitude for these men was genuine and touching. Earlier, during that crowded day, Alberto warned the others that as representative of the anthropology department of the University of Santiago he was in personal charge of the welfare of the Indians and that they must not study the women, which of course they did as soon as the ship was out of sight.

The third male, Lucho, was the healthiest. He was to come aboard the *Gloria* with Alberto, Luis, and myself, as guide, to search the tortuous channels of the north for the missing sea otter hunters. Lucho knew every square inch of the labyrinthine waterscape, charted or uncharted, and just where the hunters were likely to have gone. In fact, they might well have told him, but if so, he did not volunteer the information. Our cook had sent his son, Lucho Chico, to feed us, and the Air Force its German-Araucanian corporal and a large young recruit with very red cheeks.

Although 8:00 A.M. was our zero hour, we did not get off until 8:30 because the anchor cable slipped off its drum on the first and second attempts to weigh anchor. At 10:30 we reached the Angostura Inglese (English Narrows). There we saw the tide spouting out at us like steam water from a millrace. We had to turn back to find a safe anchorage and wait four to six hours for another try, so we anchored at 11:05 A.M. in a small bay across the channel from the entrance to Beauchamp Fjord. There Luis shot two ducks. At 3:30 P.M. we passed through the English Narrows and overtook a big Chilean tanker, and saw a seal. At 4:30 we anchored in Liberta Bay, Puerto Gray. The captain and Lucho saw some freshly cut stumps, which meant that Alakalufs had been there quite recently, for this was one of their camping places.

About five o'clock the next morning, Friday, September 4, while I was lying in bed awake, I saw Lucho arise silently from his bunk and carefully remove all nonstationary objects from the table—like the salt, pepper, cutlery, and butter dish—and place them on the floor near the cupboard door, as if in anticipation of trouble. Then he went on deck.

A little more than an hour later, I could feel the motor turn over, and crash-crunch, the *Gloria* keeled over with a strong list to starboard, and the butter dish slid rapidly across the floor, slopping out a trail of its melted contents in its wake.

Alberto and Luis, barefooted and in their pajamas, were up the ladder in half a flash. I crawled out, dressed, made sure I had my passport, traveler's checks, cash, jackknives, matches, flashlight, and cameras. Only then did I come up, to be greeted derisively by Alberto and Luis, who were hopping around on deck in their bare feet, trying to keep warm.

"Look at him, he shaved before he came up," cried Alberto. "What good will you be over in that jungle, in your bare feet and pajamas?" I retorted, adding, "This is not my first shipwreck, and it may not be my last."

Then I turned to Lucho and asked him in a quiet tone of voice, "Why didn't you tell us we were going to hit that rock?" "Because nobody asked me," he said.

As soon as we were hung up on the rock, the bosun said, "This is a good time to wash the deck," and they did. I only wished that they had cleaned out the hold as well, because it was getting quite high, particularly as our Chileans did not always go out on deck to relieve themselves, but used the garbage pail behind the ladder, and it had slopped over when we struck the rock. That is what, in essence, the pisso-potto business of the previous evening had been about.

As the *Gloria* pulled herself off the rock in the rising tide, Alberto led a cheer for the skipper, a Spanish version of "hip hip hooray," in which we all heartily joined.

We passed Williams Island and Middle Island without finding any Indians, and Lucho was under full instructions to volunteer any useful information in advance without waiting to be asked. At 6:00 P.M. we anchored in a small bay of the Rowley Peninsula, hoping the next morning to pass the Smith Peninsula and to turn east up to Río Baker, where Lucho thought the otter hunters might be camped.

At 10:30 P.M. a huge sea lion appeared on the starboard bow, and the corporal shot and killed it. The captain would not stop to recover it, for he had a schedule to meet, so the animal died for nothing. The corporal explained that he wanted the skin for himself and the meat for the Indians' dogs (or really for the Indians themselves). He was reprimanded and confined to the galley—not a bad brig—until he timidly emerged, only to discover at 3:15 P.M. that he was wanted because the captain was lost, having already gone up one wrong channel and come back again.

Only the corporal and Lucho knew these waters, and the corporal alone could be counted on to volunteer needed information. At 4:30 we stopped the ship off the southern end of Vargas Island to take aboard a one-eyed half-Araucanian hermit and his dog. The hermit had landed there eight years before to hunt nutria and had turned to woodchopping. He had not spoken to a living soul for seven months, and was full of pent-up chatter. He wanted to hitch a ride to Río Baker, which he could find almost with his one eye blindfolded, and he said he knew where the otter hunters had gone.

We didn't have to go very far. Rounding another corner of Vargas Island, we sighted two canoe loads of Indians and their dogs just taking off from a cove. In the first one were six men, one woman, and several dogs, the Indians all talking Spanish to each other to make us think they were Chilotes, until they spied Lucho leaning over the rail. One man and the woman boarded the *Gloria* and we took both canoes in tow.

We kept on to the mouth of the Río Baker, where we found a small medical station of three or four houses run by a naval medic from Valparaíso whose grandfather was an Englishman. He and his wife received mail from a naval vessel once every three months. He arranged with an enterprising pioneer-settler named Renaldo Sandoval to sell us a four-year-old ox for the Chilean equivalent of U.S. forty dollars. This took all of my Chilean money. Mr. Sandoval butchered an ox and the crew hung its two halves up in the shrouds to be dissected as required.

This purchase was made necessary because our cook had unwittingly miscalculated his supply of provisions before leaving Punta Arenas. Someone had told him that North Americans loved white potatoes, and he had laid in too many. But no one had told him that on the first day out two of the physiologists would decide to race each other in a weight-losing contest by eating only meat. And that was why I had to buy the ox.

The next morning, Sunday, September 6, I was up at six. All was quiet. The inlet was calm as a millpond, the bottoms of the houses draped in mist, over which their rooftops protruded. Bright and early the medic and his wife and two-and-a-half-year-old daughter came aboard to say good-bye, thinking that we were about to leave, as we had planned. Sighting my white hair, the child jumped into my arms crying: "*Abuelo! Abuelo!* (Grandfather! Grandfather!)," the word I had been forbidden to use among the Alakalufs. It took considerable prying and many tears to get the poor child ashore.

Meanwhile, the Alakalufs' boats had to be hoisted on deck— dogs, seal meat, and all. In one of them the sole female occupant set up a tarpaulin as a tent and stayed there, with her dogs, for the rest of the voyage, at least while I was in sight. One of the boats had a barrel full of assorted meat and bones, which included not only sea otter, but also at least one dog. The seal fat particularly was already getting pretty high. I could not see where they had put the controversial sea otter skins.

But we did not get off until 12:45 P.M., largely because of Alberto. He had sent an armload of cartons of the expedition's cigarettes ashore, to God knows whom, and given one chocolate bar each to the Indians. Then he dressed me down roundly because I reprimanded the corporal for having shot the seal. It was his place to reprimand the corporal, not mine. In fact, he was in command of that Indian-seeking expedition, and of the entire expedition as well, Hammel or no Hammel.

Having delivered himself of these pronouncements, he led two youthful Río Bakerites whom he had invited aboard down into the hold, at this point barely rivaling the deck in its fetid odor, and he kept them down there until Captain Delgado, who was impatient to cast off, sent a message below ordering the visitors ashore. Alberto rejected this order, whereupon Delgado asked me, as leader of the present expedition, to eject the visitors. This I promptly did, with neither pain nor displeasure, leaving the expected shouts of wrath behind me.

After this salvo, the *Gloria* pushed on at full speed without incident until dark. At that point we were at the place that the weather maps showed to be the rainiest spot in Chile, and just to prove they were right, the skies opened and poured buckets after buckets of cold water on the *Gloria,* extinguishing all the lights except for a small flame in a kerosene lantern.

I sealed all my documents in plastic, took what was left of my money, my flashlight, and bowie knife, and went on deck with everyone else. As he crossed the beams of our torches, Alberto could be seen running madly in all directions. Quite miraculously, the captain steered us into a snug harbor at 9:15 P.M. Everyone was exhausted from the excitement of having navigated in absolute darkness—everyone except our pilot, Lucho, who had slept through it all on the deck, dry and warm in my Gloucester fisherman's outfit which I had loaned, and later gave, to him.

On Monday, September 7, Labor Day, the lights were on at 4:30 A.M. I climbed on deck and pissed over the taffrail beside the mate. The Alakalufs' heads were sticking out from under tarpaulins, the seal meat was stinking, the dogs whining. At 4:40 the captain started off at full speed forward, for the sky was cloudless and every star was shining. I went below and Alberto, who had no watch, asked me anxiously, "What time is it?" I told him. He piddled in the garbage pail behind the ladder, sacked up again, and went back to sleep. I looked around for the disinfectant that Chris Andersen and I had bought in Punta Arenas, but couldn't find it. Being at the end of my olfactory rope, I picked up the pail, carried it up the ladder, and dumped its contents overboard as a present to the gulls.

By 9:45 A.M. our two noblemen were still dead to the world. We were really making knots with a following wind, and the skipper told me that if we kept this up we would hit the English Narrows on the high tide. We did, at 12:45, riding right through without a pause, and arrived at Puerto Eden around 2:30 P.M., crowned with success. Lucho had found the otter hunters; the captain had brought them back.

After the excitement of the chase, the rest of the Alakaluf expedition seemed like a letdown. The physiologists performed their expected routines methodically and like clockwork, except for one untoward event. A young otter hunter named Julio, whom we had brought back on the *Gloria* and who had, according to Alberto, been copulating with one or more women all of the next day, was wired for the cold tent that very night and panicked. He ran naked up the slope of the mountain behind the post with the rectal thermometer still inserted, until finally the wire that was trailing behind him caught in some bushes and pulled the thermometer out. Others brought him food and clothing, and he remained on the mountain, where we could see his campfire at night, until we left. Luckily, I had measured and photographed him in advance.

While measuring the men, I found to my surprise that they all had blue genitalia, caused by deep-lying pigment, with no superficial pigment to produce the color brown. These men were bearded, like many Northwest Coast and California Indians, and Carlos, who had been the leader of the otter hunters and a relatively young man, sported a goatee.

Their body build was suitable for modern cold adaptation, but not to any extreme degree. The physiologists' ultimate discovery, if I may be pardoned for oversimplification, was that the Alakalufs have a high basal metabolism capable of burning up many calories per day of animal fats, which they consumed in their native cultural condition. They also grew old prematurely. For further details, these studies have been published in the appropriate scientific journals.

When we were ready to leave, the piece of grit in my eye bothered me more and more until it became infected and I was afraid of becoming a Cyclops. I hurried home as fast as I could, and just in time.

26. *Return to Gloucester*

I was elected president of the American Association of Physical Anthropologists in 1961 for a two-year hitch. I did not want the job but foolishly accepted it. Never having run a meeting before, I bought a copy of Robert's *Rules of Order* and unsuccessfully tried to memorize it. T. Dale Stewart, M.D., Ph.D., the more or less permanent secretary-treasurer, knew how to handle a meeting. He sat beside me to coach and to steer me.

The next annual meeting was held in Philadelphia in May 1962. I chaired some of the sessions and the annual business meeting. We finished the latter fairly quickly because I managed to stave off some resolutions that Dale and I considered to be none of our business. I told their sponsors that the only resolution I would accept was one thanking our host institution for its hospitality.

After the annual dinner, in the University Museum, I made a brief, innocuous presidential address and was ready to go home and to bed, quite fatigued; many of those from other cities also made haste to leave, despite the fact that some of the younger men clamored for an extra session at once because they had some very important unfinished business to bring up. This of course was the usual trick that minorities use to get their way. I had already sniffed a gamy scent in this, and so had the chief janitor, when one of them had asked me if we had a mimeograph machine and I had told him to ask the engineer. After a conference with me, the janitor alerted his ground crew to cut the lights after I should raise my right hand, and the conspirators would stumble out in confusion. Unfortunately for my OSS-type scheme, I saw more men than I had expected, and some were old friends.

The resolution the young men were proposing was for our association to censor and to condemn officially Carleton Putnam— ex-chairman of the board of Delta Airlines, biographer of Theodore Roosevelt, and a son of a New York federal judge—for having written a small book called *Race and Reason,* which the American Bar Association had endorsed, as had Senator Richard B. Russell, chairman of the Armed Services Committee.

I was involved in that I was related to the author through both the Carletons and the Putnams. He had sent me a copy, and I had read it. I had seen nothing actionable in it.

It was not the lad who had asked for the copying machine that proposed the resolution, but my own student and collaborator, Stanley Garn, of whom I was fond.

My surprise was double, not only to see Stanley make the proposal, but also at its subject. I expected them to want to vote that all races were of equal intelligence, one that Dale and I had floored. Indeed, they did begin talking about this, but I looked at Monty Cobb, who was sitting in the front row right corner seat. Monty looked at me and said, "But we don't know, do we?"

I said, "No, Monty, we don't."

Monty was Professor W. Montagu Cobb, professor of anatomy at Howard University, my predecessor as president of the association then in session, and later the head of the NAACP.

Once he and I had brought the meeting back on beam, I asked the audience how many had read Carleton Putnam's book? Just one. What did he think of it? Not much. How many had heard of it before? Only a few hands were raised. Yet these people were prepared to vote to censure Carleton Putnam.

Only the man who had read the book and hadn't liked it very much had a right to an opinion. I told the others that in no uncertain terms, and how I was ashamed of them. Instead of collapsing from fatigue, I felt a sudden upsurge of energy. Larry Oschinsky, seated in the second row, wrote me later that he could see my testosterone rising.

There they were, some of them old and trusted friends, apparently as brainwashed as Pavlov's puppies, or as most of the social anthropologists. As Khrushchev had boasted, beating his shoe upon a table in the United Nations, the Communists did not need to fight us. They could rot us from within. I could see it all as in a horrid dream.

Instead of giving the hand signal to my friends lurking in the doorway, I told my fellow members that I would no longer preside over such a craven lot, and resigned the presidency. I would leave them to vote whatever resolution they wished, but not in my name.

The next day I was in a partial coma, but we packed, packed, packed. Gordon and Jane Bowles drove out to see us. Gordon reported that after my departure they had voted to pass the resolution, and—I thought he said—accepted my resignation. Some time later I saw the resolution in print over my signature. I asked Gordon about this and he said I had misunderstood him. I probably did, because Gordon is a Quaker and incapable of lying. Carleton Putnam called me too—he had seen it before I did.

The day after Gordon's visit Lisa and I and our cat drove to West Gloucester. I fell asleep on the Merritt Parkway in Connecticut while driving; luckily the car stopped on the median strip. I resigned from the University Museum, no part of which had had anything to do with my decision. They had always treated me with consideration and kindness. Several sympathetic persons, some in positions of influence and authority, including Kermit Roosevelt, Sr., wrote or phoned me to ask me if the rumor were true that the University of Pennsylvania had fired me for talking about race. I assured them that the rumor was false on both counts and that I had left of my own volition.

I then retired *de facto* at the age of fifty-eight, but *de jure* at fifty-nine, because the University Museum gave me a terminal sabbatical. Now I could prowl the creeks in my boat, take care of my fruit trees during the proper seasons, and listen to the wind howl in northeast storms. Once a week I could visit my mother in Wakefield, and we could keep her here with us when she pleased.

These were my hopes and thoughts. One glance at my calendar for May 1972 shows that my plans were torpedoed in advance. Not only did we have to move, but also page proof on *The Origin of Races* arrived, I took part in a Ph.D. oral exam in Philadelphia and a three-day meeting of a National Science Foundation panel in Washington. I received constant telephone calls, a two-day visit from two *Life* magazine research girls, and visits from others: my mother, Lisa's French aunt, and a Belgian physical anthropologist.

What really worried me was that some simple, honest, loyal, blue-collar-working Yankee neighbors had been sneakily approached by some FBI men who asked them insinuatingly if I were a Communist, or had shown any tendencies in that direction. One of the neighbors embarrassedly told me about these queries, with apologies for having bothered me.

I soon found out that I had been about to be asked to a high-level conference in Washington to discuss the possible reaction of the American public to the revelation that H-bombs release strontium 90. Would they panic à la Orson Welles and flee? Or stand their ground like men?

The first meeting took place in an amphitheater of the old State Department building, where President Eisenhower addressed us. He swore like a trooper, which irritated me a little because he had reprimanded me when I was in Corsica, after the battle of Tighime Pass, because I had used the word "fanny" to describe the part of me that had been grazed by a German jet-plane bullet. It was, he had said, unmilitary language. As I remember it, the first meeting made little progress.

For the second, to be held at Camp David, we assembled on the White House lawn, where we were loaded on three helicopters, each with a Marine seated on a box inside an open door. The shrinks were in number two, I was in number three, and I do not remember who was in number one. About halfway along the route we passed over a field of fat black Angus bulls. Number one made it, but number two tipped on the side the Marine wasn't sitting on, and the chopper landed in the middle of the bulls. My chopper signaled ahead for orders. We were told to proceed as planned and that number one would discharge its passengers and return to rescue the shrinks.

When the latter arrived they sat down with their notebooks and wrote out the memories of their feelings during their adventure. After the conference some of them went back by taxicabs.

I shall not, to this day, reveal what we said, nor who was there except myself, nor what the verdict was. My feeling was that old-fashioned Americans of northern European stock do not scare easily or quickly, but I seem to have been overruled because no announcement was made, and subsequent public behavior seems to have vindicated me in the sense that the knowledge of the danger of atomic clouds soon became commonly known and no riots arose.

Our people are bothered by local alarms about leaky atomic power plants and hidden chemical dumps that cause genetic defects. Our reactions are more anger than fear; our response is action rather than hysteria.

27. *The Origin of Races*

After our return from India in the spring of 1957 I requested and received a grant from the National Science Foundation (NSF 9321) for two years' work on my projected *Races of the World*. There was no question of its being published. My contract with Knopf for *The Story of Man* contained an option for my next two books. Nor was there any doubt of my obligation to tell the exact objective truth, when spending the foundation's money. I could neither exaggerate my findings for the "racists" nor minimize them for the "egalitarians"—two ill-definable words.

The 1971 *Oxford English Dictionary* does not mention *racist*. It makes *egalitarian* an adjective, meaning "that asserts the equality of mankind," without reference to race. The unabridged Webster's Third of 1961 defines a racist as "one who advocates racism," or "a doctrine or social system based on racism." A purist might define *racist* as a person who studies race, just as a botanist studies botany. Webster's Third also devotes 64 lines (approximately 640 words) to the definition of race, not including athletic events. The one that suits my purpose best is "a division of mankind possessing traits that are transmittable by descent and characteristic as a distinct human type, as Caucasian, Mongoloid, race."

Webster's Third gives two different definitions for egalitarianism: (a) "a belief that all men are equal in intrinsic worth and entitled to the rights and privileges of their society," and (b) "the belief that men are born equal in aptitudes and capacities (Plato's view of human nature was such as to be clearly opposed to egalitarianism)."

The first definition expresses a legal position. The second shows an ignorance of genetics, which Plato's logical mind adumbrated. I did not need to be a Plato to foresee the slings and brickbats that some egalitarians would hurl at me as soon as my proposed book was off the press, and another hurdle faced me from the publishing angle.

My trade editor at Knopf, Harold A. Strauss, and I agreed that my new book would be too technical for the trade department, and had to be published as a text, for assignment to college students. Therefore our contract was drawn out and signed in those terms. This is the way things were when I named the first chapter "The Taxonomy of Human Variation."

Just as I was getting rolling, I received a phone call from New York. It was a Mr. Sutton. He was the new text-department manager. The one I had dealt with before had left. Mr. Sutton wanted to come to Philadelphia to talk with me. This was unusual—for Knopfian conferences, I had always gone to New York.

When he arrived, Mr. Sutton invited me to lunch. This too was unusual. Harold Strauss had always eaten a sandwich at his desk. I didn't need to be lubricated with martinis to talk business.

So I replied to his invitation, "No, Philadelphia is *my* town. I'll take *you* to lunch." I took him to the Art Alliance, a club, where we were surrounded by my friends and their guests.

There he told me, amid the clattering of plates and the sonic blend of many voices, that he was going to break my contract. Nobody was interested in reading about race.

When I told Harold about this he said that he would have to turn it into a trade book, which might take a lot of editing. Before long we agreed that it had to be split into *The Origin of Races* and *The Living Races of Man.*

Harold made me simplify technicalities by writing "Wha da?" in the margins. This I could usually manage. Cutting out the academic weasel words was harder. "It would appear that . . ." and "Unless I am mistaken it seems . . ." etc., etc., were flushed down the drain. I had to be damned well sure that what I said was one hundred percent correct.

Once Harold had finished and I had made what corrections I could without violating veracity, a talented young copy editor took the bit in her teeth. She was trying, it seemed, to lower the IQ level of my readers to about two thirds of her own. She wasn't trying to censor me—in fact, her efforts had the opposite effect, to put my little birdie out at the very end of its limb.

It was fortunate that my script was typed on the best heavy bond paper. Otherwise her scribblings in soft lead pencils, and my erasures of them, with indignant remarks from both parties, would have worn holes in it. Could our dialogue have been left and reproduced, it would have made juicier reading than the text itself. After the job was finished, the lady quit Knopf. But I was left holding the bag. She was a brave girl, and I hope she found a less taxing job.

The hefty volume of 729 pages, not counting fore and after matter and 32 plates, was an expensive production for a moderate price. Its bibliography exceeded 500 titles (all used), and it had four tables of measurements and indices, 53 line drawings (all by Lisa*), and thirteen maps by Rafael Palacios, a consummate cartographer. All in all, it was a deluxe job.

Perhaps half of the data I needed was at hand. Much of it I had researched in order to write the pertinent papers published earlier. What I needed next was the basic thread that drew together the divergent evolutionary pathways of the races of mankind.

It came to me one night, at 2 A.M. It struck me like a bolt of lightning, in a dream. I leaped out of bed and dashed to my study to write it down.

Not only were time and energy related dimensions. The third factor was, of course, space. If space and energy were variable, time had to be variable too. I am sure that this was old hat to cosmic physicists, but it was new to me.

In all of the compilations I had seen of fossil men, they were listed on a scale of time, with little mention of whence they had come. No one had paid much attention to geography. But in my work on the cultures of the world, I had found that culture areas curiously followed the faunal areas of P. L. Sclater (1857) and A. R. Wallace (1876). Sclater had charted them by the distribution of birds, Wallace by that of animals in general.

Then I plotted the list of all known fossil specimens on the Old World part of the global map, with corrections made for the situation during the Pleistocene, because Sclater and Wallace had been concerned with the present-day climate, which is that of an interstadial. Four of the areas designated were presumably out. No race (in the sense of subspecies) of man had originated in the New World or in the Australian fauna region, or in Madagascar. I was limited to the Palearctic, Ethiopian, and Oriental. Each of these, however, was also divided by both geographical and climatic barriers.

Not only the glaciers at their maxima, but also the mountain spine of central Asia, from the Himalayas to the Tian Shan to the Altais and Siberia, split the Palearctic down the middle into an eastern and western zone. The eastern was Mongoloid territory to the north and Australoid south of the mountains of South China. Java, where several important finds had been made, was connected to the mainland of Asia during periods of high ice, when the oceans of the earth were low.

The western Palearctic was only a fringe, a twisted ribbon of frostfree land from the coast of Norway down to Spain, the shores of the

---

Her scales were left out.

Mediterranean, and the Black Sea, with a possible pocket or two in central Europe, and a loop around the southern Caspian Sea, where I had spent so much effort to discover early man. It ran around the shore of Asia Minor to the Arabian Desert and northern Afghanistan, where first I and then Louis Dupree had dug with the same idea in mind.

Of southern Arabia I was dubious because it lay in the Ethiopian faunal area. As a rule, people follow the animals they are accustomed to hunting. I saw no boundary between what I believed to be the Capoid country in North Africa and the Congoid country south of the Sahara. But I soon learned that, before the fourth cataract of the Nile had been cut through by the impounded waters from the African Lakes, what is now the southern Sudan had been a huge, shallow lake too. Now it has shrunken to Lake Chad. And so had been the Congo Basin before the Congo waters had eroded the eastern equatorial rim of Africa down to Stanley Falls. I knew there had to be such barriers, but I didn't find out about either of them (the cataracts and Stanley Falls) until after the publication of *The Origin of Races.*

Thus I had narrowed the habitable parts of the Old World during the Pleistocene into five possible cradles of man. And furthermore, the archaeological map fitted this system too. West of the Arakan Hills in Burma, which I named Movius's Line after its discoverer, the sequence went from chopping tools to hand axes to Mousterian to Levalloisio-Mousterian until about the time of the Upper Paleolithic in Europe and western Asia. After that it lost its overall uniformity and branched. Even the Upper Paleolithic techniques of Europe and western Asia may have been invented independently in more than one center. In North Africa the Aterian, with its tanged points and flakes retouched on both sides, showed that the blade cultures of the more northerly regions had not penetrated until toward or after the end of the last northern glaciation.

Somebody other than Caucasoids may well have made these artifacts, but who could they have been? There was only one major race left unaccounted for, that of the Bushmen and Hottentots, who had inhabited South Africa when the Boers arrived around 1600, and whose remains Louis Leakey had found in mounds at Homa in East Africa on the East African highland corridor.

These men had been artists who carved and painted on rocks in the Sahara and all the way down to the Cape of Good Hope. A French paleontologist, Camille Arambourg, had found skeletal remains of high antiquity of Ternifine in Algeria, consisting of one parietal bone and three lower jaws. Both the jaws and the teeth resembled those of *Sinanthropus* in China more than they did anything geographically in between. So did the upper jaw fragment and teeth that I had found in the High Cave in 1939.

What were Mongoloids doing in North Africa during the middle and late Pleistocene? Except for their peppercorn hair and steatopygia, the Bushmen resembled Mongoloids closely, both in their body proportions and in the flatness of their faces, not to mention their Mongoloid eye folds. Both their implements and rock art resembled the North African Upper Paleolithic and later. I had noted Mongoloid-looking Berbers in the Atlas in 1926 when Mary, Limnibhy, and I had crossed the High Atlas in winter, and in snow. Also, the Harratin, or agricultural serfs of the Berber landlords on the southern side of the Atlas seemed to be a Bushman-Negro population. Some of the nomadic Berbers had told me that these Harratin had been yellow-skinned before having mixed with slaves only a few generations ago.

What about the Negroes? The acid soil of the tropical forest had left no bones. But the Broken Hill skull and long bones had clearly Negro features, and resembled the Saldanha skullcap found in South Africa. Both were associated with stone tools that antedated those of the Bushmen. Africa was still a poorly documented continent, but what we had pointed in a single direction.

The Bushmen's ancestors had moved southward out of the Sahara along the cool, East African corridor, from Cap Spartel to the Cape of Good Hope, which is why I called them Capoid, following my principle of using geographical rather than physically descriptive or cultural terms.

Having specified my geographical regions, I listed the known human fossil remains in each one according to their supposed chronology. Some had been dated by carbon 14, others by the new argon 40 method, a few by deep-water isotopes, but most were still dependent on plain geological position and by the association with them of the accompanying animal bones, by the fluorine test. Then I measured every specimen, cast, or scale drawing as accurately as the material permitted. My measurements were mostly of crania, lower jaws, and teeth. I chose these measurements for two purposes.

The first was to see how well they would fit into the framework proposed by Professor Ernst Mayr at the Cold Spring Harbor Symposium of 1950 that I had attended and at which I had read a paper. Professor Mayr proposed that we should abandon all the current typological nomina for fossil hominids—such as *Pithecanthropus erectus, Sinanthropus pekinensis, Homo rhodesiensis, Homo neanderthalensis*—that split early races into different genera, and should lump them in the genus *Homo,* with a paternal and a filial species, *Homo erectus* and *Homo sapiens.*

Erectus included all the small-brained, big-toothed, chinless, mostly earlier, specimens. *Sapiens* included the mostly later, and anatomically modern, kinds of people, plus the Neanderthals. My measurements fitted Professor Mayr's twofold framework very well.

My second purpose was to see how the racial differences detectable between the specimens also fitted into that framework. In every human subspecies, or major race, both *erectus* and *sapiens* forms were represented. An exception was the racial dwarfs, who are a subrace anyhow, and are without known *erectus* ancestors either because the latter had been full-sized or because they live on lateritic soil, which destroys their bones and also influences their glands to keep them small.

So far I forged ahead, except for one mistake. Instead of calling *erectus* and *sapiens* species, I referred to them as grades, which is not a Linnaean term. In the *Origin's* glossary, *grade* is defined as "In this book, an evolutionary level or status through which one or more phyletic animals (or plants) may pass."

Another mistake was in my inability to have the last word on the first page of the last chapter of the first printing of the first edition. What the copy editor had me say was, ". . . at the beginning of our record, over half a million years ago, man was a single species, *Homo erectus,* perhaps already divided into five geographical races or sub-species. *Homo erectus* then evolved into *Homo sapiens* not once but five times, as each subspecies, living in its own territory, passed a critical threshold from a more brutal to a more *sapient* state."

The copy editor won, bless her soul, before she resigned. Only the first edition of a book gets reviewed. On page 29 I had shown in a diagram how the critical threshold might have been crossed any number of times from one to five, in the first four cases by peripheral gene flow, otherwise known as interracial mating along territorial boundaries. What could have kept a hunting party of *sapiens* men from taking advantage of *erectus* females? The males would deliver the genes for higher brain power, the females the makings of physiological adaptation to the local environment.

In the second edition of *The Origin of Races* I changed the injudicious phrasing of that fatal sentence to: "*Homo erectus* then gradually evolved into *Homo sapiens,* as each subspecies, living in its own territory, underwent advantageous genetic changes due to a process impossible to specify from the meager evidence at hand."

This defused sentence was printed only after the first edition had gone to press three times. No evidence has come to me that any of my detractors read it.

The "process impossible to specify from the meager evidence at hand" is spelled out diagramatically in Figure 1 on page 29. Number 3 would be the Caucasoid, Number 4 the Mongoloid, Number 5 the Australoid, Number 2 the Capoid, and Number 1 the Congoid. We cannot yet be sure of exactly what happened.

Whether the race in question passed the *erectus-sapiens* threshold by independent mutation or by peripheral gene flow is of less importance in the reader's mind than the relative date when each transition took place. The implication is that whoever came first is thereby best, a logical fallacy because in some environments climatic pressures cause some subspecies to become adapted more rapidly than they do in others. This also leads to a certain snobbishness as to whose ancestors became *sapiens* first.

It makes a difference in status whether your ancestors came over on the *Mayflower* or on an immigrant ship in the early 1900s, all else being equal. When I wrote that our Caucasoid ancestors crossed Ernst Mayr's species threshold some two hundred thousand years earlier than the ancestors of some Africans seem to have done, and it was published in an elegant Borzoi book by Alfred Knopf, I knew that I was in for trouble—not from American or other so-called blacks, but from their so-called white protagonists. The trouble could not come before October 15, the publication date, and after November 20 Lisa and I would be abroad.

I had five months and one week of grace, so to speak, before five weeks of preliminary duty as a target. On Monday, May 7, four days after our return to Gloucester, the page proof came. I spent May 10 and 11 in Washington on a National Science Foundation committee. Every day that I was home one or more of *Life*'s bright young lady researchers telephoned me, and one of them spent two days here going over slides. In Philadelphia, I cut two sets of five *What in the World?* television shows. I attended two funerals—one that of my favorite aunt; wrote an article on race for Scott, Foresman; hosted Carl Jr., Janet, their numerous children and animals; and visited two doctors. More pertinent to this chronicle, I wrote an article entitled "Growth and Development of Social Groups," to be delivered to the sixteen invited members of a CIBA symposium in London. Writing this article kept me so busy that I do not remember any abrasive criticism of the *Origins* before our departure. If there was any, I ignored it.

28. *Man's Future and Jebel Ighud*

As most western Europeans and many Americans know, CIBA is a giant pharmaceutical manufacturing corporation in Switzerland. It had and probably still has a large building on a large square in London. Therein it housed its guests and held scientific symposia paid for by the CIBA Foundation. To attend a conference called "Man and His Future," they gave Lisa and myself first-class air tickets that allowed us side trips to Scandinavia, France, and Morocco.

We left Boston on November 20, arrived in Shannon early in the morning of the twenty-first, hired a taxi, and rode along the coast through Clare until we came in sight of Galway Bay, and back again through Ennis. The scenery was magnificent, the people and cattle sturdy. We hopped to London late in the afternoon, and spent the next four days shopping and visiting friends, including Cyril and Gwendolyn Darlington. This meant a train ride to Oxford.

Professor Darlington held, among other titles, that of keeper of the Oxford Botanic Garden. He was also a cofounder of the journal *Heredity*. Like some other botanists, Cyril had found it useful to compare the more easily detected genetic rules that govern plants with the less accessible mechanisms of human genetics and of history. His conclusions left him vulnerable to egalitarians. We had much to talk about. His magnum opus, *The Evolution of Man and of Society,* was not published until 1969, but in 1962, drawing on my memory of our conversations, I believed that he carried many of its ideas in his capacious mind.

The symposium opened at four o'clock in the afternoon on Monday, November 26, with tea. Present were most if not all of the twenty-five invited members; some of their wives; the director of the foundation, Gordon Wolstenholme; and some of his staff. I had never seen so many famous persons packed together into one room. J. B. S. Haldane had flown up from India. He sat beside a keg of Bass Ale that had been ordered at his special request. When he stood up and started to walk around I inadvertently touched him. He recoiled, saying that I had injured his back.

Francis Crick, the codiscoverer of the spiral helix, was very pleasant. Then, or perhaps later, he mentioned the fact that the building was steam-heated. He and other Oxonians were dressed in thick Harris tweed suits, probably over long woolen underwear. They thought that the heating had been laid on for the Americans, but the director assured them that it was to please the Swiss. Gregory Pincus, the father of the pill, had just come back from Greece. He said that he had had no luck there, because the Greeks wanted as many babies as possible. One other day when Lisa wanted to go shopping, Jacob Bronowski, historian and master of all trades, gave her a lift in his canary yellow Rolls-Royce.

At five o'clock, just after tea, Sir Julian Huxley delivered the first of sixteen papers. It was entitled "The Future of Man—Evolutionary Aspects." For me to try to abstract it here would do it ill justice. I can only note that he mentioned Teilhard de Chardin's noosphere, at that time a fashionable subject; the dependence of human progress on a procession of ideas: ecology, new drugs, population control, the population explosion, birth control; and a need for a rise in global IQ. In general, Sir Julian's paper was a stimulating overview of what the symposium was about.

On Wednesday, November 28, at 9:30 A.M. I began to read my paper, "Growth and Development of Social Groups." It came to a little less than three thousand words, divided into an untitled introduction and seven following sections: Human Evolution; Pre-Sapiens Behaviour, the Differentiation of Institutions; Energy Consumption and Institutional Complexity; Control of Social Equilibrium; Evolution and Diffusion in the Growth of Societies; The Relative Flexibility of Social Systems; Social Evolution and Environment; and finally Race and Social Evolution.

Sir Julian's delivery of his paper had been followed by discussion, and so was mine, although neither lot has been recorded in the official publication of the symposium, *Man and His Future.* In my case, galley proof had been sent to me in Morocco, and I returned it promptly. In my diary I noted that Haldane had approved it heartily, and Bronowski had liked all of it except the last part, on race. He was a tiny man, almost a dwarf, with a huge, globular head topped with tightly curled, black hair. Had I been his twin, I wouldn't have liked it either.

After the symposium we took the night express to Cornwall, where Lisa had followed her father around when he was creating his magnificent paintings of cliffs and waves breaking on them, of St. Ives in the mist and in the sunlight, but where I had never been, except in family memories. She led me to her father's sites, and I took color slides of the same scenes, as accurately as possible.

The train had carried us to Penzance, only seven miles east of Land's End. That is where Paul Dougherty had done most of his Cornish painting. Two miles south of Penzance lay Mousehole. In Mousehole, Michael Howard had a house. He was the son of G. Wren Howard, Jonathan Cape's first partner. Michael drove us in a tiny car through narrow sunken lanes to an Iron Age village where people lived in stone-walled rooms hardly long enough to lie down in. Then he took us to a circle of upright stones, a cromlech. Within its bounds grazed a large black stallion, like King Arthur's steed. No one bothered it. It was sacred—like the king himself, whom one could almost see; Excalibur; and, faintly, the Holy Grail.

Then Michael drove us to Land's End, when dusk was falling. In the gift shop I heard one woman say to another: "Remember, tonight meets the coven."

Back at Michael's house in Mousehole, he asked me what I was writing. I told him that I intended to finish the *Races of the World* trilogy, but it would take a long time. Then he asked me about my life so far, and I told him.

"You must write your autobiography," he said, speaking as my publisher of thirty years. I told him that I would, and that is the origin of the book you are reading.

After that our stay in Cornwall consisted of the usual search for ancestors' graves. I found some of them but not others. I did not find my great-grandfather's birthhouse. Later my cousin Billy Coon found it, in Probus, halfway between Truro and St. Austell. It is a solid two-story granite building with a wing containing a grapevine six inches thick.

On the last day of November we flew to Copenhagen, where we dined with Dr. and Mrs. Helge Larsen on reindeer meat. Helge had dug early-man sites in Alaska with Froelich Rainey and Louis Giddings, who was also in Copenhagen. The next day Helge guided us in the Royal Museum, where we met the world-renowned ethnographer Dr. Kai Birket-Smith, who was the museum's director. He too had written a world history, *The History of Culture*.

In the museum I saw, among other rare things, an elaborate exhibit of houses, boats, and other artifacts from the Nicobar Islands, a chain between the Andamans—forbidden to us—and the northern tip of India. The islands had belonged to Denmark before being ceded to India.

Lisa wanted to go to Hälsingborg in Sweden to see her Grandmother Lund's house. I wanted to buy a long-distance portrait lens for my Hasselblad camera to take sneaky pictures with in Morocco. Louis Giddings, with his wife Bets, drove us over in his small Volkswagen bus.

This was my first view of the Danish countryside, all twenty-five miles of the way to Helsingor, where he boarded the car ferry in a pea-soup fog. How the captain piloted us through the North-Sea-to-Baltic traffic I cannot understand, except that blue eyes are said to be best in fog.

We saw Lisa's grandmother's house, I bought my lens, we had lunch, and we got back safely although Louis, who had not driven on the left before, had some close calls. Later on, in the USA, he had a real collision and was killed. He was a fine gentleman, an excellent archaeologist, and a splendid father and husband.

On December 6 we flew to Paris, with much to do before leaving for Morocco on the eighth. The Morocco plan was that I had written the new director of antiquities at Rabat, Dr. Georges Souville, telling him that under the University Museum's aegis I hoped to return to Morocco during the winter of 1962–3, and sought his permission to search and to excavate wherever I could find the most promising cave, most likely in the region of Cap Spartel. There I knew that I could muster skilled and reliable workmen. Souville had written me a favorable reply. My hope was, of course, to find some more skulls and bones of ancestral Bushmen.

We found a reasonably priced hotel and went to see Lisa's paternal aunt and her husband, Francois Trives, an old soldier and plantation owner in Indochina. When he learned of my connection with the Darlan assassination twenty years before, I found it hard to leave. Then we went to the Musée de l'Homme to call on Robert Gessain, who was about to leave for the Senegal. He let me prowl through the museum's pictures file and order copies of any that I wanted to use in my next book, *The Living Races of Man*.

After lunch in the museum we went to see François Bourlière, the zoologist, who was writing a picture book of animals for Alfred Knopf. Quite casually he loaned me a reprint of an article by Arambourg on a skull found near Safi in Morocco, still apparently in the hands of Professor Emmanuel Ennouchi of the department of geology, University of Rabat, dated June 18, 1962. Its pictures and measurements were *not* Neanderthal, as Arambourg had written. It was just what I had planned to look for. (If I used exclamation points, I would use one now.)

At 9:15 A.M. on Saturday the eighth I called Professor Henry V. Vallois at the Institut de Paleontologie Humaine, whereof he was the director and the likeliest man to know about this new cranium. A girl's voice told me to call after 9:30, but I was very tired, and called from France Trives's apartment at noon. Vallois said, "I have the cranium three meters from my hand. You can see it at three P.M."

I answered that unfortunately we had to be on a plane at 4:30, and he replied, "Hélas, not enough time," and added: "I will try to keep it for you until you get back."

Henri Vallois is a very prompt and meticulous man. The reason for his delay was glaucoma. My grandfather, my brother Maurice, and I have all had it. In 1962 Henri Vallois had to begin taking drops in his eyes in the morning, and what he meant was that he would not be able to see the cranium before 3 P.M. Professor Arambourg was in Morocco, and already at the site, studying the animal bones.

We flew a fine flight over the Pyrenees. My student and successor as expert on the Rif, David Montgomery Hart, met us at the airport. He drove us to his and his wife Ursula's house in Temara. David was teaching Islamic history and culture to Arabs in the University of Rabat. From their house he drove us to our hotel in Rabat.

The next day being Sunday, we relaxed and ambled about, seeing what was new in Rabat, and on Monday morning we went to the American Embassy to collect our mail, which included a letter from Harold Strauss saying that *The Origin of Races* was selling nicely. We met George Souville in his museum, and he was both frank and gracious. He gave me a letter of introduction to the official in charge of Goulimine in the far south asking him to see that we be given proper lodging for one or two nights. He also helped me rent a car. He called Ennouchi, who came and drove us to his museum, where he proudly showed us several mounted skeletons of elephants, his specialty, and then a cast of the fossil cranium from Jebel Ighüd. It was not a Neanderthal, but a proto-Bushman, with heavy brow ridges and other bony ridges, a *sapiens* in brain size, but still mostly *erectus* in morphology. Dr. Emmanuel Ennouchi, it seemed to me, was a little too enthusiastic over my visit. He obviously had some chip on his shoulder, and needed a new friend. He was a Jew from the south of France, and I suspect that from my name he thought me Jewish too.

On Tuesday the eleventh I rented an air-cooled front-wheel-drive Citroën at 8:30 in the morning, and we drove up to Tangier, taking a new coast road that carried us to a short branch leading to the caves. There we saw Little Absalem, among others, who led us through the caves like tourists, to show us what they had done. Little A. had an eighth child, which he indicated by a finger joint on a middle finger.

We had trouble finding the Buckinghams. El-Farhar had been abandoned, its windows broken. Win and Ellen were living in cottages with about ten students at the American School, boarding in. We took a cottage. It was cold and damp, and I caught cold. I was asked to give a lecture and to do other things I didn't do. But I did go to Dean's bar, where Dean said, softly, "Quite a lot of people of your period have been here lately."

Before leaving Tangier I drove to the caves several times, and once into the former Spanish Zone to Ksar es Sghir (the Small Castle), which had been forbidden territory during the Spanish regime. Nothing of note was visible there except a few fishing boats.

The last time we went to the caves we inspected the Pig Cave. During our earlier excavations this shelter had been used as a piggery by a Spanish swineherd, and all the Muslims had avoided it. With Moroccan independence, the swineherd had been evicted and the cave cleaned of its porcine effluvia. It was now *hallal*, the Muslim equivalent of kosher. I could hire what was left of my old gang and others like them to dig it. It was a big cave, its mouth fifteen meters or fifty feet wide and six feet high, facing westward toward the ocean. Also it was situated high enough so that every rise in the Pleistocene level may not have flooded it.

It was a good bet, but I had to return to Rabat to get permission, and still wanted to see the site of Jebel Ighud. We drove back to Rabat by a circuitous route, skirting the hills and watching for caves all the way, but we found none. A letter from Harold Strauss awaited me, saying that over five thousand copies of *Origin of Races* had been sold, this not counting the text edition or book clubs. The same mail contained proof of my CIBA paper and its comments. It had been waiting for me too long, which is probably why the discussion was not published.

We did not leave Rabat for Jebel Ighud until Saturday, December 22. I had caught a bad cold in Tangier and in Rabat it had turned into a fever, with strange dreams. That day we drove to Safi on the coast, the port where the barite from Jebel Ighud was loaded on freighters. We slept at the beautiful Hotel Marhaba. It was almost empty, while all the hotels in Marrakesh and the Atlas Mountains were jammed for Christmas.

After a good night's sleep we were up and out early on a secondary road running southeast to a small place called Chemaia. There we found a gendarme who gave us a ragged guide. We drove back northwestward about fifteen kilometers to a side road. At first it was blacktop, then dust, over two streams that had to be forded, with people pushing. Eventually we reached the mine's office and found there its director, a young Norman named Guy Lozano.

He fed us a splendid lunch and told us the story of the skull. Two free-lancing prospectors, one of whom was named Mohammed ben Fatmi, had found it in a tunnel. They had carried it to him, and he had given it to a postman, who had had it sent to Rabat, where the central post office had given it to Dr. Ennouchi, who had no more discovered it than I had.

Later Dr. Ennouchi had come there and dug some animal

bones out of a face of breccia without, it seems, asking from what spot the cranium had been removed. Only a few weeks before our arrival Professor Arambourg had visited the site, but stayed only a few minutes. He seems not to have asked either.

M. Lozano drove us in a two-horsepower Citroën wall climber to the site, where we found Mohammed ben Fatmi and his partner waiting for us. We had to walk through a tunnel about ten feet long into an open cavity of presumably barite-bearing stone. On the left, the interesting side, was first a rounded boulder seated on some reddish-brown soil, from which it threatened to fall at any moment; on the right was the breccia that Ennouchi was said to have been extracting bones from.

I asked Mohammed ben Fatmi in Arabic where the skull had come from, and he pointed to the soil under the boulder. Then I asked him, "Have you any more skulls of the Sons of Adam?"

"Of course," he said, like Lucho on the *Gloria*, when nobody had asked him.

Mohammed pushed us aside and picked up several pieces of skull vault. They had been freshly broken, perhaps when Dr. Arambourg had stepped on them. There could well be more in the soil still under the boulder, and Mohammed offered to crawl in after them.

"Not you," said I. "I am old and you are young. Allah has the date of my death written in his golden book. If I die it is by his will. *Allahu akbar.*"

I crawled under, pulled out a few more pieces, a flint point, and a few small animal bones, and packed the human bones in one specimen bag with cotton, and the other objects in a tin box. M. Lozano drove us back to his office and I drove down to Marrakesh, missing my way several times, until we reached a hotel in Gueliz, a suburb of the city, where David Hart had reserved us a room.

These events took place on December 23. We returned to Rabat on New Year's Day, 1963, to find a cable from my older son, heralding his sixth child's birth, no sex stated. He is Richard Goodale Coon, named for his mother's mother's second husband and his father's mother's father.

What happened between these events had nothing at all to do with the Jebel Ighüd story, but with traveling over the southland where, among other things, I met the paramount chief of the Ait Atta, and at least one of his goums that had been with Colonel de la Tour and me at the battle of the Pass of Tighime in Corsica.

During this week I had glued together the eighteen pieces of cranium constituting Jebel Ighüd Number 2. They formed a perfect left half of an adolescent specimen, sex at that moment indeterminable. We named it Ezra. As young crania do, it looked more fragile and modern than adult specimens. All of these details could be determined after I got it to a professional laboratory and a first-class human anatomist like Vallois or Larry Angel in the Smithsonian.

That was the problem that Souville and I faced when I showed it to him. He and I agreed that I should carry it to Paris, and if Vallois said so, to America. Our chargé d'affaires agreed. I wrote a letter to Ennouchi telling him what I was doing, and posted it. Souville got us on a jet prop to Paris by having two poor students going back to school bumped. He sent us to the airport in a conspicuous official station wagon with two tough drivers. We got through the formalities without question, and I sat with Ezra in a small box on my knees all the way to Paris, and then to Vallois's laboratory.

His eyes were working; he had put his drops in early. He inspected Ezra carefully and listened intently to my story. Then he looked at me and asked, "Why don't you take it to America?"

I hesitated, forgetting that he who hesitates is lost. "I think that you had better keep it here and study it," I answered.

A few weeks after I went home, Ennouchi flew to Paris, walked into Vallois's laboratory, picked up the originals of both Jebel Ighud Number 1 and Number 2, and carried them back to Rabat. After I was home he bombarded me with a succession of very formally worded letters accusing me of breaking all the rules of scientific behavior. He wrote as if he were imitating some eighteenth-century French style, and I answered him in plain Yankee English. He posted his by sea mail that took a month to reach me; I sent mine by air mail that arrived in a few days.

A year or two later this jerky chain was broken. At a conference in the Canary Islands he is alleged to have said that I had sent two Arab workmen under a rock that had fallen and killed them both. This was told me by an American friend who was present. I had heard the same rumor about Ennouchi, without firm verification. These reports terminated our correspondence. But he must have gone or sent someone under the rock, because he later published J. I. Number 2's right frontal bone and a juvenile mandible.

The *Catalogue of Fossil Hominids, Part I, Africa,* British Museum (Natural History), 1967, states on page 38 that the originals of both are at the laboratory of geology, University of Rabat, but temporarily in Professor Valois's care in Paris, while the cast are in the Natural History Museum in Paris. I was one of the four authors of that section of the *Catalogue.*

Both Ennouchi and Souville left Morocco long ago. Professor Vallois is still alive. I wish him *la bonne chance.* He gave me one, so to speak, but I muffed it.

29. *A Scientific Discussion*

As Harold's letters had told me, the initial trade sales of *Origin* were excellent. The October 25 publication date was far too late for that year's text adoptions. The jacket blurbs proffered high praise from Sir Julian Huxley, George Gaylord Simpson, Ernst Mayr, Bill Howells, Bill Straus of Johns Hopkins, Larry Angel of the Smithsonian, Bill Krogman of the University of Pennsylvania, J. Franklin Ewing, S. J. of Fordham (our jolly priest of *What in the World?*), and Daniel A. Poling, editor of the *Christian Herald* magazine. If Knopf had sent a review copy to my friend Rabbi Nelson Glueck, we would have had both science and religion cornered.

Everything was going fine until *The Saturday Review* asked Professor Theodosius Dobzhansky of Columbia to review *Origin*. Dobzhansky wrote a review about sixteen hundred words long, and sent me a carbon copy of it. It was sarcastic, abusive, and, I believed, defamatory. It accused me of being a racist, and even worse, of having confused the concepts of subspecies and grade, as discussed in Chapter 27. I telephoned the editorial office of *The Saturday Review* and the editors rejected Dobzhansky's review. Instead they published a few extracts from the book, and a fine, hearty review by Margaret Mead. Dobzhansky meanwhile had sent other carbon copies to G. G. Simpson and Ernst Mayr, both of whom told him politely that he was wrong; both had given my publisher favorable quotes.

His next move was to offer his original review to the editors of *The Scientific American*, who published it in its May 1963 issue.

On April 5 Morton Fried, a Columbia anthropology professor, sent a three-page mimeographed flyer to eighty-four teachers of anthropology who might have adopted *Origin* as a text. Two other pages listed their names and addresses.

Among these names were those of several of my friends, two of whom sent me copies of Fried's clandestine message. It contained proposals to hire a copywriter to prepare advertisements to place, not in *The New York Times,* but in the *Daily News,* and in half a dozen key southern newspapers. "There is going to be extreme difficulty raising funds for such a project. Here I have no talents whatsoever, and Dobzhansky seems no better off. I think it might be possible to get funds from such outfits as the Anti-Defamation League of B'nai B'rith or other similar organizations. This raises another question. Obviously, by even writing this letter from Columbia, I am playing into the hands of Putnam and his ilk who believe Columbia to be the absolute fountainhead of subversion. . . . We may be sure that the Putnamites will spill their filth on any institution that becomes involved, but the more people and the more places the sillier will be his position."

After a few questions about how to organize his committee, he ended his conspiratorial plea with good news: "I am going off to Taiwan for fourteen months beginning this June."

Having read this document twice through, I called up Conrad Arensberg in his office at Columbia. He told me that he had received a copy and had thrown it in the wastebasket. Then, as chairman of the anthropology department, he summoned both Fried and Margaret Mead into his office. What was said I neither know nor care. I have heard from Fried but twice since then. Once he requested my permission to rerun one of my old papers in a new edition of a reader he had edited, adding something that I interpreted as "I am sorry." The second time was indirectly through my granddaughter Elizabeth Eliot Coon, some four or five years ago. She took a course with him, and he asked her if she and I were related. She said I was her grandfather. He gave her an A− (not that she didn't deserve it, for she is a smart young woman).

While Fried's paper was still circulating, or a little later, and whether or not he had anything to do with it, Henry Schwarzchild of the Anti-Defamation League wrote a letter to *The New York Times* about four inches of a column long, challenging me to answer him in the same paper. With the passage of time I forgot what his challenge was, but I answered him, and sent a copy to Harold Strauss, who remarked: "Henry Schwarzchild doesn't know what your book is all about."

The *Times,* alas, never printed it, because they received it at the beginning of a printers' strike that lasted several weeks, and all the letters to the editor were shelved, mine permanently, and I couldn't have cared less. All this nonsense was tedious, made more so when *Current Anthropology,* the organ of the Wenner-Gren Foundation, reprinted Dobzhansky's *Scientific American* review, plus a pompous companion piece by Ashley Montagu. I ignored the first, and answered only the latter's argument about the size of Anatole France's brain, compared to Turgenev's. The size was reckoned by dry weight. France's brain was very dry and very light, Turgenev's fresh and juicy. This tedious argument went on and on until Sol Tax, the editor, wrote me that if we didn't quit it would go on forever.

Montagu's last blow that I know of was apparently delivered on *Kup's Show,* in a Chicago television station on the evening of September 13, 1969. According to a youthful auditor, who wrote me about it, "Montagu said how ridiculous on racial superiority and inferiority you were," and "Montagu also placed much emphasis on your name—which, when I checked it up, is apparently a very old English name."

Montagu and I have known each other since 1936, the year of the Harvard Tercentenary. He is a professional anatomist, and has written some excellent early books. As far as I can remember, the 1969 TV show was his last missile, and all else being equal, this will be my last retort. *Pax nobiscum.*

But Dobzhansky would give me no peace, not even a truce. His last substantial attack on me, called "Bogus Science," appeared in *The Journal of Heredity* early in 1968. My reply, entitled "Comment on 'Bogus Science,'" followed in the September-October number of the same journal. It runs to about four hundred words. Among these are:

You published a review of Carleton Putnam's book, Race and Reality, *by Theodosius Dobzhansky. The latter devoted one fifth of his space to reiterating for the nth time his denunciation of my book . . . following which he castigates me, also for the nth time, for not having repudiated Mr. Putnam's quotation of one brief statement in my book. . . . Dobzhansky states that "It is the duty of a scientist to prevent misuse and prostitution of his findings." I disagree with him. It is the duty of a scientist to do his work conscientiously and to the best of his ability, which is exactly what I have done and shall continue to do, and to reject publicly only the writings of those persons who, influenced by one cause or another, have misquoted him, as Dobzhansky repeatedly has done with my work, for reasons best known to himself.*

Were the evolution of fruit flies a prime social and political issue, Dobzhansky might easily find himself in the same situation in which he and his followers have tried to place me.

Carleton S. Coon

It may be briefly added that Dobzhansky's dislike of me was not limited to verbiage, but also included conspicuous physical avoidance and even rudeness. At an academy meeting in Washington I walked down the center aisle of the conference room, looking for a seat. He was sitting on an aisle seat on the left. I paused to say hello to him and he brushed me away like a fly.

Later, at a Wenner-Gren meeting in Chicago, I entered the building it was held in and saw Dobzhansky just inside the doorway, dressed in a tuxedo, and leaning over to shake hands with each member as he came in, as if he were the host. He ignored me. At dinner I was seated on George G. Simpson's right. We were holding a pleasant conversation when Dobzhansky forced his body between mine and the person's at my right. Leaning over me, and making me spill my food, he interrupted my conversation to talk to George Simpson, who was a very sick man and had to leave the conference before it was over.

My reply to "Bogus Science" was the last shot I can remember in our silly war. On May 9, 1975, I raised a flag of truce by writing the following letter.

Dear Professor Dobzhansky: This morning I have been rereading your beautifully written Mankind Evolving, *and once more I am touched by its inscription: "To Dr. C. S. Coon, with warmest regards from the author."*

At present I am writing my memoirs, and as I approach the years that followed, I would like to say as little as possible about what happened, and to state that we have buried the now-rusty hatchet.

I have dug its grave, and hope that you will agree that I may drop it in. With warmest regards to Mrs. Dobzhansky and yourself.

Carleton S. Coon

On December 19, 1975, Professor Dobzhansky died in Davis, California. Mrs. Dobzhansky had predeceased him. He left one daughter, Sophie Coe, the wife of Professor Michael Coe of Yale, and several grandchildren.

He did not answer my letter. I do not know why, nor do I need to know. In a few pages I have said more than I said I would say, because it belongs to history.

History also should include a sober explanation of our different ways of reasoning. Dobzhansky believed that new species evolve out of old ones by fortuitous combinations of mutations. He had studied mutation rates in fruit flies that produce several generations in a year; in man this takes a century. A species-forming combination of such mutations would be a rare event. For a male and female with compatible combinations to find each other would be even rarer. Therefore the copy-edited statement I quoted earlier would be impossible.

He may be excused for not having heard of the discovery of codons by Jacques Monod and A. Lwoff in 1961. A codon is a combination of three molecules which, in passing through the bloodstream, shunts itself off its own line onto the transfer RNA train, thus affecting the growth of special organs. In 1975, the year of Dobzhansky's death, this discovery was applied to human races by M.-C. King and A. C. Wilson, with significant results.

These discoveries greatly simplified the concept of speciation. I was equally unaware of Monod's and Lwoff's work, but it is now described in certain high school textbooks. Dobzhansky should not be faulted for his omission. He was busy on his own projects. My technique was not, of course, the conventional one of proceeding step by step at random, ignoring educated hunches. As explained in Chapter 27, it was to view evolution as an orderly process on a three-dimensional grid of energy, space, and time. Once we learned what had happened, the exact mechanisms became less important. If none of us had thought intuitively, we might all still belong to Ernst Mayr's once proposed and now accepted species, *Homo erectus.*

30. *Four Meetings*

From about the time that I was gluing Jebel Ighud Number 2 together until a month after my mother died, four meetings and/or conferences were held on the subject of race, with me or my name involved in each of them.

During our absence in Morocco, Dobzhansky, whom I shall recall to the stage for a brief moment, took the trouble to denounce me in his presidential address to the American Association for the Advancement of Science. Not to be outdone by this performance, Professor Sherwood L. Washburn followed suit. He had taken his master's degree at Harvard in 1935 and his doctorate there in 1940, mostly under Hooton, but I believe that he took one half course under me. Until Hooton's death in 1954, Sherry had briefed his students about Hooton's mistakes, but after the 1955 conference in the Rhodesias I became the object of his barbs.

Both Earnest and I had heard of these reports through the student grapevine. Hooton took it harder than I did. Personally I wished that Sherry had told me personally what I had said or done wrong so that I might have corrected my mistakes in the future, but he never did, and I was a little surprised by his coming out in the open in his presidential address to the American Anthropological Association shortly after Dobzhansky's discharge. At first he forbade publication of his speech, but some of my local friends who had been there told me about it nonetheless. A watered-down version of it was published later in a pamphlet entitled *Race and Intelligence,* edited by Melvin Tumin of Princeton University, whose introduction started: "Do Negroes and whites in the United States differ significantly in their native mental equipment?"

Most of the fifty-six pages were criticisms of Carleton Putnam's writings, while only the last seven were Washburn's contribution. He mentioned my work only once, ". . . in *The Origin of Races,* I think that the great antiquity of races is supported neither by the record nor by evolutionary theory." My copy had been sent me by Henry Schwarzchild. Sherry also set up a number of nameless straw men and knocked them down; e.g., "The Bushmen have been described as the result of a mixture between Negro and Mongoloid. Such a statement could only have been put in the literature without consideration of migration routes."

He didn't give a clue as to who was supposed to have said what that he contradicted. But Sherry agreed with me, if only inadvertently: He said that the Bushmen were a separate race.

Poor man. Had he only published his address I could have answered him in his own language, just two Yankees chatting together over a quart of ale, and he in exile on the Pacific coast.

In anticipation of such a chat, I had prepared my own presidential address for the upcoming meeting of the American Association of Physical Anthropologists in Boulder, Colorado. It was to meet jointly with the archaeologists, and I was still president because my outfit had refused to accept my resignation in Philadelphia.

As I was sitting on a sofa skimming over my notes for my presidential address, a colleague of Sherry Washburn sat beside me.

"What are you reading?" he asked.

"Oh, just the notes for my presidential address."

"May I read it?"

"Yes."

Then he said, "I have to drive to the Denver airport to pick up Sherry."

He left alone, and alone he returned. All I had written in my notes was that as Sherry had mentioned me in his address a few months earlier, I felt the right to mention him in mine, and so forth, all in good humor.

Neither the archaeologists nor the physical anthropologists had a presidential address. The man who had organized the meeting spoke for both of us.

Our part of the meeting went smoothly. There were no resolutions, except as to where the next meeting should be held. A Spanish-born Mexican anthropologist suggested Mexico City. So I said, *"Todos que quieren ir a Méjico dicen sí! Otros non!"*

The *sí*'s won. Many of them went. I stayed home, having little trust in Montezuma.

As we were leaving our motel room with our baggage, a chambermaid said gloomily to one of our distinguished anatomists, a missionary's son from China, "These anthropologists and archaeologists do a lot a drinking but very little fucking."

I am sorry that Sherry didn't come to Boulder. We might have gotten together profitably, as we should have done long before. Between his critical capacity and my imagination and exuberance, who knows? I would like to re-create the day when he snapped my picture on Kandahar Island, just above Victoria Falls, in which I stood next to a sign saying, ALL WILD ANIMALS ARE DANGEROUS.

On that day two British dowagers who were walking there heard a crashing in the woods. "Those miserable Americans," one said to the other, "are terribly noisy."

Out of the island's sylvan cover walked a pair of elephants that had swum over from the mainland. We Americans, like the ladies, had come by boat.

The next meeting that I attended worthy of notice in this context was the second UNESCO conference on race, held in Moscow. The first had been chaired by Montagu. Whoever was in charge decided that another one was needed. One day in June 1964, a young man came to see me. He was the assistant director, and he invited me to attend. The meeting was to be in Moscow. We talked it over in the middle of the Essex River in my boat.

He assured me that the subject of the meeting was to be race in general, and its members would not be asked to vote on the prime question of the intellectual equality or inequality of different races. I am sure that he was sincere in this assurance. I agreed to go on that condition. On July 13 my UNESCO contract arrived, permitting both Lisa and me to go. It was to begin on the eighth of August. I set about immediately to get plane reservations, but when the time came for us to leave, our Soviet visas hadn't come, and they didn't until after the conference had started. We arrived at 4 P.M. on August 10, the third day. When the conference was over, we were sent home at once. One of the Russian delegates stood at the airport, waving us good-bye as our plane took off clumsily, like a gooney bird.

For the first two days we spoke on general subjects. Then those outside the inner circle were packed off to see the paintings and the Scythian gold in the Hermitage. I had seen them before, but Lisa hadn't, and she and two French friends were constantly being told to move on when they gazed at the Renoirs and Van Goghs. After we had been led crouching through brick dungeons, I received a special favor. The American Indian rooms at the Ethnographic Museum were opened especially for me, who, unbeknownst to them, was not an Americanist. The lady curator had done a splendid job.

When we got back to Moscow, the stay-behinds had changed the agenda. Because we had been so competent in discussing race in general, we need not put the question off until the next year, as previously planned, but must vote about who was brighter than whom at once.

At this point I arose. I said that I had been deceived. There was no one here, said I, who knew about the workings of the human brain.

(Kotchekova did, and so did Rensch from West Germany, but neither spoke up. I had been mistaken.) Then the lady interpreter had a fit. "I can't understand your English! You're not speaking English, you're speaking American!"

So I said, "Then I'll speak in French," and I did, though it was a bit rough on some of the local anthropologists who understood my American better than my French.

After a while some bigwig commissar came to address us. He stated there was no racial difference in intelligence because Anatole France had a small brain while Turgenev had a big one. Somewhere I had heard that rot before. I sat there mumbling, "Balls! Balls!" while the interpreter looked at me in perplexity. My British neighbor Barnicot, across the table, said, "Quite, and just look at the difference between the two men's work."

Darryl Ford, the editor of *Africa* and world authority on "black" cultures, did not speak. He just wet one index finger and ran it around the rims of several waterglasses filled to various levels and emitting various tones.

That evening we were all supposed to dine on shashlik and other Caucasian delicacies in a Georgian restaurant, but Gyorgi Debetz, who until then had said very little, invited Lisa and me to his apartment. He took us in a taxi to a building on the outskirts of the city, then up an elevator in a tiny open wire cage to a small two- or three-room apartment, where we were greeted by his lovely wife. In a corner of another room lived a cousin of one of them and his wife, waiting more or less indefinitely for an assignment to Arkhangelsk.

Gyorgi apologized when they served us sausages instead of shashlik, and vodka instead of wine. After he had plied me with iced spirits and downed enough himself, he set about his task of persuading me to vote that all races were of equal intelligence. I may be wrong, but I sensed that to him, his success might be the lesser of two evils.

We finally got down to the point of perhaps excluding Bushmen and Australian aborigines from this generalization, when Gyorgi said, "What does it matter, there are very few of either of them, and they may soon become extinct."

When the vote came, except for one Chilean observer who didn't have a vote, everyone else but me held up a hand, some at half-mast. When two Africans and one Hindu, both highly intelligent and friendly scientists, looked at me, I may have wiggled a finger or two involuntarily. The whole thing was getting ridiculous.

As we were walking out the Hindu said, "You are the nicest

man I have ever met." Then I remembered that some of the British had called Hindus black.

When I got home I discovered that the newspapers had included me among the signers, and the telephone began ringing: "Why the hell did you do that?"

The brainwashers called it an act of insincerity. And the man who had talked with me on the Essex River resigned.

A wonderful meeting of minds. A model for world peace.

Whether I had wanted to or not, I never signed anything. My hosts had trotted me out of the country before I had a chance.

31. The Living Races of Man

Before the meetings mentioned in the last three chapters had been held, I started work on *The Living Races,* it being volume two of my projected opus, *Races of the World,* originally financed as stated in Chapter 27. To those sponsors I still felt obliged to tell the truth impartially, although the funds had long ago run out.

In writing part of it I was helped by a fellow anthropologist teaching at Harvard, Edward E. Hunt, Jr., domiciled five miles away. He knew about teeth, palm prints, physiology, and blood, and had access to libraries in Cambridge and Boston, thus saving me much time; his brain also held an exhaustive bibliography.

The book has 320 pages of text, plus 47 of front and hind matter, and 128 plates of 183 portraits of persons of all races. The first 208 pages of text describe the peoples of the earth, their cultures, and languages, with their known histories. The anatomy and physiology take up only 112 pages. It was in this part mostly that Hunt participated. Any reader who disliked this second part could skip it and enjoy the portraits, many of which were stunning. To avoid insulting anyone, I had chosen only handsome subjects, in their normal dress, hairdos, and/or ornaments.

In the second section, global maps of temperature, relative humidity, rainfall, total annual hours of sunlight, and seasonal and spatial variations in water-vapor pressure are presented. They were drafted by Vincent Kotschar, cartographer of the American Geographical Society. We also used Matthew Luckeish's chart of amounts of solar radiation of all pertinent wavelengths reaching the earth, and their absorption by ozone, water vapor, free oxygen, and carbon dioxide.

We applied these data to the racial differences in skin color and of the production of vitamin D from ultraviolet, and its role in turning inert calcium into bone. At the time we wrote *The Living Races* much less was known of this process than is known now. It will be explained in the forthcoming terminal volume of my *Races of the World* trilogy, entitled *Racial Aptitudes.*

Each race's skin is adapted to receiving the same amount of ultraviolet, more or less, in the climate in which it evolved. Where the ultraviolet load is minimal, the skin needs little pigment to make strong bones. Where the load is maximal, the skin needs much more pigment to avoid rickets, and mothers with rickety pelvises lose their babies. Robert M. Neer, M.D., of the Massachusetts General Hospital discovered the ways this complicated sequence works.

We had done rather poorly on stature. I traced its peak in different races along the winter frost line in the Northern Hemisphere, but in the Southern there was no front line except in the Andes. I had forgotten that in 1936, in his book *Race, Sex, and Environment,* my friend Jack Marrett showed that in all races stature depends on the mineral content—from calcium to trace elements—of the soil the people's food is raised on, with, it may be added, due allowances for heat and cold adaptation, as in the short Alakalufs and the bean-pole Nilotic Negroes.

Skin color was not uniquely racial either. Both Mongoloids and Bushmen had become yellow independently, Australoids and Negroids black. Nor did it go with skulls and body skeletons necessarily. Thus the Somalis could be Caucasoid in face and build and Negroid in pigmentation, and the same combinations could be found among the cattle-herding Masai and Tutsi (Watussi). The bones of men of the same race had been found by Louis Leakey in Gamble's Cave, to which he led a few of us in 1955.

Before I began to write *The Living Races,* fair-haired Australian aboriginal children and women had been found and studied in the desert. There was no chance of European admixture. Like the tawny coats of desert mammals, it seemed to be a mutation that let the hair reflect solar heat instead of absorbing it.

Our job was not just to document racial differences, but if possible to explain them. Some seemed quite simply inherited: eyeball size largest in blacks, medium in whites, and smallest in Mongoloids; whether ear wax is gooey or crumbly—these are two examples. Reactions to the wavelengths of sunlight at different latitudes, the amounts of oxygen at different altitudes, the amount of sweating needed to facilitate body-heat loss under different degrees of water-vapor pressure, as well as differences in cold adaptation, all were taken into account.

Chapter 9, only thirteen pages long, was given to the subject of "Race, Blood, and Disease." This brevity scandalized some reviewers, who had come to think that blood groups had become the only valid criteria of race. Originally Ed Hunt had written this chapter in the length of a fair-sized book of its own. Harold Strauss had said, "Cut it, and make it comprehensible to the layman." This is what I tried to do.

The reason why it seemed simpler to me than to Hunt was

because I had considered blood-group studies the back door to racial classification. In my Moroccan series, I found absolutely no correlation between the ABO groups, which I had taken, and any metrical or morphological character. As far as I was then concerned, they had nothing to do with race. Ilse Schwidetsky, in Germany, had made the same discovery in 1962, just when I began *The Living Races*. She had covered not just Morocco, but the world.

Now William Boyd (my Harvard classmate) and G. E. Mourant in London, who had first mapped the distribution of blood groups, had decided to classify races on this basis. This work is still being done, particularly by L. L. Cavalli-Sforza, who uses the most refined mathematical techniques of genetic analysis.

These men were and are right, in a sense. The blood groups furnish an alternative way of classifying races, geographically correlated, to a certain extent, with those classified by the totality of other evidence. They are useful in establishing paternity. They are much more useful in the role in terms of which they were first discovered—saving lives through blood transfusions. It was no accident that Drs. Boyd and Mourant were hematologists and immunologists.

But blood groups have a special function—to protect the body from intrusions of foreign matter, particularly organisms that produce specific diseases. Two alleles of the first-discovered and best-known system, ABO, inhibit different diseases. A blocks smallpox, and B plague. OO is geographically associated with the absence of these two people killers, as among most of the American Indians when first discovered. Our righteous ancestors reduced some of the native tribes of the Americas more by contagion than with rum or rifles. In a seminal article in the *American Anthropologist* in 1975, K. L. Beals and A. J. Kelso clearly showed by a pair of maps that the fancy blood groups, including ABO, run by levels of political complexity that reflect degrees of crowding and of urban insanitation. The cleanest "savages" have the least protection, possibly because in their native state they move camp before their filth can catch up with them. In France, where ABO groups have been studied for several generations, O has risen in modern, sanitized communities.

But I wander from the text, to return to a subject to which I am understandably allergic: racial differences in intelligence. Having been put through that wringer by brainwashers, what I wanted to do least in *The Living Races* was to write about it. Cowardice did not stop me, nor Ed Hunt's egalitarian disposition, but sheer fatigue, combined with the conviction that if I wrote about it at all, few readers would even glance at the rest of the book.

So, like an idiot, I had written in the introduction,

Racial differences imply differences in intelligence, a subject so laden with emotion that its mere mention evokes unsolicited acclaim and feverish denunciation. Even without reference to the brain or to intelligence, the simple statement that races exist drives a small coterie of vocal critics into a predictable and well-publicized frenzy.

I hope but do not expect that all reviewers will read the whole book and not just this introduction. . . . I also formally request that no one shall quote this book as ammunition for or against any cause whatsoever. . . .

That plea boomeranged. Some took it as an evasion of responsibility, others as a whitewash for complicity in a crime of their own invention. The former explanation was probably closer to the truth. I promised myself to complete the trilogy, should I survive, with a short book on the brain and behavior. In the early 1960s I didn't have the data. I hope that it will be published soon after the book you are reading is available.

Chapter 10, the penultimate, may have attracted more than its share of readers because it dealt with the local, domestic scene. Its title is "The Racial History of Man Since 1942." On page 302 we wrote:

In the census of 1790, [our first] . . . in Massachusetts, one of the most solidly English states, names are listed that still appear in the telephone books of the same communities. There were then 989 families of Smiths, 340 of Whites, 187 of Adamses. The Putnams numbered 80, the Eliots, variously spelled, 62, the Emersons 58. Among the top Boston Brahmin families of later periods, only 27 Forbeses, 16 Lowells, 9 Cabots, and one Saltonstall appear. The Gaelic contingent included 150 names beginning with Mc, 60 Kelleys, 8 Murphys, 6 O'Briens, and 3 Sullivans.

So the Kelleys outnumbered all the proto-Brahmins lumped together. In the current telephone books, the Kellys still win.

A few statistics follow about the American Negroes.

[They] are taller than the West Africans by two or three inches and American Negro males are slightly shorter than white Americans, whereas Negro women are taller than white women. Among American Negroes, heads are longer and broader than among Africans. In comparison with the Africans, the American Negroes have longer and broader faces and longer and broader noses. Many of the American Negroes are lighter skinned.

Two estimates of the proportions of white genes in the total Negro population give a figure of about 30 percent. A third that is later and uses more genetic markers than the others seems the likelier. It is about 20 percent.

In the latest available at our time of writing, dated at 1963, P. L. Workman, limiting his studies to the Negroes of Evans and Bullock Counties, Georgia, a particularly concentrated Negro area, and using fifteen genetic polymorphisms, found the European component there to be only 10.4 percent.

Mrs. Caroline Bond Day, who was working in the physical anthropology laboratory at Harvard while I was a graduate student and young instructor, made an elaborate study of 346 Negro-White families by combining genealogical and anthropological data, including family portraits, and covering prominent families like her own and those of Walter White and W. E. B. Du Bois. Some were the results of very old mixtures, and measured their racial components in thirty-seconds; and some of these included Indian ancestors, who did not show up in the blood groups taken later on similar persons, perhaps because the Indians were probably all of group O.

Doris Zemurray, later to become Mrs. Stone, and a professional Maya archaeologist, used to hang around the bone lab, keeping Mrs. Day company. I spent as much time as I could there, too, as Hooton's surrogate, helping Mrs. Day, who received my suggestions most gratefully.

Chapter 11, the last, is entitled "The Future of the Races of Man," and subtitled, "Every Man a Genius and the Centaur's Return." It is half joke, half fantasy. In it I toyed with some of the ideas expressed at the CIBA conference of 1962 by J. B. S. Haldane, Joshua Lederberg, Gregory Pincus, and others, about slicing chromosomes with nana-knives (microscopic scalpels) to make transgeneric hybrids to serve as seal-human frogmen, building sperm banks that Hermann Muller had begun and William Shockley has revived; my own idea was to re-create black and white centaurs who could play polo with each other forever, thus stalemating interracial troubles. Needless to say, the reception of this idea was largely unfavorable, if any, but that did not bother me because I was tired of race and did not write about it again for another decade.

On November 18, 1965, at the height of the Christmas shopping season, *The New York Times Book Review* section printed a full-page notice of *The Living Races of Man*. Beneath a photograph of its jacket it read in boldface: "This is the most controversial report on *Homo sapiens* since

Darwin came on the scene. It concerns that touchy, explosive, confused subject—RACE."

In smaller type: "In this remarkable book Dr. Carleton S. Coon . . . reaches some startling conclusions that pull all the myth-balanced props out from under the racists."

When I read that, I said to myself: "My word, I have fallen between two stools."

But there was a third. The editor of *The New York Review of Books* soon ran a triple-header review of three books: mine, a reprint of an 1810 tract on race, and the third edition of Ashley Montagu's *Man's Most Dangerous Myth, The Fallacy of Race,* in paperback. After a lengthy mass of persiflage the reviewer wrote, "I judge Professor Coon's volume to be a total waste of time."

The reviewer was Professor, now Sir, Edmund Leach, head of the Cambridge, England, school of social anthropology.

Among his gems he wrote, "It is to Professor Coon's discredit that he should seem to support his purported scientific classification with 128 [wrong, 183] photographs in which the *Caucasians* are posed in shirt-sleeves and 'civilized' haircuts, whereas most of his other categories appear as bare-arsed savages."

Tut tut, my noble knight. I had only two "bare-arsed" photographs, both to illustrate steatopygia, Greek for fat buttocks. Not all the "Caucasians" had modern haircuts. In very few of them were shirt-sleeves showing.

What would Professor Leach have had me do? Take along with me a barber and a wardrobe assistant? How could I have persuaded my "savages" (his pejorative term) to be shaved and shorn and then dressed up before being photographed—in the case of the steatopygious Hottentot woman, probably after having been exhumed? Or should I have taken pictures of all the "Caucasians" bare-arsed, and had the book banned or boosted as pornography?

Meanwhile in Paris, Professor Henri V. Vallois, keeper of Jebel Ighud Numbers 1 and 2, devoted three pages of *L'Anthropologie* to his own review of my new book. He outlined it in detail and excused me for not having taken the brain into consideration because (my translation), "it was the desire to avoid interpretations that could interpose an emotional [passionel] element. All the [physical] anthropologists consulted have, in other respects, been unanimous in praising M. Coon's book and to felicitate its author for having thus presented the study of the real human races in a tableau so documented and full of new ideas. To these eulogies I associate myself without hesitation."

But he had one qualification. He didn't think that language was as great a barrier to gene flow as I had made out, especially in the earliest periods. I agree, especially when the population involved had not yet learned to speak, or when soldiers landing on a foreign shore arrange gene flow by other signals, as I had seen in Casablanca in 1942.

In 1968, C. Maxmillian wrote a review of the book in Rumanian, in a government-sponsored publication. After a systematic review of its contents, the review ends: *"Cartea lui Coon constitute fără îndioală un moment important in istoria raseologei moderne."* I think I know what he meant.

Moving polarly, in a spiritual sense, from the iron to the kosher curtain, I find in my file a brief review in the *Jewish Chronicle.*

> *Carleton S. Coon gives a fascinating survey of biological and anthropological studies. A section on "The Rise and Fall of Elites" examines the outstanding Jewish contribution. This quotes the theory that "Jews bearing priestly names exceed the others in excellence of achievement. . . ." It has long been a practice to marry bright young men destined for the rabbinate to rich merchants' daughters and to encourage them to have large families.*

In *The Pretoria News* (South Africa), another favorable review is given. Most of it is about South Africa.

> *On the lighter side he mentions the possibility of changing skin colour by simple injections. One of his conclusions is startling: "Once the chromosome-slicing geneticists have been allowed to perform their magic, racial differences can be made to disappear." Of the Rehebother Basters of South West Africa, the author says: "Some of the Rehebothers could pass for Boers and vice versa, and a few of the Rehebothers are indistinguishable from the Hottentots." This statement appears to be rather bold and read without the background history could revoke racial feelings. It is in passages like this that the author's warning in the foreword must be heeded.* —D.M.

Most of the reviews cited above, and also those left out for lack of space, were written by outsiders. I had not yet run the gauntlet of my peers until the *CA* (star) Treatment, paid for by the Wenner-Gren Foundation, appeared in *Current Anthropology,* Vol. 8, No. 1–2, Feb.–April 1967.

"After agreement with Dr. Coon and the publisher, 50 Associates were invited to participate. The first 20 who agreed to the terms were sent the author's precis and copies of the book. . . . Thirteen responded in time. . . ."

I found that most of the reviewers reviewed only or mainly the portions of the book that fitted their own specialties. This made me quite vulnerable in many cases. Professor A. A. Abbie, chief anatomist at the University of Adelaide, denied almost everything I had written about his country's aborigines. N. A. Barnicot of London, who had been with us in Moscow at the UNESCO meeting, took almost six columns to dissect what I had written in Chapters 8 and 9, "Racial Differences in Adaptive Characters" and "Race, Blood, and Disease." J. Lawrence Angel clearly but politely criticized some of my anatomical differences, for he had dissected cadavers and I had not. He ends: "This book is incredibly condensed. It provides a needed background for critical graduate students and some social anthropologists. I shall find out soon if undergraduates appreciate it too."

Tadeucs Bielicki of Wroslaw, Poland, wrote: "*The Origin of Races* had already become (in Poland at any rate), one of the Anthropologists' Bibles. . . . This is a fascinating book, rich in ideas and full of the well-known charm of Carleton Coon's prose: verve and lucidity, erudition and imagination. Since, however, picking holes is (in politics and science, at any rate) a more fruitful activity than praising, I shall not elaborate on the book's virtues, which are many and evident, but shall concentrate on the few points which to me seem its weaknesses."

After this introduction in his second language, in which he rivaled Joseph Conrad and Bronislaw Malinowski, Bielicki dissected some of my boo-boos, particularly about Poland. Never have I been operated on by so skillful a surgeon, nor recovered so quickly and amiably.

Next on the alphabetic list was Dr. Alice M. Brues of Boulder, Colorado, a Radcliffe-Harvard Ph.D.

It requires a degree of courage to write a book on Races of Man in this era of the New Prudery, when r-ce has replaced s-x as the great dirty word. Some of the criticisms which the work will receive will reflect an adrenergic reflex to the title itself. And paradoxically, criticism will be more severe because there is nothing else like it in print and people will have to refer to it whether they agree with it or not. . . . just as our Victorian forebears did not entirely succeed in sweeping sex under the rug, so we cannot conceal forever the fact that people in different parts of the world do not look alike. Better to learn it in school than from vulgar companions around the corner!

A refreshing feature is the photographic section, which shows 130-odd individuals, enough to include not only "type" specimens of major races but a good range of variation within races. In contrast to anthropological illustrations of the older tradition, in which the subjects were too often shown in poses painfully reminiscent of the official record of a convicted felon, Coon's pictures show pleasant, interesting human beings, their dignity preserved by showing them in natural pose and expression, and clothes, if such is their usual custom. [Tut tut again, Dr. Leach!] It may be the ambition of some ultimately to feed the genes directly into a computer without the untidy intervention of the living, breathing, sometimes obstreperous phenotype. If so, it is time to reintroduce human beings as a subject matter for physical anthropology. Coon with his awareness of people and their environments and histories, is doing this.

Next came Cyril Darlington. He did not whitewash my deficiencies, including my failure to grapple with "the genetics of the origins and behaviour of stratified societies." It is not

because he doesn't know about them. . . . There are plenty of enthusiastic philosophers (or sociologists) who will take all this in their stride, but Coon is not one of them. . . . It may be argued that we should no longer speak of race at all, since the term is misused by ignorant and dangerous people. . . . Race . . . is part of the imperfect but impartial language of common sense. We therefore owe an additional debt to Coon for having taken steps to rehabilitate this forbidden word.

I will end this random (because it is alphabetical) sample of opinions with one from Gyorgi Debetz, who wrote:

The mistakes in Coon's book are few and insignificant. [These were all about data from the USSR, of which I had too little information, and one about the Kafirs of Nuristan, which I never succeeded in visiting.] The book, which summarizes an enormous amount of knowledge, presents an extremely important point of view on the role of the geographic environment. For Coon, race is not a paratype; in his point of view genetics is perfectly respected, but it is the modern genetics which, instead of rejecting the influence of the environment, regards it as an agent of selection.

Most of the seven others were favorable, some more than others. Hunt, oddly enough, joined one of the critics whose surnames began with M in objecting to something in a section of which he was coauthor. At the last minute Harold Strauss had changed the editors' status on the masthead from "Coon and Hunt" to "Coon *with* Hunt."

But he showed no signs of resentment when he and I were interviewed on a Boston radio station. It was a telephone-in-and-get-an-answer show, requiring quicker reflexes than a television interview, particularly when we couldn't see the questioners nor they us.

One question came from a colored man asking how he could disguise his voice in answering a job-opportunity advertisement in a

All of us Coons except myself, who took the picture, in front of a quince tree in front of my study in West Gloucester. Back row, standing, L to R, Howard, Katherine, William. Front row seated: Carl Jr. holding Ellen, Janet holding Richard, and Charles holding Elizabeth. The date is probably 1965–1967.

newspaper. Hunt replied that the speaker had a fine voice, so why change it?

Then a probably white man asked me, speaking as if between gritted teeth: "Have you read the Book of Genesis?"

"Yes, I answered, "in English, Greek, Arabic, and several other languages."

"Then how do you reconcile creation with evolution?"

"I don't."

Someone pulled the plug. I could have reconciled the two quite easily had I wanted to, but why bother, with a man like that?

Then I heard a syrupy voice that I recognized as a second-string false one used for concealment rather than pomposity. I had heard it just once before, with its utterer in view. I forget what he asked me, but I said: "Shut up!"—whether or not he did I'll never know, for the plug was pulled again.

While the aftermath of *The Living Races* was still in progress, my mother died, on the Fourth of July in 1964, at the age of eighty-four. The telephone rang at four in the morning, but I was waiting for it, and got to her house in Wakefield in twenty minutes.

As we were all attending the graveyard ceremony in the Coon family plot, the undertaker came up to me and whispered, "Do you realize that there is room for only two more bodies in this lot?"

My answer was, "Never mind, you can bury the rest of us standing up."

When my brother Maurice died in February 1980 we didn't need to. His handsome body had been cremated. In a sense, he lived and left the Earth in the Bronze Age.

32. The Forest and the Desert

One day in late October 1965, Edward Wharton-Tigar, my covert British associate in Tangier during the war, happened to be in New York. He walked into the Metropolitan Museum, not so much to admire the art as to examine the museum's collection of cigarette cards, for he owned one of the largest private collections in the world. As he was rounding a corner near the entrance he faced a showcase containing old Syrian glassware. Its label read: Gift of Mrs. Carleton S. Coon.

To Edward this meant that I was dead. So he called Gordon Browne at Woods Hole, Massachusetts, who told him that I was not only alive but as ornery as ever. Then Edward called me, to offer Lisa and myself a trip to Sierra Leone to look for fossil man. He could do this because he was director of Selection Trust, Ltd., a global mining company. They owned a diamond mine at Yengema, near which was a cave with a dirt floor.

So we visited him in London, flew to Freetown and—by a small, chartered plane—to Yengema, where we were placed in an air-conditioned guest house and given the use of a Volkswagen. Across the golf course from our lodge stood a row of tall, gray granite slabs, some nearly one hundred feet high. Some stood erect; others leaned upon each other like giant petrified revelers returning from a ball.

The cave itself is a deeply shaded enclosure of about 250 square meters (2,325 square feet), roofed by a giant slab lying at an angle of about 12 degrees from the floor. To the north the roof sloped to the floor, while on the south it was held up by various pieces of granite shattered in a fall. On the east it was partly closed by another slab. Its flat top had been followed by people pounding seeds in the forgotten past.

No one used this immovable bowl now, because the cave was considered holy, or magical. Noises had been heard coming from it. Because it stood on the highest piece of land thereabouts, these noises could be heard far away.

As we found out later, it was uninhabited for another reason. Each year during the rains, water flooded it from a crevice to the northeast, and it was damp the year round, with high water-vapor pressure, and too cold for the people who lived in their leaf-covered houses in the village nearby.

Within the limited area where I could stand erect without bumping my head, we probed with a miner's test rod to find where the deposit was deepest. Then we laid out an exploratory trench, followed by another one beside it. The total area covered was 40 square feet (6.4 square meters) and the maximum depth 75 inches (1.95 meters). We had trouble locating the bottom because the company's sounding rods wouldn't go deep enough, so we called it quits when we ran into a continuous floor of rotted granite—simply coarser soil than that above it. This rotted granite was what remained of earlier slabs that had fallen before the finer soil higher up.

We wondered how that soil had gotten there. Blown in? Washed in? No. A visiting geologist who shared the lodge with us examined it. It was rotten granite too, only finer than that beneath it. Where could it have come from? How could it be finer if it was younger?

The chief of exploration pointed to a crack in the roof above that I had not seen for fear of banging my head. That crack was widening imperceptibly. Someday the slab would split, crashing its half a million tons or so onto the floor. That was where the soil had come from.

From the floor surface to the rotted slabs the soil was the same, except that the top 10 to 20 centimeters was black, as is common with Neolithic soil because of the countless fires that burned on it. Between 40 and 60 centimeters down, roots from living vegetation had thrust themselves, pushing some of the mineral objects we were seeking out of place. At a depth of 170 to 175 centimeters several tubular concretions of a lateritic material were unearthed. These tubes had apparently once surrounded small tree roots, indicating a former floor level during climatic conditions comparable to the present one.

The soil was damp and sticky, almost like paste, and impossible to screen. It was also hard for me to keep to 20-centimeter levels, but we managed it.

The earth was bucketed out, and picked over on the western slope, but few pieces were found in it because it had been carefully excavated. Our crew loosened it, with my geological pick in the hand of one particularly good workman, and with cheaper substitutes that I had bought at a Syrian shop in town.

They handled everything so delicately that not a single piece was broken, including 984 stone implements, 281 potsherds, and several thousand pieces of scrap, which were picked over carefully by someone or other from the company. They wanted to make sure that none of the quartz was diamonds. None of it was.

The first workman sent to me initiated our relationship with this declaration: "You good massa, me good boy. You bad massa, me bad boy."

He was a good "boy," and so were all the rest. They came from different tribes and had to speak to each other in English, with various degrees of competence. Thus I understood nearly everything that was said.

Unlike my other crews, from Morocco to Afghanistan, they did not work at a steady pace, or silently, but furiously for an hour or two, during which times they sweated profusely, and then moved out together to warm their bodies in the sunshine. They thought the cave was too cold. To me in thin cotton shirt and shorts, its heat load was barely tolerable. Outside, I almost collapsed.

And while they were working they talked constantly, often telling jokes. One tiny man who was a Pygmy, whether he was supposed to have been or not, kept everyone laughing by his wonderful imitations of animal and bird calls, rolling his eyes, and dancing as he walked. Here was my grandfather's Pygmy, sixty years after I had seen him first. This was only logical, because Pygmies had preceded full-sized Negroes in the forest, as we knew from historical records. But once the small man was a little impish, when he made fun of the workman with my geological pick.

"Whazzamatta?" I asked.

"Toofums," the pick man said, showing his teeth. Two of his upper incisors had broken edges. This incident was soon over, and it was the only disharmonic moment in our dig.

But the overseer who sat on a canvas chair in modern city clothes was less useful than the men in the trench. In fact, he was absent much of the time, with headaches and other ailments. Before we left he asked for my address, and gave me his. He wanted to write me, he said, to remind me to send him whiskey and cigarettes. He had been educated in the Catholic mission, half a mile down the road.

Archaeologically the expedition was a success, thanks to both the Selection Trust, Ltd., and to the University Museum of the University of Pennsylvania, who cosponsored it and paid for some of the expenses.

Paleontologically, it was a total failure. Not one scrap of bone—of man, beast, bird, or fish—was found.

Mrs. Kenneth Aplin, the wife of the head of the exploration department, also taught at the mine's school. In order to teach anatomy, she had buried a dead dog to clean its bones. After a year in the earth, not a single bone remained. The forest's soil is very acid. That is why we know almost nothing about the origin of the Negroes of West Africa.

As for the archaeological sequence, all the information needed is in my detailed report, published in 1968.* It is also summarized in a review in *The American Anthropologist,* by Patrick Munson.†

We found three overlapping industries. The earliest consisted mostly of quartz, a difficult stone to fashion, which were small choppers, chopping tools, and also small chisels, which could have been used in making bone harpoon points. The latter had been found all the way from Ishango on the eastern border of the Congo (now Zaire), on the ancient lake shores and riverbanks all the way from East Africa up the Nile into Egypt, and along the southern shore of the huge predecessor of Lake Chad, to the shores of the Senegal and its southern tributaries.

Who were these watermen who killed crocodiles and hippopotamuses with harpoons? When did they live?

Working west of Lake Rudolf in 1965, the late Professor Bryan Patterson found at Kangatotha, among other human specimens yet to be described, a fragment of . . . human mandible bearing three molar teeth. Its C-14 date is 2825 B.C. The mandible is stout, heavily mineralized, and closely similar to others from Ishango on the west shore of Lake Rudolf found by de Heinzelin earlier. The three teeth are large and also similar to those from Ishango. Cranial and postcranial [the rest of the body] bones of the Ishango people show them to have been Negroes, and the jaws and teeth fit the same classification. The individual from Kangatotha was also indubitably a Negro. ‡

This tenuous evidence suggests but does not prove that Negroes may have chipped these tools, but it does not make whoever

---

*Yengema Cave Report, *Museum Monographs, The University Museum, 1968, by Carleton S. Coon, in collaboration with Harvey M. Bricker, Frederick Johnson, and C. C. Lamberg-Karlovsky.*

†*Vol. 72, No. 1, Feb. 1970, pp. 174–5.*

‡*C. S. Coon, "A Fossilized Mandibular Fragment from Kangatotha, Kenya, East Africa,"* American Journal of Physical Anthropology, *Vol. 34, No. 2, March 1971, pp. 157–163. The quotation given is the abstract of that article.*

chipped them very ancient there. Soon afterward another kind of tool material, dolerite, was introduced, mostly in the form of tiny replicas of hand axes or picks, and cleavers weighing about three and a half ounces, compared to about twenty ounces for a full-sized hand axe.* Both quartz and dolerite persisted into the black Neolithic layer, which contained polished stone axes and pottery.

The dolerite industry was similar to one from a site in northern Angola, with a carbon-14 date of 9234 ± 490 B.C. This site, Mugo, was on the southern edge of the tropical rain forest, Yengema on its northeastern border.

The Neolithic was dated in the geochronological laboratory of the University Museum in Philadelphia via its pottery. The method was thermoluminescence, new at the time but much used now, particularly to detect fakes in museum collections. The dates given us were between 1500 ± 350 B.C. and 2200 ± 470 B.C., not a long span, but one before the Iron Age had begun in that region.

After returning home, I worked out another means of dating, by the thickness of the spongy crust on the dolerite, both Neolithic and earlier. Dolerite contains iron, and iron rusts out in cakes. The crust on the dolerite polished axes was about ½ millimeter thick. As this crust was hard and gray, and it took about 1,750 years to accumulate, the spongy orange crust on the other and older dolerite pieces might be allowed at least ½ milimeter per 1,000 years to grow, and that would put the crustiest piece back to somewhere between 11,000 and 7,500 B.C., in line with Mugo.

It was also in line with Ishango dates from the Nile Valley and the shores of the former south Saharan lakes, "6,000 B.C. and perhaps earlier."† It lasted in Yengema until the floor of Yengema Cave was first flooded with water. That is how things go in Africa. Old industries never die, they just get pushed aside until they disappear.

From Freetown we flew to Accra in Ghana, where we visited another diamond mine and rode around the countryside, just seeing people and more people, visiting the university, and also seeking caves. On one such search up a steep mountain trail we came upon a clandestine al fresco bead factory. The people there were melting glass bottles, supposed to be used over again, and casting the molten fluid

---

*The exact weight of one I collected on the Libyan Desert.
†J. D. Clark, The Prehistory of Africa, Prager, New York & London, 1970, pp. 171–3.

into clay forms with sticks inside to make the holes. This was a delicate operation which required much skill.

The man in charge was tall and well-formed, with normal hands and feet, but one thing was peculiar about him. His facial features were almost identical to those of a plaster reconstruction I had made in the University Museum casting room of the Broken Hill skull. I photographed him but, having left my calipers behind, I could not measure his head. I still have the pictures, and a copy of my reconstruction. They still look much alike.

We moved on to Nigeria, to Jos in the cool highlands, a favorite British retreat from the hot and humid coast. There we saw a wonderful zoo, and a museum with archaeological exhibits. We also saw a naked man with green leaves around his loins and red berries in his hair. He was walking through the streets and market among robed Muslims and others in white men's clothes, and no one seemed to notice him. My Hausa driver said, "He is a heathen man. His village is so-and-so miles to the east."

During the night the temperature had fallen almost to freezing, but the air was dry, and that black man had been walking naked in a temperature close to 50° F. Yet the equally black men in Yengema cave couldn't take 75° F, for there the air was wet.

The next morning our driver took us to the village where the man lived. He was not there. Eight women were, all clad as the man in the market had been, except one, who was young and pretty. She wore a calabash on her head. They posed for their photographs as if they were models. When we were through the calabash woman asked for money.

While I had it in my hand, and she was stretching hers out, a new man appeared on a bicycle. He was wearing a red shirt and green shorts.

He took the money, saying angrily, "This is Friday. Why didn't you come on Sunday, when I am not at work?"

From Jos we went north to Kano, the capital of the powerful Hausa people, good Muslims in the Moroccan style. The city looked Moroccan, with a square minaret on its mosque. Our driver and interpreter were Ibos, Christians from the south. They were unpopular with the Hausas not only because of their religion, but because they were too smart. After we had left, the Hausas slaughtered many Ibos in the airport, where they were trying to get passage to their home in Biafra on the coast.

It was rumored in the city that the emir was about to emerge from his palace. The square in front of the royal enclosure was lined with people waiting for a glimpse of their ruler. The tension was relieved however, by a woman dressed in rags, who moved around in a lumbering fashion, rolled her eyes, waving her arms about, and shouted false announcements. "He is coming now! Watch out!" He didn't come, and she kept on shouting I knew not what until everyone else was laughing. She was a clown. A clown's job is to provide distraction, and she did it well.

Then we went to the tanner's pits, where men of several tribes were trampling skins together in pools of dyes. Some of the skins were cowhide, others sheep or goat, while the prize ones were python skins, one of which would fit a pit. It was just like the tanner's section in Fez or Marrakesh, except for the men's languages. Some spoke English, others French, and they asked me to interpret for them.

Once I had to change a roll of film. With both hands busy, I was surrounded by small boys, shouting and hanging sticks on tin plates. My driver chased them away reluctantly, saying, "They just wanted you to see them, sir."

And isn't that what a lot of people are doing today?

We arrived home from Nigeria on December 20, 1965, and were off again for Africa on December 6, 1966. Ths trip was a double-header, half UNESCO and half National Geographic; or, country-wise, half Chad and half Libya.

The UNESCO conference was held at Fort Lamy. Froelich Rainey had been invited to represent the University Museum, but he sent Lisa and me in his place. This gave me a chance to read a paper on the Yengema dig and to hear what others—British, French, and African—had to say about their own work in my new field, Saharan and sub-Saharan archaeology.

The conference was run by M. Leboef, who was in charge of antiquities in the new nation of Chad, with the help of Colonel Chapelle. They were both old-timers in the country, and had both become Chadian citizens. Everything ran smoothly. We attended an official banquet in which big women set whole roast sheep upon the tables, and a reception to which Bokassa, the president of the Central African Republic, marched. A small man, he wore what seemed to be a crown, and carried what seemed to be a scepter. He was flanked by a corps of burly bodyguards. He later made himself emperor, and is now in hiding, presumably in Libya.

It was a good conference. We met many fine people, including the distinguished biologist André T. Monod, who explored the desert on camelback, and amused us with his jokes.

In order to view the countryside, the people, their houses, and their ways of living, I begged three days off. In a rented car with a driver, we rode down the east side of the Chari River to Bongor, where a ferry was supposed to take us over to Cameroon. But we had to wait. An overloaded truck was stuck on the earthen ramp. It was one of a convoy smuggling arms from somewhere to somewhere else in an easterly direction. The white smugglers were frantic.

While they were dashing around madly, the ferry pilot ran his craft onto a beach upstream of the ramp and loaded us aboard. We left the other smugglers on the west bank, and when we returned two days later, the trucks were still there. Meanwhile, we had visited a game preserve, stopped at many villages, and seen people working, resting, bathing, herding cattle, and selling cotton at a fair. In the villages all the houses were alike, and also the granaries. Everything was tidy, and no one was quarreling with anyone else.

We got back to Fort Lamy just in time for another pleasant surprise. Colonel Chapelle told us that we were to fly to the Tibesti Mountains to see rock engravings. We were up at 3:30 A.M. and at the airport in time to take off at 5:00. We went aboard a World War II parachute plane, a DC-3, on several of which I had flown under different circumstances.

Many of the delegates had gone home, but still the plane was packed. Many of us were shooting 35-mm film out the windows, except one in the middle on the right side, where the view was best. That was occupied by the Nigerian delegate, who had covered his head with a scarf, rested it against the window, and gone to sleep.

We passed the eastern shoreline of Lake Chad, and followed a dry wadi bed northeastward to Largeau, a town in an oasis inhabited mainly by the Tebu and their former slaves. There we stopped for lunch, visited the market, and slid on the seats of our pants down a sand dune.

The Tebu are nomads, graded into nobles, agricultural serfs, and slaves. The nomads erect frames of sticks in the shape of oblong domes, and cover them with mats, which they transport, leaving the frames for other visits. The market was very colorful, and its people photogenic. They believe that their ancestors were the original inhabitants of the Tibesti Mountains, with their base at Bardai, to which we flew on, arriving early in the afternoon.

There we found the tricolor still flying, and a French lieutenant, who was black, awaiting us. He led us to his house, where the rest of the educated, non-native population awaited us. It was only natural that such a visit, or visitation, should cause excitement. These people had lived together like sailors in a forecastle in a windjammer rounding Cape Horn. Any company was welcome, especially a delegation from UNESCO.

Whiskey and wine flowed like water while we waited for an elaborate North African-style meal to be cooked. Everyone was chattering as if at a cocktail party, and making friends with everyone else. Lisa, however, held a sober conversation with a young schoolteacher, who asked her in the beginning, "What country are you from, madame?"

"I am from America."

"But madame, that is impossible. All the Americans are black."

Before this party had subsided, someone reminded our host that we wished to see some of the nearby rock engravings. "Oh yes," he said. So we piled into two vehicles awaiting us, just as the sun was reddening in the West. After passing through numerous date-palm groves we reached a rock wall shielded by an overhang. On the wall we dimly saw processions of people and animals—and no one had brought flash equipment. Or if someone had, I didn't see the flash.

The next morning we were up again before dawn and off in two trucks along a stony mountain road. This led us to a cliff of Paleozoic sandstone, many blocks of which had split off and fallen to the ground.

On the sandstone were depicted elephants and giraffes, both solo and in herds, as well as solitary rhinoceroses, one warthog, and numerous species of antelopes. The fauna was entirely Ethiopian, with none of the Palearctic species that had come in at the end of the Pleistocene.

It was the same fauna that still exists in East and South Africa, where they still have grass and trees on which to graze and browse. The engraving had been done with stone tools in firm, well-executed grooves, almost at right angles to the surface on their outer edges, and beveled on the inside, giving a feeling of bas-relief.

Whoever did this work was a gifted artist, or several of them. The elephants seemed to have exaggeratedly long legs and trunks; the giraffes, long legs and necks. Yet the anatomy was perfectly rendered, and the rhinos and the warthog were not exaggerated.

I wondered about these legs and necks until the next time I saw Louis Leakey, and he told me, "We have found bones of elephants and giraffes like them in our digs. They were adapted to a drier climate than we have today."

With his knowledge to back me, I feel certain that the one human figure at Enneri Gonoa, which I photographed several times to get the sunlight right, was equally correct. I have shown a black-and-white illustration of it here.*

Its simplicity and its action make it an exquisite work of art. I gazed at it as long as I could without missing the rest of the prehistoric show in this marvelous gallery.

The figure was over life-size. By its style we knew that it must have been carved at the same time as the elephants and giraffes. These animals had lived during a period of moderate rainfall, in savanna country. Such a period had been recognized as having existed during the fourth millennium B.C.†

The figure is called the Masked Hunter because its only body covering is what seems to be a mask over its head and face. In its right hand it holds an elongated object, which could be a club or a spear thrower (the former more likely, because there is no spear). One side of the outline of the weapon cuts through and overlaps the mask's outline. This is the only part of the figure where such an apparent error was committed. Did the same artist—or a different one—carve the "weapon" afterward? Or was this a see-through job; something magical? If the subject was a hunter, what animal did the mask try to fool? No animal in that art gallery had a head and face like that. Was the object in the figure's right hand really a weapon, a noose, or a wand?

To hunters, it is good to engrave replicas of animals, but why the hunter himself? For fertility? Definitely not. For initiation? Getting warmer. Could the mask be a disguise to keep the boys from recognizing their initiator? Zeroing in. And the object in his hand? Perhaps a bull roarer, to emit a loud, strident, and mysterious sound. And what was he holding against the mask's mouth in his left hand? A call such as the Ainu in Hokkaido make to call mother deer to their thirsty fawns? Or some kind of a voice disguiser to conceal the initiator's identity? We shall never know unless time rewinds itself and puts on a repeat performance.

E. Klitsch and A. Pesce, "Remarks about prehistoric sites in Southern Libya and Tibesti." In J. J. Williams, ed., South-Central Libya and Northern Chad, *Petroleum Exploration Society of Libya. Drukkerij Holland N.U., Amsterdam, 1966, pp. 69–74. See also H. Ziegert,* Climatic Changes and Palaeolithic Industries in Eastern Fezzan, Libya, *Ibid., pp. 65–68. For "Masked Hunter" see p. 74.*
†*Calculated geologically by Ziegert, op. cit., p. 65.*

Both the infantile position of the penis at rest and the proportions between the upper and lower parts of the limb—with long muscle bellies in proportion to tendons—are Bushman, not Negro, racial attributes. This rock engraving, with many other kinds of evidence, attests the presence of full-sized Bushman ancestors in the Sahara before they later became dessicated, and some of them moved southward to southern Africa.

Leaving these speculations, let us try to identify the hunter's race. His thighs are relatively longer than a Negro's in proportion to his lower legs, even if we compare him to a Nilotic, like a Dinka or Shilluk. His limb muscles are less bunchy, and their tendons shorter. Though not erect, his penis points slightly upward and forward. This is a modern Bushman trait.

I am glad the artist masked his subject's face, to let us think about what he was doing, but I also regret this censorship. But how could the artist have foreseen the importance of race in the twentieth-century in the USA?

Interspersed among the elegant animal engravings were many of Phase II, the Cattle Period, obviously drawn later, when the mountains were still covered with enough vegetation to feed the herds. They were longhorns, but also humpless, and with variegated coats. While the outlines were still carved, although in a less painstaking manner, the details of their bodies were simply pecked by hammering the walls with stones. The people looked like children's doodles, or figures made of sticks. Instead of being single, the cattle and the people were shown in groups. One might distinguish breeds of cattle, but not of men. Cattle equals wealth, and wealth outshadows groups of people. That's one way of looking at it. Or might it be more dangerous to make fun of cattle than of men?

Group III, the most recent, were Tuareg boundary marks resembling our western ranch brands. Two of them, for example, mean crow and bastard crow.

Crow   Bastard Crow

Exhiliarated by this sojourn in the mountains, we awaited with keen anticipation the second leg of our trip, to Libya. On the evening of our return to Fort Lamy we dined with Mr. and Mrs. Brewster Morris, our ambassador and his wife. They had been very kind to us throughout our stay in Chad. Mr. Morris had arranged, through our military attaché, to have us flown to Tripoli on a giant USAF transport plane, which would have otherwise gone empty.

But our flight orders came too late, and we had to take the next commercial plane to Paris and then down to Tripoli, where we were met at the airport by Bill Gresham, our USIS chief, and by Dr. and Mrs.

Ayub, the deputy director of antiquities for the desert and his charming Egyptian wife. This was their second trip to the airport to meet us and all were a little tired.

The Ayubs had previously visited Philadelphia, where the doctor had made some sort of an agreement with Froelich Rainey and then a University Museum chauffeur had driven them to our house in Gloucester. We fed them an Arab dinner, including shish kebabs, which I broiled on a grill overlooking the marsh and river. When I greased the grill with lamb fat the Ayoubs looked alarmed. "Are you sure," the doctor asked, "that isn't pork?"

We planned our trip in some detail and with much enthusiasm. Dr. Ayoub was enchanted with the Garamantes, a fair-skinned, blond people who drove chariots on the desert. They had been the ancestors of the ancient Egyptians, and of his own people, the Nubians, who now were black.

I told him that besides viewing these charioteers, whose pictures had been painted on the walls of cliffs and caves, I wanted to excavate a cave or two to look for fossil man. I also wanted to visit the Duwwuds, a relict people who harvested *Artemesia,* the brine shrimp, in a shallow salt lake. Lidio Cipriani, the Italian explorer, had visited and photographed them. According to his pictures and descriptions, they looked like the Haratin beyond the Atlas in Morocco, a possible partly Bushman relict. That too was a fine idea. Everything was great.

It still was when we arrived in Tripoli, and the Ayubs took us to a hotel. There I went to bed, for I had contracted a chest cold on our ride back from Gonoa to Bardaï. I had sat on the front seat with the driver, while the ladies and the Frenchmen huddled in the body of the truck with cloths wrapped around their necks. I had haughtily declined to do so, because I wanted to see everything I could before we left.

While I was lying abed two Arabs came to visit me. One spoke French; the other was Beshir, whose Arabic was so different from mine, and whose vocabulary was so limited, that we had a hard time understanding each other. Beshir was to be our driver down to Sebha, the capital of the southern province, where Ayub had his headquarters. He had left ahead of us, and Beshir was to drive us down when I got over my cold.

Before we left I met Al Sawyer, a petroleum explorer, who knew the desert the way a woodchuck knows his hole. He told me exactly where some caves were—and they could be reached by road. They stretched like a row of booths, as in the Syrian desert, for 15 kilometers, beginning 170 kilometers south of Serdeles, on the road to Ghat.

I also reported to Dr. Jivril, the director of antiquities, in the Castillio. There I found an old friend of mine from Baghdad. Taka Bakir, who had left his own country's service during a political disturbance. He was Dr. Jivril's deputy. My problem was to get a digging permit. It was in a morning early in Ramadhan, when almost everyone had sat up all night feasting, and now it was time to go to bed.

Dr. Jivril told me that the cabinet the permits were in was locked up.

Said Taka, "*'Andi el-muftah*" (I have the key), but Dr. Jivril ignored this remark, for why should I know Arabic? Dr. Jivril was very sleepy, and his stomach was rumbling. So he agreed to send the permit to Dr. Ayub at Sebha, who would sign it and send it back. Poor Taka, thought I as we left, carrying four hundred specimen bags that Al Sawyer had given me to hold the finds that we would excavate from the fifteen-kilometer stretch of caves.

The Land Rover was heavily loaded as we took off, with Beshir at the wheel. Down along the beautiful coast we sped, passing every vehicle—and stopping briefly at the Roman city of Leptis Magna—until we came to a fork where the pavement ended, and we turned left. Up to this point my principal trouble had been to grab the wheel every time that Beshir fell asleep. When I offered to drive, he refused indignantly. That was *his* job.

Once we were on a dirt road, with many detours into the desert on one side or the other, the trouble was bumps, which threatened to shake our kidneys out. The oases and villages began to dwindle, until we came to a place called Hun. Beshir was now fully awake, but thirsting for a cigarette. He was a chain-smoker, and had smoked throughout the previous night. Now he was just waiting for the moment when a true believer could no longer distinguish between a white thread and a black one. Then he would break the day's fast.

Beshir had no threads, but he had cigarettes and matches. He knew when to start. By the time we had arrived at Socna, his native place, his nerves were under control. He led us through a maze of alleys into the house of an old man who seemed to be a judge. He greeted us warmly, fed us, and voiced many complaints about the USIS. Where was the swimming pool that they had been promised, and the movie projectors, etc., etc.? (Later on Bill Gresham denied having made these promises.)

The next morning we rolled on to Sebha, arriving before Dr. Ayub had arisen from his bed. We made a few arrangements, visited the military, saw a Chinese doctor about my cold, and found a book by John Updike in the USIA library to puzzle the Libyans with.

The year before, when Dr. Ayub had hosted Froelich Rainey there, he had taken him to a huge field of hand axes, packed like raisins in a cake, very much like Olorgesailie in Kenya, which Louis Leakey had made into a national monument. Whenever I asked if we might see them, "Látah," he would say. And of course we never did.

On Saturday, the last day of 1966, we set off for Jarma, the seat of the Garamantes, where the antiquities department had a house. Professor Ayub rode in a red Land Rover, we in the green one driven by Beshir. A truck loaded with baggage followed us both.

On New Year's Day we visited the Roman ruins of Germa, which the Italians had excavated, along with a number of slightly Negroid skeletons. The Italians had left it in excellent condition, with little more to dig. As we were walking through a trench, I saw a hearth full of charcoal in a wall. i brought out a plastic tube to collect it in, and the custodian's eyes lit up. Now he could find the dates of the various levels, but Professor Ayub took the tube out of my hand. "I will give it to him latah," he said.

From Germa we rode over the old French road, which was pure washboard, to Serdeles, near the Algerian border. Here we met a Tuareg chief, tall, lean, and aquiline, as he should have been.

The next morning Beshir was incapacitated. He had been smoking all night, and inhaling carbon dioxide from a charcoal-burning brazier. A second Tuareg drove me and Lisa on the road toward Ghat, only 120 kilometers, or 75 miles, to the south, or no more than 60 miles to the beginning of Al Sawyer's gallery of caves. In them if I were lucky, I might solve the problem of who had inhabited the center of the Sahara during the Pleistocene.

The Tuareg and I got on well together. His Arabic was Moroccan, not Egyptian, for the linguistic boundary moved eastward as it went southward from Tunisia. and when I changed *th* into *t*, what was left of my Riffian worked too. So wonderful a conversation were we having that I forgot to count the kilometer stones. He had driven smoothly and gently, and now he eased the Land Rover into a joltless stop.

"What's wrong?" I asked. "Are we low on gasoline?"

He shook his head and pointed to the kilometer stone alongside. It said 15.

I had told Professor Ayub, the descendant of the Garamantes, that there were fifteen kilometers of caves just a little way north of Ghat. Where we had stopped was only sixty-odd miles north of the caves, over a good road—an hour and a half's drive. I had been dreaming about such caves for many years. But Professor Ayub had told the Tuareg that I had said the caves were fifteen kilometers out of Serdeles.

The carving of a long-legged elephant on a loose stone that my Tuareg driver showed me at Kilometer 15 south of Sardeles in Libya. The early post-Pleistocene elephants had to have long legs to travel great distances because their food was scarce. Louis Leakey also found their skeletons in East Africa.

The Tuareg was sad that I was unhappy. In partial compensation he led us to a rock on the back of which was carved the outline of an elephant. I took several pictures of it with my Hasselblad. No one except other Tuaregs had ever seen it before, he said.

Back at Serdeles, the expedition was ready to move across the desert, which was smoother than the road to the Acacus Mountains. Before we left, Professor Ayub remarked to me, "These oil geologists, the desert makes them imagine things, like Mr. Sawyer's caves."

For the first time I lost my temper with him. I said very little, but I did something worse than any words could convey. I smoked a cigarette, in the middle of the desert and of Ramadhan, before him and all his men. I had set a shame-compulsion on him. Saving violence, there was nothing more for me to do.

Had Beshir been there I might not have done it, but he was still upstairs and gaga, so he was left behind. The Tuareg rolled us across the smooth desert toward the Acacus Mountains, into a valley straight out of a myth, probably no more than twenty miles from Al Sawyer's caves, across the mountain crest, which looked like a dinosaur's spine.

We passed yellow dunes and red dunes until we came to a narrow gateway where an arched rock bore inscriptions in Tafinaq (Tuareg) and Arabic. At the head of the valley stood a small Tuareg camp. A few blades of grass were being nibbled by a score or so of sheep. There was no water to be seen, but the Tuaregs knew where to find it. They did not need to evade telling us, for we knew better than to ask. After all, Professor Ayub had brought along a drum or two of water for the men, and cases of soda water for us.

We camped that night, and early in the morning I examined the caves, including the one the others had slept in (Lisa and I had been put in a tent).

There we found the paintings, mostly in yellows and reds, of beautiful blondes with topknots on their heads, and men driving chariots, as well as the metal ladders left behind by Professor Fabrizio Mori, who had copied them all several years before. They are in his book,* all but one. Professor Ayub, who had not spoken to me since Serdeles, approached me and said, "There is one more that Mori didn't get." And so there was. It required a flash, and my strobe wouldn't work.

Despite all these impediments I did see the blond chariot people painted on the walls of Acacus, and they were very much like the blond Berbers all the way from the Jebel Akhadar in northeastern Libya to the Shawiya of eastern Algeria. They had none of the markings of the Mashausha on the Egyptian wall paintings. They had apparently lasted into Roman times, until chariots had given way to camels, and the camels and sheep had overgrazed the land.

A book review in *Science* December 26, 1975,† sheds a gleam of light. Apparently camels were first domesticated in northern Arabia and Syria around 1100 B.C. The Hyksos had brought horses and chariots into Egypt about five hundred years earlier. It took some time for the camel to replace the horse and chariot. This happened in the latter part of the Roman occupation, when it was difficult for them to maintain their roads, while camels could go everywhere, until phased out by trucks.

I find it hard to associate these chariot folk with the Gara-mantes, whose skeletons the Italians had found to be Negroid, and

*F. Mori, Tadrart Acacus, Arte Rupestre e culture del Sahara preistorico, *Torino, Giulio Einaude, ed., 1965.*

†The Camel and the Wheel, *Richard W. Bullett, Harvard University Press, Cambridge, Mass., 1975.*

harder still to tie them in with the Romans. I scratched around the caves a bit and found some Neolithic pottery and some basalt pebble tools. The charioteers hadn't lived there, they had just visited and left their calling cards.

To me their origin and their connection, if any, with the Riffians remains a mystery. It was a priceless experience for us, but not for the National Geographic Society, because we did not linger in Libya very long.

When we got back to Germa, Professor Ayub said that he was going to Tripoli to celebrate the Aid el-Kebir at the end of Ramadhan. Lisa and I were to wait in the expedition house until he got back, and then to excavate more Garamantes. I refused. We went to Sebha in his red Land Rover, while Beshir drove the professor there in the green one and cracked it up en route.

The only way we could get to Tripoli was to hire a whole bus. I gave Ayub a check for cash and he upped the exchange rate 25 percent. "I shall deposit this in my Swiss bank account," he said. And he gave me one hand axe as bonus.

Through the night we rode in our bus, and all the next day. On the following morning I reported to Dr. Jivril at the Castillio. The conversation indicated that Professor Ayub had taken Dr. Jivril's green Land Rover without his permission. I would have to stay on for a trial, or at least as a witness. This might take weeks, or a month. Where was Professor Ayub, anyhow?

We received bad news through the mail. Our daughter-in-law was dying in Washington, leaving six children, the oldest of whom was in school in Barcelona. Bill Gresham wheeled us out to the airport and got us aboard a waiting plane. We had been in Libya two weeks, but it seemed a century. We saw our grandson, who took the news well. We buried Jannie's ashes in West Gloucester, in a Neolithic pot from a site near Lake Urmiya. The children flew up from Washington with armfuls of flowers.

Afterward, while the Episcopal priest was sitting with us in our living room, I couldn't help making up a couplet in Arabic.

Wa hiya wakhshiyya, wa mat fil horiyya.

And she was a wild thing, and she died in a state of freedom.

33. *The Hunting Peoples*

Janet's death was followed by a pleasant invasion by six grandchildren. This made Lisa and me feel young again. It also carried an important dividend. The furor over race, then raging at its height, seemed trivial compared to the problems of the third generation.

To what could my grandchildren look forward, they and their age-mates lucky or unlucky enough to have been born on the earth in this moment of confusion and of strife? Better to look backward into the roots of men and women who lived before technology had outstripped our other faculties. So I started my research on the hunting peoples who had survived into the nineteenth and even the twentieth century. Some of them could still knap flint. If we civilized folk should blow ourselves into protoplasmic paste, might not these living hunters start the cycle over again? Might not some of our own tired seed, if any were left, steer their own course on a safer tack?

My lecture notes, diaries, and *Reader* were useful, but not enough for the job ahead. It took me nearly five years of reading and false starts to finish the book. The best sources were, as usual, eyewitness reports by keen and honest observers who were not in leg irons from having studied social anthropology. One prize gem was *Friendly Mission, The Tasmanian Journals and Papers of George Augustus Robinson, 1892–1934*. Edited by N. J. B. Plomley.*

While bucking the winter gales on a Swedish banana boat to Honduras and back, I read and abstracted its 1,071 pages. This experience drew me into an early Paleolithic, yet still familiar world, in which a man named Woorrady raped and slew his sister-in-law, because her lover had speared her husband (Woorrady's brother) through the back. Swap spears for pistols, and there we are, at 4 P.M., on TV.

George Robinson was a mason in Hobart Town, newly arrived from England. The Black War was going on. The native Tasmanians had given up compromising with the settlers, who were encroaching on their hunting grounds and particularly with the sealers, who were sneaking off their women. One white man was said to have tamped the

---

*Tasmanian Historical Research Association, Halstead Press Pty. Ltd., Kingsgrove, NSW, Australia, 1966.

tobacco in his pipe with a native's severed thumb. On the other side, the natives used to creep up to the settlers' cabins bare-handed, dragging spears between their toes, and before the settler could cock his musket, whisk! a spear in his neck.

The Tasmanians filled every qualification for the most primitive people on earth. They could not make fire, but carried torches of bark and punk with them. Should one "mob" lose its fire, even its bitterest enemies would give them a light. They had no hafted stone implements, only flake tools which might have been attributed to *Homo erectus* if found in the right geological level. They had no containers for carrying water. They had no dogs. The list of things they didn't have would fill a monograph, but one thing they *did* have: the courage and the cunning to threaten the new settlers with extermination.

The settlers had formed a militia, strung out in a "Black Line," and the natives were diminishing in numbers. So that is why George Augustus Robinson, a kindly man, was picked to round up the survivors, many still hostile, for transport to the offshore islands, where the last one died in 1876. As expected, it was despair and disease that did them in. Robinson's diaries are their obituary. Although he could never have heard of anthropology, he was one of the keenest and most objective observers that ever lived.

His laurels were shared a century later by an Austrian priest, Father Martin Gusinde. He went to the opposite ultimate refuge area of the Southern Hemisphere, Tierra del Fuego, to study the Canoe Indians. There Charles Darwin, one of the most brilliant men to whom our civilization has given birth, considered the Yaghans to be the most brutish and debased people on the earth.

Yet Father Gusinde found them to have a sensitive and intricate social organization, and a succession of initiation ordeals and ceremonies as complex as any in the world. Gusinde knew, because he passed through them all. Although simple, their technical skills made it possible for the Yaghans to live well in an inhospitable aquatic climate, the southernmost inhabited land on earth.

The Bushmen of South Africa had been studied by Sir Francis Galton; Lorna Marshall and her daughter Elizabeth Marshall Thomas, whose book *The Harmless People* is a gem of writing; and local administrators. I used all their works.

The Negritos of the Andaman Islands in the Bay of Bengal, who were ignorant of fire making and who harpooned sea turtles from canoes, had been studied by E. H. Man, an administrator; A. R. Browne, a founder of the functional school of social anthropology; and the Italian explorer-anthropologist-photographer Lidio Cipriani.

These are a few examples of the men and women whose price-less documents I had the pleasure to read and to digest.

First I wrote almost half the text of *The Hunting Peoples*, people by people, from the Tasmanians and Birhors to the Ainu, until it had passed the limits of a single book. It was the way I had done the *Reader*, and each part had internal continuity, following a single outline, but my editor called a halt.

To get it into one volume, he told me, it might be better to arrange it by subject matter, drawing examples from all the hunting peoples. So in trapping, for example, I jumped from Australia to Alaska, then down to Maine and over to Hokkaido. In rites of passage, the Australians and the Kwakiutl of Vancouver Island led the field.

Some people read only the parts about technology, illustrated by Aldren Watson's lively wash drawings. Others concentrated on the social organization, and still others on the shamans, who seemed to practice ESP, particularly clairvoyance, while in trances, and telekinesis while awake. One shaman could predict when a pregnant whale would wash ashore, another could shoot evil waves into an enemy by pointing and jerking a bone in his direction.

The shamans didn't have to worry about investigating committees, they just did what they had to do. And, from the standpoints of their customers and victims, their magic worked.

Unlike my experience with *The Origin of Races,* I had only one bout with a copy editor. It was a very important one, because it came in page proof, in the last paragraph, which many reviewers read first.

Saving our planet from human destruction, and from the destruction of life itself, is only half our problem. The other half is for us to learn how nature intended human beings to live, and to reestablish continuity with those who may still be alive after the rest of us are dead. If we succeed in the first endeavor, and fail in the second one, someday, far out in the desert, a few families of hunters may meet, and ask one another: "Where has whitefella gone?"

The copy editor changed the last four words to: *"Where have the city people gone?"*

I caught this change just in the tiniest nick of time, and called the copy editor on the telephone. Of all the reviews this book received, the majority of them quoted my statement as restored.

The one review that pleased me most was by John Hillaby, in the *New Scientist,* of London. He wrote:

Once I came close to spiritual paralysis among one of the tribes he has a lot to say about: the Mbuti Pygmies of the Eastern Congo. The occasion: a chance meeting in Epulu with two anthropologists. One, I believe, would be called a functionalist, the other a structuralist, a follower of Lévi-Strauss. . . . After glorious days in the company of seemingly happy and well-adjusted little people, forest-dwellers, who hunted duiker, pig, and occasionally okapi, I drank expensive Scotch at night, listened to near incomprehensible chatter about Hauser, Mauss, Simiand, and Durkheim. Excellent fellows all, once the pillars of their profession but not ones, I suggest, you can get much out of. . . .

But that was along ago. It wasn't until I read Kroeber and Coon and the few like them—which isn't many, that I began to get glimmerings of what anthropology was about. . . . Coon I reckon among the world's top five. . . .

Why should the wife of an Eskimo whaleboat owner walk about with a special wooden bucket several months before the hunt . . . in order to give the whale a drink of fresh water? Are all hunters crazy?

The answer, of course, is that such seemingly irrational acts serve a social purpose. Man might be defined as the only animal that needs to be insane in order to survive. When he became coldly practical, discarding his beliefs and rites, measuring and counting things accurately, building efficient machinery, inventing weapons of mass destruction, sending men to the Moon and burning more of the Earth's oxygen than its plant life can replace. Coon believes that he has also begun to warm up the wax that will seal his own fate.

The Italian edition of *The Hunting Peoples* is particularly handsome, with a title that is appetizing, at first glance, to an Anglo-American audience: *I Popoli Cacciatori*—a literal translation of the English original. Because the title of this book is the same as the Italian original of Marco Polo's book, I doubly thank my Italian publishers.

What has happened to me since *The Hunting Peoples* was published, or just before it? I taught summer school for two weeks at Boulder, Colorado; and a course on the hunting peoples at Harvard; made two trips to Central America and one to Nepal, more as a tourist than as a professional; and wrote two short books now presumably in print.

When a wild animal ages, its teeth wear down and hinder eating, and its eyes begin to fail, making it hard to see oncoming predators. With a man, dentists and doctors fill both cavities and the scavenger's role. Mine do their jobs in a most friendly way, and I salute them.

I apologize to anyone whom I may have offended unintentionally, and forgive everyone who may have done the same to me.

In his study at home, with snow showing on the leaves of a quince tree outside the window, the author poses with his old reconstruction of the male Sinanthropus that he made in Philadelphia. (Photograph by Phil Taylor)

My last line, from the *Iliad,* as might be expected, is: *Bē d'akeōn para thīna polŭphloisbōto thalāsses.*

It means, "He walked in silence on the shore of the much-roaring sea."

To the younger, Greekless generation, let me, as a shore dweller, explain that I prefer it as an exit line to the movie cliché, "He rode his faithful steed westward into the setting sun."

Better to have one's bones picked by the delicate teeth of fish than by the knifelike beaks of vultures.

Index